Plato and Plotinus on Mysticism, Epistemology, and Ethics

Bloomsbury Studies in Ancient Philosophy

Also available:

Happiness and Greek Ethical Thought, M. Andrew Holowchak
The Ideas of Socrates, Matthew S. Linck
Plato's Trial of Athens, Mark A. Ralkowski
Plotinus the Platonist, David J. Yount
The Poverty of Eros in Plato's Symposium, Lorelle D. Lamascus
The Socratic Method, Rebecca Bensen Cain

Plato and Plotinus on Mysticism, Epistemology, and Ethics

David J. Yount

BLOOMSBURY ACADEMIC
LONDON • NEW YORK • OXFORD • NEW DELHI • SYDNEY

BLOOMSBURY ACADEMIC
Bloomsbury Publishing Plc
50 Bedford Square, London, WC1B 3DP, UK
1385 Broadway, New York, NY 10018, USA

BLOOMSBURY, BLOOMSBURY ACADEMIC and the Diana logo
are trademarks of Bloomsbury Publishing Plc

First published in Great Britain 2017
Paperback edition first published 2018

A catalogue record for this book is available from the British Library.

Library of Congress Cataloging-in-Publication Data
Names: Yount, David J., author.
Title: Plato and Plotinus on mysticism, epistemology, and ethics / David J. Yount.
Description: New York : Bloomsbury Academic, 2017. | Series: Bloomsbury studies in ancient philosophy ; 7 | Includes bibliographical references and index.
Identifiers: LCCN 2016039288| ISBN 9781474298421 (hb) | ISBN 9781474298445 (epdf)
Subjects: LCSH: Plato. | Plotinus. | Mysticism. | Knowledge, Theory of. | Ethics.
Classification: LCC B395 .Y68 2017 | DDC 184–dc23 LC record available at https://lccn.loc.gov/2016039288

ISBN: HB: 978-1-4742-9842-1
PB: 978-1-3500-8218-2
ePDF: 978-1-4742-9844-5
ePub: 978-1-4742-9843-8

Series: Bloomsbury Studies in Ancient Philosophy

Typeset by RefineCatch Limited, Bungay, Suffolk

To find out more about our authors and books visit www.bloomsbury.com and sign up for our newsletters.

To my parents,
Richard
and
Pauline

Contents

Preface

In this book, I argue that Plato and Plotinus do not essentially differ on many important claims in the areas of mysticism, epistemology, and ethics. I would like to acknowledge those who considerably improved this work. First, I would like to sincerely thank my colleagues and students at Mesa Community College (especially my first two Plato classes), who have heard me discuss this book's contents for years. I would specifically like to thank Dr. Debi Campbell and Dr. Barry Vaughan, who gave me excellent comments, and Kerry Leibowitz, Cathie Gagnon, Michael Yount, and especially my wife Elaine and my three sons Alex, Elliot, and Holden, for their moral support throughout the project. Hackett Publishing graciously permitted my use of most of the Plato quotations (all rights reserved), for which I am most grateful. (See below for a statement regarding my Harvard University Press permissions.) I would like to thank Jenn Neal for her invaluable assistance in the editing of this project. I greatly benefited from Lloyd Gerson's careful reading of the manuscript and excellent comments, though we still differ in our views. I am also in debt to Robert Price, who spurred my interest in and helped me better understand Plotinus. Finally, as a small token of my thanks for everything my parents Richard and Pauline have given me in my life, I dedicate this book to them.

Dave Yount
Mesa Community College

Introduction

There are two issues I should discuss before I lay out my argument that the mysticism, epistemology, and ethics of Plotinus do not essentially differ from Plato's view. First, I will examine and assess the "Unwritten Doctrines" or "Estotericist" interpretation of Plato's work (section I). Second, I will explain the methodology and plan of my project (section II).

I. The "Unwritten Doctrines" and Esoteric interpretations of Plato

There is an interpretation alternatively referred to as the Unwritten Doctrines, Unwritten Teachings, or Esoteric view of Plato's dialogues and, of course, there are those in favor and those against the idea.[1] I need to address this view because at least one commentator[2] argues that Plotinus is an adherent of it. Let us review what the interpretation holds, and then I will stake out a position to this effect: whether one accepts this view or not, one can still find the beliefs of Plotinus in the writings of Plato, which is all that my argument requires.

The Unwritten Doctrines or Esoteric interpretation of Plato may be defined as follows:

> The modern "Esoteric" interpretation of Plato ascribes to him a more or less secret "esoteric" doctrine, consisting of a metaphysical system not to be found, at least not explicitly, in his written works, but propounded orally to his disciples in the Academy and constituting the real though hidden content of his philosophy.[3]

According to this view, we have evidence from Aristotle, Aristoxenus, Simplicius, Alexander, and Philoponous themselves that Plato had doctrines that he did not explicitly refer to in his writings, such as the Indefinite Dyad and/or the Great and Small.[4]

Witness the famous quotation from Aristoxenus on Plato's lecture on the Good Itself:

> This, as Aristotle was always saying, was the experience of most of those who heard Plato's lecture *On the Good*. Each of them attended on the assumption that he

> would hear about one of the recognized human goods—such as wealth, health, strength, and in general some marvellous happiness. When Plato's lectures turned out to be about mathematics—numbers, geometry, astronomy—and to crown all about the thesis that the good is one, it seemed to them, I fancy, something quite paradoxical; and so some people despised the whole thing, while others criticized it.[5]

Aristoxenus notoriously relates here that Plato gave an oral lecture on the Good, and more often than once. In Plato's *Republic*, the character Socrates says that he will only be able to discuss the offspring of the Good (presumably the sun in our perceptible world), and not the Good Itself.[6]

In *Physics* IV 209b11–6, Aristotle also explicitly mentions Plato's "unwritten teaching":

> This is why Plato in the *Timaeus* says that matter and space are the same: for the "participant" and space are identical. (It is true, indeed, that the account he gives there of the "participant" is different from what he says in his so-called unwritten teaching. Nevertheless, he did identify place and space.) I mention Plato because, while all hold place to be something, he alone tried to say *what* it is.

This quote presents evidence that what Plato wrote in the *Timaeus* and what he said in his unwritten teachings were two different things.

Detractors of the unwritten doctrine view, such as Cherniss,[7] argue that Aristotle should not be trusted in these matters, since he was not sympathetic to Plato's view and misinterpreted Plato elsewhere.[8]

Further, Brisson argues that Aristoxenus' account actually works against the Unwritten Teachings view, because:

> According to Aristoxenus' testimony, this lecture recalled the doctrine of dialogues (*Republic* [VI and VII] in particular) and was directed towards an audience of amateurs rather than of initiated followers.
>
> What, then, would have constituted Plato's unwritten doctrine?[9]

This is an excellent point. However, there seems to be something to the Unwritten Teachings view, since Plato does beg off giving a detailed account of the Good in the *Republic*, among other things, such as giving an account of the "father of the universe" in the *Timaeus* or the "king" in *Letter* II.[10]

Now to bring this to the forefront of the Plotinus-Plato issue: According to Tigerstedt, Neo-Platonists think that Plato holds an esoteric, *but written*, doctrine, which is not of the same kind as that of the "modern Esotericists":

> The modern Esoteric interpretation of Plato cannot be found in any ancient Platonist, least of all in the Neoplatonists, to whom Plato's entire philosophy was an esoteric doctrine, revealed to the initiated, not in any oral tradition but in the Master's written works, if read according to the rules of Neoplatonic exegesis.[11]

However, Tigerstedt argues against the modern Esoteric reading of Plato, claiming that instead of reviving the traditional Neo-Platonist (esoteric) reading of Plato, they use non-Platonic sources such as Aristotle, Aristoxenus, Simplicius, and others to try to understand Plato, and therefore fail to reach their goal:

> What in any case [modern Esotericists] have not done, is precisely what they boast of doing, viz., restoring the "traditional," i.e., Neoplatonic interpretation, for that had been destroyed once and for all in the eighteenth century. . . . The [modern Esotericists] have generally accepted the verdict of modern scholarship and refrained from systematizing the Dialogues, trying instead to depreciate their importance in favor of other sources—in direct contrast to the Neoplatonists.[12]

First, Tigerstedt initially sets up his definitions in such a way that one must be either an Esotericist (real doctrine is oral) or a non-Esotericist (real doctrine is written), but then he adds a third category (real doctrine is written and orally reinforced privately to the privileged few) and accuses the Esotericists of using non-Platonic sources to make their case. This argument is spurious because if Esotericists believe that Plato's most important doctrine is oral, and Aristotle et al. discuss Plato's oral doctrine, this does not disprove their case. More importantly, however, Tigerstedt seems to beg the question by denying that Plato's dialogues contain a system, for which I argue.[13]

Tigerstedt also criticizes the Esoteric reading as being a radical solution that disposes of the problems of the contradictions, obscurities, and gaps in Plato's view:

> Like all radical solutions of the problem of interpreting Plato, the Esoteric one ruthlessly disposes of the problem itself. There are, indeed, contradictions, gaps, obscurities, and ambiguities in Plato's works. But they do not matter. For Plato's written works do not contain his real doctrine which he taught to his disciples in the Academy and did not divulge. Fortunately, thanks to Aristotle and other ancient authors, earlier or later, this oral, esoteric doctrine can be reconstructed. It turns out [to] be a rigidly systematic, hierarchical metaphysics of Being, an "Ontology," very similar to Neoplatonism, whose direct forerunner it was. For Plotinus was in fact what he claimed to be: Plato's true heir and successor.[14]

Tigerstedt makes three main points here that should be addressed: First, I grant with Tigerstedt that it is a flawed hermeneutic to claim that there are no interpretive issues in the dialogues, and to wipe one's hands of them by arguing that Plato's real doctrine does not appear in the dialogues. But that is not my contention in this work.

Second, contrary to Tigerstedt, the Esotericist (and Neo-Platonic) view of Plato is rigidly systematic; I readily admit that I find a system in Plato's work, and I will do my best to lay it out throughout this book. The reader should decide for him or herself if these elements are contained within the dialogues or not.

Third, Tigerstedt's claim that Plotinus is Plato's "true heir and successor"—the thesis of the Esotericist—is more or less what I am aiming to defend.

In general, Tigerstedt states that the Neo-Platonic and Esoteric readings are both out of favor these days ("At the beginning of the nineteenth century, the decline and fall of the Neoplatonic interpretation of Plato was an accomplished fact");[15] similarly, there are few proponents who currently advocate these readings; and it is futile to try to revive these readings of Plato. I concede Tigerstedt's first and second points that there are in fact few writers with this take on Plato, and that the Neo-Platonic reading of Plato is out of favor; however, I do not agree that it is an "accomplished fact," and will attempt to refute that notion in this work. As for the observation that there are few proponents, I myself am a current advocate of the Neo-Platonic reading of Plato, and the paucity of fellow defenders fails to prove the implausibility of that reading. Neither of these points—nor the bold claim that it is futile to revive this approach—implies that there could not be great merit in arguing for these readings of Plato. In fact, this is partly what fuels and justifies this project.

I am not an Esotericist using Tigerstedt's criteria, since we can find plenty of concordance (or fail to find essential differences) with what Plato and Plotinus write, using Plotinus as someone who is more explicit than Plato about their ultimate teachings. However, I do agree with Tigerstedt when he notes: "Aristotle does not distinguish between an exoteric and an esoteric Platonic philosophy."[16] Thus, to boldly argue that the most important part(s) of Plato's views are exclusively oral betrays Plato's life work, as far as his dialogues are concerned. Surely there is something of doctrinal worth in the dialogues themselves.[17]

More needs to be said about Tigerstedt's assessment of the Neo-Platonic reading of Plato. First, Tigerstedt interestingly puts the Neo-Platonists into the esoteric camp of interpreters:

> The Neoplatonists properly speaking—Plotinus, Porphyry, Iamblichus, and their disciples—do not distinguish between an exoteric and esoteric Platonism. To them, there is only an esoteric one. Plato's philosophy is by them regarded as a mystery religion, revealed by the gods to Plato—and, indeed, before him to the "Ancient Theologians" . . . and through Plato to the elected few, as Proclus says in the First Book of his *Platonic Theology*. Nor do the Neoplatonists oppose Plato's oral teaching to his written work. True, they occasionally refer to his lecture *On the Good*, i.e., his metaphysics—which is what really matters to the Neoplatonists—is to be found in them. Proclus even goes so far as to assert that this teaching penetrates virtually all the Dialogues, though to a varying degree. It is only a question of reading them in the right way.[18]

Speaking only on Plotinus' behalf, this is not an accurate reading of the *Enneads*. At no time does Plotinus state that the Unwritten Teachings of Plato are more important than Plato's writings, or that Plato's writings are not important. In fact, Tigerstedt seems to contradict himself when he says that there is no difference between the exoteric and esoteric Plato, and then goes on to state that the Neo-Platonists are esotericists; that is, if Plato's view is contained in the words of Plato, then the oral teachings are presumably superfluous or redundant. What I will grant is Plotinus' belief that few people will have the vision of the Good, but Plato believes this as well, so this is not a concern. Moreover, it is not on account of Plato discussing his secret or real doctrine that Plotinus claims to have experienced the Good; it was because of dialectic and other requirements that

Plotinus met, along with his active search for the knowledge, that allowed him to experience this vision some 500 years later; thus Tigerstedt's points here are answerable.

Tigerstedt continues with the charge that Neo-Platonists found their own opinions in Plato, using metaphors, and reading Plato as Christians read the Bible:

> This attitude of the Neoplatonists should not astonish us. A great part of their extant works consisting of commentaries on the Platonic Dialogues, they could hardly be expected to declare that the writings they were interpreting did not contain Plato's innermost thought. Nor did the Neoplatonists say so, but, thanks to an ingenious method of interpretation, which has wrung an unwilling admiration from modern scholars, they succeeded in finding their own opinions in Plato. In desperate cases, there was always the last resource of allegorism. For the Neoplatonists did not read Plato as the Alexandrian philologists had read Homer, but as the contemporary Christian theologians read the Bible. The Dialogues were to the Neoplatonists Sacred Books, full of divine revelation, intelligible only to the initiated.[19]

I take issue with Tigerstedt's view that the Neo-Platonists are *both* esotericists who downplay the importance of Plato's writings in favor of his oral teachings, *and* are also people who read Plato's works as Christians read the Bible. Why, per Tigerstedt's view, would they take much stock in the writings if all that mattered about Plato's thought was his oral teachings? As to his claim that the Neo-Platonists read their views into Plato's writings, the reader should make his or her own judgment after having read the rest of this book and seeing to what extent that seems to be true, given the extent of the parallels between Plato and Plotinus' writings. Nonetheless, I agree with Tigerstedt that Plotinus—due to his experience with the intelligible region (and beyond)—sees Plato's writings as confirming the truth of his experience, and that this experience can only truly be understood by "the initiated."

Tigerstedt's understanding of the Neo-Platonist reading of Plato is that unless one takes Plato in the Neo-Platonistic way, one's view of Plato is wrong. If one applies the Neo-Platonic reading of Plato, there is unity to the interpretation and hermeneutical problems vanish; if one rejects the Neo-Platonic reading, the hermeneutical problems reappear:

> Thus, the interpretation of Plato ceases to be a problem. There is one and only one way of understanding him, and that is to study the Dialogues as interpreted by the Neoplatonists. Neoplatonism being a metaphysical system, founded by Plotinus and brought to its perfection by Proclus, the difficulty of combining Plato's various often divergent statements into a unity disappears. Only when the Neoplatonic interpretation becomes questionable or is openly rejected, the problem of Platonic interpretation emerges again.[20]

First, it is not the case that Plotinus' reading of Plato contends that there are no issues whatsoever in Platonic interpretation. There remain problems about exactly how one should take the Indefinite Dyad, if at all, in Plato's work (just to name one among many other detailed issues of interpretation laid out in the ancient philosophy journals) and it would be silly for anyone to claim otherwise. With his comment, though, Tigerstedt seems to favor leaving Plato's work disunited, especially given how he seems to delight in the challenge of the Neo-Platonic interpretation (more than one thousand) years later; he ends his commentary by stating that the Neo-Platonists' reading of Plato truly deserves the appellation "classical" or "traditional."[21] Having argued that Plato already had in place the very metaphysical system that Tigerstedt claims Neo-Platonism has (but only that this is true for Plotinus),[22] I hope to show, leaving Neo-Platonists in general aside for the present work, that Plotinus has the best reading of Plato in the areas of mysticism, epistemology, and ethics.

Admittedly, Findlay discusses Plato's "Unwritten Doctrines."[23] However, Findlay mainly argues—as Tigerstedt's Esotericists do not—that we have evidence from others around Plato at the time (especially Aristotle),[24] who can shed some light on what he was teaching "in the classroom" that did not necessarily appear in the Dialogues; for instance, the "Great and Small" and "Indefinite Dyad."[25] More importantly, Findlay believes that we can find parallels directly in Plato's writings, so he is not an Esotericist by Tigerstedt's definition, since he believes that we can read Plato's view right from the dialogues just as Plotinus does. Though I have no qualm with Findlay's use of Aristotle and others to aid in our understanding of Plato and what he may have said outside his extant writings, I will confine my project in the subsequent chapters only to what we actually find in Plato's texts, and to what we actually find in Plotinus' texts.

In sum, the Esoteric doctrine, as defined by Tigerstedt, and *not* necessarily as defended by some commentators (Findlay and Miller), is not assumed in this work because doing so is not necessary to make my argument.

II. The methodology and plan of my argument

Due to space constraints, I must ignore similarities between Plotinus' views and Aristotle, and the Pythagoreans, Stoics, Gnostics, Middle Platonists, and post-Plotinian Platonists.

To defend my view that Plato and Plotinus do not essentially differ on mysticism, epistemology, and ethics, I will use the Compatibility Principle:

> *Plato and Plotinus' views are compatible or consistent in principle if Plotinus (or Plato) writes on some subject that does not appear in Plato (or Plotinus), unless there is written evidence in a particular case that one author writes something to the effect that 'A is true' and the other author writes that "A is false."*

I aim to address and counter virtually every commentator whom I have read in English, who attempts to argue that there is an essential difference between these philosophers on the issues of mysticism, epistemology, or ethics; my argument will only be as strong as the number and quality of my responses to opponents of my thesis.

Lastly, I am trying to show that Plato and Plotinus do not have *essentially different* views, that is, differences on philosophically significant matters. For instance, they do not disagree (but in fact agree) that wisdom leads to or implies happiness, contemplation, and purity, ultimate knowledge is of the Good or One (and Forms), we gain knowledge by recollection and dialectic, we can only have opinion of perceptibles, happiness is a state of the soul, no one errs willingly, and so on, for many other epistemological and ethical claims, not the least of which is the mystical claim they each make: the most important experience a person can have is to see or know the Good or One. To hold these views is what would make one *the*, as opposed to *a*, Platonist. Again, to be clear, by claiming that there are no essential differences between their views, I am not arguing that they have identical views, since I admittedly cannot find every claim of each philosopher in the other's work. Thus, on my reading, the views of Plato and Plotinus are so similar on the issues examined here, that I cannot find an essential difference between them.

I have used the translations of Plato from Cooper's *Plato: Complete Works*, unless otherwise noted. Moreover, for the Platonic quotations, I have started them with the character or principal interlocutor who represents Plato—usually Socrates, but also the Athenian, the Stranger, Diotima—first, and then put the responses second, unless otherwise noted. For Plotinus, I have used A.H. Armstrong's translation, unless otherwise noted. I will use the standard method of referencing the *Enneads*: Ennead, treatise, chapter, and line (sans the chronological number of when a treatise was written), as follows: VI.9.1.12–13, which refers to the twelfth and thirteenth lines of the sixth Ennead, ninth treatise, and first chapter. For secondary source quotations of both works, I have taken the liberty of italicizing the names of Plato's Dialogues and the word "Enneads," as well as converting Oxford English to American English ("colour" to "color," and so on) if necessary to maintain continuity throughout the work.

In chapter 1, I describe in as much detail as possible Plato and Plotinus' view that we can have an ultimate experience or vision that amounts to knowledge of what exists, how we should live, and even the nature of knowledge itself. The requirements for the experience will also be reviewed, according to both philosophers. I will also show that, assuming that Plotinus is a mystic, Plato is best read as a mystic as well.

In chapter 2, I will analyze Plato and Plotinus' views of wisdom, knowledge, dialectic, recollection, prayer, and opinion, and show that none of these issues violate my Compatibility Principle above, and that none of these comparisons yield an essential difference between their views.

In chapter 3, I will examine Plato and Plotinus' views on ethics, that is, their takes on happiness, love, purification, and reverence, how to live (including philosophy, virtue, justice, and temperance), and how not to live (including vice, ignorance, impiety, and attachment to the body), music, art, desire for the good, not erring willingly, and pleasure and pain, showing that they do not have essentially different views thereon as well.

1

The Ultimate Experience: The Evidence of Mysticism in Plato and Plotinus

1.1 Introduction

I use the phrase "ultimate experience"[1] to designate an occurrence that transmits to its experiencer knowledge of what exists, of how we should (not) live, and even of the nature of knowledge itself; this experience is alternatively described by both Plato and Plotinus as a vision, and is purported not only to provide knowledge to its experiencer, but also to be the source of wisdom, true happiness, and virtue.

Plato and Plotinus commentators rarely address the nature of this experience—the everlasting, self-sustaining, ineffable, difficult, and rare aspects—in both philosophers' views, nor the requirements for such an experience. None of the Plotinian literature, at least in English, has a comparison of these aspects with Plato. A healthy minority of Platonic scholars believe that Plato is not a mystic; so, given that Plotinus is nearly unanimously taken to be a mystic,[2] if I can demonstrate the harmonious features of the ultimate experience for both philosophers, then we have more, if not sufficient, reason to believe that Plato is a mystic—at least in the same way in which the term applies to Plotinus.

I will review and comment on the literature regarding whether or not Plato and/or Plotinus are mystics; argue that a definition of mysticism is not required to proceed with this argument; and show the evidence for the claim that, assuming Plotinus is a mystic, both philosophers describe an experience that is sufficiently similar to classify them as mystics.

Plato and Plotinus believe that the ultimate experience:

(1) Gives the ultimate answers to the most significant philosophical questions;
(2) Is everlasting or self-sustaining;
(3) Is difficult and rare;
(4) Is ineffable; and
(5) Has at least four requirements.

I will show how my "ultimate experience" theory explains Plato's attitude toward what the multitude of non-philosophers think and would say about his philosophy and argue that interpreting Plato as a mystic can be made by an argument to the best explanation. I will also address A.H. Armstrong's and Gerson's assessments of the relative lack of importance of mysticism in the philosophy of Plotinus, objecting that interpreting Plotinus as a mystic is essential to understanding his philosophy.

Plato, Plotinus, and mysticism

Commentators—allowing them to define "mysticism" however they wish—have taken many, if not all, possible major stances on this issue (with the number of advocates for each position in parentheses):

(1) Plato is a mystic (33);[3]
(2) Plato is not a mystic (18);[4]
(3) Socrates is a mystic (2);[5]
(4) Socrates is not a mystic; (3)[6]
(5) Plotinus is a mystic; (48)[7] and
(6) Plotinus is not a mystic. (1)[8]

Obviously, the question of whether Plato and Socrates are mystics is much more controversial than the question of whether Plotinus is a mystic. I will focus on Plato's mysticism, or lack thereof, and whether what he discusses is similar to Plotinus. It is noteworthy, however, that the majority view—Plato is a mystic—does not show up in introductory philosophy texts.[9]

In his introduction to *Plato: The Collected Dialogues*, Huntington Cairns claims:

> Plato was a philosopher and a poet, but not a mystic. . . . He has been a source of inspiration to many types of mysticism but his writings have been repeatedly misread. This misunderstanding has been greatly promoted and popularized by the writings of Philo and Plotinus.[10]

Apparently, Cairns' conception of mysticism is that a mystic denies "rational order"[11] and exalts "feeling above reason."[12] I disagree with this, but first let me object here to three other points he makes.

First, referring to Plato as a poet would effectively be an insult to Plato himself, given what he claims about poets in the *Republic*; namely, that poets stir up the passions—lust and anger—instead of quelling them (*Republic* X 606d; and see the *Ion*). Cairns could be speaking of Plato's pleasant writing style and use of metaphor; however, the truth would be still more important to Plato and undoubtedly he would at least prefer "philosopher" to "poet." For instance, it does not matter how poetic one's speech is if one is not speaking the truth.[13] Also, Plato characterizes poets as having a sort of divine inspiration, without really possessing knowledge about their work (see, for example, the *Apology*, *Ion*, and *Republic*). Therefore, Plato is not a poet but a philosopher.

Second, I agree that Plato is not a mystic *if and only if* Cairns' conception of mysticism—that a mystic denies rational order and exalts feeling above reason—is correct. But here is a partial refutation of Cairns' conception of mysticism: Since, generally speaking, Plotinus is taken to be a mystic and Plato is not as universally so taken, Cairns' conception should at least pick out Plotinus as being a mystic, while also excluding Plato. However, Cairns' conception does not pass this test. In many places, Plotinus refers to "Reason-Principles" of which everything in the universe is an image; presumably these Reason-Principles ascribe a rational order to the universe. In addition, Plotinus frequently urges us to use our reason and intellect and in fact *identify with* Intellect. Moreover, he constantly gives rational arguments for his positions and never writes that emotion should take the place of reason, which one would presumably not expect from someone who exalts feeling above reason. In fact, Plotinus claims that the just soul is analogous to elders at the assembly who sit in quiet consideration, ignoring the tumult of the disorderly populace, which is itself analogous to those who are not in control of their bodies and Spirit part of their soul (VI.4.15.18–32). I will argue that there are the three parts of the soul and discuss how humans are essentially the Reason part of their soul, happiness occurs when Reason guides one's soul, philosophers follow their Reason, and that justice is a well-ordered soul where Reason rules. Someone, as Cairns alleges of Plotinus, who believes that emotions are to be exalted above reason should not make any of these claims. Furthermore, Plotinus holds that the One is beyond thought (V.3.14.18–19). Thus, Cairns' conception of mysticism is incorrect, at least as a characterization of Plotinus' view.

Third, I would argue that for any given definition of mysticism, either Plato and Plotinus both are mystics, or both are not mystics. By showing that each experience discussed by both philosophers is similar, we see that Cairns is mistaken in accusing Plotinus of misreading or misunderstanding Plato.[14] Since it is nearly unanimous that Plotinus is a mystic, I will argue that Plato is a mystic using their writings to show the similarity.

Before arguing that Plato is best construed as a mystic in a Plotinian sense, let us review some other significant statements that have been made against the view that Plato is a mystic:

(1) Some Neo-Platonists depart from Plato by insisting that knowledge of the [One] can only be acquired through a mystical vision. Neoplatonic literature is replete with detailed accounts of the [One] and its various emanations. But unless we have had such a mystical vision or are willing to trust the authority of those who claim to have had such a vision, this aspect of the world-view of the Neoplatonists is unappealing. Mysticism often leads to the opposite extreme from relativism—to an absolutism that is antithetical to the dialectical philosophy of Plato.[15]

(2) A short cut would have been mysticism—the contemplation of the inexplicable, the adoration of the unknowable. But that would have been losing "the eye of the soul." Plato is looking for the intelligible, not for an emotional intoxication.[16]

(3) In this paper it has been argued that Plato shares with the traditional mystics many features, but that it is difficult to say with confidence that his system culminates in a *nonrational or "emotional" apprehension of ultimate reality with which one becomes united*.... [I]t is evident that Plato is a thinker too multifaceted and fertile to be easily bound by our imperfect but nonetheless useful categories. He was first and foremost an exponent of philosophic reason.

His method is intuitive at its highest point, but intuition alone does not establish the claim of "mystic." Inspiration, intuition, reason: these odd companions are all aspects of Plato's method of philosophizing.[17]

(4) What is new about the Plotinian experience is that it is, first and foremost, mystical. Plato had described, in poetic, rhetorical terms, a lover's amorous agitation for his beloved: love starts out being carnal, but then, with the ascent of the soul, it serves as the motor force for an intellectual, almost scientific process. Platonic love is thus not, properly speaking, "a mystical transport."[18]

(5) The willingness to use traditional symbols for the faith that there is is something more than mechanism in the universe, explain them all. But they have been and still are endlessly quoted in the literature of superstition and mysticism by the mob of incredible twaddle-churners, fanatical and hypocritical ascetics, maudlin mystics, and table-tipping thaumaturgists who have made Platonism a byword with rational men.[19]

(6) The [Neo-Platonists] doubted in the last instance the possibility of theoretical knowledge of the ultimate basis of all being and sought a remedy in revelation received in a state of mystical ecstasy. . . . Neo-Platonism with its need of revelation instead of independent investigation . . . thus completed the suicide of philosophy.[20]

Re: (1): We will see that each philosopher describes the experience of the Good or One both as a vision and as knowledge of the Good. Moreover, I have always read Plato as an objectivist who claims that there are Forms that are eternal beings, existing whether or not we acknowledge their existence, along with souls, the World-Soul, and many others. Here I will confirm that Plotinus' statement, among others, that dialectic is the most important part of philosophy and performs the same functions in his philosophy as they do in Plato's.

Re: (2): There is evidence in both Plato and Plotinus that the Good is unknowable as well as knowable, but mysticism is not seen as a shortcut to anything; it is the culmination of years of mathematics and dialectic. Plotinus is looking for the intelligible as well in Nous and not merely emotional intoxication; lastly, as will be shown, they each claim that true happiness is a direct result of nothing other than wisdom and/or knowledge.

Re: (3): The issue of whether the ultimate experience is rational or irrational is a difficult one to settle. Plato and Plotinus each claim that dialectic is the chief way—among other requirements of the soul—for one to achieve knowledge of the Good, but also acknowledge that this is the greatest ineffable experience that anyone can have.

Re: (4): Plato and Plotinus both have the same view of love as we will see; more specifically, they agree on the details of the Ladder of Love in Plato's *Symposium*, where love moves from being physical, to intellectual, to a vision of Beauty, and they are committed to the view that one can have a transformative vision of Beauty.

Re: (5): First, I sincerely hope that I do not fit any of the ad hominem arguments Shorey uses against his opponents here, and instead urge careful consideration of Plato and Plotinus' writings before siding with Shorey on this issue. Plato is certainly saying more than merely using *symbols* for the belief that there is something more than mechanism in the universe, and this is not enough, in my view, to explain what Plato is relating in all of the "mystical" passages. He is urging us to have that experience that he describes as being ultimate, even arguing that we *desire* it. He is arguing that God and gods exist, among many other things, and not merely stating a faith, but adamantly believes (if I am not permitted to say, "know") it, and argues for gods' existence in the *Laws* (886c–99d). All of what I have said applies to Plotinus as well, of course. To briefly rebut Shorey's ascetic point, both Plato and Plotinus state the importance of asceticism in one's being a good philosopher, as will be shown.

Re: (6): As stated in my first two responses, Plotinus and Plato hold that the highest knowledge is knowledge of the Good, while at the same time referring to it as a vision, and claiming that the Good is in some sense unknowable as well, as we'll see. However true Zeller's words may be about Neo-Platonism causing the suicide of philosophy, I hope to show that Plato stressed the need for the ultimate experience no less than Plotinus. In response to Zeller, my retort is *either* that Plato destroyed philosophy—if I can show that he believes what Plotinus believes—*or* Plotinus is not one of the Neo-Platonists who destroyed philosophy.

A definition of mysticism is not required

One might demand a definition of mysticism, but there are several reasons why I wish to avoid doing so.[21] First, my definition would almost certainly not satisfy everyone; for instance, a very broad definition would include every kind of mystic[22] and hence would only beg the question in favor of my case and be useless.

Second, I trust Bussanich,[23] who argues that Stace's[24] and Zaehner's (two of the foremost experts on mysticism) definitions have been shown to be lacking. If experts in mysticism have not done an excellent job of defining mysticism, I presume I will not be successful either.

Third, defining mysticism is not necessary for this project since, regardless of the definition, Plotinus is taken to be a mystic. If I can show that Plato describes the experience in the same way as Plotinus, then the precise definition of mysticism is moot.[25]

Thus, I will try to show that Plato and Plotinus each describe the experience in similar terminology, with similar characteristics. In this work, I will not address the possibility that Plato believes that one can have a non-dual experience, such that the seer of the Good becomes one with the Good, so there is no distinction between the Good and its experiencer,[26] because I have dealt with this issue elsewhere.

Plato and Plotinus describe a similar experience

Both Plato and Plotinus describe the effects of this ultimate experience in terms that make any possible sense experience pale in comparison. Since these kinds of passages occur in both Plato and Plotinus, we are faced with the choice of either viewing both philosophers as mystics, or as non-mystics. But because Plotinus is nearly universally taken to be a mystic, the case I am making is that Plato and Plotinus describe effects of the same ultimate experience.

Plato: In a letter to the friends of Dion:

> This knowledge ["knowledge of the problems with which I am concerned" at 341c1–2] is not something that can be put into words like other sciences; but after long-continued intercourse between teacher and pupil, in joint pursuit of the subject, suddenly, like light flashing forth when a fire is kindled, it is born in the soul and straightway nourishes itself. (*Letter* VII 341c5–d2)

I read Plato as saying that unless you have had the experience of this knowledge being generated in your soul—and though "joint pursuit of the subject" may be nothing other than dialectic—words will not suffice to acquire such knowledge.

Socrates agrees with what Simmias says about having firsthand experience of divine things. Simmias says:

> I believe, as perhaps you [Socrates] do, that precise knowledge on that subject is impossible or extremely difficult in our present life, but that it surely shows a very poor spirit not to examine thoroughly what is said about it, and to desist before one is exhausted by an all-round investigation. One should achieve one of these things: learn the truth about these things or find it for oneself, or, if that is impossible, adopt the best and most irrefutable of men's theories, and, borne upon this, sail through the dangers of life as upon a raft, *unless someone should make that journey safer and less risky upon a firmer vessel of some divine doctrine*. . . .
>
> Said Socrates: "You may well be right, my friend." (*Phaedo* 85c1–d4, e1–2; emphasis added)

Socrates is agreeing with Simmias that one must "learn the truth about these things or find it for oneself," using the most irrefutable human theories, if we cannot have "some divine doctrine" (a divine word or account, implying revelation, as Fowler and Tredennick translate *logou theiou tinos*), which is a stronger vessel than the best human doctrine. Socrates, the same character that grilled the priest in the *Euthyphro* about the definition of piety, and argued that Piety was a nature that was independent of the gods, and questioned the benefits of sacrificing and praying, seems now in the *Phaedo* to simply accept Simmias' statement that we should have a divine revelation if we can. Why would he quickly agree with Simmias and not doggedly question him about that view as he did in the *Euthyphro*? My argument to the best explanation, given this and other passages in Plato, is that Socrates agrees with Simmias because Plato thinks it possible to have such a revelation. But there is more textual evidence.

In the *Symposium*, for instance, Socrates describes the vision of what Beauty is, as told to him by Diotima:

> All of a sudden he will catch sight of something wonderfully beautiful in its nature; that, Socrates, is the reason for all his earlier labors:
>
> "First, it always *is* and neither comes to be nor passes away, neither waxes nor wanes. Second, it is not beautiful this way and ugly that way, nor beautiful at one

> time and ugly at another, nor beautiful in relation to one thing and ugly in relation to another; nor is it beautiful here but ugly there, as it would be if it were beautiful for some people and ugly for others....
>
> And there in life, Socrates, ... there if anywhere should a person live his life, beholding that Beauty. If you once see that, it won't occur to you to measure beauty by gold or clothing or beautiful boys and youths—who, if you see them now, strike you out of your senses, and make you, you and many others, eager to be with the boys you love and look at them forever, if there were any way to do that, forgetting food and drink, everything but looking at them and being with them." (*Symposium* 210e4–1a5, 211d1–8)

Plato is relating several things about this experience: First, the vision of Beauty is the soul coming to an understanding of the Beautiful Itself, or the Form of Beauty. Second, the vision is something that "neither waxes nor wanes"; that is, it neither increases nor decreases in intensity. It is as if your soul is a light switch that is either in the "on" (had the experience) or "off" (have not had the experience) position. Third, if two people were to have the vision of Beauty, they would agree about what was truly beautiful. Fourth, Plato urges us that our lives should be lived ("if anywhere") in beholding that Beauty, implying that life is not worth living unless one has this vision. Lastly, the knower of Beauty learns how and in what ways the beautiful physical objects are merely copies or cheap imitations of the Form of Beauty, so she would find it ridiculous to call physical things truly beautiful and hence, would not urgently pursue them.

I will show that both philosophers seem to describe the awesome nature of seeing/knowing the Good, as well as seeing/knowing Beauty.

Plotinus:

> So we must ascend again to the Good, which every soul desires. Anyone who has seen it knows what I mean when I say that it is beautiful. It is desired as good, and the desire for it is directed to Good, and the attainment of it is for those who go up to the higher world....
>
> If anyone sees it, what passion will he feel, what longing in his desire to be united with it, what a shock of delight! The man who has not seen it may desire it as good, but he who has seen it glories in its beauty and is full of wonder and delight, enduring a shock which causes no hurt, loving with true passion and piercing longing; he laughs at all other loves and despises what he thought beautiful before; it is like the experience of those who have met appearances of gods or spirits and do not any more appreciate as they did the beauty of other bodies. (I.6.7.1–4, 12–21; adapted from A.H. Armstrong[27])

Plotinus agrees that the experience of seeing the Good[28] makes one realize that every physical beautiful thing pales in comparison. It is also clear that Plotinus is talking about an experience that one can have, and that he is agreeing with Plato's description of Beauty in the *Symposium*.

Plato: Diotima—whose account Socrates is retelling, and with whose account he agrees—also states in Plato's *Symposium* that this appearance or vision of the beautiful is *not* one kind of knowledge:

> *Nor will the beautiful appear to him* in the guise of a face or hands or anything else that belongs to the body. *It will not appear to him as* one idea [*logos*] or *one kind of knowledge* [*tis epistēmē*]. It is not anywhere in another thing, as in an animal, or in earth, or in heaven, or in anything else, but itself by itself with itself, it is always one in form; and all the other beautiful things share in that, in such a way that when those others come to be or pass away, this does not become the least bit smaller or greater nor suffer any change. (*Symposium* 211a5–b5; emphasis added)

Plato uses the phrasing "the beautiful appear[s]" to one, implying a "vision," as opposed to a "knowing experience," because while one is experiencing the Form of Beauty, one is not experiencing "knowledge" per se, but an object of knowledge. Paradoxically, however, before (*epistēmēn* at 210d7) and after (*gnōi* at 211c8) this passage, Plato admittedly also describes this experience as knowledge of Beauty.

Though I do not intend to imply that Beauty is identical to the Good on Plato's view, we can compare a similar passage about the Form of the Good in *Republic* VI, where Plato states that the Good is the source of truth and knowledge, though the Good itself is neither truth nor knowledge (*Republic* VI 508d–9a).

To sum up, I agree with Bussanich: "Plato's ultimate aim, like his predecessors, is to provide guidance toward an ultimate experience of the truth."[29] I further concur with him on the following:

> The *epopteia* is presented in *Symposium* . . . and *Phaedrus* as the culmination of an erotic, visionary ascent, but these aspects of the path are complementary to the *Phaedo* which also refers to seeing the truth and the forms (66d7, e1) and it speaks, albeit quietly, the language of desire (65c9, 66b7, 66e3). The communion of the soul with the forms in the *Phaedo*, the eroticized version of *Republic* 490b, and the vision of the forms and the Good in the cave simile all depict the *epopteia*, the transcendent experience recounted by Diotima and by Socrates himself in the palinode: "beauty was radiant to see at that time when the souls . . . saw that blessed and spectacular vision and were ushered into the mystery that we may rightly call the most blessed of all . . . and we gazed in rapture at sacred revealed objects that were perfect, and simple, and unshakeable and blissful. That was the ultimate vision, and we saw it in pure light because we were pure ourselves, not buried in this thing we are carrying around now, which we call a body, locked in it like an oyster in its shell." (*Phaedrus* 250b5–c8[30])

Plotinus: Three passages from Plotinus confirm his view that we can have an ultimate philosophical experience. First, he describes his experience:

> Often I have woken up out of the body to myself and have entered into myself, going out from all other things; I have seen a beauty wonderfully great and felt

> assurance that then most of all I belonged to the better part; I have actually lived the best life and come to identify with the divine; and set firm in it I have come to that supreme actuality, setting myself above all else in the realm of Intellect. Then after that rest in the divine, when I have come down from Intellect to discursive reasoning, I am puzzled how I ever came down, and how my soul has come to be in the body when it is what it has shown itself to be by itself, even when it is in the body. (IV.8.1.1–11)

So Plotinus claims that the experience is frequent, that he is more his soul than his body, and that the experience involves seeing beauty as a nonphysical entity. After the experience is over, Plotinus describes it:

> One should not enquire whence it comes, for there is no "whence": for it does not really come or go away anywhere, but appears or does not appear. So one must not chase after it, but wait quietly till it appears, preparing oneself to contemplate it, as the eye awaits the rising of the sun; and the sun rising over the horizon ("from Ocean," the poets say) gives itself to the eyes to see. (V.5.8.1–7)

In the sentence before this quotation, Plotinus relates that the experience is a vision of truest seeing, and in several sentences after this quotation, he states that the object of this vision is above Intellect. In the present passage, he warns that we should not think of the Good in any physical terms such as existing in time or space, or even—as he claims elsewhere—being a being at all. Plotinus also tells us that we can only prepare for this experience and wait for something to happen, which I find parallel to Plato's claim in the *Meno* that virtue is a gift from the gods.

Further, according to Plotinus we need to have this vision in order to truly realize ourselves as human beings:

> It is enough if the intellect comes into contact with it; but when it has done so, while the contact lasts, it is absolutely impossible, nor has it time, to speak; but it is afterwards that it is able to reason about it. One must believe one has seen, when the soul suddenly takes light: For this is from him and he is it; we must think that he is present when, like another god whom someone called to his house, he comes and brings light to us: for if he had not come, he would not have brought the light. So the unenlightened soul does not have him as god; but when it is enlightened it has what it sought, and this is the soul's true end, to touch that light and see it by itself, not by another light, but by the light which is also its means of seeing. It must see that light by which it is enlightened: for we do not see the sun by another light than his own. (V.3.17.25–37[31])

Plotinus thinks the soul that is unfulfilled and does not have what it sought is "unenlightened," and once it achieves its true end is "enlightened." He also claims that we cannot use our reason during the vision.

Lastly, in his biography of the life of Plotinus, Porphyry states that Plotinus united with God—the One—four times while Porphyry was with him.[32] This experience certainly does not appear to be a mathematical proof or a philosophical argument.

In summary, Plato and Plotinus seem to be describing a similar experience given their writings, and thus we seem to be warranted in referring to Plato as a mystic—given that we are already referring to Plotinus as one.

1.2 The ultimate answers to the most significant philosophical questions

Both Plato and Plotinus believe that we can have a single experience of the ultimate entity of the universe that tells us what exists (answering the ultimate question of metaphysics), that gives us ultimate knowledge (answering that we can know and what we can know—the ultimate questions of epistemology), and that tells us how we should live (addressing the ultimate question of ethics).

Plato: It is worth noting that not all commentators agree that the Good is, for Plato, the ultimate metaphysical, epistemological and/or ethical principle.[33] Let us start with a passage from the *Republic*, where Plato, summarizing his Cave Allegory, says what this experience—the vision of the Good—tells you:

> In the knowable, the last thing to be seen yet hardly seen is the Idea of Good, and, having seen it, one must conclude that it is the cause of all that is right and beautiful in everything, having brought light and its master in the visible, and having provided authoritative truth and reason in the intelligible; and that one who is to act wisely in private or public must have seen it. (*Republic* VII 517b8–c5; my translation[34])

Plato claims that the Good is the cause of everything that is good, right and beautiful, true, and rational, and even of the perceptible sun. So if the Good is the source of rightness, and if one is to act wisely, then one must see the Form of the Good.

Plato asserts that the Good is the cause of truth and knowledge, but is not itself truth or knowledge:

> So that what gives truth to the things known and the power to know to the knower is the Form of the Good. And though it is the cause of knowledge and truth, it is also an object of knowledge. Both knowledge and truth are beautiful things, but the Good is other and more beautiful than they. In the visible realm, light and sight are rightly considered sunlike, but it is wrong to think that they are the sun, so here it is right to think of knowledge and truth as goodlike but wrong to think that either of them is the Good—for the Good is yet more prized. (*Republic* VI 508d4–9a5; adapted from Grube/Reeve)

For Plato, the Form of the Good is the source of knowledge and truth. He also states that one cannot truly know goodness until one knows the Form of the Good:

> Then the same applies to the Good. Unless someone can distinguish in an account the Form of the Good from everything else, can survive all refutation, as if in a battle, striving to judge things not in accordance with opinion but in accordance with being, and can come through all this with his account still intact, you'll say that he doesn't know the Good Itself or any other good. And if he gets hold of some image of it, you'll say that it's through opinion, not knowledge, for he is dreaming and asleep throughout his present life, and, before he wakes up here, he will arrive in Hades and go to sleep forever.
>
> Yes, by god, I'll certainly say all of that. (*Republic* VII 534b8–d2; adapted from Grube/Reeve)

More importantly, Plato says that we cannot benefit from any knowledge we may have if we do not have knowledge of the Good. Socrates says:

> You have often heard that the Form of the Good is indeed the greatest thing learned, and that it is by their relation to it that just things and other things become useful and beneficial. And now you are probably aware that I am about to speak about this Form and say in addition to this, that we do not know this Form adequately; and if we do not know this Form, even if we should know especially well the other things [that is, the just things and other things] without knowing this Form, you are aware that there would be no benefit to us, just as there would be no benefit if we should possess something without the possession of the good. (*Republic* VI 505a2–b3; my translation)

So, from the earlier passage, Plato holds that the Good is the source of knowledge, and from the latter that the Good is the greatest thing to learn, without which all other knowledge, if one has any, is useless and not beneficial. For Plato, benefiting oneself is living well, and living well is happiness, and the goal of ethics is living well and being happy, so this passage entails that knowing the Good is necessary for being happy. Thus, the Good is necessary for ethical behavior; it is not merely the reason that all good things exist.

Plato also relates that one must go beyond assumptions such as are made in geometry and other deductive arts and sciences—arguably logic and deductive reasoning are meant to be included here as well—until one arrives at the unhypothetical first principle (*Republic* VI 511b–d, VII 532a–b, 533c–d), which he implies is the Good.[35] Thus the Good is the cause of knowledge, truth, and every good thing that exists, and the entity that one must know in order to know both what goodness is, and also to be a good person.

In the *Meno*, Plato says that virtue is "a gift of the gods," which is consistent with the idea that a vision or knowledge of the Good is not acquired deductively; its acquisition is attained or not, and its attainment is not assured by any means:

> If we were right in the way in which we spoke and investigated in this whole discussion, virtue would be neither an inborn quality nor taught, but comes to

> those who possess it as a gift from the gods which is not accompanied by understanding, unless there is someone among our statesmen who can make another into a statesman. If there were one, he could be said to be among the living as Homer said Tiresias was among the dead, namely, that "he alone retained his wits while the others flitted about like shadows." In the same manner such a man would, as far as virtue is concerned, here also be the only true reality compared, as it were, with shadows.
>
> I think that is an excellent way to put it, Socrates.
>
> It follows from this reasoning, Meno, that virtue appears to be present in those of us who may possess it as a gift from the gods. (*Meno* 99e4–100b4)

In addition, the *Meno* excerpt may make sense of the Divided Line passage in the *Republic*, where it is said that one must proceed beyond one's assumptions in order to have knowledge.

Moreover, Plato states that one's happiness is connected to the ordered rule of philosophic life, and that having the power of goodness is the noblest prize:

> If the victory goes to the better elements in both their minds [Reason], which lead them [that is, the lower parts of the soul—Appetite and Spirit] to follow the assigned regimen of philosophy, their life here below is one of bliss and shared understanding. They are modest and fully in control of themselves now that they have enslaved the part that brought trouble into the soul and set free the part that gave it virtue. After death, when they have grown wings and become weightless, they have won the first of three rounds in these, the true Olympic Contests. There is no greater good than this that either human self-control or divine madness can offer a man. (*Phaedrus* 256a7–b5)

These passages show Plato's belief that we can have an experience that will entail our happiness, that is the highest achievement of human life, and that involves knowing or having a vision of the Good.

Plato sums up the study of virtue and vice in a letter, stating that long and earnest labor is involved, and that knowledge that truly illuminates an object's nature is at the extremity of human effort, analogous to attempting to light a fire by rubbing sticks together:

> In short, neither quickness of learning nor a good memory can make a man see when his nature is not akin to the object, for this knowledge never takes root in an alien nature; so that no man who is not naturally inclined and akin to justice and all other forms of excellence, even though he may be quick at learning and remembering this and that and other things, nor any man who, though akin to justice, is slow at learning and forgetful, will ever attain the truth that is attainable about virtue. Nor about vice, either, for these must be learned together, just as the truth and error about any part of being must be learned together, through long and earnest labor, as I said at the beginning. Only when all of these things—names, definitions, and visual and other perceptions—have been rubbed against one

> another and tested, pupil and teacher asking and answering questions in good will and without envy—only then, when reason and knowledge are at the very extremity of human effort, can they illuminate the nature of any object. (*Letter* VII 344a2–c1)

Plotinus: Plotinus concurs with Plato that the Good is the ontological[36] source of all good things including knowledge,[37] as well as the entity that we must experience in order to be truly virtuous:[38] He agrees with Plato that the Good is the greatest thing to learn:

> The knowledge or touching of the Good is the greatest thing, and Plato says it is the "greatest study," not calling the looking at it a "study," but learning about it beforehand. We are taught about it by comparisons and negations and knowledge of the things which come from it and certain methods of ascent by degrees, but we are put on the way to it by purifications and virtues and adornings and by gaining footholds in the intelligible and settling ourselves firmly there and feasting on its contents. But whoever has become at once contemplator of himself and all the rest and object of his contemplation, and, since he has become substance and intellect and "the complete living being," no longer looks at it from outside—when he has become this he is near, and that Good is next above him, and already close by, shining upon all the intelligible world. (VI.7.36.3–15; adapted from A.H. Armstrong[39])

For Plotinus, the Good is "next above him," that is, the intellect or intelligible world, just as Plato claimed—the Good is the source of knowledge and truth, but is not itself knowledge and truth. Plotinus thinks that in "[running] up beyond beauty" and going "beyond all," (that is, seeing the Good) one sees the source of virtue:

> He was one with himself, with no distinction in himself either in relation to himself or to other things—for there was no movement in him and he had no emotion, no desire for anything else when he had made the ascent—but there was not even any reason or thought, and he himself was not there, if we must even say this; but he was as if carried away or possessed by a god, in a quiet solitude and a state of calm, not turning away anywhere in his being and not busy about himself, altogether at rest and having become a kind of rest. He had no thought of beauties, but had already *run up beyond beauty* and gone beyond the choir of virtues, like a man who enters into the sanctuary and leaves behind the statues in the outer shrine; these become again the first things he looks at when he comes out of the sanctuary, after his contemplation within and intercourse there, not with a statue or image but with the Divine itself; they are secondary objects of contemplation. But that other, perhaps, was not a contemplation but another kind of seeing, a being out of oneself and simplifying and giving oneself over and pressing towards contact and rest and a sustained thought leading to adaptation, if one is going to contemplate what is in the sanctuary. But if one looks in another way, one finds nothing. These are images; and this, therefore, is how the wise among the expositors of holy things express in

> riddles how that god is seen; and a wise priest who understands the riddle may make the contemplation real by entering the sanctuary; and even if he has not been there, and thinks that this sanctuary is something invisible, and the source and the principle, he will know that he sees principle by principle and that like is united with like. And he will neglect none of the divine properties which the soul can have even before the vision, and will seek the rest from the vision; and the rest, for him who has *gone beyond all*, is that which is before all. (VI.9.11.8–35; emphasis added[40])

We glean that Plotinus holds that there is a source of beauty and virtue, and that it is possible to know one's source and principle, which is what we crave.[41]

Taken together with the Platonic passages, the last two Plotinian quotations make Anton's claim about Plotinus faulty: "He could only use Plato to borrow a ladder to climb above Beauty, above all Forms, including the Form of the Good, and finally touch the One . . ."[42] While Plotinus certainly claims that a person can come to see or touch the One that is beyond being (that is, the One is beyond the Forms) we saw that Plato makes the same kinds of claims about the Good: The Good is the source of the Forms, Beauty, and knowledge, and the ultimate goal is to have a vision or gain knowledge of the Good.[43]

Lastly, Plotinus states that the vision of the highest is the greatest experience that the soul can undergo,[44] since no other experience can really compare:

> When the soul has good fortune with it, and it comes to it, or rather, being there already, appears, when that soul turns away from the things that are there, and has prepared by making itself as beautiful as possible and has come to likeness (the preparation and the adornment are clearly understood, I think, by those who are preparing themselves) and it sees it in itself suddenly appearing (for there is nothing between, nor are there still two but both are one; nor could you still make a distinction while it is present; lovers and their beloveds here below imitate this in their will to be united), it does not still perceive its body, that it is in it, and does not speak of itself as anything else, not man, or living thing, or being, or all (for the contemplation of these would be somehow disturbing), and it has no time for them nor wants them, but it has been seeking it, and meets that when it is present, and looks at that instead of itself; but it has not even time to see who the soul is that looks. There, truly, it would not exchange this for anything in the world, not even if someone handed over the whole universe to it, because there is nothing still better, and nothing that is more a good; for it does not run up higher, and all the other things are on its way down, even if they are in the realm above. So then it has the ability to judge rightly and to know that this is what it desired, and to establish that there is nothing better than it. For there is no deceit there; or where could it find any thing truer than truth? What it speaks, then, is that, and it speaks it afterwards, and speaks it in silence, and in its happiness is not cheated in thinking that it is happy; and it does not say it is happy when the body tickles it, but when it has become that which it was before, when it is fortunate. But it says it in contempt of all the other things in which it delighted before, offices or powers or riches or

> beauties or sciences, and it would not have spoken if it had not met better things than these; it is not afraid, either, that anything may happen to it, since it does not even see it while it is with that; but if all the other things about it perished, it would even be pleased, that it might be alone with this; so great a degree of happiness has it reached. (VI.7.34.8–38[45])

This vision is the key to the soul's happiness for Plotinus, just as Plato stated in the earlier excerpts. These passages taken together leave me wondering about Meijer's[46] claim that contemplation of the Ideas is the Platonic ideal, whereas experiencing the One is the ideal for Plotinus, as well as Mayhall's[47] claim: "Much that is central is not, in its Plotinian form, to be found in Plato at all." It is best to postpone evaluation of Mayhall's statement until the claims concerning epistemology (especially dialectic) and ethics have also been reviewed.

In sum, Plato and Plotinus are committed to there being an experience that tells us what exists, what we can know, and how to live. We also saw that not all commentators agree on what the Good is for Plato, or that Plotinus describes the experience in the same way as Plato does.

1.3 The everlasting and self-sustaining experience

Plato and Plotinus both claim that the ultimate experience is everlasting—neither increasing in knowledge nor decreasing from knowledge to forgetfulness—and is self-sustaining. In short, one does not lose the fruits after undergoing the ultimate experience. (Few commentators even mention this aspect of the experience.)

Plato: First, Plato says that knowledge comes about from an experience, which is best interpreted together with what is described in the *Republic* as a vision of the Good:

> This knowledge ["knowledge of the problems with which I am concerned" at 341c1–2] is not something that can be put into words like other sciences; but after long-continued intercourse between teacher and pupil, in joint pursuit of the subject, suddenly, like light flashing forth when a fire is kindled, it is born in the soul and straightway nourishes itself. (*Letter* VII 341c5–d2[48])

Given that Plato devoted himself to the study of philosophy, and argued that knowledge of the Good was the most important thing to learn, we can safely infer that Plato has in mind by "the subject" the Good or knowing the Forms, and he implies candidly outside of his usual dialogic form that the experience is a self-sustaining one: the Greek for "straightway nourishes itself" (Post translates it "at once becomes self-sustaining") is *auto heauto ēdē trephei*.

A good number of Platonic scholars have questioned the authenticity of *Letter* VII (and others), so we might wonder if there is anywhere else in the certainly authentic[49] dialogues where we find Plato claiming that one can have a self-sustaining or everlasting experience of the Forms. Indubitably there is, which should give support to the authenticity of *Letter* VII at least, or make doubters less vehement on this point of contention. There is evidence for the everlasting aspect of the experience in the *Symposium* and the *Laws*.

In the *Symposium*, Socrates relates Diotima's speech to others, and implicitly agrees with Diotima:

> ["]But how would it be, in our view," she said, "if someone got to see the Beautiful itself, absolute, pure, unmixed, not polluted by human flesh or colors or any other great nonsense of mortality, but if he could see the divine Beauty itself in its one form? Do you think it would be a poor life for a human being to look there and to behold it by that which he ought, and to be with it?" (*Symposium* 211d8–2a2)

Diotima implies that humans who behold Beauty Itself can live richly with it for their whole life, which attests to the everlasting and unforgettable aspect of the experience.[50]

For Platonic evidence on this point, in the *Laws*, the Athenian Stranger implies that one can "capture" the "highest good" and spend one's remaining life in its possession:

> Nothing that nature gives a man is better adapted than his soul to enable him to avoid evil, keep on the track of the highest good, and when he has captured his quarry to live in intimacy with it for the rest of his life. (*Laws* V 728c9–d2)

Thus, Plato, in his letters and dialogues holds that once one has an experience or vision of the Good and/or Beauty, one never loses the fruits of that encounter.

Plotinus: Plotinus states that even if someone who has seen the Good were to be tortured in the Bull of Phalaris,[51] that person still does not lose sight of it, implying that it is not something one can forget, and that once experienced, it is always present. Keeping in mind that the "greatest study" for Plato and Plotinus is the "learning about it beforehand" (as Plotinus puts it at VI.7.36.6) about the knowledge of the Good:

> The good man's activities will not be hindered by changes of fortune, but will vary according to what change and chance brings; but they will all be equally fine, and perhaps, finer for being adapted to circumstances. . . . But the "greatest study" is always ready to hand and always with him, all the more if he is in the so-called "Bull of Phalaris"—which it is silly to call pleasant, though people keep on saying that it is; for according to their philosophy that which says that its state is pleasant is the very same thing which is in pain; according to ours that which suffers pain is one thing, and there is another which, even while it is compelled to accompany that which suffers pain, remains in its own company and will not fall short of the vision of the universal good. (I.4.13.1–3, 5–12)

So even a soul in the Bull of Phalaris "remains in its own company and will not fall short of the vision of the universal good." Interestingly, Plotinus also claims that the presence of the Good in the one who possesses it remains, even while one is asleep:

> The Good, since it was there long before to arouse an innate desire, is present even to those asleep and does not astonish those who at any time see it, because it is always there and there is never recollection of it; but people do not see it, because it is present to them in their sleep. (V.5.12.11–4)

Thus, both Plato and Plotinus hold that once one experiences the Good (and/or Beauty, in the case of Plato), one never loses the presence that is gained by that experience.

1.4 The difficult and rare experience

Far from claiming that the experience or vision of the Good or Beauty is easy or frequently enjoyed, both philosophers claim that the ultimate experience is very difficult, and is therefore rare. I have no issues with the commentators who mention the difficulty and rarity of the experience.[52]

Plato on difficulty: There are many passages in which Plato claims that the vision of the Good and/or Beauty, and becoming a good or virtuous person is a difficult and even painful experience.[53] In a passage from the Cave Allegory, Plato says that a prisoner released from the Cave who was forced to see the fire and reality in the cave would be "pained" [*algoi*] (*Republic* VII 515c8) and "irritated" [*aganaktein*] (*Republic* VII 516a1). Of course, the cave is a metaphor for reality, and the eyes represent the mind of the possible knower, so having pain in one's eyes represents experiencing psychological pain at realizing that reality is not what one once thought it was. Shortly after these references to pain, Plato says:

> And if someone dragged him away from there by force, up the rough, steep path, and didn't let him go until he had dragged him into the sunlight, wouldn't he be pained and irritated at being treated that way? And when he came into the light, with the sun filling his eyes, wouldn't he be unable to see a single one of the things now said to be true?
>
> He would be unable to see them, at least at first. (*Republic* VII 515e6–6a4)

So the released prisoner of the cave feels pain when he sees the fire while still in the cave, and, after a "rough, steep" ascent through the cave to the outside, feels pain again at the true light of the sun. Analogously, Plato claims that the potential Good-knower comes to feel pain as he or she attempts to possess knowledge.

Lastly, in the Cave Allegory, Plato relates difficulties after the released prisoner comes to know the Good and returns to the cave (namely, deals with the public):

> Before his eyes had recovered—and the adjustment would not be quick—while his vision was still dim, if he had to compete again with the perceptual prisoners in recognizing the shadows, wouldn't he invite ridicule? Wouldn't it be said of him that he'd returned from his upward journey with his eyesight ruined and that it isn't worthwhile even to try to travel upward? And, as for anyone who tried to free

> them and lead them upward, if they could somehow get their hands on him, wouldn't they kill him?
>
> They certainly would. (*Republic* VII 516e8–7a7)

Thus, Plato states that the knower of the Good will appear ridiculous to most people, and may annoy most people so much that they may want to kill him or her.

Plato claims that even the "blessed gods" themselves with their excellent chariots—souls—have a steep ascent, and that it only gets more difficult for "other chariots," which are presumably humans:

> When they ["the blessed gods" at 247a4] go to feast at the banquet they have a steep climb to the high tier at the rim of heaven; on this slope the gods' chariots move easily, since they are balanced and well under control, but the other chariots barely make it. The heaviness of the bad horse drags its charioteer toward the earth and weighs him down if he has failed to train it well, and this causes the most extreme toil and struggle that a soul will face. (*Phaedrus* 247a8–b6)

Thus the toil and struggling of humans is much more than what the blessed gods deal with, though the blessed gods still have a challenge.

Further, in addition to Socrates who mentions that the wondrous vision of the very soul of beauty is a result of "all of his previous labors" (*Symposium* 210e6; my translation), Plato says in a letter to Dionysius that this experience is typically difficult:

> Perhaps you once heard something from someone and providentially started on the track of the answer, but then, thinking you had it safe, neglected to fix fast the proofs of it, which now dart here and there about some object of your fancy, whereas the reality itself is quite different. You are not alone in this experience; I assure you that everyone at first hearing is affected in just this way, and though some have more difficulty than others, there is almost no one who escapes with but little effort. (*Letter* II 313b4–c5)

So Plato claims that almost everyone has difficulty understanding what his view of the truth is, which implies that it is all the more difficult for one to actually understand (not merely intellectually).[54]

Plato also refers to becoming a good person as an important struggle, which is only accomplished if one knows the Good:

> Yes, for the struggle to be good rather than bad is important, Glaucon, much more important than people think. Therefore, we mustn't be tempted by honor, money, rule, or even poetry into neglecting justice and the rest of virtue. (*Republic* X 608b4–8[55])

Plato also says:

> I disregard the things held in honor by the majority of people, and by practicing truth I really try, to the best of my ability, to be and to live as a very good man, and

> when I die, to die like that. And I call on all other people as well, as far as I can—and you especially I call on in response to your call—to this way of life, this contest, that I hold to be worth all the other contests in this life. (*Gorgias* 526d5–e4[56])

So the pursuit of the human good exceeds all other contests. Plato also puts this point in a similar way when he says several times that the gods have "put sweat between us and virtue":

> Some [poets] harp on the ease of vice, as follows:
> *Vice in abundance is easy to get;*
> *The road is smooth and begins beside you,*
> *But the gods have put sweat between us and virtue,*
> and a road that is long, rough, and steep. (*Republic* II 364c6–d3[57])

Via the Athenian in the *Laws*, Plato gives a fuller version of Hesiod's saying:

> People who are anxious to attain moral excellence with all possible speed are pretty thin on the ground and it isn't easy to find them: most only go to prove the wisdom of Hesiod's remark that the road to vice is smooth and can be traveled without sweating, because it is very short; but "as the price of virtue," he says,
> *The gods have imposed the sweat of our brows,*
> *And long and steep is the ascent that you have to make*
> *And rough, at first; but when you get to the top,*
> *Then the rugged road is easy to endure.* (*Laws* IV 718d7–9a2)

Plato also claims that when he tells the truth to an arrogant person—that he must "[work] like a slave to attain" the truth and live a life of reason—it will not be easy for this person to hear that message:

> And if someone approaches a young man in that condition ["he (who) exalt(s) himself to great heights and (brims) with pretension and pride that is empty and lacks understanding" at 494d1–2] and gently tells him the truth, namely, that there's no understanding in him, that he needs it, and that it can't be acquired unless he works like a slave to attain it, do you think that it will be easy for him to listen when he's in the midst of so many evils?
>
> Far from it. (*Republic* VI 494d4–8[58])

In meeting Dionysius, Plato actually came across a person with just these qualities:

> When I arrived, I thought my first task was to prove whether Dionysius was really on fire with philosophy, or whether the many reports that came to Athens were without foundation. Now there is a certain way of putting this to the test, a dignified way and quite appropriate to tyrants, especially to those whose heads are full of half-understood doctrines, which I saw at once upon my arrival was particularly the case with Dionysius. You must picture to such men the extent of the undertaking,

> describing what sort of inquiry it is, with how many difficulties it is beset, and how much labor it involves. For *anyone who* hears this, who *is a true lover of wisdom, with the divine quality that makes him akin to it and worthy of pursuing it, thinks that he has heard of a marvelous quest that he must at once enter upon with all earnestness, or life is not worth living*; and from that time forth he pushes himself and urges on his leader without ceasing, until he has reached the end of the journey or has become capable of doing without a guide and finding the way himself. This is the state of mind in which such a man lives; whatever his occupation may be, above everything and always he holds fast to philosophy and to the daily discipline that best makes him apt at learning and remembering, and capable of reasoning soberly with himself; while for the opposite way of living he has a persistent hatred. (*Letter* VII 340b1–d6; emphasis added.[59])

So only certain characters of persons will be able to put up with all the study and hard work in order to master philosophy. Overall then, there is overwhelming support for the claim that Plato thinks that doing philosophy properly, or being a good person, or coming to know the Good, is the hardest and most valuable struggle one can undertake in this life.

Plotinus on difficulty: Plotinus describes in superlative terms the difficulty in attaining the vision of the Good or One, using, as Plato did, the metaphors of a contest, a struggle, an ascent, among others. Note that in the following passage, where he likens the work to be done to a contest, "this" in the first sentence and "That" in the last sentence refer to attaining the ultimate experience:

> Here the greatest, the ultimate contest is set before our souls; all our toil and trouble is for *this*, not to be left without a share in the best of visions. The man who attains this is blessed in seeing that "blessed sight," and he who fails to attain it has failed utterly. A man has not failed if he fails to win beauty of colors or bodies, or power or office or kingship even, but if he fails to win this and only this. For this he should give up the attainment of kingship and of rule over all earth and sea and sky, if only by leaving and overlooking them he can turn to *That* and see. (I.6.7.30–9, emphasis added[60])

So this is a most stern and utter combat that one must undergo in order to have the ultimate experience, and Plotinus passionately urges his reader to renounce everything perceptible post haste. His use of the words "toil and trouble" implies that this is a difficult contest, echoing Plato's claims. Plotinus also declares that, for the soul, while incarnated on earth, "there are many hindrances here below to arriving at perfection" (II.9.17.47–8).

Keep in mind that when each philosopher makes claims such as "few men are truly good" or "the man of virtue is rare," this is equivalent to their claiming that few people have the ultimate experience, since we saw above that on Plato and Plotinus' view, knowledge of the Good or a vision of the Good is necessary for one's being good, happy, virtuous, and living well.

Plato on rarity: Here is additional evidence that few people will understand what beauty is:

> In fact, there are very few people who would be able to reach the Beautiful Itself and see it by itself. (*Republic* V 476b10–1; adapted from Grube/Reeve[61])

The perfect philosopher is rare:

> I suppose that everyone would agree that only a few natures possess all the qualities that we just now said were essential to becoming a complete philosopher and that seldom occur naturally among human beings ["courage, high-mindedness, ease in learning, and a good memory" at 490c9–10]. Or don't you think so?
>
> I certainly do. (*Republic* VI 491a8–b3)

Of course, for Plato, the perfect philosopher would know the Good. There are many other similar passages, where Plato discusses the rare qualities to be found in the guardians, or rulers of the ideal state—again, where the ultimate requirement is that they know the Good: *Republic* VI 495b, 503d–e, and especially 503b–c.

In the *Phaedrus*, Plato also claims that there are few people who will come to know things as they really are—Forms—just as he stated of Beauty in *Republic* 476b:

> Justice and self-control do not shine out through their images down here, and neither do the other objects of the soul's admiration; the senses are so murky that only a few people are able to make out, with difficulty, the original of the likenesses they encounter here. But beauty was radiant to see at that time when the souls, along with the glorious chorus (we were with Zeus, while others followed other gods), saw that blessed and spectacular vision and were ushered into the mystery that we may rightly call the most blessed of all. (*Phaedrus* 250b1–c1[62])

In addition, Plato states that few will recollect what we all have previously contemplated, and even the souls that do will be startled by the images of the Forms:

> Nature requires that the soul of every human being has seen reality; otherwise, no soul could have entered this sort of living thing. But not every soul is easily reminded of the reality there by what it finds here—not souls that got only a brief glance at the reality there, not souls who had such bad luck when they fell down here that they were twisted by bad company into lives of injustice so that they forgot the sacred objects they had seen before. Only a few remain whose memory is good enough; and they are startled when they see an image of what they saw up there. Then they are beside themselves, and their experience is beyond their comprehension because they cannot fully grasp what it is that they are seeing. (*Phaedrus* 249e4–50b1)

Furthermore, Plato claims that all men have a share in true opinion, but understanding—here, the quality of being able to know the Forms—is only possessed by (the gods and) a small group of humans:[63]

> If understanding and true opinion are distinct, then these "by themselves" things definitely exist—these Forms, the objects not of our sense perception, but of our understanding only. But if—as some people think—true opinion does not differ in any way from understanding, then all the things we perceive through our bodily senses must be assumed to be the most stable things there are. But we do have to speak of understanding and true opinion as distinct, of course, because we can come to have one without the other, and the one is not like the other. It is through instruction that we come to have understanding, and through persuasion that we come to have true belief. Understanding always involves a true account while true belief lacks any account. And while understanding remains unmoved by persuasion, true belief gives in to persuasion. And of true belief, it must be said, all men have a share, but of understanding, only the gods and a small group of people do. (*Timaeus* 51d3–e6)

Plato also says that it is not easy to find people who want to become truly good:

> People who are anxious to attain moral excellence with all possible speed are pretty thin on the ground and it isn't easy to find them. (*Laws* IV 718d7–e1[64])

He adds later in the *Laws* that few people even seem to know what the nature and potency of the soul is, among other things:

> It's the *soul*, my good friend, that nearly everybody seems to have misunderstood, not realizing its nature and power. Quite apart from the other points about it, people are particularly ignorant about its birth. It is one of the *first* creations, born long before all physical things, and is the chief cause of all their alterations and transformations. (*Laws* X 892a2–7)

If few know the soul, presumably even fewer would know the Forms and/or their source.

Lastly, Plato says that, due to the rarity of the proper nature, it is best not to tell too many people about his philosophy:

> I do not think that the "examination," as it is called, of these questions would be of any benefit to men, except to a few, that is, to those who could with a little guidance discover the truth for themselves. (*Letter* VII 341e1–3)

In sum, Plato believes that few people really understand the Forms and true goodness, and therefore few people are happy. The difficulty and rarity help to explain why it is not surprising that many people both are not familiar with this experience and also why many people have not had this ultimate experience, assuming there is such a thing.

Plotinus on rarity: Plotinus implies that the experience is rare by claiming that few people become "godlike," which for Plotinus means having an experience of the One.

He says, "the fact is that man has the middle place between gods and beasts, and inclines now one way, now the other, and some men become like gods and others like beasts, and some, the majority, are in between" (III.2.8.9–11).

In another passage, Plotinus claims that having the ultimate vision is a birthright of all, but few choose to use that birthright:

> Shut your eyes, and change to and wake another way of seeing, which everyone has but few use. (I.6.8.25–7[65])

So both Plato and Plotinus think that the ultimate experience is both difficult to attain, and rare among humans.

1.5 The ineffable experience

Both Plato and Plotinus believe that the vision of the Good or One is ineffable,[66] which, according to Kellenberger, has four categories or senses. To say that the mystical object is ineffable is to say that it:

(1) Cannot be shown or revealed to those who have not seen or experienced it;
(2) Cannot be imparted or transferred to others who have not directly experienced it;
(3) Defies expression, that no adequate report of its contents can be given in words; and
(4) Transcends our concepts.[67]

These categories can aid in understanding ineffability, but I will not verify each of these in the philosophies of Plato and Plotinus, who seem to focus on senses (2) and (3) more than the others.

A roughly equal amount of commentators note the ineffable character of the ultimate experience in Plato and Plotinus' works.[68] Interestingly, while no commentator that I am aware of argues against the presence of ineffability in Plotinus, A.E. Taylor makes such an argument vis-à-vis Plato's corpus.

Plato: In *Plato: The Man and his Work*, Taylor connects mysticism with ineffability and then switches to discussing myths in Plato:

> All the mystics insist on the point that the direct vision of supreme reality is not only incommunicable; it cannot even be recalled in memory when the moment of vision has passed. You are sure that you "saw"; you cannot tell what you saw even to yourself. This is the real reason why, as Burnet says, Plato never uses "mythical" language about the "forms," but only about things like the soul, which he regards as half real, partly creatures of temporality and change. We should note, however, that the supreme reality which is apprehended in the culminating vision is never said in Plato to be God, but always the supreme "form." It is the *good* which is the Platonic and Socratic *ens realissimum*.[69]

Taylor then declares his puzzlement about Plato's view of God. In a later work, however, Taylor makes two relevant and revealing statements:

> For the Platonic *philosophy* the myths can hardly be said to have any direct significance. . . . The notion, common since the days of Neo-Platonism, that the myth is the appropriate form in which to symbolize truths too sublime for rational comprehension, is entirely foreign to Plato. It is precisely when he is dealing with what he regards as the ultimate realities that his language is most "scientific" and least mythical.[70]

It seems Taylor believes that Plato uses myths (which implies ineffability for Taylor) about the soul because Plato regards the soul as only being half-real, but he does not use myths in relation to the Forms—or the Form of the Good—because he believes they can be rationally comprehended. If this is correct, however, a defender of Taylor's view would have to explain the "ineffability" passages quoted below that deal directly with the Forms (*Republic* VI 506d7–7a6, VII 533a1–5, *Timaeus* 28c3–5, 48c2–d4, *Statesman* 285d10–6b2, and *Letter* VII 341b7–e3, 342e2–3a4).

Some of those who deny the "mystical reading" of Plato claim that *Letter* VII is not authentic. However, the interpretive move of claiming inauthenticity—purely on the ground of content—has two problems: it only explains one letter and not the other similarly worded passages in unquestionably authentic dialogues; and to my knowledge, there is no credible stylometric data to suggest that Plato is not its author. I am assuming that *Letter* VII is authentic, but this is not essential for my project, given that Plato makes the same kinds of claims in dialogues whose authenticity have not been questioned.

In several passages Plato asserts that he cannot really explain this ultimate source in words—one cannot adequately describe the ultimate experience and any description of it is not equivalent to one's experiencing it. In the *Republic*, a dialogue that is certainly authentic, right before the Sun Simile, the Line Analogy, and the Cave Allegory, Plato more than hints that he will not be giving a full account of the Good:

> Let's abandon the quest for what the Good Itself is for the time being, for even to arrive at my own view about it is too big a topic for the discussion we are now started on. But I am willing to tell you about what is apparently an offspring of the Good and most like it. Is that agreeable to you, or would you rather we let the whole matter drop?
>
> It is. The story about the father remains a debt you'll pay another time.
>
> I wish that I could pay the debt in full, and you receive it instead of just the interest. So here, then, is this child and offspring of the Good. But be careful that I don't somehow deceive you unintentionally by giving you an illegitimate account of the child.
>
> We'll be as careful as possible, so speak on. (*Republic* VI 506d7–7a6; adapted from Grube/Reeve)

These "ineffable" passages beg the question: Why would Plato not be able to tell us more about the Good? For if it is his view that a true dialectician is able to give a full account of the Good (*Republic* VII 534b–d), and every good thing that participates in it, why would he not give such an account? It seems that Plato has more in his mind about the Good than he is sharing in the dialogues. One interpretation is that he does not have knowledge of the Good and is just waxing philosophical. A better interpretation is that he knows the Good but chooses not to disclose everything he knows about it. Why? Mainly because he could not put it into much more apt words even if he tried, and the multitude would think him ridiculous (see the section, "Plato and Plotinus' attitude toward the hoi polloi" below). This latter interpretation would also explain Plato's frequent use of myth and metaphor.

The challenge to my opponents who would take the first "waxing philosophical" interpretation is to explain what is going on here and in the rest of these passages that follow. Why, for example, would Plato discuss the criteria of knowledge and link the vision of the Good to that knowledge, if he is simply waxing philosophical? Plato himself also says, "I suspect that it's a lesser crime to kill someone involuntarily than to mislead people about fine, good, and just institutions" (*Republic* V 451a5–7). If Plato had the integrity to teach students in his Academy, and even brilliant ones such as Aristotle with whom he disagreed, then we should not interpret his ideas as mere fantasies that he used to mislead people about his real views on the good, honorable and just cities and people therein. Plato could be wrong, but it is implausible to accuse him of amusing people with hyperbole as opposed to honestly articulating his beliefs.

When Plato is reviewing the Sun, Line and Cave passages again, he writes:

> You won't be able to follow me any longer, Glaucon, even though there is no lack of eagerness on my part to lead you, for you would no longer be seeing an image of what we're describing, but the truth itself. At any rate, that's how it seems to me. That it is really so is not worth insisting on any further. But that there is some such thing to be seen, *that* is something we must insist on. (*Republic* VII 533a1–5)

So we see Plato expressing his wish that he be able to tell Glaucon (and presumably anyone who wanted to know more about the Good) exactly what the Good is, but that he will not be able to do this. Why does Plato not show Glaucon the "truth itself" as "it seems to me" and how does Plato know that we must insist that "there is some such thing to be seen"? My explanation is that Glaucon has not had this experience, and so would not know what Plato is really trying to describe, and that it is therefore something that one must experience for oneself.

Interestingly, Plato elsewhere ascribes ineffability to entities other than the Good. In the *Timaeus*, Plato says something about what is impossible to give an account of: "Now to find the maker and father of this universe [*to pan*] is hard enough, and even if I succeeded, to declare him to everyone is impossible" (*Timaeus* 28c3–5).[71] I interpret this maker and father as God or the Demiurge.

Also in the *Timaeus*, Plato claims that he will not be able to discuss the first principle(s) of all things in the same way in which he is addressing other topics:

> For the present I cannot state "the principle" or "principles" of all things, or however else I think about them, for the simple reason that it is difficult to show clearly what

> my view is if I follow my present manner of exposition. Please do not expect me to do so then. I couldn't convince even myself that I could be right to commit myself to undertaking a task of such magnitude. I shall keep to what I stated at the beginning, the virtue of likely accounts, and so shall try right from the start to say about things, both individually and collectively, what is no less likely than any—more likely, in fact, than what I have said before. (*Timaeus* 48c2–d4[72])

Plato is notifying the reader that he is doing his best to tell us what he thinks and his explanation will be probable, but that he will not be able to tell us about the first principle(s) adequately.

Here is Plato's explanation from the *Statesman* as to why it is so difficult in principle to discuss the Forms, versus perceptibles:

> I think the majority of people fail to recognize that for some of the things there are, there are certain perceptible likenesses which are there to be easily understood, and which it is not at all hard to point out when one wants to make an easy demonstration, involving no trouble and without recourse to verbal means, to someone who asks for an account of one of these things. Conversely, *for those things that are greatest and most valuable, there is no image at all which has been worked in plain view for the use of mankind, the showing of which will enable the person who wants to satisfy the mind of an inquirer to satisfy it adequately, just by fitting it to one of the senses.* That is why one must practice at being able to give and receive an account of each thing; for the things that are without body, which are finest and greatest, are shown clearly only by verbal means and by nothing else, and everything that is now being said is for the sake of these things. But practice in everything is easier in smaller things, rather than in relation to the greater.
>
> Very well said. (*Statesman* 285d10–6b2; emphasis added)

Admittedly, Plato speaks of one's ability to "give and receive an account of each thing," but he also mentions one aspect of the intellection of the Forms, that the person who knows or believes the Forms can force the neophyte to perceive them for himself.[73] So Plato gives us a justification as to why explaining even the Forms, let alone the experience of the Good, is ineffable, or something not easily described in words: Forms are immaterial, and one's reason must discover them.

I believe that Plato refers to the experience of the Good in the following passage in the disputed *Letter* VII. Plato says that, unlike in certain studies where a subject can be articulated, there is no way of putting into words the knowledge of the problems with which he concerns himself—presumably philosophical problems such as are discussed in the dialogues:

> So much at least I can affirm with confidence about any who have written or propose to write on these questions, pretending to a knowledge of the problems with which I am concerned, whether they claim to have learned from me or from others or to have made their discoveries for themselves: it is impossible, in my opinion, that they can have learned anything at all about the subject. There is no

> writing of mine about these matters, nor will there ever be one. For this knowledge is not something that can be put into words like other sciences; but after long-continued intercourse between teacher and pupil, in joint pursuit of the subject, suddenly, like light flashing forth when a fire is kindled, it is born in the soul and straightway nourishes itself. And this too I know: if these matters are to be expounded at all in books or lectures, they would best come from me. Certainly I am harmed not least of all if they are misrepresented. If I thought they could be put into written words adequate for the multitude, what nobler work could I do in my life than to compose something of such great benefit to mankind and bring to light the nature of things for all to see? But I do not think that the "examination," as it is called, of these questions would be of any benefit to men, except to a few, that is, to those who could with a little guidance discover the truth by themselves. (*Letter* VII 341b7–e3)

Plato is making several claims related to my thesis: it is difficult to write adequately about this subject but that he could do it best; he thinks that it would be a great achievement to be able to convey the nature of things to everyone; and Plato does not think that it is worth the trouble to inform everyone of his worldview, since most people are not able or willing to discover the truth. Note, however, that these statements do not come as an interpretive surprise, since Plato has already said similar things in the dialogues.

On the ineffability of one's deepest thoughts Plato also says:

> These things [name, definition, image, and knowledge, at 342b2–3], moreover, because of the weakness of language, are just as much concerned with making clear the particular property of each object as the being of it. On this account no sensible man will venture to express his deepest thoughts in words, especially in a form which is unchangeable, as is true of written outlines. (*Letter* VII 342e2–3a4)

Some Platonic commentators seem to be uncomfortable with the plausibility of ineffability, but consider that many experiences seem to be ineffable or beyond words: even everyday happenings. For example, I have been on an amusement ride that drops you straight down for about one and a half seconds. To tell someone else exactly what that is like would seem to be impossible. To say that, for instance, it was fun, that I have never been on another ride like it, or that my stomach had butterflies afterwards, really does not begin to describe what that ride is actually like. Even to describe what something "is like" is, by definition, not to describe what the experience *is*. The person for whom I'm describing this experience might reply, "Yes, I had fun when I went to an adventure movie too, but I doubt this is what you are trying to describe, right? Also, I've had butterflies in my stomach around certain members of the opposite sex, or when I'm in trouble with my parents." Can you really put these experiences into words adequately enough? Thus, my hypothesis that Plato had an experience of the ultimate nature of reality—since these are the subjects to which he devotes himself—excellently explains why he makes the statements he does about its ineffability.

Plotinus: Obviously alluding to Plato's Cave passage—presuming that the One is metaphysically equivalent to the Good—Plotinus agrees with Plato that the One and the experience cannot be spoken of or written about, but he urges everyone to have the vision for themselves:

> Every beautiful thing is posterior to that One, and comes from it, as all the light of day comes from the sun. Therefore, Plato says, "It cannot be spoken or written," but we speak and write impelling towards it and wakening from reasonings to the vision of it, as if showing the way to someone who wants to have a view of something. (VI.9.4.10–4[74])

Plotinus also warns that the reader should keep in mind the phrase "as if" when he attempts to describe the Good:

> One must go along with the words, if one in speaking of that Good uses of necessity to indicate it expressions which we do not strictly speaking allow to be used; but one should understand "as if" [*hoion*] with each of them. (VI.8.13.47–50)

Plotinus explains that the best one can say is that the One is unnameable and the best we can experience with respect to the One is a vision, as opposed to knowledge:

> This "what it is like" must indicate that it is "not like": for there is no "being like" in what is not a "something." But we in our travail do not know what we ought to say, and are speaking of what cannot be spoken, and give it a name because we want to indicate it to ourselves as best we can. But perhaps this name "One" contains [only] a denial of multiplicity. This is why the Pythagoreans symbolically indicated it to each other by the name of Apollo, in negation of the multiple. But if the One—name and reality expressed—was to be taken positively it would be less clear than if we did not give it a name at all: for perhaps this name [One] was given it in order that the seeker, beginning from this which is completely indicative of simplicity, may finally negate this as well, because, though it was given as well as possible by its giver, not even this is worthy to manifest that nature; since that cannot be heard, nor may it be understood by one who hears, but, if at all, by one who sees. But if the seer tries to look at a form, he will not know even that. (V.5.6.22–37[75])

In sum, Plato and Plotinus[76] both discuss the ineffability of stating the Ultimate Source of Being or of All Things.[77] Evidence of this ineffability in Plato runs counter to A.E. Taylor's claim that Plato did not believe the ultimate experience was ineffable, but only the soul.

1.6 Requirements for the ultimate experience

What does each philosopher say about what one needs to do in order to have this experience? I will show that they agree on the following major requirements:

(1) Purify oneself; that is, do not focus on bodily needs;
(2) Be relatively virtuous or good;
(3) "Convert" one's soul to view the Forms via practicing dialectic;
(4) Unify oneself; that is, have all soul parts work together, following one's Reason; and
(5) Possess intelligence, a good memory, and a natural affinity for philosophy.

Many commentators discuss one or more of these requirements, but the notable exceptions—where others are mentioned that are questionable and/or where it is argued that Plato and Plotinus have differing views on the requirements—will be mentioned in the appropriate places. I will examine differences with Sinnige and Organ, who argue that Plato and Plotinus have different requirements.

Plato: *Purify oneself.*[78] In the *Phaedo*, there are three passages where Plato advocates for something that seems similar to meditation, and that the true philosopher who wishes to know the Forms will dissociate from the body as much as possible. First, he states that the soul needs to be left alone from bodily distractions in order to truly contemplate:

> When then, he asked, does the soul grasp the truth? For whenever it attempts to examine anything with the body, it is clearly deceived by it.
> True.
> Is it not in reasoning if anywhere that any reality becomes clear to the soul?
> Yes.
> And indeed the soul reasons best when none of these senses troubles it, neither hearing nor sight, nor pain nor pleasure, but when it is most by itself, taking leave of the body and as far as possible having no contact or association with it in its search for reality.
> That is so.
> And it is then that the soul of the philosopher most disdains the body, flees from it and seeks to be by itself?
> It appears so. (*Phaedo* 65b9–d3)

He calls the avoidance of the body "purification," seeming to suggest meditation:

> And does purification not turn out to be what we mentioned in our argument some time ago, namely, to separate the soul as far as possible from the body and accustom it to *gather itself and collect itself out of every part of the body and to dwell by itself* as far as it can both now and in the future, freed, as it were, from the bonds of the body?
> Certainly. (*Phaedo* 67c5–d3; emphasis added)

He describes the true philosopher, again mainly in terms of asceticism:

> No one may join the company of the gods who has not practiced philosophy and is not completely pure when he departs from life, no one but the lover of learning.

> It is for this reason, my friends Simmias and Cebes, that those who practice philosophy in the right way keep away from all bodily passions, master them and do not surrender themselves to them; it is not at all for fear of wasting their substance and of poverty, which the majority and the money-lovers fear, nor for fear of dishonor and ill repute, like the ambitious and lovers of honors, that they keep away from them.
>
> That would not be natural for them, Socrates, said Cebes.
>
> By Zeus, no, he said. Those who care for their own soul and do not live for the service of their body dismiss all these things. They do not travel the same road as those who do not know where they are going but, believing that nothing should be done contrary to philosophy and their deliverance and purification, they turn to this and follow wherever philosophy leads. (*Phaedo* 82b10–d7)

Be (relatively) virtuous or good: Though it is infrequently noted,[79] Plato implies in the Sun Simile that one must be a good person in order to know/see the Forms: First, the eye cannot see visible objects such as a tree without the sun—analogously, the soul (or mind) cannot know the Forms without the Form of the Good. Second though, the eye must have a nature akin to the sun in order to be able to see things such as trees—analogously, the soul must have a nature akin to the Good in order to be able to know the Forms. In other words, just as the eye must be "sunlike" as he says at *Republic* VI 508b, the soul must be "goodlike" in order to know the Forms.

Here is another more direct passage:

> The philosopher always uses reasoning to stay near the form, *being*. He isn't at all easy to see because that area is so bright and the eyes of most people's souls can't bear to look at what's divine. (*Sophist* 254a8–b1)

Thus most people cannot bear to gaze at absolute goodness, whereas the reasoning philosopher is presumably better equipped for such an experience.

Further, there is a passage in the *Laws* that supports the view that one must be good in order to know the Forms:

> So what conduct recommends itself to God and reflects his wishes? There is only one sort, epitomized in the old saying "like approves of like" (excess apart, which is both its own enemy and that of due proportion). In our view it is God who is preeminently the "measure of all things," much more so than any "man," as they say. So if you want to recommend yourself to someone of this character, you must do your level best to make your own character reflect his, and on this principle the moderate man is God's friend, being like him, whereas the immoderate and unjust man is not like him and is his enemy; and the same reasoning applies to the other vices too. (*Laws* IV 716c1–d4[80])

Thus, assuming God is good, humans need to be godlike (good) in order to truly be following God; additionally, they need to be temperate and just, which is also godlike.

"Convert" one's soul to view the Forms via practicing dialectic: After the Cave Allegory in the *Republic*, Plato claims that a potential knower/seer of the Good needs to convert, shift, or turn his or her soul towards the vision, as the soul already has within it the power to have such an experience:

> But our present discussion, on the other hand, shows that the power to learn is present in everyone's soul and that the instrument with which each learns is like an eye that cannot be turned around from darkness to light without turning the whole body. This instrument cannot be turned around from that which is coming into being without turning the whole soul until it is able to study that which is and the brightest thing that is, namely, the one we call the Good. Isn't that right?
>
> Yes.
>
> Then education is the craft concerned with doing this very thing, this turning around, and with how the soul can most easily and effectively be made to do it. It isn't the craft of putting sight into the soul. Education takes for granted that sight is there but that it isn't turned the right way or looking where it ought to look, and it tries to redirect it appropriately.
>
> So it seems. (*Republic* VII 518c4–d8; adapted from Grube/Reeve[81])

Plato repeats the requirement that we should not attach ourselves to bodily pleasures to know the Forms (see *Republic* VII 519a) and then puts forth the educational regimen for his ideal rulers. Plato requires his rulers to study: "calculation and arithmetic,"[82] "geometry,"[83] of "plane surfaces" and "revolving solids" (solid geometry),"[84] "astronomy,"[85] and, most importantly, "dialectic"[86]—which we can infer from *Republic* VII 533b1–d4 is the art that speedily and effectively turns or converts the soul, and from 534e2–5a1 is the highest study.

Unify oneself: Moreover, Plato strongly implies that in order to be happy, a good philosopher, and just, a person must be unified, by which he means that one's parts of the soul[87] work together, following Reason—the highest and best part of the soul.[88]

Possess intelligence, a good memory, and a natural affinity for philosophy: Lastly, Plato explains how important it is for one who is anxious to attain the truth about virtue and vice to have intelligence, a good memory, and an inborn affinity with philosophy and justice:

> In short, neither quickness of learning nor a good memory can make a man see when his nature is not akin to the object, for this knowledge never takes root in an alien nature; so that no man who is not naturally inclined and akin to justice and all other forms of excellence, even though he may be quick at learning and remembering this and that and other things, nor any man who, though akin to justice, is slow at learning and forgetful, will ever attain the truth that is attainable about virtue. Nor about vice, either, for these must be learned together, just as the truth and error about any part of being must be learned together, through long and earnest labor, as I said at the beginning. (*Letter* VII 344a2–b3)

This sums up Plato's view of some of the most important requirements[89] of the person who wishes to know the Good and consequently be happy.

Plotinus:[90] *Purify oneself*: Just as Plato argued that the earnest seeker of the Good, the true philosopher, should pay little attention to the needs of the body and purify oneself in order to become divine, so Plotinus also claims that we need to retreat from the realm of sense and become one (thus reaffirming the "unify oneself" requirement):[91]

> In proportion as the soul goes towards the formless, since it is utterly unable to comprehend it because it is not delimited and, so to speak, stamped by a richly varied stamp, it slides away and is afraid that it may have nothing at all. Therefore it gets tired of this sort of thing, and often gladly comes down and falls away from all this, till it comes to the perceptible and rests there as if on solid ground; just as sight when it gets tired of small objects is glad to come upon big ones. But when the soul wants to see by itself, seeing only by being with it and being one by being one with it, it does not think it yet has what it seeks, because it is not different from what is being thought. But all the same this is what one must do if one is going to philosophize about the One. Since, then, that which we seek is one and we are considering the principle of all things, the Good and the First, one must not go far away from the things around the primary by falling down to the last things of all, but as one goes to the primary one must lift oneself up from the things of sense which are the last and lowest, and become freed from all evil since one is hastening to the Good, and ascend to the principle in oneself and become one from many, when one is going to behold the Principle and the One. Therefore one must become Intellect and entrust one's soul to and set it firmly under Intellect, that it may be awake to receive what that sees, and may by this Intellect behold the One, without adding any sense-perception or receiving anything from sense-perception into that Intellect, but beholding the most pure with the pure Intellect, and the primary part of Intellect. (VI.9.3.4–27[92])

Note that Plotinus tells us that souls gladly retreat from confronting the formless by descending to the familiar perceptible surroundings; we must focus on bringing over nothing whatever from sense and essentially become Intellect if we hope to see the "pure Intellect"; and one's being pure is essentially equivalent to one's being freed from the body.

Plotinus again emphatically states that bodily pleasures are to be avoided in the pursuit of the ultimate experience, and instead one must turn inward to attempt to make the discovery:

> Just as it is said of matter that it must be free from all qualities if it is going to receive the impressions of all things,[93] so much more must the soul be without form if there is going to be no obstacle settled in it to its fulfillment and illumination by the first nature. But if this is so, the soul must let go of all outward things and turn altogether to what is within, and not be inclined to any outward thing, but ignoring all things (as it did formerly in sense-perception, but then in the realm

> of Forms), and even ignoring itself, come to be in contemplation of that One. (VI.9.7.12–21[94])

Plotinus warns us to get beyond the appearances, or we will be like dreamers who desire the dream and shun waking life:

> Reverse your way of thinking, or you will be left deprived of God, like the people at festivals who by their gluttony stuff themselves with things which it is not lawful for those going in to the gods to take, thinking that these are more obviously real than the vision of the god for whom they ought to be celebrating the festival, and take no part in the rites within. Yes, in these our rites also the god, since he is not seen, creates disbelief in his existence in those who think that that alone is obviously real which they see only with the flesh; as if people who slept through their life thought the things in their dreams were reliable and obvious, but, if someone woke them up, disbelieved in what they saw with their eyes open and went to sleep again. (V.5.11.11–22[95])

Plotinus considers virtue, purity, and asceticism necessary for the experience:

> One of us, being unable to see himself, when he is possessed by that god brings his contemplation to the point of vision, and presents himself to his own mind and looks at a beautified image of himself; but then he dismisses the image, beautiful though it is, and comes to unity with himself, and, making no more separation, is one and all together with that god silently present, and is with him as much as he wants to be and can be. But if he returns again to being two, while he remains pure he stays close to the god, so as to be present to him again in that other way if he turns again to him. In this turning he has the advantage that to begin with he sees himself, while he is different from the god; then he hastens inward and has everything, and leaves perception behind in his fear of being different, and is one in that higher world. . . . How then can anyone be in beauty without seeing it? If he sees it as something different, he is not yet in beauty, but he is in it most perfectly when he becomes it. If therefore sight is of something external we must not have sight, or only that which is identical with its object. This is a sort of intimate understanding and perception of a self which is careful not to depart from itself by wanting to perceive too much. (V.8.11.1–12, 19–24[96])

Be (relatively) virtuous or good [and] *unify oneself*: Plotinus agrees with Plato on these two requirements: Unless one is virtuous or good to a sufficient extent (though neither philosopher is precisely clear on how virtuous one must be), one may not see or know Beauty (or beyond that, the Good).[97] Moreover, a person who desires to see or know Beauty must be unified or become "one."[98]

> When it is just awakened it is not at all able to look at the brilliance before it. So that the soul must be trained, first of all to look at beautiful ways of life: then at beautiful works, not those which the arts produce, but the works of men who have

> a name for goodness: then look at the souls of the people who produce the beautiful works. How then can you see the sort of beauty a good soul has? Go back into yourself and look; and if you do not yet see yourself beautiful, then, just as someone making a statue which has to be beautiful cuts away here and polishes there and makes one part smooth and clears another till he has given his statue a beautiful face, so you too must cut away excess and straighten the crooked and clear the dark and make it bright, and never stop "working on your statue" till the divine glory of virtue shines out on you, till you see "self-mastery enthroned upon its holy seat." If you have become this, and see it, and are at home with yourself in purity, with nothing hindering you from becoming in this way one, with no inward mixture of anything else, but wholly yourself, nothing but true light, not measured by dimensions, or bounded by shape into littleness, or expanded to size by unboundedness, but everywhere unmeasured, because greater than all measure and superior to all quantity; when you see that you have become this, then you have become sight; you can trust yourself then; you have already ascended and need no one to show you; concentrate your gaze and see. (I.6.9.1–24[99])

So Plotinus holds that one must make oneself beautiful, a unified, good person, in order to see Beauty, but mentions God and the Good presumably as part of the same vision. He continues:

> This alone is the eye that sees the great Beauty. But if anyone comes to the sight blear-eyed with wickedness, and unpurified, or weak, and by his cowardice unable to look at what is very bright, he sees nothing, even if someone shows him what is there and possible to see. For one must come to the sight with a seeing power made akin and like to what is seen. No eye ever saw the sun without becoming sun-like, nor can a soul see Beauty without becoming beautiful. You must become first all godlike and beautiful if you intend to see God and Beauty.[100] ... That which is beyond [the Forms, Intellect, essence] we call the nature of the Good, which holds Beauty as a screen before it. So in a loose and general way of speaking the Good is the primary beauty. (I.6.9.24–34, 37–40; adapted from A.H. Armstrong[101])

Plotinus is essentially explaining Plato's Sun Simile, that one must be "goodlike" in order to see the Good—or alternatively, as it is put here, become godlike in order to see God.

"Convert" one's soul to view the Forms via practicing dialectic: Plato and Plotinus both discuss a necessary conversion, or turning, of the soul. Plotinus examines the concept as follows:

> You will increase yourself then by rejecting all else, and the All will be present to you in your rejection; but if it is present in your rejection and does not appear when you are with the other things, it did not come in order to be present, but you went away when it was not present. But if you went away, it was not from it—for it is present—and you did not even go away then, but were present and turned the opposite way. (VI.5.12.27–9)

Several commentators allude to this turning inward,[102] but none of them explicitly mention Plato and Plotinus' agreement on this issue.

Plotinus concurs with Plato that mathematics is important to the attainment of the vision as well as dialectic:

> The philosopher—he is the one who is by nature ready to respond and "winged," we may say, and in no need of separation like the others. He has begun to move to the higher world, and is only at a loss for someone to show him the way. So he must be shown and set free, with his own good will, he who has long been free by nature. He must be given mathematical studies to train him in philosophical thought and accustom him to firm confidence in the existence of the immaterial—he will take them easily, being naturally disposed to learning; he is by nature virtuous, and must be brought to perfect his virtues, and after his mathematical studies instructed in dialectic, and made a complete dialectician. (I.3.3.1–10)

While it is true that Plato discusses solid geometry and astronomy, and Plotinus only mentions mathematics, there is nothing to indicate in Plotinus' work that he would not agree with Plato that these studies would be helpful and/or required to be learned in the ideal state, which is the context in which Plato promotes these studies. Plato and Plotinus do agree that the highest and most important study is dialectic.[103]

Possess intelligence, a good memory, and a natural affinity for philosophy: If one does not possess intelligence, one will not be able to satisfy the mathematics requirement—or that of dialectic, for that matter. A similar argument can be made concerning the good memory. And lastly, without a natural affinity for philosophy, practicing dialectic concerning the immaterial will be difficult if not impossible.

A final poetic passage sums up Plotinus' view of the search for the ultimate experience: It is as if we need to prepare ourselves by making ourselves beautiful, virtuous, and unified and wait for the experience to happen:

> One should not enquire whence it comes, for there is no "whence": for it does not really come or go away anywhere, but appears or does not appear. So one must not chase after it, but wait quietly till it appears, preparing oneself to contemplate it, as the eye awaits the rising of the sun; and the sun rising over the horizon ("from Ocean," the poets say) gives itself to the eyes to see. (V.5.8.1–7[104])

I should review two arguments against my position that Plato and Plotinus have the same requirements for the ultimate experience. The first comes from Sinnige:

> What we find in Plato's dialogues is descriptions of an intellectual process of ascent. There is no reference, as in Plotinus, to the personal experience of being caught up into another form of existence. What Plotinus describes is a movement of transformation in which the existence of the whole individual person is implied, not simply a development of philosophical knowledge. Plato's philosophical system and Plotinus' description of mystical surrender move in different worlds.

> The stress on getting away from the senses is found in both, but it has a different meaning. In Plato the way out is through knowledge and philosophy. It is a rational process. In Plotinus it is an existential process, which has its roots in the deepest of human emotions, not in theoretical distinctions.[105]

Contra Sinnige, I have several replies: First, it does seem that Plato is telling us that one personally experiences a transformation into another form of existence—an existence where one's Reason rules over the other parts of the soul, where one is truly virtuous. Also, the Cave Allegory makes clear that once one comes to know the Good, the released prisoner's life and attitude toward humanity is transformed. Second, since (as we'll see) Plato and Plotinus both value dialectic equally as a means to achieving the ultimate experience, we cannot say that Plotinus focuses on the emotions as opposed to theoretical distinctions, knowledge, or philosophy; all these latter methods are also emphasized in Plotinus.

In addition, Sinnige claims that Plato and Plotinus disagree about who is eligible for this ultimate experience:

> As a consequence only the trained philosopher [in "Plato's system"] could partake in the contemplation of the transcendent world. The great mass of non-intelligent citizens were scornfully placed by Plato in the category of useful servants. In Plotinus the divine creative power of the universe is omnipresent, and every human being may find their way to contemplate it. Plotinus says that this is due to a faculty that is in the possession of everyone, though few do use it.[106]

This is not a sound argument, because Plotinus claims, along with Plato, that the ultimate experience is difficult and rare. Undergoing what is necessary is not easy, which explains on both philosophers' views why few people will achieve this goal. Plotinus nowhere states that everyone is a philosopher; on the other hand, both Plato and Plotinus do claim that we all have the potential of recollecting the truth. Plato says that we are all likened to prisoners in his Cave Allegory; that is, we all "know" the truth in some sense, and can, if we are brave and continue to practice philosophy (and purify, unify, and beautify ourselves), eventually see or know the Good. So Sinnige's charge that it is only on Plotinus' view that every human being *may* find their way fails to convince as being a difference between his view and Plato's.

In another objection, Sinnige states: "The journey inward in the human soul [in Plotinus] coincides with the spiritual journey to the origins. This is one more theory that is not found in Plato's philosophy."[107] I hope to show that Plato believes, just as Plotinus does, that the individual soul can return to Nous by the use of Reason, to contemplate the Forms and know the Good. If, according to Plato, we can know and see the Good, and the Good is ultimately the source of all (good) things that exist, then in what sense are we not returning to our origins if we come to know it, on Plato's view?

The second argument comes from Organ, who claims that there is a difference between the requirements of the two philosophers: "Whereas for Plato virtue is to be attained through activities in the political affairs of the city state, for Plotinus the quest involved retreats into the countryside, discussions in classrooms, and silent meditations."[108] However, in the *Republic*, Plato is merely detailing the best way in which to bring about the vision of the Good; I suggest that the political training is only a necessary part of the future rulers' training because they will be *rulers*. For instance, the regimen in the *Republic* does not negate what is said in the other dialogues about purifying the soul and virtue. Plato obviously emphasizes dialectic, also implying the "classroom" discussions that he assuredly had in the Academy, as seen in the *Republic*. Additionally, meditation or something akin to it seems to appear in both thinkers' views. Thus, Organ's claim is not convincing.

In sum, both Plato and Plotinus agree that, to have the ultimate experience, one must be a good person, shun bodily pleasures, turn one's soul in the proper direction, study mathematics, and practice dialectic. There is thus no indication that they disagree about what activities or inward work the seeker should pursue.

1.7 Plato and Plotinus' attitude toward the hoi polloi

Plato and Plotinus have similar attitudes toward the general population (hoi polloi, the multitude, the many) and their thoughts about the true philosopher pursuing knowledge of the Good.

Plato: Plato warns about what the multitude (or unreleased prisoners) will think about the prisoner who attempts to make the rough ascent to the Sun—the Form of the Good. For convenience, I will refer to this released prisoner who ultimately sees the Sun as the "Good-knower." Plato has Socrates discuss the Good-knower who returns to the cave:

> And before his eyes had recovered—and the adjustment would not be quick—while his vision was still dim, if he had to compete again with the perpetual prisoners in recognizing the shadows, wouldn't he invite ridicule? Wouldn't it be said of him that he'd returned from his upward journey with his eyesight ruined and that it isn't worthwhile even to try to travel upward? And, as for anyone who tried to free them and lead them upward, if they could somehow get their hands on him, wouldn't they kill him? (*Republic* VII 516e8–7a6[109])

Here we see three different, negative reactions: the Good-knower will provoke ridicule by average people (non-philosophers), the non-philosophers will think the Good-knower has ruined his mind, and the average people might try to kill the Good-knower who attempts to aid others in pursuing the knowledge of the Good.

In the *Phaedrus*, while delineating the fourth kind of madness, Plato says:

> [The philosopher] stands outside human concerns and draws close to the divine; ordinary people think he is disturbed and rebuke him for this, unaware that he is possessed by god. Now this takes me to the whole point of my discussion of the fourth kind of madness—that which someone shows when he sees the beauty we

> have down here and is reminded of true beauty; then he takes wing and flutters in his eagerness to rise up, but is unable to do so; and he gazes aloft, like a bird, paying no attention to what is down below—and that is what brings on him the charge that he has gone mad. (*Phaedrus* 249c8–e1[110])

These passages show Plato's awareness that most people will think that a philosopher who is seeking a vision of Beauty or the Good is quite unstable.

Moreover, as we already saw, Plato did not think that this experience was an everyday occurrence. There is also evidence that he realized that most people would not understand if he were to be more explicit: "Only take care that these letters do not fall into the hands of uninstructed men. Nothing, I dare say, could sound more ridiculous to the multitude than these sayings, just as to gifted persons nothing could be more admirable and inspiring" (*Letter* II 314a1–5). Plato also writes that he was initially troubled not to have met anyone else who had made the discovery about "the first" (312d7):

> I had never met anyone who had discovered this truth, and that most of my own study was devoted to it. (*Letter* II 313b3–4)

This suggests that Plato is worried about the fact that this experience is so rare and that he has not seen or heard others discuss its possibility; if he were to walk about Athens and tell others about it, he could expect to be ridiculed, and perhaps even killed. After all, Socrates was executed merely for *questioning* others about virtue and goodness; we can imagine worse for Plato if—assuming he had knowledge, for the moment—he would have walked about Athens *declaring* his knowledge of life, the universe and everything.

I agree with these additional related points: First, Findlay[111] notes: "The philosopher is deemed mad by the multitude, but he remains a man possessed, divinely inspired." Second, Gaiser[112] plausibly hypothesizes that Plato gave his Lecture on the Good to protect his life and Academy (which was mildly under attack after the Dion-Syracuse incidents), because he was aware that Anaxagoras and Protagoras were charged with impiety (as Socrates was), and due to the public's disdain of public societies: "the best defense against such hostility is to satisfy the curiosity of the opponents."[113] Third, Organ[114] states that Plato wrote myths partly in response to the political climate and his unwillingness to be involved politically in Athens.

Thus, Plato's depiction of the multitude's attitude toward the Good shores up the idea that he had some kind of mystical experience that itself signaled how out of the ordinary the experience was, relative to the average person.

Plotinus: Plotinus only indirectly alludes to what most people will think about philosophers:

> The fact is that man has the middle place between gods and beasts, and inclines now one way, now the other, and some men become like gods and others beasts, and some, the majority, are in between. (III.2.8.9–11)

It stands to reason that if most people do not become godlike, then they would not think of philosophers as being normal and thus would not necessarily respect them. There is only one other relevant passage, where Plotinus gives an analogy as to how Reason can be overtaken by one's appetites and emotions, likening Reason to a "best advisor" who fails to dominate in a public meeting:

> Perplexity and variety of opinions belong to the gathering [of our various parts and passions]: from our best part the right account of the matter is given to the common gathering, and is weak because it is in the mixture, not by its own nature. But it is as if in the great clamor of an assembly the best of the advisors does not prevail when he speaks, but the worse of those who clamor and shout, but he sits quietly unable to do anything, defeated by the clamor of the worse. . . . In the best man, the man who separates himself, the ruling principle is one, and the order comes from this to the rest. (IV.4.17.20–7, 33–4)

Presumably the greater populace would not be the best advisor, and so Plotinus would probably agree with Plato that most people would not agree with the philosopher's priorities and views.[115]

Judging the evidence suggesting that Plato believes that we can and should have an ultimate experience of the Good; do these claims prove that Plato is a mystic?

1.8 Interpreting Plato as a mystic: The argument to the best explanation

I contend that Plato is best interpreted as being a mystic, in the same sense in which commentators use the term positively to describe Plotinus' writings, while also defending the prized place of rationality and philosophy therein. I have already shown that a sizable minority (eighteen) argues that Plato is not a mystic. In contrast, no English-language commentator explicitly argues that Plotinus is not a mystic. My argument is thus directed to those Platonists with the minority view.

Why would a person as intelligent as Plato commit himself to some unconventional, unproven views? For example, how could Plato think that our souls already have knowledge of the Forms in between incarnations, so that what people call learning is really nothing other than recollection? How could Plato have written that we would be pained in our ascent toward a vision of the Good? How could Plato know that a vision of the Good was possible? Why would the Good be beyond and the source of being? How does he know that the Good is the source of knowledge and truth, but is neither of them?

I see at least four possible answers to the thrust of these kinds of interpretive questions: First, Plato may be deliberately deceiving us, pretending to imagine how knowledge might be,[116] though he himself only has an opinion about this account. Second, Plato may be mentally ill but felt the need to share his delusions. Third, Plato may be using the transcendent Good (for one instance) as an explanatory entity, just as specialists do with neutrinos, God, black holes, or the unconscious. So he would not need to have had a direct experience of the Good to claim that it is necessary to explain what it is posited to explain; namely, there is nothing prior to it and it is absolutely first. Lastly, Plato may have actually had this experience, and is being deliberately evasive at times, realizing—as he strongly implies in the Cave Allegory—that people will think him and his view ridiculous, and therefore has the character Socrates say more than once that he only has an *opinion* of the Good, the cave outing,[117] and that he is not sure about being able to see the Good.

I reject the first explanation that Plato is deliberately deceiving us, because Plato himself says, "I suspect that it's a lesser crime to kill someone involuntarily than to mislead people about fine, good, and just institutions" (*Republic* V 451a5–7). He does discuss the possibility of the noble lie, for the purpose of the guardians' keeping the lower classes believing that they are valuable in performing their roles within the state (*Republic* III 414b–5e). However, this lie is "noble" precisely because it keeps the just form of the state; the "lie" does not mislead the citizens of the ideal state about what is good, noble or just. In the noble lie, Plato is saying that there are different kinds of people, each fit for different tasks, and that each of them is valuable to ensure the preservation and goodness of the state (415d–e). Plato consistently says that it is impossible for one to adequately talk of the Good, or the Father of All, or of the subjects to which he devotes himself. This subject is obviously important to him—the central point of his metaphysics and epistemology—and so there is no reason to attribute maliciousness to him in this section of the *Republic*.

I reject the second explanation that Plato is mentally ill for three reasons: he writes rationally both before and after the material on the Good; there are no accounts of his life where he was taken to be mentally ill by anyone, not even by those who strongly disagreed with his philosophical views; and he taught Aristotle and many others in his Academy; thinking that Plato is insane does all of these other students a disservice, as well as implying their collective incompetence, which is highly implausible.

I reject the third explanation that Plato is only positing the Good, for instance, as an explanatory entity and as a way of having an entity that is absolutely first. He does not dryly announce that there must be a first principle—he describes the experience in all-encompassing, life-changing terms (as does Plotinus, incidentally). Ignoring what Plato says about the Good for a moment, what is or should be particularly spectacular about a philosopher declaring that there is an entity that is absolutely first? After all, many philosophers posit God as the first mover, or the First before all else, but without saying anything else about whether we can experience that God, or what it is like to ascend to knowledge of God. Second, this view does not account for Plato's repeated insistence of ineffability in matters related to the Good; if all he was trying to say was that there must be an absolute first, Source of All Things, then why didn't he just say that and move along to other topics? In short, this view does not explain all of the textual phenomena.

Since *most* commentators take Plotinus to have, or at least claim to have, experienced the Good or One, the argument to the best explanation would include Plato as well, since Plato seems to share Plotinus' enthusiasm for one's having the vision of the Good by adding these other, non-philosophical features (the passionate descriptions and awe of the interlocutors specifically in Plato's case).[118]

Thus, I endorse the fourth view, that Plato had an experience of the Good. I concur with Bowe, except that I extend what he says about the interpretation of the *Republic* to the whole of Plato's text: "We are considering a point of interpretation where to deny Plato's mystical tendencies closes the peripheral vision necessary for an appreciation of the movement of the text."[119] I also generally agree with Inge:

> We have here an outline of a philosophy of mysticism, of the Platonic or Neoplatonic type, in which a firm knowledge of ultimate truth is obtained by spiritual vision or insight, which is its own evidence. It is not based on rationalist argument, nor on scientific knowledge of the laws of nature. Spiritual things are spiritually discerned, and no appeal lies from the affirmations of the spirit to any facts of nature. Naturalism and positivism are denied a hearing. The witnesses to the truths of the spiritual life are the specialists in divine knowledge, the mystics.[120]

In my opinion, Inge goes a bit beyond what Plato and Plotinus actually hold, because they both want to rationally justify their worldviews and demand the use of dialectic to achieve knowledge of the Good. As I have shown though, they both claim that this experience is ineffable, which lends itself to mysticism.

Therefore, the best explanation of these phenomena seems to be that Plato had an experience that cannot be fully argued for or explained, either in writing or in speech. Whereas Plato, at least in his extant works, wrote in dialogues and was relatively vague about the experience, Plotinus wrote in non-dialogic prose and is direct about what he experienced. Moreover, they both emphasize rationality as a requirement before the experience,[121] the awesome emotion during it, and the subsequent knowledge and rationalizing thereafter. Therefore, the commentators who wish to drive an interpretive wedge between Plato and Plotinus on the emotional versus rational components of the experience are mistaken.[122] Those who ridicule mysticism and then attribute it only to Plotinus but not to Plato are mistaken as well.[123]

Some interpreters of Plato such as Rosalyn Weiss[124] think that Plato uses myths whenever he cannot give a rational account of his beliefs.[125] Though that may be true in some cases of Plato's use of myth (even though he argues for recollection in the *Phaedo*), we should ask ourselves why Plato would be so rational and then claim to believe some unconventional, possibly even irrational beliefs.[126] So on the one hand, Plato is rational. His early so-called "Socratic" dialogues contain many brilliant arguments, and there are those who spend their academic careers mainly studying those arguments, trying to sort them out and giving a compatible account of them. Moreover, Plato did such an excellent job of criticizing his own theory of Forms in the *Parmenides* that some commentators have argued that he rejects the theory at that point in his philosophical career. On the other hand, Plato claims that once one has a vision of Beauty, one will no longer yearn to look at beautiful youths and love them as one did before (*Symposium* 211d1–8). Or he seems to believe, as Plotinus does, that human souls choose their lives and that a guardian spirit is assigned to each person to ensure that he or she will carry out their life's plan. The question is, why would Plato commit himself to these views, when all that would philosophically be required is to argue that Forms exist, that souls are immortal, and that perceptible things are images of Forms? In short, *why does Plato believe these things*? How could someone this rational believe in something like guardian spirits with no apparent evidence, or without even a good dialectical exchange or proof? How does *he* know that we recollect the *Forms*?

My answer is that we can best interpret Plato as purporting to have had an experience that most people have *not* had, but *could* have if they were so interested, were brave, determined, good, and actively pursued this investigation in the appropriate way. He is saying knowledge is possible not because it is *theoretically* possible, or because the existence of knowledge would fit in well with the rest of his theory, or because he *wants* there to be knowledge of such and such a kind, but because he actually *has* knowledge.[127]

Here is a plausible explanation of why Plato would not directly state that he has knowledge: Who would accept such a declaration from Plato, or anyone else for that matter? Also, given that Socrates was supposedly executed because of the *questions* he asked, would it be wise or prudent for Plato to write out in declarative prose that he has knowledge of the Good, virtue, God, everything else that exists, and of how we should live? Moreover, if you were to have an experience of knowledge, which told you what exists, what we can know, and how we should live, (how) would you go about telling others of that experience? It seems reasonable that Plato is doing his best to tell us indirectly *that* he had an experience, or a vision, or a knowing, and *what* he experienced, saw, or knew.

Not all Plotinian commentators accept the view attributed to Plotinus—that the ultimate experience is and should be the goal of all human behavior, though few will use their abilities to attain it. I will examine several commentators' take on this issue and show that Plotinus' experience played a central role in his philosophy as well as in his endorsement of Plato's.

1.9 The explanatory importance of mysticism in the philosophy of Plotinus

Even among those who claim that Plotinus is unquestionably a mystic, commentators differ on the role that Plotinus' mystical experience plays in his philosophy. The two basic positions seem to be either that his philosophy can be explained and understood without reference to his experience (A.H. Armstrong,[128] Bréhier, Gerson, Katz, and Turnbull), or that his experience informed his philosophy, and played a central role in shaping his philosophy (A.H. Armstrong,[129] Bussanich, Dillon, Dodds, Katz, Kenney, Majumdar, More, Organ, and Rist). My position is that Plotinus' experience plays a significant role in determining his metaphysics, epistemology, and ethics.

Several commentators make the point that Plotinus' mystical experience does not play a crucial role in what his philosophy is, and that we can basically study his view without reference to his experience. A.H. Armstrong seems to change his view on this issue, starting out as follows:

> Plotinus himself is very far from basing his doctrine of the One on his mystical experience. He presents it, as he presents all his philosophy, as based on the authority of Plato . . . but still more on hard honest rational discussion and purely

> intellectual insight into the nature of reality.... He does not rely on experience to prove that there is such a principle as the One. Like all the greatest mystics, he interprets and judges his mysticism in the light of that doctrine about the supreme realities which he believes to be true on other grounds.[130]

Armstrong seems to argue that Plotinus does not believe the One exists or has a certain nature due to his experience of it (which Armstrong does not doubt), but that he believes it because of Plato's writings and rational discussion about it. Note Armstrong's position here, because he seems to change it, as we'll see later. It is my contention that Plotinus had the experience first, which resulted in his "knowing" that the One, Nous, Forms, and the All-Soul existed, and that this subsequently resulted in his believing that Plato is correct. However, to the reader of the *Enneads*, it will seem as if Plotinus is arguing philosophically that the One exists, so I have sympathy for Armstrong's view here—though I ultimately reject it.

In his *Plotinus*, Lloyd Gerson does a superb job of laying out Plotinus' views on epistemology, metaphysics, and ethics, and the book is an excellent work on Plotinus in general. However, it is only in the last chapter that Gerson explains why he has not mentioned "an important feature of [Plotinus'] philosophy, namely, his mysticism."[131] His explanation: "I have hitherto found no need to introduce the concept of mystical experience and related concepts in order to explain anything in Plotinus. This may surprise some who simply assume that mysticism is more or less what Neo-Platonism is all about," and he states that he only wants to challenge this assumption for Plotinus, and not the other Neo-Platonists.[132] He continues:

> Sharing in the life of Intellect or contemplation of Forms can, for example, be explained along Aristotelian lines. That is, Plotinus is talking about the life that Aristotle says god has always and we have occasionally. And no one supposes that Aristotle is being a mystic when he does this. It is true that Plotinus' account of the details of this life is importantly different. But it is still an account based on similar concepts.[133]

Gerson recognizes that Plotinus' explanation is "importantly different" from Aristotle's view but that it is also similar. No one considers Aristotle to be a mystic, because Aristotle never discusses knowing the nature of God in anything other than a theoretical (via contemplation) or logical (there must be a first mover, first cause) way. Gerson's attempt to explain away Plotinus' many references to the vision of the Supreme, and its transforming one's life and causing true happiness in everyone who has it, regrettably misses the essential point of Plotinus' philosophy. After all, Plotinus strongly avers that if you fail to have this experience, you fail utterly (I.6.7.30–9).[134] It is my contention that Plotinus has the view he has—as does Plato—precisely *because* he experienced the vision of the One or Good that he writes about. This also explains why the two philosophers have such similar philosophies, and agree on countless details like reincarnation, guardian spirits, and more.

Gerson also discusses the connection between Plato and Plotinus' thought in this context:

> Much of what Plotinus has to say about the One is inspired by Plato and based on arguments which have a lot more to do with scientific realism than they do with mysticism. The elements of Plotinus' thought that can usefully be labeled "mystical" are rather easily isolated from his other epistemological doctrines.[135]

Plato and Plotinus hold that having the experience or vision of the One or Good is necessary and sufficient both for knowledge and happiness. Both adhere to the doctrine of scientific realism with their view that the Forms are objects of knowledge; however, they both imply that one cannot obtain and/or benefit from this knowledge unless one knows—has "seen"—the Good. Additionally, Gerson is failing to mention all the Platonic passages that state or imply that we can have a vision of the Good and that this is what we truly desire.

Gerson also dismisses Porphyry's account of Plotinus attaining union with the One four times while they knew each other, because of the experience's ineffable nature.[136] However, we see similar patterns of ineffability in Plato and Plotinus along with a sincere desire to relate as much information as possible about it.

Lastly, Gerson argues that the experience of the One is "transitory" and possibly "enduring," but not "eternal" as Plotinus describes the activity of Intellect.[137] He also reasons that: "Since these [mystical] experiences are only intimations of the eternal life of Intellect, it is implausible to suppose that they represent the summit of the philosopher's quest."[138] However, both thinkers hold that the ultimate experience is self-sustaining for the experiencer; Plotinus even implies that one does not lose its fruit even during sleep or while being tortured in the Bull of Phalaris. Moreover, the ultimate experience is not necessarily an eternal contemplative activity of one's own intellect, as that activity is in the Intellect or Nous. One should not conflate these two activities. It is quite plausible to think that for Plotinus and Plato the ultimate experience is the summit of the philosopher's quest.

I will briefly address the commentators with whom I agree. First, A.H. Armstrong states, seemingly contra his position in 1945 ("Plotinus himself is very far from basing his doctrine of the One on his mystical experience"):[139]

> I do not think that anyone who really studies the [*Enneads*] without prejudices or preconceptions can deny that it was genuine and that it was good and valuable, and not a pathological state or a psychological aberration. There is no doubt, too, that it had a very important influence on his conception of the One.[140]

If Plotinus' experience had an important influence on his conception of the One, then it is difficult to understand how Plotinus "is very far from basing his doctrine of the One on" it. Nonetheless, I agree with Armstrong's change of position.

Bussanich rightly takes "Plotinus' intellectual and emotional intensity"—quoting *Life* 14.2–4—to mean: "Plotinus' metaphysical doctrines are often rooted in his own experience, which in turn shapes his manner of expression."[141] I also concur with his warning that it is a mistake to reject the mystical dimension of Plotinus' thought as anti-philosophical.[142]

Dillon puts it excellently here:

> Plotinus is not, however, just a fearless analytic philosopher. He does also have an aspect which a modern philosopher would, I think, find disconcerting: he has *been there*, by which I mean that he gives one the overwhelming impression of a man who has actually *experienced Nous*, and even the One, and is desperately seeking to express, in coherent philosophical terms, what he has beheld.[143]

In sum, I examined Plato and Plotinus' view that the ultimate experience is the most important experience one can achieve in this lifetime, the importance of having this ultimate experience, and whether they believe (or know) what they claim because of their experiences. Contra Gerson et al., I cannot see how a Plotinian interpreter can make a convincing case that Plotinus has the views he does from anything other than having had the ultimate experience. My case should only be strengthened once we see the similarities of their views on every major—and even on many of what may be considered minor—issue, in the areas of epistemology and ethics.

1.10 Summary

Both Plato and Plotinus claim that these ultimate experiences share many features: First, it provides answers to the chief philosophical questions, such as what there is, what one can know, and how one should live. Second, the experience is everlasting and self-sustaining, in that if one experiences it, one never forgets it and it is ever present. Third, it is difficult to experience it and a rarity among humans. Fourth, it is ineffable—if one experiences a vision of the Good, one will not be able to detail the experience except perhaps to say that it was the greatest experience that gave one knowledge of the Source of All Things, happiness, and similar things. Fifth, they both agree about what it takes for someone to have the ultimate experience: virtue, control of bodily pleasures, the turning of one's soul in the proper direction, the studying of mathematics, and the practicing of dialectic.

Plato expresses concern about revealing what this experience is like, having witnessed Socrates' execution by Athenians, which indicated that people would think him ridiculous if he blatantly told them what he knew. This also lends credence to the view that Plato had some kind of experience which he understands most people will think is a form of madness.

I argued that Plato should best be interpreted as a mystic, contra Cairns in his introduction of *The Collected Dialogues of Plato* (and others), because it explains why Plato seems so rational on the one hand, but seemingly willing to leave rationality behind on issues such as recollection, reincarnation, guardian spirits, and other views. If Plato had the ultimate experience, it would help explain this particular apparent inconsistency in his thought.

Finally, Gerson and others discuss the unimportance of mysticism in Plotinus' thought, and the possibility of essentially ignoring his mysticism in order to understand his view; contra Gerson, I hold that Plotinus' mysticism plays a major role in his thought, and that it is precisely the ultimate experience that causes Plotinus and Plato to not essentially disagree on virtually every major and minor philosophical issue.

2

Epistemology: Plato and Plotinus on Knowledge

2.1 Introduction

Plato and Plotinus do not essentially differ on these epistemological views:

(1) Intellect/Nous/Being has wisdom, humans become godlike with the aid of wisdom, good men are wise men, wisdom leads to or implies happiness, wisdom implies contemplation and purity, and wisdom ensures the beneficial use of virtues;
(2) Ultimate knowledge is of the Good (or the One), pure or true knowledge has the Forms and not perceptibles as its objects, there is a significant difference between theoretical and practical knowledge; the knower is awake and the opiner is dreaming, and knowledge is vastly superior to opinion;
(3) The surest way of attaining knowledge is to practice dialectic;
(4) The soul recollects what it already knows from the interlife (life between incarnations) and therefore rationalism is true;
(5) Prayer is useless without relevant action and right opinion; and
(6) Opinion is inferior to knowledge and has perceptible objects as its cognitive object.

2.2 Wisdom

Both Plato and Plotinus (and the translators of their works) use or translate both σοφία and φρόνησις as "wisdom," though φρόνησις can be and is translated as "practical wisdom," "thought," "intelligence," and similar such words. To highlight the fact that both philosophers mostly use these words interchangeably, I will place "[*sophia*]" after the word wisdom in the quotes from Plato and Plotinus when the Greek word is σοφία or one of its derivatives; "[*phronēsis*]" will be placed after wisdom to indicate φρόνησις or one of its derivatives.

I claim that Plato and Plotinus endorse the following claims concerning wisdom:

(1) Intellect/Nous/Being has wisdom;
(2) Humans become godlike with the aid of wisdom;
(3) Good men are wise men;

(4) Wisdom leads to or implies happiness;
(5) Wisdom implies contemplation and purity; and
(6) Wisdom ensures the beneficial use of virtues.

Intellect/Nous/Being has wisdom

Plato:[1] The first relevant passage is in the *Sophist*, where Plato is arguing with the Friends of Forms who are not willing to concede any life, change, movement, or soul to the Forms or the Forms' realm. Plato refers to "that which is perfectly real" (or "that which wholly is" on White's translation), which must be taken as the territory of the Forms—the intelligible realm (or what Plotinus refers to as Nous or Intellect)—and affirms its possession of wisdom:

> Are we really to be so easily convinced that change, life, soul, understanding have no place in that which is perfectly real—that it has neither life nor wisdom [*phronēsis*], but stands immutable in solemn aloofness, devoid of intellect [*nous*]?
>
> That, sir, would be a strange doctrine to accept.
>
> But can we say it has intellect [*nous*] without having life?
>
> Surely not.
>
> But if we say it contains both, can we deny that it has soul in which they reside?
>
> How else could it possess them?
>
> But then, if it has wisdom [*phronēsis*], life, and soul, can we say that a living thing remains at rest in complete changelessness?
>
> All that seems to me unreasonable.
>
> In that case we must admit that what changes and change itself are real things.
>
> Certainly. (*Sophist* 248e7–9b4; adapted from Cornford)

So Plato states that *that which is perfectly real* must have wisdom.

Secondly, in the *Philebus*, Plato states that there is a cause ["of no small significance"] that is most justly called wisdom [*sophia*] and reason [*nous*]:

> We had better pursue the alternative account and affirm, as we have said often, that there is plenty of the unlimited in the universe as well as sufficient limit, and that there is, above them, a certain cause, of no small significance, that orders and coordinates the years, seasons, and months, and which has every right to the title of wisdom [*sophia*] and reason [*nous*].
>
> The greatest right.(*Philebus* 30c2–8[2])

So Plato holds that Nous or intellect has wisdom and that Nous and wisdom are causes that order and coordinate the years, seasons, and months.

Plotinus:

> The greatness and power of this wisdom [*sophia*] can be imagined if we consider that it has with it and has made all things, and all things follow it, and it is the real

> beings, and they came to be along with it, and both are one, and being is wisdom [*sophia*] there. But we have not arrived at understanding this, because we consider that the branches of knowledge are made up of theorems and a collection of proportions; but this is not true even of the sciences here below. (V.8.4.44–51; adapted from A.H. Armstrong[3])

This passage, in its reference to life in Intellect and real Being, also bears a striking resemblance to *Sophist* 248e7–9b4:

> Life holds no weariness for anyone when it is pure: and how should that which leads the best life grow weary? This life is wisdom [*sophia*], wisdom not acquired by reasonings, because it was always all present, without any failing which would make it need to be searched for; but it is the first, not derived from any other wisdom; the very being of Intellect is wisdom: it does not exist first and then become wise. For this reason there is no greater wisdom: absolute knowledge has its throne beside Intellect in their common revelation. (V.8.4.34–40)

Note that Plotinus states that the wisdom of Nous is not acquired by reasonings; Rappe generalizes that: "the Neoplatonists insisted that wisdom could be located only outside all texts and outside all language."[4] Contra Rappe (considering only Plotinus' view), he justifies his claim that Nous' wisdom was not acquired by reasonings, *because it was always present without any failing*; but Plato certainly holds that Nous is always present (eternal) and perfect, just as the Forms are eternal. I concede, however, that the ultimate experience that grants wisdom to humans to the extent possible is ineffable; but given that both philosophers hold that our words refer to Forms, our words can and do indeed refer to wisdom.

Humans become godlike with the aid of wisdom

Plato:

> A man should make all haste to escape from earth to heaven; and escape means becoming as like God as possible; and a man becomes like God when he becomes just and pure, with wisdom [*phronēseōs*]. (*Theaetetus* 176a8–b2; adapted from Levett/Burnyeat[5])

Further, I share two relevant views with J. Armstrong here: Plato holds that the ideal life of becoming like God "involves knowledge of the Good itself";[6] and Plato's identification of God with Nous entails that becoming like God commits one to improving the sensible world;[7] I extend this view to Plotinus as well.

Thus, Plato holds that we become divine or godlike by becoming just via wisdom.

Plotinus: Plotinus echoes Plato:

> We become godlike "if we become righteous and holy with the help of wisdom [*phronēseōs*]," and are altogether in virtue. (I.2.1.4–5[8])

I will briefly address Anton, Hadot, and Rist's objections. First, Anton argues that virtue for Plotinus has a new meaning:

> The new meaning [of] this virtue shifted to being an instrument for understanding the goal of the return to the One. It also redefined *philosophia* as the love of a new wisdom whose mission is to sustain the desire for the great ascent. With Plotinus, *sophia* must perform radically new tasks, beyond what Plato and Aristotle, and definitely beyond what the Stoics expected.[9]

Plato agrees with Plotinus that the highest goal for humans is to acquire knowledge of the Good. So wisdom does not need to perform new tasks, and there is no new love of wisdom in Plotinus that we do not already find in Plato.

Second, Hadot[10] summarizes: "Such is the wisdom of Plotinus. It is a mystical wisdom, which has no meaning for whomever has not experienced divine union." First, see my reply to Anton which applies equally here, and second, I've just shown that both philosophers refer to wisdom as the means to becoming godlike.

Third, Rist argues:

> Plotinus, then, was convinced both by theory and by practice that [*homoiōsis theōi*] led to the mystical union. Plato, on the other hand, supposed that it led to contemplation of the Forms and to an intuitive grasp of the Form of the Good. The difference is obvious.... There is all the difference in the world between contemplation and union in the Plotinian sense.[11]

Rist downplays Plato's emphasis of one's gaining knowledge of the Good here in favor of contemplation of the Forms. Plotinus believes that dialectic, which involves moving from Ideas and through Ideas is the most important part of philosophy as well, so the difference between the two philosophers here is exaggerated.[12]

Good humans are wise humans

Plato: In Plato's corpus, several passages serve my purpose. The first is in the *Laches*: "Every one of us is good with respect to that in which he is wise [*sophia*] and bad in respect to that in which he is ignorant" (194d1–2). The better a human is, the wiser she is, and vice versa; this passage implies that the best is also the most wise.

The second passage is in the *Menexenus*: "All knowledge cut off from justice and the rest of virtue has the look of low cunning, not wisdom [*sophia*]" (246e7–7a2; adapted from Ryan); this implies that wisdom is more than mere possession of knowledge, requiring the wise person to be just and virtuous. From elsewhere in Plato's work we know that in order to be just and virtuous, one needs to know the Good, so we can infer that there is a connection between one's being wise and one's knowing/seeing the Good.

The last passage is from the *Phaedo* and shows that wisdom is the source of the virtues and true goodness, from which we can infer that if one is good, one is wise:

> I fear this is not the right exchange to attain virtue, to exchange pleasures for pleasures, pains for pains and fears for fears, the greater for the less like coins, but that the only valid currency for which all these things should be exchanged is wisdom [*phronēsis*]. With this we have real courage and moderation and justice and, in a word, true virtue, with wisdom [*phronēsis*], whether pleasures and fears and all such things be present or absent. Exchanged for one another without wisdom [*phronēsis*] such virtue is only an illusory appearance of virtue; it is in fact fit for slaves, without soundness or truth, whereas, in truth, moderation and courage and justice are a purging away of all such things, and wisdom [*phronēsis*] itself is a kind of cleansing and purification (*Phaedo* 69a6–c3)

Hitchcock claims that Plato changes his mind from the time that he wrote this *Phaedo* passage, upon writing the *Republic* 505c passage:

> Socrates also raises an objection to the view endorsed at *Phaedo* 69a–c that the good is wisdom. When asked what kind of wisdom, those who hold this view are compelled to say that it is wisdom about the good, a ridiculous reply because "they reproach us for not knowing the good, and then speak as though we did know" (505c1–2). The objection is new in Plato's writings, and suggests a recantation of his earlier position.[13]

The *Phaedo* passage only claims that when one possesses wisdom, it makes possible courage, temperance, integrity and true goodness. Plato does not say there that wisdom is the Form of the Good (or that wisdom is knowledge *simpliciter*, which is what the *Republic* passage in question concerns). However, if wisdom is the knowledge/vision/experience of the Good (as Plotinus and I interpret Plato as holding), then these passages are consistent; to merely claim that knowledge is good, without knowing whether it is knowledge *of* the Good,[14] is not sufficient. And the Good is beyond being, so *perhaps* it is even unknowable (though Plato says it's knowable elsewhere). In any case, we do not have to read Plato as rejecting an earlier belief.

Plotinus: There is one key passage in the *Enneads* to show that the good person is wise:

> Plato was right in maintaining that the man who intends to be wise [*sophia*] and in a state of well-being [*eudaimona*] must take his good from There, from above, and look to that good and be made like it and live by it. He must hold on to this only as his goal, and change his other circumstances as he changes his dwelling-place, not because he derives any advantage in the point of well-being [*eudaimonein*] from one dwelling-place or another, but guessing, as it were, how his alien covering will be affected if he lodges here or there. (I.4.16.10–7[15])

Admittedly, the beginning part of this passage is only showing that the person who wants to be wise and happy must look to the Good; however, Plotinus also states that one must be made like it and live by it. If one lives by the good and is made like the good, we can infer that one is good (to the extent possible for humans), and that one is thereby wise.

Wisdom leads to or implies happiness

Note that for both philosophers, happiness is a state or disposition and not a process or an action.

Plato: I will use a passage from the early dialogues that gets much attention from Platonic and Plotinian commentators due to their lack of being mentioned by Plotinus as often as other dialogues. In the *Euthydemus*, Plato says that we need to become wise in order to be happy:

> Since we all wish to be happy, and since we appear to become so by using things and using them rightly, and since knowledge was the source of rightness and good fortune, it seems to be necessary that every man should prepare himself by every means to become as wise [*sophia*] as possible. (*Euthydemus* 282a1–6[16])

In the *Meno*, Plato essentially repeats the point made in the *Euthydemus*, that so-called goods and virtues are only good or beneficial to one if one is wise. He lists temperance, justice, courage, intelligence, memory, and munificence at *Meno* 88a7–8, and virtue at 88d2. Plato generalizes the principle as well, saying: "all that the soul undertakes and endures, if directed by wisdom [*phronēsis*], ends in happiness, but if directed by ignorance, it ends in the opposite" (88c1–3).

So Plato believes that wisdom produces happiness, and that if one is happy, one is wise.[17]

Plotinus: We have just seen Plotinus argue that in order for one to be wise and happy, one must look to the Good and be made like It and live by That (I.4.16.10–7). There are other indirect passages that support this view. In the first passage, Plotinus implies that the position of Plato's *Euthydemus* and *Meno* is correct:

> But suppose there were two wise [*sophia*] men, one of whom had all of what are called natural goods and the other their opposites, shall we say that they both have well-being equally? Yes, if they are equally wise. Even if one is good-looking and has all the other advantages which have nothing to do with wisdom, or in any way with virtue and the vision of the best, or with the best itself, what does that amount to? (I.4.15.1–6[18])

Plotinus' answer implies Plato's view in the *Euthydemus* and *Meno* is correct, that wisdom helps you use other things wisely for happiness; but—more importantly for our immediate purposes—whether or not one possesses natural goods, if one is wise, then one is happy.[19]

Wisdom implies contemplation and purity

Plato: Besides *Phaedo* 69a6–c3, I can adduce two passages that equate wisdom with contemplation and/or purification. First, in the *Phaedo*, Plato states that contemplation, that is, the soul's investigation "by itself" of the realm of the pure—the Forms—is called wisdom (79d1–7). Second, Plato connects purity with wisdom in the *Laws*:

> That body should sate itself with body he'll think outrageous; his reverence and respect for self-control, courage, high principles and wisdom [*phronēsis*] will make him want to live a life of purity, chaste lover with chaste beloved. (*Laws* VIII 837c3–d1; adapted from Saunders)

Here Plato states that if one puts contemplation before passion, and worships wisdom, one will live in purity in body and soul.[20]

Plotinus: Plotinus boldly states that wisdom consists in the contemplation of Intellect's contents:

> Wisdom [*sophia*], theoretical [*theōriai*] and practical [*phronēsis*], consists in the contemplation of that which intellect contains; but intellect has it by immediate contact. There are two kinds of wisdom, one in intellect, one in soul. That which is There [in intellect] is not virtue, that in the soul is virtue. (I.2.6.12–5; the first three brackets are mine[21])

Near the end of the second passage, Plotinus states that the happy person (here rendered "well off") possesses the dignity of wisdom and the purity of good:

> If anyone does not set the good man up on high in this world of intellect, but brings him down to chance events and fears their happening to him, he is not keeping his mind on the good man as we consider he must be, but assuming an ordinary man, a mixture of good and bad, and assigning to him a life which is also a mixture of good and bad and of a kind which cannot easily occur. Even if a person of this sort did exist, he would not be worth calling well off [*eudaimōn*]; he would have no greatness in him, either of the dignity of wisdom [*sophia*] or the purity of good. (I.4.16.1–9[22])

We can also infer from the presumption that the intelligible realm is pure that if one is wise, at least one is as pure as is humanly possible.

Wisdom ensures the beneficial use of virtues

Each thinker claims wisdom as the cognitive state or soul feature that ensures virtues such as temperance, justice, courage, and the like are beneficial for one's soul and not somehow harmful. In fact, it appears that they both hold that one's being wise is the same as being virtuous; I focus here on the claim that wisdom aids in making virtues advantageous.

Plato: We see these kinds of claims made, for example, in the *Meno*, *Symposium*, *Republic*, and *Laws*; from the *Meno*:

> All the qualities of the soul [temperance, justice, courage, intelligence, memory, and munificence at 88a7–8] are in themselves neither beneficial nor harmful, but accompanied by wisdom [*phronēsis*] or folly they become harmful or beneficial. This argument shows that virtue, being beneficial, must be a kind of wisdom [*phronēsis*]. (*Meno* 88c6–d3[23])

Thus, virtue is a sort of wisdom, and goods of the soul ("virtues") become advantageous with the presence of wisdom.

Plotinus: Plotinus examines the "lower kinds of virtue" or "civic virtues"—justice, temperance, and courage, as applied to the ruling of a state or the role of a citizen therein:

> Can the lower kinds of virtue exist without dialectic and theoretical wisdom [*sophia*]? Yes, but only incompletely and defectively. And can one be a wise man [*sophia*] and a dialectician without these lower virtues? It would not happen; they must either precede or grow along with wisdom. One might perhaps have natural virtues, from which the perfect ones develop with the coming of wisdom [*sophia*]. (I.3.6.14–9[24])

So Plotinus holds that wisdom implies that one has these virtues, and that one develops perfect or full virtue with the coming of wisdom.[25]

2.3 Knowledge

Plato and Plotinus agree that the ultimate knowledge is of the Good (or the One), that the objects of knowledge in general are the Forms and not perceptibles, that there is a distinction between theoretical and practical knowledge, that the knower is awake and the opiner is dreaming, and that knowledge is vastly superior to opinion.

Plotinus mentions a Platonic passage on knowledge:

> About the knowledge there—which Plato observed and said "that which is not a knowledge different from that in which it is," but how this is so, he left us to investigate and discover, if we claim to be worthy of our title [of Platonists]. (V.8.4.52–5)

Here, Plotinus might have in mind the *Parmenides*, where Plato objects to his own view as follows:

> Wouldn't knowledge that belongs to us be of the truth that belongs to our world? And wouldn't it follow that each particular knowledge that belongs to us is in turn knowledge of some particular thing in our world? (*Parmenides* 134a9–b1)

Subsequently, Plato responds to his own objection with:

> He seems to have a point; and, as we said, he is extraordinarily hard to win over. Only a very gifted man can come to know that for each thing there is some kind, a being itself by itself; but only a prodigy more remarkable still will discover that and be able to teach someone else who has sifted all these difficulties thoroughly and critically for himself. (*Parmenides* 135a5–b2)

Evidently Plotinus claims himself to be worthy of the title of Platonist, because, in many places, he has talked about investigating, discovering, and knowing the Supreme and what that is like.

Ultimate knowledge is of the Good

Plato and Plotinus hold that ultimate knowledge is of the Good, which also makes the Good the greatest thing to learn. I also raise the following issues:

(1) The Good is the source of truth and knowledge;
(2) The Good is the unhypothesized principle or the topmost entity of the Divided Line Analogy;
(3) "Vision" and "touch" metaphors are used alternatively for expressing knowledge of the Good;
(4) Knowledge of the Good is non-discursive; and
(5) Paradoxically, it may be possible that no knowledge may be had of the Good.

Plato:[26] In the *Republic*, Plato says that we must know the Form of the Good to get any benefit or use out of anything else (including any other knowledge), and that the Form of the Good is the most important thing to know, learn, or possess:

> You have often heard that the Form of the Good is indeed the greatest thing learned, by using which both just things and other things become useful and beneficial. And now you are probably aware that I am about to speak about this Form and say in addition to this, that we do not know this Form adequately; and if we do not know this Form, even if we should know especially well the other things [that is, the just things and other things] without knowing this Form, you are aware that there would be no benefit to us, just as there would be no benefit if we should possess something without the possession of the good. (*Republic* VI 505a2–b3; my translation[27])

There are many important claims made in this passage: the Idea of Good is the greatest thing to learn; just things and every other possession become useful only with reference to the Good and/or one's possession of the Good; and if we do not know the Good, even if we know other things or Forms, it will not benefit us to have such knowledge.

We can further affirm that this is Plato's view because knowledge of the Good is the highest epistemological achievement of the released prisoner in the Cave Allegory: "In the knowable realm, the Form of the Good is the last thing seen, and it is reached only with difficulty" (*Republic* VII 517b8–c1; adapted from Grube/Reeve).

Unsurprisingly, not all Platonic commentators agree that Plato's claim that ultimate knowledge is of the Good is so obvious. For instance, Luban[28] states: "The doctrine of the Good is best understood as an ontological, not a moral or axiological doctrine." Luban does not even raise the notion of the Good's playing a role in epistemology there.[29] Contra Luban, however, Plato assigns the chief epistemological role to the Good.

Plotinus: Plotinus agrees with Plato that knowledge of the Good is ultimate and that the Good is the greatest thing to be learned:[30]

> The knowledge or touching of the Good is the greatest thing, and Plato says it is the "greatest study," not calling the looking at it a "study," but learning about it beforehand. We are taught about it by comparisons and negations and knowledge of the things which come from it and certain methods of ascent by degrees, but we are put on the way to it by purifications and virtues and adornings and by gaining footholds in the intelligible and settling ourselves firmly there and feasting on its contents. But whoever has become at once contemplator of himself and all the rest and object of his contemplation, and, since he has become substance and intellect and "the complete living being," no longer looks at it from outside—when he has become this he is near, and that Good is next above him, and already close by, shining upon all the intelligible world. (VI.7.36.3–15; adapted from A.H. Armstrong[31])

Thus Plotinus holds that knowledge of the Good is the greatest thing to learn, and he certainly confirms here that he agrees with Plato on the importance of attaining knowledge of the Good.

Let us now reply to two commentators with whom I disagree on this issue, though there are others:[32] First, Katz[33] emphasizes that: "the Plotinic [sic] vision is ontological, not epistemological, in character. This means that it involves not only the enlightenment of the subject but also the disclosure of ontologically superior objects." My first reply is that Plotinus states that we can know the One (and I will later show that knowledge of the Good/One also entails one's happiness for Plotinus), so we cannot deny that the Plotinian vision has an epistemological character to it. My second reply is that Katz's charge is puzzling, because he states both that the vision is not epistemological in the first sentence, and then that "enlightenment" is involved in the vision.

Second, Zeller makes two similar statements that I take issue with, the first of which will represent them both: "The neo-Platonists doubted in the last instance the possibility of theoretical knowledge of the ultimate basis of all being and sought a remedy in revelation received in a state of mystical ecstasy."[34] Plotinus does in fact state that knowledge of the Good is ultimate (and also that the Good is the basis of being).

Thus, I have shown that both thinkers aver that knowledge of the Good is the ultimate knowledge attainable.

The Good is the source of truth and knowledge

Plato: As many commentators do not seem to dispute,[35] Plato states that the Good is the source of knowledge and truth as well, in part of the Sun Simile. In *Republic* VI 507c–8c, Plato makes an analogy between the sun, the eye, and the power to see, on the one hand, and the Good, the soul, and power to know on the other: The eye cannot see visible objects such as a tree without the sun; analogously, the mind cannot know the Forms without the Form of the Good. At *Republic* VI 508b, Plato also implies that the eye must have a nature akin to the sun in order to be able to see things such as trees; analogously, the soul must have a nature akin to the Good to be able to know the Forms. At this point, Glaucon asks Socrates to explain further, and Socrates continues:

> So that what gives truth to the things known and the power to know to the knower is the Form of the Good. And though it is the cause of knowledge and truth, it is also an object of knowledge. Both knowledge and truth are beautiful things, but the Good is other and more beautiful than they. In the visible realm, light and sight are rightly considered sunlike, but it is wrong to think that they are the sun, so here it is right to think of knowledge and truth as goodlike but wrong to think that either of them is the Good—for the Good is yet more prized.
>
> This is an inconceivably beautiful thing you're talking about, if it provides both knowledge and truth and is superior to them in beauty. (*Republic* VI 508d4–9a7; adapted from Grube/Reeve)

Plato's main point here is that the Good is the source of truth and knowledge, and similar to truth and knowledge, but is not identical to either, and is better than both.

Plotinus: First, note that commentators do not seem to mention this point in Plotinus. Nonetheless, in the following passage, Plotinus agrees in principle with Plato that the One (or Good) is the source of knowledge:

> The perplexity arises especially because our awareness of that One is not by way of reasoned knowledge or of intellectual perception, as with other intelligible things, but by way of a presence superior to knowledge. The soul experiences its falling away from being one and is not altogether one when it has reasoned knowledge of anything; for reasoned knowledge is a rational process, and a rational process is many. The soul therefore goes past the One and falls into number and multiplicity. One must therefore run up above knowledge and in no way depart from being one, but one must depart from knowledge and things known, and from every other, even beautiful, object of vision. For every beautiful thing is posterior to that One, and comes from it, as all the light of day comes from the sun. (VI.9.4.1–11[36])

After acknowledging that he is discussing the One, that is, "that which is prior to what is most honorable among real beings" (VI.9.5.24–5), and realizing that he has just mentioned that it in fact has no fitting name, but if we must name it, "One" is perhaps most apt, he continues:

> This [the One] is difficult to know for this reason, but can be better known from its product, substance (*ousia*)—and it is intellect which leads to substance—and its nature is of such a kind that it is the source of the best and the power which generates the real beings, abiding in itself and not being diminished and not being one of the things which it brought into being. (VI.9.5.33–8[37])

So Plotinus states that knowing the One is difficult, but that it is better known from its products, which implies that the One causes the possibility of knowledge, as Plato says. Thus, assuming for now that the One is the Good for both philosophers, Plotinus agrees with Plato that the Good is the source of knowledge.

Plotinus believes that the One or Good is the source of truth. Here he is urging the seeker to concentrate on the pure form and come to be in the intelligible realm:

> For he will see an intellect which sees nothing perceived by the senses, none of these mortal things, but apprehends the eternal by its eternity, and all the things in the intelligible world, having become itself an intelligible universe full of light, illuminated by the truth from the Good, which radiates truth over all the intelligibles. (IV.7.10.32–8[38])

Truth thus streams from the Good, according to Plotinus.

Plotinus agrees with Plato that the Good makes knowledge possible, where the following sight and light metaphors are clearly intended to refer to knowledge and truth:

> This is why that Good is said to be the cause not only of substance but of its being seen. And just as the sun, which is cause for sense-objects both of their being seen and their coming into being, is also in some way cause of sight—and therefore is neither sight nor the things which have come to be—in this way also the nature of the Good, which is cause of substance and intellect and light, according to our analogy, to the things seen there and the seer, is neither the real beings nor intellect but cause of these, giving by its own light thinking and being thought to the real beings and to intellect. (VI.7.16.22–31)

Thus the Good is the cause of substance [*ousia*] and Intellect (and truth—"light"), and the cause of Being's ability to be seen/known. He is also essentially affirming the Sun Simile points made by Plato.[39]

Therefore, both philosophers affirm that the Good is the source of truth and knowledge.

The Good is the unhypothesized principle or the topmost entity of the Divided Line Analogy

Even though Plotinus does not mention the Divided Line Analogy explicitly, he alludes to different levels of understanding, and thoroughly agrees with Plato that dialectic is the best method to bring one to knowledge of the Good, where dialectic is mentioned by Plato as being the cognitive activity practiced in the topmost section of the Line.

Plato: On my account of the Divided Line Analogy (*Republic* VI 509d–11e),[40] Plato divides a line into four segments and ascribes four powers (image-thinking, opinion, understanding, and intellect) to four different cognitive objects (shadows or reflections of perceptible objects, perceptible objects, mathematical objects improperly conceived, and Forms), in different ratios and proportions to one another. The relevant part of this passage for the Good, however, is where Socrates states why geometry, mathematics and the kindred sciences and methods are not the highest study, but only qualify as second behind dialectic or intellect. Socrates states that mathematicians use "hypotheses, proceeding not to a first principle but to a conclusion" (*Republic* VI 510b5–6); in the highest section of the line, "it makes its way to a first principle that is *not* a hypothesis, proceeding from a hypothesis but without the images used in the previous subsection, using forms themselves and making its investigation through them" (VI 510b6–9). Plato states that there is a beginning or first principle that is *not* a hypothesis, implying that it transcends assumption, and shortly thereafter claims that dialectic is the study that aids one in arriving at this first principle:

> Understand that, by the other subsection of the intelligible, I mean that which reason itself grasps by the power of dialectic. It does not consider these hypotheses as first principles but truly as hypotheses—but as stepping stones to take off from, enabling it to reach the unhypothetical first principle of everything. Having grasped this principle, it reverses itself and, keeping hold of what follows from it, comes down to a conclusion without making use of anything visible at all, but only of Forms themselves, moving on from Forms to Forms, and ending in Forms. (*Republic* VI 511b3–c2; adapted from Grube/Reeve)

From this passage, Plato believes that we can ascend to an unhypothetical first principle, a starting point that requires no assumption, and that once attained, one can run through other ideas and relate this starting point to the other ideas. Plato is claiming in the Divided Line Analogy that the Good is at the top of the line and perhaps somehow above it—that is, the cause of the line, the cause of being, the uppermost section, but beyond being, to be consistent with what we learn in the Sun Simile. The Good is the unhypothetical first principle to which we must ascend, which is consistent with everything we have seen Plato say about the Good thus far, even if we have not so ascended.[41]

Plotinus: Plotinus also believes that the One or Good is the unhypothesized principle, and by implication, the topmost entity of the Divided Line Analogy.[42]

The Good is the ultimate object of knowledge for Plotinus. Since he states that the Supreme is the cause of the cause (VI.8.18), and that the Good or One is the cause of the Forms and substance (VI.9.5.33–8, VI.7.16.22–31, and see I.7.1.20–8), Plotinus believes that the Good is that beyond which nothing else is, and is the Source of All Things. Plotinus also holds that the Good is the source of the Intellect (VI.7.16.22–31), which is consistent with the Good's being the unhypothesized First Principle. In sum, if, in Plotinus' view, the One is the First, and the Source of any and everything else including Forms, and therefore is the starting point of all, that highest principle is functionally equivalent to the first principle of the Divided Line Analogy.[43]

Thus, I have adequately demonstrated that Plato and Plotinus aver that the Good is the unhypothesized principle or the topmost entity of the Divided Line Analogy. Let us now examine a feature of the Good's causation.

"Vision" and "touch" metaphors are used alternatively for expressing knowledge or experience of the Good

Both philosophers use vision and touch metaphors to refer to the knowledge or experience of the Good. This is an issue because some Plotinian scholars have claimed that only Plotinus uses or emphasizes the touch metaphor, and from there argued that Plato and Plotinus do not have the same view of knowledge of the Good. Both of these sense metaphors will aid us in examining exactly what kind of knowledge one gains of the Good (non-discursive), as well as whether these philosophers are using these metaphors to allude that knowledge of the Good is not possible.

Plato: Let me affirm Plato's use of the vision metaphor first,[44] briefly giving two quotations from *Republic* VII as representative of all of them. First, in the summary of the Cave Allegory, Plato says: "In the knowable, the Idea of Good is the last thing to be seen, but hardly" (517b8–c1; my translation). Second, Plato states: "It is our task as founders, then, to compel the best natures to reach the study we said before is the most important, namely, to make the ascent and see the good" (519c8–10).[45]

This passage helps confirm Plato's use of the "touch" (or "contact" or "grasp") metaphor in reference to Forms:[46]

> Won't it be reasonable for us to plead in his defense that it is the nature of the real lover of learning to struggle toward what is, not to remain with any of the many things that are believed to be, that, as he moves on, he neither loses nor lessens his erotic love until he grasps [*hapsasthai*][47] the being of each nature itself with the part of his soul that is fitted to grasp it [*ephaptesthai*], because of its kinship with it, and that, once getting near what really is and having intercourse with it and having begotten understanding and truth, he knows, truly lives, is nourished. (*Republic* VI 490a8–b6[48])

Admittedly, Plato does not explicitly refer here to the Good per se; nonetheless the context is clear enough that the Good is one of the natures that can be known along with the being of "each nature itself."

Thus, Plato uses a vision metaphor to refer to the experience of the Good, and uses "touch" or "grasping" metaphors in contexts where Forms are present.

Plotinus: That Plotinus uses the vision metaphor to describe the experience of the Good is not controversial:[49] "Now in the intelligible world the soul also sees the Good through Intellect" (IV4.4.1).[50]

As with Plato, Plotinus uses a touch metaphor in relation to the Forms,[51] but more specifically uses it when examining the claim that the Good is the greatest thing to learn: "*The knowledge or touching of the Good* is the greatest thing" (VI.7.36.3–4; emphasis added).[52]

Representing a few commentators' opinions about Plotinus and the touch metaphor,[53] I will cite Miles, who argues against Bos:

> Bos writes, "I am of the opinion that [Platonism's] essence must be located in man's aspiration to leave behind the experiential situation of tension and struggle which results from never-ending differences of opinion, and to reach a level of knowledge and science which will once and for all put an end to all struggles and schism." True, Bos claims to characterize "Platonism" rather than Plotinus specifically, but, as Platonism's foremost interpreter, Plotinus is included in his generalizations. Yet Plotinus believed that human access to the way the world is is only achieved by a fundamentally ineffable experience of vision/touch.[54]

Miles curiously refers to Plotinus as the foremost interpreter of Plato, but then claims that Plotinus (and thus implies not Plato) believes that in order to access the way the world is, one must have an ineffable experience involving vision or touch. Since Plato himself uses both of these metaphors, and as I have covered many additional parallels in their descriptions of the ultimate experience including ineffability, however, I can confidently refute Miles' implication that Plotinus somehow has a different view from Plato.

Plotinus uses vision and touch metaphors to allude to experiencing the Good, and therefore, both philosophers refer to the cognitive encounter with the Good alternatively as knowledge, vision, and/or touching of the Good. One possible implication of the use of these alternate metaphors is the allusion that perhaps, strictly speaking, one *cannot* have knowledge of the Good (see below).

Knowledge of the Good is non-discursive

The knowledge that Plato and Plotinus urge us to gain is non-discursive or intuitive in nature, as opposed to, say, a conclusion that we can reach by argument.

If my analysis holds, it implies that both philosophers believe that we cannot pass on the ultimate experience's nature directly to those who have not experienced it for themselves. Plato and Plotinus also describe the experience of the Good as a vision (and/or touching) and not merely knowledge, which lends credence to the view that they believe that the experience is non-discursive.

Plato: Several commentators have already made this argument or statement, and I agree with them.[55] One argument against the non-discursive view is that Plato states that one will not be a true dialectician unless one can give an account of the Good (*Republic* VII 534b–d). The best rebuttal, I think, à la Lachterman[56] and Mohr,[57] is to claim that there is a difference between a true dialectician who can give an account of the Good because he has experienced it, and for the listener of that account to be able to come to know the Good just from listening to the account. As I have shown, there are other requirements for this experience other than only practicing dialectic. Lastly, on the premise that the Good is the most important thing to learn, as is shown to be true for Plato, if it were possible for Plato to have written out an argument that gives one the knowledge thereof, he certainly would have done so (cf. *Letter* VII 341b–2a). However, on my reading of the *Republic* and *Letter* VII, the Good does not seem to be the kind of thing that one can arrive at knowledge of via argument.

Thus, we have good reason to believe that Plato believes that knowledge of the Good is non-discursive.

Plotinus:[58]

> The perplexity arises especially because *our awareness of that One is not by way of reasoned knowledge or of intellectual perception, as with other intelligible things, but by way of a presence superior to knowledge. The soul experiences its falling away from being one and is not altogether one when it has reasoned knowledge of anything; for reasoned knowledge is a rational process, and a rational process is many.* The soul therefore goes past the One and falls into number and multiplicity. One must therefore run up above knowledge and in no way depart from being one, but one must depart from knowledge and things known, and from every other, even beautiful, object of vision. For every beautiful thing is posterior to that One, and comes from it, as all the light of day comes from the sun. (VI.9.4.1–11; emphasis added[59])

I grant that Plotinus definitely states in this passage that the experience of the One is *not* knowledge but superior to it. But what he seems to be saying in the context is that it is an object of vision unlike the other objects of vision—but it remains an object thereof, which is consistent with his statements about its being a vision above; and it is not a rational, reasoned process, which is precisely to say that it is a non-discursive experience. Thus, my point is proven, even if I have opened another can of worms: How can the experience of the Good be knowledge (as Plotinus states) and yet not be knowledge, as he seems to state here? I will examine this paradox in the next section.

Mayhall disagrees with my view and describes the essence of Platonism as follows:

> The essence of Platonism is its exhibition of the very type of a metaphysical philosophy particularly directed toward a transcendent reality. With this goes the rationalistic side of the Platonic tradition, a belief in the power of thought directly to grasp transcendent realities, as shown in Platonic theories of universals and of mathematical objects; thus logic and mathematics are seen as providing keys to the structure of the universe.[60]

Contrasting this characterization with Plotinus' view, he concludes:

> Plotinus' work, then, is more dogmatic and less tentative than Plato. It is concerned with constructing a system for which Plato's dialogues could provide "proof-texts." Much that is central is not, in its Plotinian form, to be found in Plato at all.[61]

However, Plotinus has the same rationalistic side of the Platonic tradition with his endorsement of dialectic, mathematics, and repeated arguments in favor of Plato's view (as opposed to constant appeals to the experience as the only defense). Moreover, Plato does not simply state that if one knows math and practices science, then one knows the truth of everything and has thereby reached the goal. As with Plotinus, the goal is clearly to experience the Good and obtain knowledge, vision, or a grasp thereof, if possible. I thus repudiate Mayhall's statement that *the* central claim of Plotinus is not found in Plato.

Therefore, I have shown that, for both philosophers, knowledge of the Good seems to be non-discursive.

Paradoxically, it may be possible that no knowledge may be had of the Good

The subject of the Good is the most paradoxical in Plato and Plotinus' thought; let us look at the issue of whether knowledge of the Good is *not* possible for both philosophers. Friedländer notes and describes the paradox here:

> At last, still another dimension becomes visible above the level of being. As the cause of becoming is not itself becoming, so the source of being is not itself being. Then we encounter the highest paradox: not itself being, but beyond being. While there is still knowledge about being, though not purely conceptual knowledge, there can be no knowledge about what is "beyond" being. . . . There is a paradoxical tension in this antithesis: on the one hand, the *Logoi*, and only the *Logoi*, are the keys to the world of being—"It appeared to me as if one ought to seek refuge in the *Logoi*, and perceive through them the true nature of being" (*Phaedo* 99e)—on the other hand, above this world of being towers that which is beyond everything and, therefore, cannot be grasped even by the *Logoi*.[62]

However, Hardie, Rawson, Ross, and Shorey have all found that Plotinus' view differs from Plato's on this very point, so I will take up the objections of Rawson and Ross after examining Plotinus' view. I will also examine Rist's warning about possible inconsistencies in Plato's view and the trap that this sets for later Platonic interpreters, including Plotinus.

Plato: Noting that the Good is the greatest thing to learn and *knowledge* of the Good is non-discursive, I can make the following points to expose the clues that, for Plato, the Good is a fishy sort of philosophical entity, in the sense of its being unknowable.[63]

First, remember the vision and touch passages above, which imply that he is trying to get away from the idea that we can *know* the Form of the Good but that it is more of an experience.[64] Also, compare what Plato says about the vision of Beauty in the *Symposium* (which is also referred to as knowledge of Beauty):[65]

> *Nor will the beautiful appear to him* in the guise of a face or hands or anything else that belongs to the body. *It will not appear to him as* one idea [*logos*] or *one kind of knowledge* [*tis epistēmē*].[66] It is not anywhere in another thing, as in an animal, or in earth, or in heaven, or in anything else, but itself by itself with itself, it is always one in form. (*Symposium* 211a5–b2; emphasis added[67])

If the vision of Beauty is not knowledge, we have the same sort of paradox mentioned for another important Form, which implies that the same kind of thing may be true on Plato's view of the Good as well (especially given that the Good is said to be not being, but beyond being).

Second, recall the non-discursive nature of the experience of the Good. If the experience is intuitive and not the same thing as arriving at a conclusion, then this implies again at the very least that this experience is not the same as deducing the Good from logical premises. A suggestion that combines the first and second points is that we have a vision of the Good, which then becomes knowledge after we have begun to think discursively again, but I cannot cite a supporting text so I merely suggest it here.

Lastly, in part of the Cave Allegory summary, Plato says: "in the knowable, the Idea of Good is the last thing to be seen, but hardly" (*Republic* VII 517b8–c1; my translation),[68] which implies that the Good technically may not be known, but that a glimpse of the Good will give its seer enough understanding to see the layout of the universe, as it were, and understand the source of goodness.

We are left with the impression that Plato both states that knowledge of the Good is possible and yet that it somehow is not. Fortunately for my project, we find Plotinus saying the same thing.

Plotinus: I will briefly summarize the passages that insinuate that we cannot know the Good or One: Regarding VI.9.4, note that Plotinus acknowledges the perplexity of the issue first, and *then* states: "Our awareness of that One is not by way of reasoned knowledge … as with other intelligible things, but by way of a presence superior to knowledge" (VI.9.4.1–3).[69] Similar to Plato's claims concerning knowledge of the Good, Plotinus claims that the One is difficult to know at VI.9.5.33–8.

Thus, Plotinus holds in some places that we cannot have knowledge of the Good or One.

As noted above, Gadamer,[70] Hardie,[71] Rawson, Ross, and Shorey[72] all argue that Plotinus' view of an unknowable Good or One distinguishes his view from that of Plato's. In Rawson's argument against Plotinus' view that the Platonic Good is beyond being, he raises three problems against this Plotinian interpretation. Here is the third, which is related to the (un)knowability of the Good:

> The most significant difficulty of Plotinus' interpretation is that it makes the Good unknowable in principle, because Book V demands that only "what *is* completely, is completely knowable" (477a). If the Good has no share of being,

> then the Good is unknowable. But the Good is the most important thing to learn .... and no other knowledge can be of use to us without knowledge of it (505ab). This certainly suggests (though it does not strictly entail) that the Good can be known. To be sure, Plato emphasizes the difficulty of knowing the Good, but this seems in the end to highlight the possibility that the Good can, "after all," be known.[73]

In the end, Rawson seems merely to be highlighting the paradox noted here, as opposed to resolving it by claiming at the quotation's end that the Good *may* be known for Plato though this proposition is "not strictly entail[ed]" by what Plato says. After all, as Rawson says, if "the Good has no share of being, then the Good is unknowable," and Plato claims that the Good is not being, but beyond being at *Republic* VI 509b, then it is not unwarranted to conclude that the Good *may* be unknowable, which is all I am noting here. In sum, Rawson is merely noting that Plotinus' interpretation is paradoxical, but then leans toward one of the paradox's options for Plato (that the Good is knowable), while ignoring the same kinds of statements that Plotinus makes on this issue (that the Good *is* knowable).

I move now to Ross' objection:

> The question remains whether Plotinus may not be right in holding that Plato meant to set up as that which is most completely real a completely unknowable One, and as derivable from it a One which is an object of knowledge. Perhaps in all his works the passage which comes nearest to corresponding to this view is that in the *Republic* in which the Idea of the good is said to be more exalted than knowledge; but it seems to me that what Plato meant by that is not that it is unknowable but that it is a presupposition of knowledge, and that it can be known only in part; that in part it can be known is said in the *Republic* itself [505a2].[74]

My argument against Ross relies on my argument that the Good of the *Republic* is equivalent to the One in the *Parmenides*. But for now I can still say that Ross has not accounted for *Symposium* 211a5–b2, where "knowledge" of Beauty is transformed in the next paragraph to a "vision of" Beauty that is "not knowledge," which suggests that we cannot simply assert that we can have knowledge of Beauty. Analogously, if the Good is said to be the source of the Forms and not a being, then knowledge of the Good would seem to be quite impossible, leaving us with a metaphor of a seeing or a grasping of it. Yet I can still agree with Ross that the Good is a presupposition of knowledge and that a vision of it somehow yields knowledge, because I have certainly noted that Plato and Plotinus claim that knowledge of the Good is possible.

Lastly and more generally, Rist notes the problem of inconsistency in Plato's dialogues and the problem for later interpreters such as Plotinus:

> If, however, the Platonic dialogues themselves contain unresolved contradictions, either explicit or implicit, then clearly by enlarging upon certain portions of the corpus and neglecting the rest, one could produce a system which, though more

> consistent than that of Plato, would by this very consistency be open to the charge of being unplatonic.[75]

I take Rist's point and hope to show that whatever Plato says—consistently or not—about the major issues and entities in his philosophy, Plotinus also does, as this current issue of whether or not we can have knowledge of the Good shows.[76]

I conclude by merely noting that both philosophers state (or heavily imply) in different parts of their writings that we can and cannot have knowledge of the Good or One. An objector cannot point to this fact with respect to only one philosopher in an attempt to show that the other philosopher has a different view. I leave the resolution of this paradox to be resolved by someone else at a later time—that is, if it has not already been resolved by arguing that the Good must be experienced non-discursively in order to understand or grasp its nature.

Let us now turn to the much less controversial claim that the Forms are objects of knowledge.

(Pure or True) Knowledge has the Forms (and not perceptibles) as its objects

I will examine Plato and Plotinus' claims that pure or true knowledge has the Forms as its objects and then consider the objection that Plato may not believe what he states elsewhere about the possibility and nature of knowledge because he only opines it. However, the claim that knowledge is of the Forms is not meant to conflict with both philosophers' claims that knowledge of the Good or One is supreme.

Plato: The most direct passage on this point occurs in the *Phaedrus*, where Plato claims that true knowledge is knowledge of the "place beyond heaven" and of Forms:[77]

> The place beyond heaven—none of our earthly poets has ever sung or ever will sing its praises enough! … What is in this place is without color and without shape and without solidity, a being that really is what it is, the subject of all true knowledge.… On the way around [the soul] has a view of Justice as it is; it has a view of Self-control; it has a view of Knowledge—not the knowledge that is close to change, that becomes different as it knows the different things which we consider real down here. No, it is the knowledge of what really is what it is. (*Phaedrus* 247c3–4, c6–d1, d5–e2[78])

In the next passage from the *Phaedo*, Plato emphasizes the use of pure thought alone to understand pure realities (the Forms), independent of the whole body:

> He will do this ["grasp that thing itself" and "come closest to knowledge" at 65e3–4] most perfectly who approaches the object with thought alone, without associating any sight with his thought, or dragging in any sense perception with his reasoning, but who, using pure thought alone, tries to track down each reality pure and by itself, freeing himself as far as possible from eyes and ears, and in a word, from the whole body, because the body confuses the soul and does not allow it to

acquire truth and wisdom whenever it is associated with it. Will not that man reach reality, Simmias, if anyone does?

What you say, said Simmias, is indeed true. (*Phaedo* 65e7–6a10)

Plato reaffirms this view that the soul makes its investigation using the Forms themselves and only Forms in the Divided Line Analogy of the *Republic*:

In one subsection, the soul, using as images the things that were imitated before, is forced to investigate from hypotheses, proceeding not to a first principle but to a conclusion. In the other subsection, however, it makes its way to a first principle that is *not* a hypothesis, proceeding from a hypothesis but without the images used in the previous subsection, using Forms themselves and making its investigation through them. (*Republic* VI 510b5–9; adapted from Grube/Reeve[79])

Thus, for Plato, (pure or true) knowledge is of the Forms, and not perceptible objects.

Plotinus: I can now affirm Plotinus' agreement that true knowledge is of the Forms, and then respond to an objection from Harris that both philosophers do not hold the same view.[80] In the first passage, Plotinus confirms Plato's view that the unaided intellect works only with unities within the soul:

When one considers the nature of any particular thing one must concentrate on its pure form, since what is added is always a hindrance to the knowledge of that to which it has been added.... But if purification causes us to be in a state of knowledge of the best, then the sciences which lie within become apparent, the ones which really are sciences. For it is certainly not by running around outside that the soul "sees self-control and justice," but itself by itself in its understanding of itself and what it formerly was, seeing them standing in itself like splendid statues all rusted with time which it has cleaned. (IV.7.10.27–30, 40–7)

Plotinus confirms this view of Plato's, that there is true knowledge in the soul that is not sense knowledge and is of the Forms:

There must be true knowledge in the souls which are in us, and these are not images or likenesses of their Forms as things are in the sense-world, but those very Forms themselves existing here in a different mode. (V.9.13.9–11[81])

Two final passages will confirm the Plotinian view that true knowledge is of Being:

For we and what is ours go back to real being and ascend to that and to the first which comes from it, and we think the intelligibles; we do not have images or imprints of them. But if we do not, we are the intelligibles. If then we have a part in true knowledge, we are those; we do not apprehend them as distinct within ourselves, but we are within them. (VI.5.7.1–6[82])

Thus, in Platonic fashion, Plotinus conveys the point that the Forms have independent existence such that when we apprehend them, we do not see them as being in us per se, but existing on their own. And (where "the things which truly exist" obviously refer to the Forms):

> All things come from contemplation and are contemplation, both the things which truly exist and the things which come from them when they contemplate and are themselves objects of contemplation, some by sense-perception and some by knowledge or opinion; and ... actions have their goal in knowledge and their driving-force is desire of knowledge. (III.8.7.1–5)

So Plotinus believes that (pure or true) knowledge is of the Forms.

Harris, however, objects to the view just laid out: "Plotinus' view is even more radical than Plato's, since he does not set the knower off from his objects, as do Plato and Aristotle, but rather makes the intelligible universe within the subject as the object for knowledge."[83] I have several replies: First, as we'll see in the recollection section below, Plato believes that all of us (humans) already have knowledge of the Forms somehow—presumably not consciously—in our souls. Second, Plato implies that Form-knowers have Forms in their souls (where "clear model" is certainly a Form):

> Do you think, then, that there's any difference between the blind and those who are really deprived of the knowledge of each thing that is? The latter have no clear model in their souls, and so they cannot—in the manner of painters—look to what is most true, make constant reference to it, and study it as exactly as possible. (*Republic* VI 484c6–d1)

Third, since the Forms and the soul are immaterial, then they are akin; since the soul already knows the Forms in some sense (to make recollection possible), then why would the Platonic intelligible universe not be somehow "within the subject as the object of knowledge"? Moreover, if Plato does not agree with this view, why does he state that temperance is *self*-knowledge, when that virtue involves knowledge of a *Form*, Temperance, and for one to actually know how to *benefit* from that knowledge, one must know the Form of the Good? These claims all imply that we come to know ourselves—or "our" intelligible universe, which is the same for everyone—as we ascend to knowledge of the Good, on Plato's view just as much as in Plotinus' view.

Thus, both thinkers hold that pure or true knowledge has the Forms as their objects and that the Forms somehow are in one's soul.

Theoretical knowledge versus practical knowledge

Plato and Plotinus each discuss "pure" and/or "true" knowledge; but in other passages they also distinguish this kind of knowledge from "applied knowledge" or "sense knowledge," which is employed when one uses geometry to build a house, for instance.

Plato: Plato makes a distinction between true knowledge of the Forms on the one hand, and technical knowledge involved in crafts in the *Philebus*:

> Knowledge differed from knowledge [*epistēmē dē epistēmēs diaphoros*]—one having regard to the things that come into being and perish, the other to those that do not come into being nor perish, but are always, unchanged and unaltered. Reviewing them on the score of truth, we concluded that the latter was truer than the former. (*Philebus* 61d10–e4; Hackforth[84])

Plotinus: Plotinus can also be said to claim that there are two kinds of knowledge,[85] one purer and the other (more aptly named opinion) dealing with the sense objects:

> As for the kinds of knowledge which exist in a rational soul, those which are of sense-objects—if one ought to speak of "kinds of knowledge" of these; "opinion" is really the suitable name for them—are posterior to their objects and likenesses of them; but those which are of intelligible objects, which are certainly the genuine kinds of knowledge, come from Intellect to rational soul and do not think any sense-object. (V.9.7.1–6)

Therefore, Plato and Plotinus claim that there is theoretical knowledge and practical knowledge, and that the former is more true or authentic.

Knowers are awake; opiners are dreamers

Plato and Plotinus both used the metaphor of knowing being equivalent to one's being awake, and opining being equivalent to one's mistaking a dream for reality.

Plato:

> What about someone who believes in beautiful things, but doesn't believe in the Beautiful Itself and isn't able to follow anyone who could lead him to the knowledge of it? Don't you think he is living in a dream rather than a wakened state? Isn't this dreaming: whether asleep or awake, to think that a likeness is not a likeness but rather the thing itself that it is like?
>
> I certainly think that someone who does that is dreaming.
>
> But someone who, to take the opposite case, believes in the Beautiful Itself, can see both it and the things that participate in it and doesn't believe that the participants are it or that itself is the participants—is he living in a dream or is he awake?
>
> He's very much awake.
>
> So we'd be right to call his thought knowledge, since he knows, but we should call the other person's thought opinion, since he opines?
>
> Right. (*Republic* V 476c2–d7; adapted from Grube/Reeve[86])

Plotinus:

> This, then, is our argument against those who place real beings in the class of bodies and find their guarantee of truth in the evidence of pushings and strikings and the apparitions which come by way of sense-perception; they act like people dreaming, who think that the things they see as real actually exist, when they are only dreams. For the activity of sense-perception is that of the soul asleep; for it is the part of the soul that is in the body that sleeps; but the true wakening is a true getting up from the body, not with the body. Getting up with the body is only getting out of one sleep into another, like getting out of one bed into another; but the true rising is a rising altogether away from bodies, which are of the opposite nature to soul and opposed in respect of reality. Their coming into being and flux and perishing, which does not belong to the nature of reality, are evidence of this. (III.6.6.65–77[87])

In Plato's view, the person who does not believe that beauty is an abstract object—but who instead believes that beauty is many physical instances, for example, a beautiful woman or piece of music—is not awake; similarly, Plotinus says that he has been discussing "those who place real beings in the class of bodies and find their guarantee of truth in the evidence of pushings and strikings and the apparitions which come by way of sense-perception."

Thus, both philosophers believe that, metaphorically, there are two basic states one can be in, either awake (knower of the Forms), or dreaming (not believing Forms exist, but believing that the perceptible is real).

Knowledge versus opinion

Plato and Plotinus both hold that knowledge is concerned with Being, the Forms, or the real, while opinion is concerned with perceptible objects, things which constantly come into being and perish.

Plato: Plato makes a significant distinction between knowledge and opinion in the *Republic*, claiming that they are different faculties, and as such, have different objects as well (that is, knowledge has the Forms for its objects; opinion has perceptible things as its objects) (V 477b–8b).[88] Plato claims that opiners experience beautiful and just things and actions, and believe that they are what beauty and justice really are, and they do not believe that beauty itself and justice itself are immaterial, eternal, immutable Forms—here, "the things themselves":

> As for those who study the many beautiful things but do not see the Beautiful Itself and are incapable of following another who leads them to it, who see many just things but not the Just Itself, and so with everything—these people, we shall say, opine everything but have no knowledge of anything they opine.
>
> Necessarily.
>
> What about the ones who in each case study the things themselves that are always the same in every respect? Won't we say that they know and don't opine?

That's necessary too.

Shall we say, then, that these people love and embrace the things that knowledge is set over, as the others do the things that opinion is set over? Remember we said that the latter saw and loved beautiful sounds and colors and the like but wouldn't allow the Beautiful Itself to be anything?

We remember, all right.

We won't be in error, then, if we call such people lovers of opinion rather than philosophers or lovers of wisdom and knowledge? Will they be angry with us if we call them that?

Not if they take my advice, for it isn't right to be angry with those who speak the truth. (*Republic* V 479e1–80a10; adapted from Grube/Reeve)

Plato then points to the difference between knowledge and opinion:

> Let's agree that philosophic natures always love the sort of learning that makes clear to them some feature of the being that always is and does not wander around between coming to be and decaying. (*Republic* VI 485a10–b3)

Several times, Plato also raises the idea that his ideal rulers, the guardians, will require knowledge and not mere opinion about the good, the beautiful, and the just (see *Republic* VI 484c–d, and *Laws* XII 965b and 966a–b). Lastly, in the Allegory of the Cave, Plato tells the person who exits the cave and sees the sun (namely, the person with knowledge of the Good) and returns: "Because you've seen the truth about fine, just, and good things, you'll know each image for what it is and also that of which it is the image" (*Republic* VII 520c3–6).[89] Thus, the person with knowledge will know what the objects of opinion (images) truly are, and in what way they are images or copies of the Forms, the true realities.

In the *Timaeus*, Plato makes a distinction between the Forms and sense objects, attributes reasoned accounts and understanding to that which always is, and attributes opinion to sense objects:

> As I see it, then, we must begin by making the following distinction: What is *that which always is* and has no becoming, and what is *that which becomes* but never is? The former is grasped by understanding [*noēsei*], which involves a reasoned account. It is unchanging. The latter is grasped by opinion, which involves unreasoning sense perception. It comes to be and passes away, but never really is. (*Timaeus* 27d5–8a4)

In the *Symposium*, Socrates tells Phaedrus that his description of Love might fool the ignorant, but not those who know:

> Your description of [Love] and his gifts is designed to make him look better and more beautiful than anything else—to ignorant listeners, plainly, for of course he wouldn't look that way to those who knew. (*Symposium* 198e6–9a2)

Socrates implies that one who knows will not be easily swayed from their knowledge, whereas if someone has mere opinion, that person will be much more easily impressed and therefore swayed by rhetoric or sophistry.

Thus Plato finds a difference between knowledge and opinion in their faculties—infallibility and not using one's senses versus fallibility and using one's senses, respectively, and objects and Forms versus perceptibles, respectively.

Plotinus:[90] Plotinus begins by saying that there are two kinds of knowledge, but then states that one kind is more aptly named opinion or surface-knowing, whereas the other kind is true knowledge:

> As for the kinds of knowledge which exist in a rational soul, those which are of sense-objects—if one ought to speak of "kinds of knowledge" of these; "opinion" is really the suitable name for them—are posterior to their objects and likenesses of them; but those which are of intelligible objects, which are certainly the genuine kinds of knowledge, come from Intellect to rational soul and do not think any sense-object. (V.9.7.1–6[91])

As far as the "different faculty" aspect of Plato's view goes, Plotinus seems to affirm that in principle:

> One must perceive each thing by the appropriate organ, some things with the eyes, others with the ears, and so on. One must believe, also, that one sees other things with the intellect, and not think that intellectual perception is seeing or hearing, which would be like insisting that the ears should see and that sounds do not exist because they are not visible. (V.5.12.1–5)

And more directly:

> Knowledge and sense-perception, of which one is related to the object known and the other to the object perceived. (VI.1.6.11–3[92])

So Plotinus claims that opinion has perceptibles as its object, as well as that knowledge and opinion are different faculties with different objects.

Rist[93] argues that Plotinus does not have the same view of *pistis* (conviction, not faith) as Plato: "That Plotinus admits the validity of knowledge by [*pistis*] is evident from *Ennead* 6.9.10.6." However, Plotinus is merely discussing the experience or the vision of the One, and saying that we should seek proof by this kind of evidence, neither of which conflicts with Plato.

To conclude, we can see that Plato and Plotinus do not essentially differ in their views on knowledge and opinion; that is, they each believe that ultimate knowledge is of the Good; (pure or true) knowledge has the Forms (and not perceptibles) as its objects; there is a meaningful distinction between theoretical knowledge and practical knowledge; knowers are awake; opiners are dreamers; and knowledge and opinion are different faculties with different objects.

2.4 The importance of dialectic

Both Plato and Plotinus claim that dialectic is the supreme science of the Forms, and ultimately leads one to the knowledge of the Good when coupled with one's being virtuous. I will be arguing against many commentators who argue that Plotinus and Plato do not have the same view of dialectic, so this topic is especially controversial.[94] The main issues are whether dialectic has the same end for both philosophers, and whether it performs the same function.

Plato: I agree with the commentators who hold that Plato apparently had a unified (non-developmental) view; roughly, dialectic is used by philosophers[95] to collect and divide the Forms[96] to reach the truth[97] and/or knowledge[98] of the Good.[99] Plato explicitly mentions dialectic in eight[100] of his twenty-eight dialogues and implicitly in the *Parmenides* (given his account of dialectic).

In the *Euthydemus*, Socrates states that reasonable geometers, astronomers, and calculators should hand over their discoveries for use by dialecticians:

> No art of actual hunting, he said, extends any further than pursuing and capturing; whenever the hunters catch what they are pursuing they are incapable of using it, but they and the fisherman hand over their prey to the cooks. And again, geometers and astronomers and calculators (who are hunters too, in a way, for none of these make their diagrams; they simply discover those which already exist), since they themselves have no idea of how to use their prey but only how to hunt it, hand over the task of using their discoveries to the dialecticians—at least, those of them do so who are not completely senseless. (*Euthydemus* 290b7–c6)

In the *Cratylus*, Plato defines the dialectician as "someone who knows how to ask and answer questions" (390c10–1) and the director of the legislator as to what to name everything and how to name it properly (390d5–7). In the *Gorgias*, Socrates chides Polus for having neglected dialectic even though Polus was well trained in rhetoric (471d–e).

In the *Republic*, Plato writes the most about dialectic, and connects its goal to knowing the Form of the Good. He first mentions it in the Divided Line Analogy (VI 509d–11e), as a study that questions assumptions, works only with the Forms (as opposed to perceptible diagrams or writing, for instance), and is more valuable than other arts and sciences (such as geometry and arithmetic mentioned at VI 510c2–3):

> By the other subsection of the intelligible, I mean that which reason itself grasps by the power of dialectic. It does not consider these hypotheses as first principles but truly as hypotheses—but as stepping stones to take off from, enabling it to reach the unhypothetical first principle of everything. Having grasped this principle, it reverses itself and, keeping hold of what follows from it, comes down to a conclusion without making any use of anything visible at all, but only of Forms themselves, moving on from Forms to Forms, and ending in Forms.

> I understand . . . that you want to distinguish the intelligible part of that which is, the part studied by the science of dialectic, as clearer than the part studied by the so-called sciences, for which their hypotheses are first principles. (*Republic* VI 511b3–c7; adapted from Grube/Reeve[101])

Dialectic is more true and exact than geometry and other sciences because geometry does not question its assumptions but merely deduces conclusions from them, and uses visible diagrams to do its work; dialectic questions assumptions until one cannot question one's assumptions any further and arrives at an unhypothetical first principle, the Form of the Good. Notice that this passage in the *Republic* is completely consistent with the *Euthydemus* passage, which claims that the dialectician uses the conclusions of geometers, astronomers, and calculators.

When Plato is recounting the Allegory of the Cave and connects the goal of practicing dialectic with the Good, he shows that the first principle mentioned in the last *Republic* passage is the Form of the Good:

> Isn't this at last, Glaucon, the song that dialectic sings? It is intelligible, but it is imitated by the power of sight. We said that sight tries at last to look at the animals themselves, the stars themselves, and, in the end, at the sun itself. In the same way, whenever someone tries through argument and apart from all sense perceptions to find the being itself of each thing and doesn't give up until he grasps the Good Itself with understanding itself, he reaches the end of the intelligible, just as the other reached the end of the visible.
>
> Absolutely.
>
> And what about this journey? Don't you call it dialectic?
>
> I do. (*Republic* VII 532a1–b5; adapted from Grube/Reeve)

It is clear from the Allegory of the Cave and absolutely not controversial that the sun of the Cave Allegory is a symbol of the Form of the Good, since Plato himself connects these ideas at *Republic* VII 517a8–c5. Plato is a bit more emphatic about dialectic's being the only study that will be able to reveal this knowledge:

> Mustn't we also insist that the power of dialectic could reveal it ["the truth itself" at *Republic* VII 533a3] only to someone experienced in the subjects we've described and that it cannot reveal it in any other way?
>
> That too is worth insisting on.
>
> At any rate, no one will dispute it when we say that there is no other inquiry that systematically attempts to grasp with respect to each thing itself what the being of it is. (*Republic* VII 533a8–b3[102])

From this passage, we discover that dialectic "systematically attempts to grasp" what each thing is, in addition to questioning assumptions and working only with Forms. Plato adds yet another qualification of what a dialectician is able to do:

> Do you call someone who is able to give an account of the being of each thing dialectical? But insofar as he's unable to give an account of something, either to himself or to another, do you deny that he has any understanding of it?
>
> How could I do anything else? (*Republic* VII 534b3–7)

So dialectic enables one to give an account of the being of each thing. Not surprisingly, when Plato puts all the studies that his ideal rulers, the guardians, will pursue in order to be the best rulers, he states that dialectic is the queen of all the arts and sciences:

> We've placed dialectic at the top of the other subjects like a coping stone and . . . no other subject can rightly be placed above it. (*Republic* VII 534e2–4)

At this point in the *Republic*, Plato states that the guardians will need to spend five years studying dialectic (VII 539d–e). Then Plato writes that ascending from the cave of ignorance, which is brought about by dialectic, is a conversion of the soul and is true philosophy (VII 521c), which implies that dialectic itself is true philosophy, since only dialectic leads one to the first principle, the Good.

Moving to yet later dialogues, Plato mentions dialectic in the *Phaedrus* as well, in a much more poetic way than in the *Republic*, after arguing that a knower of the just, noble, and good will not write about these things, but instead find amusement in sowing gardens of letters:

> Socrates, you are contrasting a vulgar amusement with the very noblest—with the amusement of a man who can while away his time telling stories of justice and the other matters you mentioned ["the man who knows what is just, noble, and good" at 276c3–4].
>
> That's just how it is, Phaedrus. But it is much nobler to be serious about these matters, and use the art of dialectic. The dialectician chooses a proper soul and plants and sows within it discourse accompanied by knowledge—discourse capable of helping itself as well as the man who planted it, which is not barren but produces a seed from which more discourse grows in the character of others. Such discourse makes the seed forever immortal and renders the man who has it as happy as any human being can be.
>
> What you describe is really much nobler still. (*Phaedrus* 276e1–7a5)

Here we have another feature of a dialectician, that she selects the proper soul to work in which to plant discourse founded on knowledge, words that will benefit that soul.

In the *Sophist*, Plato defines one of the functions of dialectic as dividing according to kinds:

> Aren't we going to say that it takes expertise in dialectic to divide things by kinds and not to think that the same Form is a different one or that a different Form is the same?
>
> Yes. (*Sophist* 253d1–4; adapted from White)

This definition of dialectic is significant to Plato because there are also several passages in the *Phaedrus* in which he discusses the Method of Division as well as bringing "seeing together things that are scattered about everywhere and collecting them into one kind . . . defining each thing" (265d3–5).[103]

Interestingly,[104] in one of the latest dialogues, Plato describes dialectic in such a way that it harkens back to Socrates' life, and Socrates' account of the Athenians' experience with Socratic dialectic:

> They cross-examine someone when he thinks he's saying something though he's saying nothing. Then, since his opinions will vary inconsistently, these people will easily scrutinize them. They collect his opinions together during the discussion, put them side by side, and show that they conflict with each other at the same time on the same subjects in relation to the same things and in the same respects. The people who are being examined see this, get angry at themselves, and become calmer toward others. They lose their inflated and rigid beliefs about themselves that way, and no loss is pleasanter to hear or has a more lasting effect on them. Doctors who work on the body think it can't benefit from any food that's offered to it until what's interfering with it from inside is removed. The people who cleanse the soul, my young friend, likewise think the soul, too, won't get any advantage from any learning that's offered to it until someone shames it by refuting it, removes the opinions that interfere with learning, and exhibits it cleansed, believing that it knows only those things that it does know, and nothing more. (*Sophist* 230b4–d4[105])

In an unsurprising passage, Plato equates the dialectician with the true philosopher:

> You'll assign this dialectical activity only to someone who has a pure and just love of wisdom. (*Sophist* 253e4–5)

Plato again avers the superiority of dialectic, and of the reasonable people who judge it to be truer than any other:

> The power of dialectic would repudiate us if we put any other science ahead of her.
>
> What science do we mean by that again? . . .
>
> [Dialectic is] the discipline concerned with being and with what is really and forever in every way eternally self-same by far the truest of all kinds of knowledge. (*Philebus* 57e6–8, 58a2–5)

First, Anderson[106] states that dialectic's power in Plato's philosophy lies in its form of inquiry, but not as a set of conclusions. I would argue that, since dialectic leads one to the knowledge of Forms, if we can think of Forms as conclusions, then dialectic does in fact lead to conclusions. While one is "collecting and dividing" the Forms, however, one is not necessarily arriving at conclusions.

Second, Sayre[107] contrasts Plato's view of dialectic in the *Republic* versus the *Philebus*, heavily implying that in the *Republic* but not in the *Philebus*, the Good can be reached by dialectic.[108] However, this would be an argument from silence, since Plato admittedly does not claim in the *Philebus* that the goal of dialectic is the Good, but without a claim that denies this, we cannot know for certain.

In conclusion, Plato holds that dialectic uses the conclusions of geometry, mathematicians, and other sciences; determines what each thing really is, or its essence; and questions assumptions, using only ideas—that is, Forms—until its practitioner arrives at knowledge of the Form of the Good, the unhypothesized first principle. At this point, the dialectician, having knowledge, is a true philosopher, and can give an account of what each thing's essence really is, choose the proper soul to whom to give images (words) of her knowledge, and expose inconsistencies in interlocutors' beliefs. For all of these reasons, Plato values dialectic as the highest of all studies.

Plotinus: Plotinus has the same view of dialectic, and the same respect for it, as Plato.[109] For instance, in his treatise devoted to dialectic, Plotinus asks:

> What art is there, what method or practice, which will take us up there where we must go? Where that is, that it is to the Good, the First Principle, we can take as agreed and established by many demonstrations. (I.3.1.1–4)

So Plotinus agrees with Plato that the goal is the Form of the Good. Plotinus proceeds to answer the question of what discipline has this goal, agreeing with Plato that dialectic is the necessary study to understand the first principle,[110] and also his agreement that mathematics plays a role in one's education as well as dialectic:

> The philosopher—he is the one who is by nature ready to respond and "winged," we may say, and in no need of separation like the others. He has begun to move to the higher world, and is only at a loss for someone to show him the way. So he must be shown and set free, with his own good will, he who has long been free by nature. He must be given mathematical studies to train him in philosophical thought and accustom him to firm confidence in the existence of the immaterial—he will take to them easily, being naturally disposed to learning; he is by nature virtuous, and must be brought to perfect his virtues, and after his mathematical studies instructed in dialectic, and made a complete dialectician. (I.3.3.1–10)

Having confirmed that Plotinus believes that the end of dialectic is the Good, I can show that Anton is incorrect when he states that, since each philosopher has a different philosophical end, they conceive of dialectic differently as well:

> Plato and Plotinus, however, identified [dialectic] as the proper method of philosophy for the attainment of wisdom. Yet it would seem odd if two metaphysical positions which differ in their respective conceptions of the ends of the philosophical enterprise present no differences at all in their conceptions of the method by which they reach their truths and complete their speculative work.[111]

Since I have shown that each philosopher describes the philosophical end as being the same—the knowledge or vision of the Good, and both claim that dialectic is the proper method, it is difficult to see why dialectic must be different on each view.

Plotinus also agrees that when one has practiced dialectic correctly and achieved its end or goal, one knows the essence of all beings, that dialectic's ultimate object is the Good, and that dialectic uses the conclusions of other sciences:

> What then is dialectic, which the former kinds of men as well as philosophers must be given? It is the science which can speak about everything in a reasoned and orderly way, and say what it is and how it differs from other things and what it has in common with those among which it is and where each of these stands, and if it really is what it is, and how many really existing things there are, and again how many non-existing things, different from real beings. It discusses good and not good, and the things that are classed under good and its opposite, and what is the eternal and what not eternal, with certain knowledge about everything and not mere opinion. It stops wandering about the world of sense and settles down in the world of intellect, and there it occupies itself, casting off falsehood and feeding the soul in what Plato calls "the plain of truth," using his method of division to distinguish the Forms, and to determine the essential nature of each thing, and to find the primary kinds, and weaving together by the intellect all that issues from these primary kinds, till it has traversed the whole intelligible world; then it resolves again the structure of that world into its parts, and comes back to its starting-point; and then, keeping quiet (for it is quiet in so far as it is present There) it busies itself no more, but contemplates, having arrived at unity. It leaves what is called logical activity, about propositions and syllogisms, to another art, as it might leave knowing how to write. Some of the matter of logic it considers necessary, as a preliminary, but it makes itself the judge of this, as of everything else, and considers some of it useful and some superfluous, and belonging to the discipline which wants it. (I.3.4.1–23)

Notice the connections here as well to the Divided Line Analogy: when one is practicing dialectic, one proceeds beyond the arts such as geometry which work from unquestioned assumptions, and only uses Ideas and proceeds through Ideas. Note also the similarity to Plato's *Phaedrus* (276e1–7a5), which was set up with the statement that the philosopher should leave writing behind as a focus of his philosophy, and instead practice dialectic.

Plotinus also agrees with Plato that dialectic entails the collecting and dividing of Forms, as we have seen Plato hold in the *Phaedrus*. Besides Plotinus' references to the Method of Division (at I.3.4.12–3) as well as collection ("weaving together by the intellect all that issues from these primary kinds" at I.3.4.14–5), we can find further confirmation, at least of collection:

> Intellect gives clear principles to any soul which can receive them: and then it combines and interweaves and distinguishes their consequences, till it arrives at perfect intelligence. (I.3.5.1–4)

Several commentators[112] claim that Plotinus does not think of dialectic as a discipline that collects and divides; this quotation and the previous one, however, show that Plotinus does in fact hold that dialectic collects and divides Forms as part of its function.

Next, Plotinus affirms that dialectic is the most precious part of philosophy, which is certainly compatible with Plato. After quoting *Philebus* 58d6–7, namely, that dialectic is the purest part of intelligence and wisdom, Plotinus asks:

> Surely philosophy is the most valuable thing? Are dialectic and philosophy the same? It is the valuable part of philosophy. For it must not be thought to be a tool the philosopher uses. It is not just bare theories and rules; it deals with things and has real beings as a kind of material for its activity; it approaches them methodically and possesses real things along with its theories. (I.3.5.8–13)

In the next passage, Plotinus confirms that dialectic has knowledge of the truth, and not of propositions, which is compatible with Plato's view of Forms, as they are not claims to be known, but beings of essential natures. For Plotinus, dialectic is a practice that exposes inconsistencies, implying that it is a rational discursive process,[113] as Plato claimed at *Phaedrus* 276e1–7a5:

> [Dialectic] does not know about propositions—they are just letters—but in knowing the truth it knows what they call propositions, and in general it knows the movements of the soul, what it affirms and what it denies, and whether it affirms the same thing as it denies or something else, and if things are different from each other or the same; whatever is submitted to it it perceives by directing intuition, as sense-perception also does, but it hands over petty precisions of speech to another discipline which finds satisfaction in them. (I.3.5.17–23)

Thus, contra those commentators who claim that Plotinus' endorsement of dialectic is mainly to encourage emotional,[114] supra-logical,[115] non-epistemological[116] experience, Plotinus confirms that dialectic is a rational method, just as Plato states.

In the last Plotinian dialectic passage, he again states how precious dialectic is to philosophy, not only in its use of mathematics, but in ethics, and to understand what matter is, a view with which Plato obviously concurs. Ultimately, as on Plato's view, dialectic induces the virtue of wisdom:[117]

> So dialectic is the valuable part. Philosophy has other parts; it also surveys the nature of the physical world with assistance from dialectic, as the other skills use arithmetic to help them; though natural philosophy stands closer to dialectic in its borrowing: in the same way moral philosophy derives from dialectic on its contemplative side, but adds the virtuous dispositions and the exercises which produce them. The intellectual virtues have principles from dialectic almost as their proper possession; although they are with matter most of their principles came from that higher realm. The other virtues apply reasoning to particular experiences and actions, but practical wisdom is a kind of

> superior reasoning concerned more with the universal; it considers questions of mutual implication, and whether to refrain from action, now or later, or whether an entirely different course would be better. Dialectic and theoretical wisdom provide everything for practical wisdom to use, in a universal and immaterial form. (I.3.6.1–14[118])

I will briefly consider several objections against my view that Plotinus has the same view of dialectic as Plato.

First, Anton says that Plotinus transforms Plato's dialectic: "[Plotinus' dialectic] therefore seeks to incorporate Plato's dialectic as it is transformed into the search for what is beyond to the unity of all knowledge, namely 'The Real,' the source of all Goodness and all being, God and One."[119] Plato and Plotinus both claim above that dialectic has as its ultimate end, the knowledge or vision of the Good, which is the source of knowledge and truth.

Second, Bréhier[120] claims that in Plotinus' philosophy, dialectic remains "sterile" and is "transformed into a metaphysical reality." I see no evidence of either point (however metaphysically real Plotinus' conception of dialectic is, so is Plato's). Perhaps Bréhier is noting that Plato's dialogues enliven the spirit of dialectic, but if so, this fails to show in itself that Plotinus does not have the same attitude toward dialectic.

Third, Dodds claims that Platonic dialectic can only tell us what the One is not:

> The concept of the One *can* be reached, as Plotinus fully recognizes, by a purely dialectical regress; and the element of personal mysticism is absent, so far as I know, from the fragments of the Neopythagoreans (until we reach Numenius) and of the old Academy. Dialectic, however, as we see in the *Parmenides*, can only tell us what the One is not. This tedious accumulation of negatives may content the metaphysician; but, as Inge says somewhere, one cannot worship the alpha privative.[121]

Both philosophers state that dialectic has the Good as the goal. Additionally, dialectic in the *Parmenides* does not result only in negations of the One; in the Second Hypothesis (142a–55e), for instance, Parmenides concludes that the One has being, is one, is in time, and there can be knowledge, opinion, and perception of it, among other things. If Dodds intends to argue that the Good/One is said to be unknowable by Plato, the same can be said of Plotinus' view.

Fourth, Harris states: "[Plotinus] accepted Aristotle's dialectical method as superior to that of Plato and basically followed it even though he did specifically reject Aristotle's categories."[122] After a cursory search for Aristotelian dialectic,[123] I can verify neither that Harris is correct that Aristotle had his own version of dialectic nor that Plotinus employed Aristotelian dialectic.[124]

Fifth, Meijer attempts to explain Plotinus' failure to mention dialectic in his treatise on Beauty [I.6.9]:

> There are no dialectics that lead to Beauty. The Idea of Beauty can only be known by immediately recognizing from one's memory of the original contact one had

> with the Idea of Beauty (*Phaedrus* 250 B ff.). On the other hand, dialectics (as, for example, developed in the *Republic*) pave the way back to the other Ideas. So it is understandable that in [I.6.9] Plotinus leaves out any form of dialectics.[125]

My replies are, first, that Plato does not explicitly state that one should use dialectic to gain knowledge of Beauty either, in the *Symposium*, for instance; but both Plato and Plotinus say the same kinds of things about dialectic in general. Moreover, as Meijer implies, Plotinus also does not explicitly require dialectic for knowledge of Beauty, so there is not necessarily an incompatibility here. Second, as we'll see, Plato and Plotinus agree on the rungs of the Ladder of Love, the summit of which culminates in knowledge or a vision of Beauty, so they appear to agree on the necessary steps to ascend to knowledge of Beauty.

Sixth, Pistorius argues against my view:

> Plotinus was an idealist, and as such he followed Plato in his belief that there was an ideal archetype of the visible universe. But he did not, like Plato, reach that world by the ladder of concepts. For Plato the ideas were knowable by the discursive reason. Even the highest idea, the archetype or idea of ideas, could be reached by the process of human thought. Not so Plotinus. He does not go from the visible to the invisible, from the particular to the universal, but from the universal to the particular. The Intellectual-Principle or the world of ideas, is for him the self-apparent ultimate reality and it needs no proof.[126]

First, Plotinus has indeed claimed that we move from the physical to the non-physical Ideas (see I.3.4.1–23 and I.3.6.1–14). Second, both philosophers agree that one's use of dialectic can achieve knowledge of the Forms. Third, on the reaching of the highest idea (the Good) with dialectic, they again agree, with the caveat that the Good may not be known. Fourth, Plotinus does not claim that one moves from the universal to the particular; instead he states that we go from sensibles to the Forms, and ultimately to the Good, which is the source of all Forms. In that sense, and according to both philosophers, the Good is universal, so in that sense Pistorius is correct. Fifth, given that Nous or Intellect is the realm of Ideas for both philosophers,[127] and as such, is the ultimate reality (qua Being) for them both as well. However, they both argued for the existence of the Intelligible realm and/or Forms, so Pistorius' charge that Plotinus assumes that it needs no proof is also untrue.

Lastly, Rist[128] points out this paradox: "Dialectic can tell us about the Good *qua* Form, but the Good *qua* 'beyond Being' must be grasped by an intuition, albeit an intuition which only the dialectician can hope to possess." According to Rist, both philosophers make these claims. However, he continues:

> The real difference between Plato and Plotinus here is that although Plato describes the Good as "beyond Being" and thus apparently puts it in a different category from the other Forms, in practice when speaking of dialectic, he tends to forget this distinction. Plotinus does not, and by thus by seizing upon one aspect of a Platonic paradox he succeeds in producing a theory which is more coherent than,

and distinct from that of his Master. Plato usually regards the Form of the Good as a Form rather than as something "beyond Being," and this means that it is perfectly limited and defined.[129]

So I take the objection to be that Plotinus, though making Plato's view more coherent, differs from Plato's dialectic view by focusing on the Good's being beyond being, and ignoring that it is usually described by Plato as a Form. However, as Rist mentioned, Plato states both that the Good is a Form and that it is not, and Plotinus refers to the Good as an Idea as well;[130] so it can be argued that both philosophers are equally paradoxical on this issue, no matter which aspect they seize upon or emphasize.

In sum, contra many commentators (while agreeing with many others), Plotinus and Plato agree about the purpose[131] and importance of dialectic as a method for one's coming to have knowledge of the Form of the Good, as well as its role in using the conclusions of mathematics and other sciences.

2.5 The doctrine of recollection

The doctrine of recollection (*anamnēsis*) states that as our souls between incarnations have knowledge of Forms (reality, or the Beings), when we, as currently incarnate human beings, seem to "learn" something that *is* (such as what "Double" is; a Form, according to Plato and Plotinus), we are really recollecting what we already know, unconsciously or subconsciously. In other words, coming to have conscious knowledge of the Forms while incarnated is recollecting. Recollection assumes at least three things: our souls are immortal, Forms exist, and reincarnation is true.

This issue is surprisingly controversial for both philosophers' works. On the Platonic side, for instance, there are commentators who argue that Plato does not actually believe in recollection, by claiming either that it is a sham doctrine and therefore only a myth, that he discounts it, or that he does not mention the doctrine when he should.[132] From the Plotinian side, I address objections that Plotinus does not have the same view of recollection as Plato.

Since rationalism is the view that there is innate knowledge, that is, knowledge that we possess at the time of our birth, or before, whenever we see Plato or Plotinus claim that the soul has knowledge before its birth, he will then qualify as being a rationalist. We will find, not surprisingly, that both Plato and Plotinus are rationalists.

Plato: Though some commentators seem to agree that Plato takes recollection seriously,[133] others take the opposite view. For instance, R. Weiss says that the doctrine of recollection is a "sham doctrine" that Plato does not really believe, and thus it is nothing more than a "myth."[134] Contra Weiss, there are several excellent reasons for thinking that Plato believes that recollection is true and that it is neither a myth nor a sham doctrine.

First, Plato not only mentions that the doctrine of recollection is true in the *Meno*, but he also uses recollection to prove the immortality of the soul and takes four pages attempting to prove its truth convincing Cebes and Simmias in the *Phaedo* from 72a–6a.

Second, Plato takes pains to confirm the truth of recollection at *Phaedo* 91e5–2a5.

Third, Plato further discusses recollection in some detail in *Phaedrus* from 248e–9c, and again in the late dialogues: See *Statesman* from 272d–3d and *Philebus* from 34a–c. If the *Meno* were the only dialogue in which Plato had mentioned his doctrine of recollection, Weiss' view would have much more merit and perhaps one could explain the doctrine away as a silly notion that Plato dismissed and matured from; however, given that the doctrine appears in four other dialogues, two of which are middle and two late (whereas the *Meno* is usually taken to be a dialogue on the cusp between early and middle, a so-called "transitional dialogue"), it does not seem to be a view that Plato ever dismissed.

Rawson[135] also posits the view that Plato is not serious about the doctrine of recollection, at least in some dialogues. He begins by claiming that it is an underappreciated puzzle why Plato should ignore his doctrine of recollection so often. The fact that Plato does not bring up a view when and where other commentators believe that he should is not an argument that he has in fact abandoned that view.[136] Before Rawson refers to recollection as "a naively extravagant doctrine that has been dismissed by most philosophers ever since,"[137] he makes these claims, all of which I will deny:

> In the *Meno*, Socrates introduces recollection at secondhand from vague and dubious sources (81a–b), then discounts as questionable all but its encouraging practical implications (86b–c).[138] In the *Phaedrus*, recollection is the centerpiece of a fantastic rhetorical display that begins with teasing disclaimers [242b–244a] and is later straightforwardly disowned as playful and potentially misleading (262d, 265b).[139]

On the *Meno* interpretation: First, citing priests and priestesses as the sources for his view of recollection is parallel to Socrates' citation of Diotima in the *Symposium* as "a woman from Mantinea . . . who was wise about many things besides [Love]" (*Symposium* 201d2–3). Thus Rawson's charge that priests and priestesses are dubious sources is itself dubious. On the contrary, I believe that Plato is merely attributing his beliefs to "experts" because he does not have an argument that can entirely convince non-believers either of a vision of Beauty or of recollection, respectively. But to analogously claim that Plato in the *Symposium* does not believe that a vision of Beauty is possible because Diotima is a disreputable source is not interpretively plausible.

Second, on Socrates' discounting everything but the practical push to inquire as questionable (*Meno* 86b–c), he may be aware that most people will not take his slave boy demonstration as a knock-down argument in favor of recollection, as is the case even today. But this does not imply (per Rawson) that Plato himself does not believe the theory is correct, and indeed the slave boy did recollect what double is during the demonstration.

On the *Phaedrus* interpretation: First, at 242b–4a, Socrates is exhibiting his usual Socratic irony and humility before telling us what he really thinks. He then says that he needs to purify himself (243a)—which he takes seriously elsewhere—so we should not interpret this as a joke. Then he states at 243d4–5 that, "I want to wash out the bitterness of what we've heard with a more tasteful speech"; we have no reason to take this as a teasing disclaimer, and Rawson is conveniently ignoring this to make his case. Moreover, at 243c1–2, Socrates has already referred to "shameless ... speeches," so when he again refers to "two speeches" at 262d1, should we not take him as referring to *those* two speeches, *before* Socrates begins to discuss recollection? Further, even if I grant that one of the two speeches referred to by Socrates at 262d1 is the one that contains recollection, *Phaedrus* 262d is far from clearly denigrating recollection per se when Socrates says: "In fact, by some chance the two speeches do, as it seems, contain an example of the way in which someone who knows the truth can toy with his audience and mislead them" (*Phaedrus* 262c10–d2). For Socrates denies there that he possesses any oratorical skill: "certainly *I* don't possess any art of speaking" (262d5–6). And if recollection is an oratorical joke, then what do we make of its role in the *Phaedo* to aid in proving the existence of Forms? At this point, taking Rawson's line seriously, Plato's chief ontological entities (or better yet, the Good Itself of the end of *Republic* VI and the beginning of VII) can be called into question, which is quite implausible, given Plato's definite references to Forms in the remainder of his work and the obvious importance Plato assigns the Good.

Regarding *Phaedrus* 265b6–c1: "We used a certain sort of image to describe love's passion; perhaps it has a measure of truth in it, though it may also have led us astray. And having whipped up a not altogether implausible speech, we sang playfully, but also appropriately and respectfully." First, it says they *may* have been led astray, not that they *went* astray. Second, since *the description of love's passion* was possibly over the top, the best candidate(s) for what they may have got wrong is something involving the lover's experience. The parts about the gods' experience with their chariots is not necessarily being called into question; the claim that some human souls have seen much and some have seen little is consistent with the Myth of Er in *Republic* X, where souls are said to drink different amounts from the river of forgetfulness. In short, if Plato is giving up his entire theory of recollection here, he should tell us exactly what is wrong with it and show the way in which this disavowal affects his other beliefs that he still holds; for example, the immortality of the soul and the Forms.

Thus, it is far from clear that Rawson is correct about Plato's downplaying, if not outright rejection, of his theory of recollection.

Plato first mentions the theory of recollection in the *Meno* as a response to Meno's Paradox,[140] and presents it as a plausible theory that he heard from priests and priestesses. Here is how he describes some of the underpinnings of the theory:

> As the soul is immortal, has been born often and has seen all things here and in the underworld, there is nothing which it has not learned; so it is in no way surprising that it can recollect the things it knew before, both about virtue and other things. As the whole of nature is akin, and the soul has learned everything, nothing prevents a man, after recalling one thing only—a process men call learning—discovering everything else for himself, if he is brave and does not tire of the search, for searching and learning are, as a whole, recollection. (*Meno* 81c5–d5)

Shortly after this, Meno asks Socrates to teach him what recollection is (which is ironically put, since Socrates has said that there is no teaching or learning, only recollection). Socrates then gives a demonstration of doubling a square with a slave boy of Meno's who had never been taught geometry before, where the boy knows what double is, and knows what figure he is looking for, but as the exercise continues, he cannot give the way in which to double the initial square. At the end of the exercise, the boy apparently has knowledge of doubled squares (*epistēmēn* at 85d9 and see *Phaedo* 73a7–b2, quoted below), but he recovered this knowledge for himself through questioning, and this implies that no one taught him this knowledge in this lifetime, so it must have come from before he was "a human being" as Plato says at *Meno* 86a6. He then summarizes his argument about recollection and his response to Meno's Paradox:

> If the truth about reality is always in our soul, the soul would be immortal so that you should always confidently try to seek out and recollect what you do not know at present—that is, what you do not recollect?
>
> Somehow, Socrates, I think that what you say is right.
>
> I think so too, Meno. I do not insist that my argument is right in all other respects, but I would contend at all costs both in word and deed as far as I could that we will be better men, braver and less idle, if we believe that one must search for the things one does not know, rather than if we believe that it is not possible to find out what we do not know and that we must not look for it.
>
> In this too I think you are right, Socrates. (*Meno* 86b1–c3)

Lastly, Plato states that recollection involves tethering or shoring up one's true opinions:

> For true opinions, as long as they remain, are a fine thing and all they do is good, but they are not willing to remain long, and they escape from a man's mind, so that they are not worth much until one ties them down by (giving) an account of the reason why. And that, Meno my friend, is recollection, as we previously agreed. (*Meno* 97e6–8a5)

In the *Phaedo*, Plato writes the most about recollection. He introduces the theory of recollection in the voice of Cebes, but the rendition thereof is entirely consistent with what we saw in the *Meno*:

> Furthermore, Socrates, Cebes rejoined, such is also the case if that theory is true that you are accustomed to mention frequently, that for us learning is no other than recollection. According to this, we must at some previous time have learned what we now recollect. This is possible only if our soul existed somewhere before it took on this human shape. So according to this theory too, the soul is likely to be something immortal. (*Phaedo* 72e1–3a3)

Plato then describes precisely what went on in the slave boy example in the *Meno*, namely that Socrates asked the right questions such that the slave boy would recollect what he already knew, and Socrates used diagrams which convinced the boy:

> When men are interrogated in the right manner, they always give the right answer of their own accord, and they could not do this if they did not possess the knowledge and the right explanation inside them. Then if one shows them a diagram or something else of that kind, this will show most clearly that such is the case. (*Phaedo* 73a7–b2)

Plato then argues for another kind of recollection, where seeing an object that one in the past closely associated in one's mind with another person can remind one of that person; for example, Socrates' seeing Simmias reminds him of Cebes:

> Do we not also agree that when knowledge comes to mind in this way, it is recollection? What way do I mean? Like this: when a man sees or hears or in some other way perceives one thing and not only knows that thing but also thinks of another thing of which the knowledge is not the same but different, are we not right to say that he recollects the second thing that comes into his mind?
>
> How do you mean?
>
> Things such as this: to know a man is surely a different knowledge from knowing a lyre.
>
> Of course.
>
> Well, you know what happens to lovers: whenever they see a lyre, a garment or anything else that their beloved is accustomed to use, they know the lyre, and the image of the boy to whom it belongs comes into their mind. This is recollection, just as someone, on seeing Simmias, often recollects Cebes, and there are thousands of other such occurrences. (*Phaedo* 73c5–d11)

Shortly after 74a–5e, Plato continues with a lengthy argument in favor of recollection based on the existence of Forms and our knowledge of them. Socrates and Cebes then agree that learning is recollection (76c) and much later, Cebes states that he found this theory remarkably convincing at the time and Simmias claims that he agrees with Cebes, adding that he would be surprised if he ever changed his mind about it (91e–2a).

Simmias gives us the last quotation from the *Phaedo*, which is interesting because he is explicit that for recollection to be true, the soul needs to have knowledge of the ultimate standard of reality, and he believes that the soul indeed has such knowledge:

> The theory of recollection and learning, however, was based on an assumption worthy of acceptance, for our soul was said to exist also before it came into the body, just as the reality does that is of the kind that we qualify by the words "which truly is," and I convinced myself that I was quite correct to accept it. (*Phaedo* 92d6–e2)

Plato also mentions recollection in the *Phaedrus*, *Statesman*, and *Philebus*.[141] In the *Phaedrus*, Plato actually limits recollection to humans:

> A soul that never saw the truth cannot take a human shape, since a human being must understand speech in terms of general Forms, proceeding to bring many

> perceptions together into a reasoned unity. That process is the recollection of the things our soul saw when it was traveling with god, when it disregarded the things we now call real and lifted up its head to what is truly real instead. (*Phaedrus* 249b6–c4; adapted from Nehamas/Woodruff)

In the cosmological view put forth in the *Statesman*, Plato states that souls' recollection is dim of the instruction it received from God (273a–b).

Wrapping up the Platonic passages, in the late dialogue the *Philebus*,[142] Plato distinguishes memory from recollection through Socrates' conversation with Protarchus:

> And do we not hold that recollection differs from memory?
>
> Perhaps.
>
> Does not their difference lie in this?
>
> In what?
>
> Do we not call it "recollection" when the soul recalls as much as possible by itself, without the aid of the body, what she had once experienced together with the body? Or how would you put it?
>
> I quite agree.
>
> But on the other hand, when, after the loss of memory of either a perception or again a piece of knowledge, the soul calls up this memory for itself, we also call all these events recollection.
>
> You are right. (*Philebus* 34b2–c3)

Plato defines recollection in an interesting, yet ultimately similar way here in the *Philebus*: that which has been experienced by the soul together with the body is a sense experience that the soul recognizes (that is, the rational part of the soul processes a sense datum), which is in turn dealt with by the soul by itself—as a Form—is recollection. Also, recollection is the recovering of a memory, so memory is obviously not equivalent to recollection.

Thus, Plato holds that recollection is the process of discovering knowledge that the soul had before birth, by using one's senses to remind themselves that the perceptible examples of their sense experience are not Absolute Standards. And yet, since we know these Standards, we can know that we are not learning these things in this lifetime, but merely recollecting them.

Plotinus:[143] Plotinus has at least ten passages[144] that directly assume and refer to recollection, and several where that doctrine is implied, such as where he says that the soul has an "ancient knowledge" in I.6.2.[145] One of Plotinus' first references to recollection shows that he agrees with Plato that the soul has "everlasting knowledge" of the "authentic reality of each thing," that is, the Forms, and has the capability of recollection:

> The intellection of the authentic reality of each thing which the soul derives from itself, from the contemplations within it, and from recollection [*anamnēseōs*], gives

> it an existence prior to body and makes it everlasting because it has everlasting knowledge. (IV.7.12.8–11)

Plotinus gives his best description of recollection in V.3, "The Knowing Hypostases and the Transcendent," as involving dialectic; judging, combining, and distinguishing sense perceptions to recognize the impressions and adapt them, culminating in the wisdom of recollecting the Forms:

> The reasoning power in soul makes its judgment, derived from the mental images present to it which come from sense-perception, but combining and dividing them; and, as for the things which come to it from Intellect, it observes what one might call their imprints, and has the same power also in dealing with these; and it continues to acquire understanding as if by recognizing the new and recently arrived impressions and fitting them to those which have long been within it: this process is what we should call the "recollections" of the soul. (V.3.2.7–14)

As for Gerson's concern:

> Plotinus seems to make little use of this [recollection] doctrine as it is explained in the *Meno* and the *Phaedo*. In the *Meno*, Socrates accounts for the slave-boy's ability to arrive at a true belief about the answer to a mathematical problem by recollection (85ce). That is, through questioning, the true belief is "stirred up like a dream" in him. In the *Phaedo*, Socrates argues that one's ability to judge sensible equals as somehow deficient with respect to equality depends on our having had prior knowledge of the Form of Equality (73cff.). In both passages recollection plays an active role in judgments made about sensible particulars. Strictly speaking, the issue for Plotinus is not prior knowledge.[146]

I have three responses to Gerson's concern: First, after the mathematics demonstration in the *Meno*, though Socrates makes some hypothetical statements about the slave boy's putative knowledge, he actually states (implicitly in a question) that the slave boy has *knowledge* (*epistēmēn*), and not true belief: "Must he not either have at some time acquired the knowledge he now possesses, or else have always possessed it?" (85d9–10). Socrates' question assumes that the slave boy now possesses knowledge; his question is whether the slave boy acquired it or always possessed it. Thus, Gerson is not stating the whole case. Second, we can equally read Plotinus as saying that recollection plays an active role in making judgments about the particulars because one will be able to recognize the similarities and differences among the old impressions and the Forms themselves, just as on Plato's view. Third, as for Gerson's comment that the issue is not prior knowledge for Plotinus, the latter does state that there must be true knowledge of the Forms in our souls, as Plato does, which is one of the prerequisites for recollection:

> There must belong to an individual soul that is really a soul some kind of righteousness and moral integrity, and there must be true knowledge in the souls

> which are in us .... not images or likenesses of their Forms as things are in the sense-world, but those very Forms themselves. (V.9.13.7–12[147])

This quotation also addresses a confusing concern that Inge has:

> In "Recollection," which gives actuality to the notions which the Soul possessed only potentially, "time is not present." Plotinus transforms Plato's "Recollection" into a doctrine of innate ideas potentially present. Memory is always of something which the Soul has experienced, not of something innate.[148]

I am confused about Inge's concern because I have already shown that both Plotinus and Plato state that recollection is of Forms that are actually present to the recollecting soul. Thus, Plotinus is hardly transforming Plato's view on this point. Moreover, Plato states that memory and recollection are not the same thing (*Philebus* 34b2–c3). Plotinus implies that there are two kinds of memory: earthly memory of things that happened via our senses, and recollection, which is a memory of the Forms not involving time, which alludes to his and Plato's belief that the Forms are eternal, as is the soul's possession thereof:

> The soul must not be said to remember, either, in the sense in which we are speaking of remembering, the things which it possesses as part of its nature, but when it is here below it possesses them and does not act by them, particularly when it has just arrived here. But as for its activity, the ancients seem to apply the terms "memory" and "recollection" to the souls which bring into act what they possessed. So this is another kind of memory; and therefore time is not involved in memory understood in this sense. (IV.3.25.27–35)

In another passage, he exhorts the reader: "if you have seen yourself beautiful, remember [*anamnēsthēti*] them" (V.8.2.45–6),[149] which implies that we must recollect from within us what we already know about beauty.

Plato states that we use our senses in the process of recollection, in order to come to know the Forms; Plotinus also affirms this. I confirm the senses' role in recollection, and show that Plotinus is so convinced of recollection and what is recollected, that he hyperbolically declares that no one could deny recollection unless he or she has "neither ... understood this world here nor seen that higher world":

> Even in pictures those who look at the works of art with their eyes do not see the same things in the same way, but when they recognize an imitation on the level of sense of someone who has a place in their thought they feel a kind of disturbance and come to a recollection [*anamnēsin*] of the truth; this is the experience from which passionate loves arise. But if someone who sees beauty excellently represented in a face is carried to that higher world, will anyone be so sluggish in mind and so immovable that, when he sees all the beauties in the world of sense, all its good proportion and the mighty excellence of its order, and the splendor of form which is manifested in the stars, for all their remoteness, he will not

> thereupon think, seized with reverence, "What wonders, and from what a source?" If he did not, he would neither have understood this world here nor seen that higher world. (II.9.16.43–56)

In another passage, Plotinus states that we can use recollection to come to know eternity after first identifying what time—eternity's likeness—is: "If someone, before contemplating eternity, should form a picture in his mind of what time is, it would be possible for him, too, to go from this world to the other by recollection and contemplate that of which time is a likeness, if time really has a likeness to eternity" (III.7.1.20–5).

Plotinus also compares those whom Plato calls "lovers of sights and sounds" (*Republic* V), who worship the beauty of earth only and do not believe Forms exist, with those who use recollection to recollect what Beauty really is. In the same passage, moreover, he diagnoses those who fail to recollect, content with beautiful images:

> It is true, certainly, that those who are moved to generation here below are content to have the beauty here below, the beauty which is present in images and bodies, since the archetype is not present to them which is responsible for their loving even this beauty here below. And if they come from this beauty here to the recollection of that archetype, this earthly beauty still satisfies them as an image; but if they do not recollect, then, because they do not know what is happening to them, they fancy this is the true beauty. (III.5.1.30–6[150])

In other passages, Plotinus questions why some are quicker than others at recollecting and answers that the soul needs to be poised and prepared (IV.6.3); he then asks, "What is it, then, which has made the souls forget their father, God, and be ignorant of themselves and him, even though they are parts which come from his higher world and altogether belong to it?" (V.1.1.1–3).

Pistorius argues that Plotinus and Plato did not have the same view of recollection:

> We know, of course, that Plato toyed with the doctrines of rebirth and remembrance, and also that he regarded the two theories as mutually inclusive. Plotinus, on the other hand, not only refused to accept remembrance on the part of the soul of the life before bodily death, but he even denies the possibility of any remembrance whatsoever in the Ideal World. It is very clear that he does not accept the Platonic theory of remembrance. Had Plotinus viewed the doctrine of rebirth with any favor, he would at least have attempted to disprove the mutual inclusion of the two doctrines. I believe that I am justified in saying that the passages where rebirth is apparently accepted by Plotinus, either refer to popular belief or the theories of other philosophers.[151]

For now, we can argue that Plotinus clearly accepts recollection, assuming "remembrance" is recollection, and only denies memory of the Forms, because they are timeless and eternal, which we saw Plato do as well in the *Philebus*. It is unclear why Plotinus would need to argue for the mutual inclusion of the two doctrines, if it is clear—and it is, as I hope I have shown in the case of recollection—that Plotinus accepts both doctrines. Why can he not allow the reader to make the inference that these views (and many other related views) go hand-in-hand, without assuming that he must not have accepted Plato's doctrine of recollection? Finally, it is simply not the case that Plotinus is only referring to popular belief or other philosophers' theories when he refers to recollection, as the related quotations show.

Thus, both Plotinus and Plato hold that recollection is an important task of the philosopher, which involves using the senses to remember what sense objects are only copies or imitations of; namely, the Forms. Lastly, then, note that I have implicitly confirmed that both philosophers are rationalists.

2.6 Prayer

Plato and Plotinus both have the view that prayer can help a virtuous person who is working toward a goal, but that, in the end, it will not help but will harm the vicious person who does not help him or herself. As with meditation[152] and divination,[153] Platonic commentators rarely, if ever, mention prayer.

Plato: First, Plato tells us that Socrates said the following immediately before drinking the hemlock:

> One is allowed, indeed one must, utter a prayer to the gods that the journey from here to yonder may be fortunate. This is my prayer and may it be so. (*Phaedo* 117c1–3)

So Socrates made a prayer, and no one questioned whether it would do any good for him to do so. There is also another prayer that Socrates makes in the *Phaedrus*—though I leave it an open question as to whether the following is Plato's prayer, a general Athenian prayer, or a prayer that Plato heard Socrates make at some point:

> O dear Pan and all the other gods of this place, grant that I may be beautiful inside. Let all my external possessions be in friendly harmony with what is within. May I consider the wise man rich. As for gold, let me have as much as a moderate man could bear and carry with him. (*Phaedrus* 279b8–c3)

Admittedly, we do not know and Plato wisely does not claim that Socrates' prayer was answered, though he did state in the last line of the *Phaedo* that Socrates was the best—bravest, wise, and most upright—man he and his friends knew (118a17).

Also in the *Phaedrus*, Plato claims that families can rid themselves of ancient curses by prayer and worship:

> Madness can provide relief from the greatest plagues of trouble that beset certain families because of their guilt for ancient crimes: it turns up among those who need a way out; it gives prophecies and takes refuge in prayers to the gods and in

> worship, discovering mystic rites and purifications that bring the man it touches through to safety for this and all time to come. So it is that the right sort of madness finds relief from present hardships for a man it has possessed. (*Phaedrus* 244d5–5a1)

Plato in the *Statesman* defines priests as those who know the proper forms of prayer, and this view is not contested or refuted:

> The class of priests, in its turn, has—as custom tells us—expert knowledge about the giving through sacrifices of gifts from us to the gods which are pleasing to them, and about asking from them through prayers for the acquisition of good things for us. I imagine that both of these things are parts of a subordinate art.
>
> It appears so, at any rate. (*Statesman* 290c8–d4)

In the *Laws*, Plato says that only the good people will have their prayers answered, so to be consistent, the family in the *Phaedrus* passage should comprise good people. In the *Laws* passages, Plato refines his view somewhat to include a distinction between good and bad prayer, what should be prayed for, and so on. In this first passage, Plato argues—via Megillus, who is summing up the Athenian's view—that we should pray for practical wisdom, and not that everything should follow our desire:

> Your point, I take it, is that you should demand your own way in your prayers only if your wishes are supported by your rational judgment—and this, a rational outlook [*phronēsei*], should be the object of the prayers and efforts of us all, states and individuals alike.
>
> It should indeed. (*Laws* III 687e5–8a1)

Thus one who is not following one's Reason should not pray for anything other than wisdom. Plato gets more specific in the next passage, and relates that a praying man without intelligence actually endangers himself:

> I maintain that, if you lack wisdom, praying is a risky business, because you get the opposite of what you want. (*Laws* III 688b6–c1)

Plato states what he refers to as the finest and truest doctrine about praying—it benefits the good and is done in vain by (and harms) the bad person:

> In our view it is God who is preeminently the "measure of all things," much more so than any "man," as they say. So if you want to recommend yourself to someone of this character, you must do your level best to make your own character reflect his, and on this principle the moderate man is God's friend, being like him, whereas the immoderate and unjust man is not like him and is his enemy; and the same reasoning applies to the other vices too.
>
> Let's be clear that the consequence of all this is the following doctrine (which is, I think, of all doctrines the finest and truest): If a good man sacrifices to the

gods and keeps them constant company in his prayers and offerings and every kind of worship he can give them, this will be the best and noblest policy he can follow; it is the conduct that fits his character as nothing else can, and it is his most effective way of achieving a happy life. But if the wicked man does it, the results are bound to be just the opposite. Whereas the good man's soul is clean, the wicked man's soul is polluted, and it is never right for a good man or for God to receive gifts from unclean hands—which means that even if impious people do lavish a lot of attention on the gods, they are wasting their time, whereas the trouble taken by the pious is very much in season. So this is the target at which we should aim. (*Laws* IV 716c4–7a4[154])

Note that Plato emphasizes prayer as part of being in constant company with the gods; this is an important point because, as I will address in the conclusion, Plotinian commentators tend to believe that Plotinus (and not Plato) took from the Stoics the idea that there is cosmic or universal sympathy, which is the basis of magic and prayer.[155] However, Plato seems to say that resonating with the gods' realm is possible via prayer and sacrifice, and, generally speaking, it just makes sense ontologically that the immaterial—especially the good, temperate person appealing to a good, temperate God or gods, given the "like approves of like"[156] principle—will somehow be connected sympathetically with all the immaterial, the Forms, God, gods, guardian spirits, the All-Soul, and individual souls.

So Plato believes that prayer is efficacious if one is a good person and asks for intelligence and the virtues (as Socrates requested temperance in the *Phaedrus* prayer).

Plotinus:[157] Plotinus does claim that prayers are answered when the petitioner is like God (as Plato said in the *Laws* 716c4–7a4 passage), but does not explicitly claim that bad people will *not* have their prayers answered. In the first passage, Plotinus differentiates prayer from being charmed by spells:

We must not think that other kinds of prayers either are freely and deliberately answered: for people charmed by spells do not act with free deliberation. (IV.4.40.27–9)

Plotinus confirms that he agrees with Plato's view that it is when a petitioner is like God that a prayer is answered:

When a man prays to a heavenly body, some influence comes from it upon him or upon another person. (IV.4.40.32)

And:

But the sun, or another heavenly body, does not hear his prayers. And that which he prays for comes about because one part is in sympathetic connection with another, just as in one tense string; for if the string is plucked at the lower end, it has a vibration at the upper. (IV.4.41.1–4)

Plotinus explains why even people who are not perfect can have a prayer answered:

> One thing is benefited and harmed by another because it is naturally so disposed, and by the arts of physicians and magicians one thing is compelled to give something of its power to another. And in the same way the All gives to its parts, both spontaneously and if someone else magically attracts [its power] to a part of it; for it lies at the disposal of its parts by its own natural disposition, and so the one who makes the prayer is no alien. But *if the man who prays is evil, there is no need to be surprised; for the wicked draw water from the streams and that which gives does not know itself to what it gives, but only gives*; but all the same that which is given is also co-ordinated with the nature of the All; so that if someone takes what he ought not from what lies at the disposal of all, justice pursues him by an inevitable law. (IV.4.42.6–19; emphasis added)

What Plotinus is saying is still compatible with what Plato says, since Plotinus still implies that the one who prays "is no alien" to the gift that will be given, implying again the likeness to which both Plotinus and Plato have alluded.

Now let us focus on the italicized portion of the passage: Plotinus implies there that the bad person may in fact benefit (at least temporarily) from praying, because the gods only give, but do not discriminate between receivers, as a stream gives water indiscriminately. The possible problem here is that Plato has said that the bad person is not fit for prayer, that prayer will not be helpful to such a person, and that their sacrifices and prayers are in vain because no good man or god could be benefited by them (*Laws* IV 716d–7a). However, Plotinus' points here remain in principle compatible with Plato's main idea, based on the last phrase in the quotation above: Even if a bad person somehow has a prayer answered—and Plato did not state that a bad person's prayer *cannot be answered*, but only that it would not be noble, good, and helpful toward the happy life at 716d—and temporarily benefits from that prayer, justice will hunt him down and make him ultimately pay the penalty. Lastly, Plotinus still states that "justice pursues him by an inevitable law" if a bad person does get anything apparently good, implying a similarity with Plato's point that a bad person only gets bad results from prayer.

Plotinus claims that one who is not actively trying to achieve a goal cannot use prayer:

> It would not be right for a god to fight in person for the unwarlike; the law says that those who fight bravely, not those who pray, are to come safe out of wars; for, in just the same way, it is not those who pray but those who look after their land who are to get in a harvest, and those who do not look after their health are not to be healthy; and we are not to be vexed if the bad get larger harvests, or if their farming generally goes better. (III.2.8.36–42)

It is on the basis of this passage and other similar ones in III.2.8–9 that A.H. Armstrong makes the next assessment:

> When we turn to the Plotinus passage [III.2.8–9] we find ourselves in an entirely different world of thought. The uselessness of prayer, not only in the case of the

> wicked but also in that of the weak and inefficient [III.2.8], is due to the inexorability of the natural law. . . . Those who go contrary to nature, to the unified rhythm and ordered arrangement of the cosmos as a whole, even if it is not through their own fault, will suffer for it.[158]

I agree with Armstrong's view except for two caveats: first, given that Plotinus does state that prayers can benefit the good person; and second, Plato in the *Laws* implies—by stating that God is the measure of all things, and then stating that the "rule" is as follows—that divine law dictates that good people will benefit from prayer and that the bad will harm themselves.[159]

Thus, Plato and Plotinus both believe in the efficacy of prayer, under certain circumstances, and even that certain things should and should not be prayed for.

2.7 Opinion

Having already covered Plato and Plotinus' views on knowers being awake and dreamers being asleep, true opinion versus knowledge, and the distinction between knowledge and opinion, I will focus here on their views concerning opinion. Plato and Plotinus both hold that opinion is midway between ignorance and knowledge, and that opinion has sense objects as its cognitive objects.

Plato: Let us start with Plato, from the *Symposium*, where "correct judgment" translates *hē orthē doxa* (true opinion):

> Correct judgment, of course, has this character: it is *in between* understanding [*phronēseōs*] and ignorance.
>
> True, said I, as you say. (*Symposium* 202a8–10)

Plato similarly states in the *Republic* that opinion is between ignorance and knowledge:

> If something could be shown, as it were, to be and not to be at the same time, it would be intermediate between what purely is and what in every way is not, and that neither knowledge nor ignorance would be set over it, but something intermediate between ignorance and knowledge?
>
> Correct.
>
> And now the thing we call opinion has emerged as being intermediate between them?
>
> It has. (*Republic* V 478d5–12[160])

Earlier in the *Republic*, Plato also states that persons who do not believe that Forms exist—"lovers of sights and sounds"—do not and will not know what beauty is, and their mental state is best called opinion:

> The lovers of sights and sounds like beautiful sounds, colors, shapes, and everything fashioned out of them, but their thought is unable to see and embrace the nature of the Beautiful Itself.
>
> That's for sure . . . .
>
> So we'd be right to call his thought knowledge, since he knows, but we should call the other person's thought opinion, since he opines?
>
> Right. (*Republic* V 476b4–9, d5–7; adapted from Grube/Reeve)

The next passage wraps up Plato's view concerning opinion:

> As for those who study the many beautiful things but do not see the Beautiful Itself and are incapable of following another who leads them to it, who see many just things but not the Just Itself, and so with everything—these people, we shall say, opine everything but have no knowledge of anything they opine.
>
> Necessarily . . . .
>
> Shall we say, then, that these people love and embrace the things that knowledge is set over, as the others do the things that opinion is set over? Remember we said that the latter saw and loved beautiful sounds and colors and the like but wouldn't allow the Beautiful Itself to be anything?
>
> We remember, all right.
>
> We won't be in error, then, if we call such people lovers of opinion rather than philosophers or lovers of wisdom and knowledge? Will they be angry with us if we call them that?
>
> Not if they take my advice, for it isn't right to be angry with those who speak the truth. (*Republic* V 479e1–6, 479e10–80a10; adapted from Grube/Reeve[161])

In sum, if one does not hold that Forms exist, one is a lover of opinion and not a possessor of knowledge. In Book VI, Plato actually refers to leadership of any government by a lover of opinion is akin to a blind person leading others, and uses that point to argue in favor of having rulers who have "the knowledge of each thing that is":

> Do you think, then, that there is any difference between the blind and those who are really deprived of the knowledge of each thing that is? The latter have no clear model in their souls, and so they cannot—in the manner of painters—look to what is most true, make constant reference to it, and study it as exactly as possible. Hence they cannot establish here on earth conventions about what is fine or just or good, when they need to be established, or guard and preserve them, once they have been established.
>
> No, by god, there isn't much difference between them.
>
> Should we, then, make these blind people our guardians or rather those who know each thing that is and who are not inferior to the others, either in experience or in any other part of virtue?
>
> It would be absurd to choose anyone but philosophers, if indeed they're not inferior in these ways, for the respect in which they are superior is pretty well the most important one. (*Republic* VI 484c6–d10)

Plato begins his Cave Allegory with two levels of opinion: the prisoners believing shadows of figures (of horses and humans, say) being cast by a fire are the natures of horses, humans, and so on, and the released prisoners who see the fire, the figures being carried by others, who again believe that these figures are the natures of horses or humans. In reality, Forms are what are the real natures of everything that is, and everything else we experience are copies or resemblances of these Forms:[162]

> Next, I said, compare the effect of education and of the lack of it on our nature to an experience like this: Imagine human beings living in an underground, cavelike dwelling, with an entrance a long way up, which is both open to the light and as wide as the cave itself. They've been there since childhood, fixed in the same place, with their necks and legs fettered, able to see only in front of them, because their bonds prevent them from turning their heads around. Light is provided by a fire burning far above and behind them. Also behind them, but on higher ground, there is a path stretching between them and the fire. Imagine that along this path a low wall has been built, like the screen in front of puppeteers above which they show their puppets.
>
> I'm imagining it.
>
> Then also imagine that there are people along the wall, carrying all kinds of artifacts that project above it—statues of people and other animals, made out of stone, wood, and every material. And, as you'd expect, some of the carriers are talking, and some are silent.
>
> It's a strange image you're describing, and strange prisoners.
>
> They're like us. Do you suppose, first of all, that these prisoners see anything of themselves and one another besides the shadows that the fire casts on the wall in front of them?
>
> How could they, if they have to keep their heads motionless throughout life?
>
> What about the things being carried along the wall? Isn't the same true of them?
>
> Of course.
>
> And if they could talk to one another, don't you think they'd suppose that the names they used applied to the things they see passing before them?
>
> They'd have to.
>
> And what if their prison also had an echo from the wall facing them? Don't you think they'd believe that the shadows passing in front of them were talking whenever one of the carriers passing along the wall was doing so?
>
> I certainly do.
>
> Then the prisoners would in every way believe that the truth is nothing other than the shadows of those artifacts.
>
> They must surely believe that. (*Republic* VII 514a1–5c3)

The lowest level of the Cave is where the prisoners are looking at the shadows, and taking them to represent what is real; this is analogous to the lowest level of the Divided Line Analogy, which is image-thinking (*eikasian*). The better level within the cave, or the realm of opinion (*pistin*), is when the prisoner is able to see the fire, the puppeteers (or carriers), the puppets, and things carried, and as before, the prisoners believe, once their "eyes" adjust, that they are now experiencing and understanding what is real.

Moving on to later dialogues, Plato makes two claims from the *Timaeus*. The first confirms that opinion is of perceptible objects: "Perceptible things are grasped by opinion, which involves sense perception. As such, they are things that come to be, things that are begotten" (28b8–c3). The second associates belief with becoming: "What being is to becoming, truth is to convincingness [*pistin*]" (29c3). These sentences go a little way to show that Plato did not in fact change his view of opinion (on the objects and nature of those objects of opinion), at least between the middle dialogues and later dialogues.

The last Platonic quotation discusses the difference between, and origin of, true and false opinions:

> If memory and perceptions concur with other impressions at a particular occasion, then they seem to me to inscribe words in our soul, as it were. And if what is written is true, then we form a true judgment [*doxa alēthēs*] and a true account of the matter. But if what our scribe writes is false, then the result will be the opposite of the truth.
>
> I quite agree. (*Philebus* 39a1–b1)

So for Plato, as he argued in *Republic* V, opinion has as its objects perceptible things, which are things that change constantly and are copies of unchangeable, eternal, immaterial Forms.

Plotinus:[163] Plotinus refers to opinion as "that which is known by sense-perception" but discusses the questions that can arise concerning its veracity:

> For there is a lack of confidence about even those objects of sense-perception which seem to inspire the strongest confidence in their self-evidence, whether their apparent existence may be not in the underlying realities, but in the ways the sense-organs are affected, and they need intellect or discursive reason to make judgments about them; for even if it is agreed that they are in the underlying sense-realities which sense-perception is to grasp, that which is known by sense-perception is an image of the thing, and sense-perception does not apprehend the thing itself: for that remains outside. (V.5.1.12–9[164])

Note that Plotinus substitutes in the phrase "their apparent existence" as a way of describing the objects of "that which is known by sense-perception," and raises the idea that opinions might lie within individuals and not be accurately representing the object(s) sensed. This is fully compatible with Plato's Cave passage. The next passage explicitly states that opinion is a result of sense perception, and when we see Forms imitated in sense objects, we have sense perception thereof, and hence we have opinion, versus knowledge:

> If one grants that the objects of thought are as completely as possible outside Intellect, and that Intellect contemplates them as absolutely outside it, then

> it cannot possess the truth of them and must be deceived in everything it contemplates. For they would be the true realities; and on this supposition it will contemplate them without possessing them, but will only get images of them in a knowledge of this sort. If then it does not possess the true reality, but only receives in itself images of the truth, it will have falsities and nothing true. If, then, it knows that what it has is false, it will admit that it has no part in truth; but if it does not know even this, and thinks it has the truth when it has not, the falsehood in it will be doubled and will set it far away from the truth. (This is the reason, I think, why there is no truth in the senses, only opinion: opinion is opinion because it receives, and what it receives is different from that from which it receives it.) (V.5.1.50–65)

Plotinus not only claims that opinion is of sense perception, but also that one does not possess knowledge or the truth of sense objects, and that sense objects are images of the "true realities," which he holds to be Forms. In the next passage, Plotinus mimics some of the language of Plato's Cave Allegory by arguing that what passes for the most real is most truly non-existent. This is consistent with Plato's claims that the prisoners will be upset when the knower of the Good urges them to be released and see the truth, and that they will ridicule the knower of the Good and even try to kill him or her (where the "First" referred to here is the equivalent of Plato's Good):

> Do not, then, seek to see with mortal eyes this as our account describes it, nor to see that it is in the way in which someone would expect it to be who assumes that all things are perceived by the senses, by which supposition he eliminates that which is most real of all. For the things which one thinks are most real, are least real; and the [materially] large has less genuine existence. But the First is the principle of existence and, again, more authentic than substantial reality. (V.5.11.5–11)

Thus, we can conclude that Plotinus and Plato agree on the nature of opinion, what it is, what its objects are, and its inferiority to knowledge of the Forms, or truly authentic Being(s).

2.8 Summary

Both Plato and Plotinus hold that wisdom is a kind of super-knowledge, that it is knowledge of the Good that allows us to benefit from any other knowledge.

Moreover, they claim that ultimate knowledge is of the Good (or One), that knowledge is of the Forms, knowers are awake, opiners are akin to dreamers, and that knowledge is vastly superior to opinion.

Both philosophers also agree that dialectic is the supreme method or practice of philosophy that allows us to know the Good and that in gaining conscious knowledge of the Forms, we recollect what we already unconsciously knew. The latter claim amounts to an additional agreement that rationalism is true. Each declares that prayer is useless without relevant action and right opinion, let alone one's being a good person as they conceive it.

Lastly, they both claim that opinion has perceptible objects as its objects; namely, these objects constantly "become" and change, and since knowledge can only be had of immutable objects, knowledge cannot be had of perceptible objects.

3

Ethics: Plato and Plotinus on Happiness, How to Live, and How Not to Live

3.1 Introduction

Plato and Plotinus do not essentially differ on ethics concerning at least these points: the nature of happiness, love, purification and reverence, the way in which we should live (philosophy, virtue, justice, and temperance), the way in which we should not live (vice, ignorance, impiety, and over-concern for the body), music and musicians, arts and artisans, desire for the good, the impossibility of erring willingly, and pleasure and pain.

Assuming that the Good is the source of ethical truth,[1] note the connection between personal identity and ethics for Plato and Plotinus. That is, ethics for these thinkers (and other Greek thinkers in general) is a matter of something being good for a person, so we should address their view as to what a person is. This turns out to be a complex analysis, but both philosophers believe that there are three parts of the soul—Reason, Spirit, and Appetite—the latter two being mortal; we are also more our soul than our bodies in general and more specifically more our Reason (the divine part of us) than either Spirit or Appetite (the mortal soul parts). However, depending on one's character, one can operate more due to Spirit and/or Appetite than from Reason, or vice versa.

This leads to questions, such as, if I am essentially Reason, do I have any uniqueness and what role would my personality play, if any? After all, what would make me unique if I (who equal Reason, use "myself" to) merely access the immutable Forms, just as any other philosopher who has seen the Good, according to Plato and Plotinus? What exactly would it be that benefits from, say, being temperate and not drinking alcohol while driving? My answers are bound to be contentious, but I believe that both philosophers would argue that there can still be uniqueness in one's Reason due to one's life experiences, memories, current situation, and so on, but that uniqueness per se is not important to these men. Remember that they have also argued that in some sense all souls are one: Plotinus also posits Forms of individuals.[2] My Reason (or I) would benefit from having access to the Forms because (their view goes) I would then know what exists, what is possible to know, and the way in which it is best for me to live, not to mention that I would know myself, which is also described by them as (part of) temperance.

There are other questions related to vice: Why does vice make *me* worse, if I am only Reason? More specifically, if I am an intelligent embezzler, how does this damage my Reason (or, *per hypothesi*, who I am)? From my understanding, Plato and Plotinus would answer that the presence of vice automatically implies a lack of proper functioning of Reason, a lack of knowledge of good and bad, and therefore one will also lack virtue and will perform actions and have thoughts that will lead to their unhappiness. A vicious person can go a long way towards destroying their Reason, in the sense of not paying attention to Reason, or subordinating its aim at the best to the acquisition of wealth, as in our example, or sex, or any number of things (honor, power, and/or other external goods). Both philosophers concede that one can be intelligent without being virtuous, so the presence of intelligence does not by itself indicate that one has a healthy Reason part of the soul.

Recall my arguments that are relevant to Plato and Plotinus' ethical views: each philosopher urges us to know the Good or the One, since it is the ultimate experience and the goal of philosophy. Moreover, having this ultimate experience amounts to wisdom, and we should practice dialectic, the highest study within philosophy. Lastly, we can have a transformative vision of Beauty,[3] it is possible to know God via philosophy,[4] evil is a privation, must always exist, and haunts our mortal nature.[5]

3.2 On happiness

For both Plato and Plotinus, the goal of life is happiness. The Greek for happiness, *eudaimonia*, is probably best translated as "thriving" or "flourishing," versus happiness; keeping this in mind, I have adapted Armstrong's rendering of *eudaimonia*—"well-being"—as "happiness" or "happy," depending on the context.[6]

Happiness is also linked with virtue, using one's reason, and knowing the Good. More specifically, Plato and Plotinus agree on the following issues: happiness is a direct result of or nothing other than wisdom and/or knowledge; happiness is possessing the beautiful and the good, and that the good are happy; happiness is a direct result of or nothing other than possessing virtue(s); happiness occurs when Reason always guides the soul; happiness is a state as opposed to a process; and misfortunes do not seriously affect the good man or Sage who is happy.

Happiness is a direct result of or nothing other than wisdom and/or knowledge

Plato: In the *Charmides*, even though the conclusions about temperance and knowledge are admittedly far from conclusive, Plato has Critias agree that a house is well-run and a city well-governed if guided by temperance, and that the temperate fare well and therefore are happy (171e5–2a3); in the same passage Socrates claims (and Critias agrees) that the advantage of temperance is to know what one knows and what one does not know (*Charmides* 172a4–6).[7]

Clinias agrees that, as knowledge provides good fortune and rightness, and using things rightly leads to happiness, then we should try to become as wise as possible:

> Since we all wish to be happy, and since we appear to become so by using things and using them rightly, and since knowledge was the source of rightness and good fortune, it seems to be necessary that every man should prepare himself by every means to become as wise as possible—or isn't this the case?
>
> Yes, it is, he said. (*Euthydemus* 282a1–7)

Plato continues to hold this view: using wisdom to guide one's action leads to happiness:

> In a word, all that the soul undertakes and endures, if directed by wisdom, ends in happiness, but if directed by ignorance, it ends in the opposite?
>
> That is likely. (*Meno* 88c1–4)

Lastly, in Plato's summation of the Cave Allegory: "Anyone who is to act wisely [*emphronōs*] in private or public must see it,"[8] where "it" refers to the Good. We can be interpretively sure that Plato connects knowing the Good with happiness by what he says at *Republic* VI 505a2–b3, about the lack of knowledge of the Good implying the loss of benefit of any possession or knowledge of anything else, as well as his statement that the guardians will have to know the Good in order to properly order the Kallipolis to be happy, at *Republic* VI 506a4–8.

Plotinus: Plotinus agrees that knowledge of the Good implies one's knowledge of happiness and one's being happy:[9]

> When the soul has good fortune with it, and it comes to it, or rather, being there already, appears.... There, truly, it would not exchange this for anything in the world, not even if someone handed over the whole universe to it, because there is nothing still better, and nothing that is more a good; for it does not run up higher, and all the other things are on its way down, even if they are in the realm above. So then it has the ability to judge rightly and to know that this is what it desired, and to establish that there is nothing better than it. For there is no deceit there; or where could it find any thing truer than truth? What it speaks, then, is that, and it speaks it afterwards, and speaks it in silence, and in its happiness is not cheated in thinking that it is happy; and it does not say it is happy when the body tickles it, but when it has become that which it was before, when it is fortunate. (VI.7.34.8–9, 21–38)

Plotinus also agrees with Plato that being wise is equated with being happy:

> Plato was right in maintaining that the man who intends to be wise[10] and in a state of happiness must take his good from There, from above, and look to that good and

> be made like it and live by it. He must hold on to this only as his goal, and change his other circumstances as he changes his dwelling-place, not because he derives any advantage in the point of happiness from one dwelling-place or another, but guessing, as it were, how his alien covering will be affected if he lodges here or there. (I.4.16.10–17; adapted from A.H. Armstrong)

Plotinus may be referring to *Republic* VI 505a–b, 506a, and the Sun Simile and Cave Allegory, in order to legitimately interpret Plato as teaching that to be happy, one is to draw his good from the Supreme; after all, there is nothing more Supreme in Plato's philosophy than the Form of the Good.

Plotinus also claims that happiness is possible for humans (I.4.4), though he notes that Nous has the perfect life and all other lives are phantoms of life and incomplete lives in comparison (I.4.3). Lastly, while in the context of arguing that plants can also be happy, Plotinus denies that happiness is founded on the life of Reason for all beings (I.4.2). Nonetheless, Plotinus does believe that for humans, happiness occurs when Reason always guides the soul in the proper way.

In sum, both Plato and Plotinus claim that knowledge of the Good and wisdom result in happiness, or just that they are the ingredients for happiness.

Happiness is the possession of goodness and beauty; and the good are happy

Plato: Plato writes that the one who is to be happy must not only get possession of good things (wealth, health, beauty, good birth), but also use them, or there is no benefit from having them (*Euthydemus* 280d–e).[11]

Plato avers that human happiness is possessing the beautiful and the good:

> By calling anyone "happy," don't you mean they possess good and beautiful things?
>
> Certainly. (*Symposium* 202c10–2[12])

Technically, this passage only shows that Plato believes that the happy possess good and beautiful *things*, as opposed to the Forms. However, Diotima also words this issue in this way:

> Can we simply say that people love the good?
>
> Yes, I said.
>
> But shouldn't we add that, in loving it, they want the good to be theirs?
>
> We should. (*Symposium* 206a3–8[13])

Moreover, we have already seen that Plato states that the good is a possession that allows us to benefit and gain use from other knowledge and possessions (*Republic* VI 505a2–b3).

Plato also holds that if one is or possesses good, one is happy (*Gorgias* 470e9–11, *Symposium* 204e–5a),[14] and that if one is not good, then one is not happy (*Laws* V 743c4).[15]

Plotinus: For Plotinus' part, he states that happiness requires fullness of life, and that a happy person possesses the Good (and not merely the good):

> If then the good life belongs to what has a superabundance of life (this means what is in no way deficient in life), happiness will belong only to the being which lives superabundantly: this will have the best, if the best among realities is being really alive, is perfect life. So its good will not be something brought in from outside, nor will the basis of its goodness come from somewhere else and bring it into a good state; for what could be added to the perfect life to make it into the best life? (I.4.3.25–31; adapted from A.H. Armstrong[16])

What about the beautiful; does Plotinus agree that the happy person also possesses the beautiful? Evidence for this agreement can be inferred from Plotinus' claims that implanting goodness and introducing order and beauty into an ugly soul makes it virtuous (III.6.2), and that if one is happy, one possesses the Good. For it follows that if one is happy, one possesses both good and beauty on Plotinus' view.

Plotinus claims that the good are happy, and more specifically, that *only* the good are happy:

> Punishment certainly follows; and it is not unjust that someone who has come to be this sort of person should suffer the consequences of his condition; people must not demand to be well off who have not done what deserves happiness. Only the good are well-off; that, too, is what gives the gods their happiness. (III.2.4.44–8; adapted from A.H. Armstrong[17])

Thus, Plato and Plotinus believe that the happy possess the good and beauty, and that the good are happy.

Happiness is a direct result of or nothing other than possessing virtue(s)

Plato: Socrates says:

> It's necessarily very much the case, Callicles, that the self-controlled man, because he's just and brave and pious, as we've recounted, is a completely good man, that the good man does well and admirably whatever he does, and that the man who does well is blessed and happy. (*Gorgias* 507b8–c5)

In other words, one's possessing the virtues implies that one is good, and also happy.

In Plato's *Menexenus*, he claims that if one is happy within oneself (that is, a happiness that does not hang in suspense with other men or with one's fortune), one's life is ordered for the best and one is temperate, valiant, and wise (248a1–4).

The just man is said to live well and therefore to be blessed and happy (*Republic* I 353e10–4a2). Plato states that we must have a solid faith: "We must always know how to choose the mean in such lives and how to avoid either of the extremes, as far as possible, both in this life and in all those beyond it. This is the way that a human being becomes happiest," (*Republic* X 619a5–b1) which implies that temperance and justice produce the greatest happiness for man.

Plato again confirms that the temperate, wise, courageous life is superior in rightness and virtue, and also unreservedly happier than the opposite:[18]

> The self-controlled, the wise and the courageous, experience pleasure and pain with less intensity and on a smaller and more restricted scale than the profligate, the fool and the coward. The first category beats the second on the score of pleasure, while the second beats the other when it comes to pain. The courageous man does better than the coward, the wise man than the fool; so that, life for life, the former kind—the restrained, the courageous, the wise and the healthy—is pleasanter than the cowardly, the foolish, the licentious and the unhealthy.
>
> To sum up, the life of physical fitness, and spiritual virtue too, is not only pleasanter than the life of depravity but superior in other ways as well: it makes for beauty, an upright posture, efficiency and a good reputation, so that if a man lives a life like that it will make his whole existence infinitely happier than his opposite number's. (*Laws* V 734c3–e2)

Two further passages are of note in the *Laws*: First, Plato claims via the Athenian that the indispensable condition for happiness is not to wrong others, or ourselves, which is presumably a characteristic of justice (VIII 829a1–3). Second, Plato claims that the happy person will only get as many riches as rectitude and temperance will permit, valuing money for the sake of the body, and the body for the sake of the soul (IX 870b2–c1).[19]

Plotinus: Plotinus discusses implanting goodness in the soul, and introducing order and beauty where there is evil and ugliness, making virtue a harmony (III.6.2), which implies that one's soul at the end of this implantation is just and good. If one is good, one is happy. Plotinus also confirms Plato's point in the *Menexenus* that it is possible for one to be happy within oneself when he states that we must "try to find self-sufficiency in the matter of well-being" (I.4.5.23–4). Plotinus also confirms the contrapositive: if we are not happy, it is due to a lack of courage for the battle:

> If, then, it is possible for souls to be happy in this All, we must not blame the place if some are not happy, but their own incapacity, in that they have not been able to take a noble part in the contest for which the prizes of virtue are offered. (III.2.5.1–4; adapted from A.H. Armstrong)

Lastly, Plotinus confirms Plato's view that "the man who intends to be wise and in a state of happiness must take his good from There, from above, and look to that good and be made like it and live by it" (I.4.16.10–3; adapted from A.H. Armstrong), because if one makes oneself like to the Good, one must become good, which is what it is to possess virtue—and hence happiness—for Plotinus.

In sum, both philosophers believe that happiness results from virtue, or co-exists with virtue.

Happiness occurs when Reason always guides the soul

Plato and Plotinus each affirm that if Reason consistently guides the soul, that soul is happy. This is essentially equivalent to the claim that the just person is happy, so I will not spend much time confirming this point.

Plato: Reason is here rendered as "the better elements in . . . their minds":[20]

> If the victory goes to the better elements in both their minds, which lead them to follow the assigned regimen of philosophy, their life here below is one of bliss and shared understanding. They are modest and fully in control of themselves now that they have enslaved the part that brought trouble into the soul and set free the part that gave it virtue. (*Phaedrus* 256a7–b3[21])

Note, too, that Plato seems to equate happiness with temperance, virtue in general, and one's being set free.

Plotinus: Interestingly, Plotinus is concerned to allow happiness for plants as well, so he makes a statement that happiness is not necessarily the life of Reason:

> Those who say that [happiness] is to be found in a rational life, not simply in life, even life accompanied by sensation, may very likely be right; but we ought to ask them why they posit happiness only in the case of rational living things. "Do you add the 'rational' because reason is more efficient and can easily find out and procure the primary natural needs, or would you require reason even if it was not able to find them out or obtain them?" (I.4.2.31–8; adapted from A.H. Armstrong; my brackets[22])

But when discussing human happiness, which is the context in which I am discussing Reason, Plotinus certainly believes that when Reason guides us, we are happy philosophers. Plotinus implies that he is committed to the view that when Reason rules, a person is good (because when the converse is true, he is evil):

> It is like when in an assembly the elders of the people sit in quiet consideration, and the disorderly populace, demanding food and complaining of other sufferings, throws the whole assembly into an ugly tumult. Now if people like this keep quiet and a speech from a sensible man gets through to them, the multitude settles to a decent order and the worse has not gained the mastery; but if not, the worse is master and the better keeps quiet, because the tumultuous mob could not receive the word from above, and this is the vice of city and assembly. But this is also the vice of man; he too has in himself a populace of pleasures and lusts and fears,

> which gain the mastery when a man of this kind surrenders himself to a populace of this kind; but whoever enslaves this mob, and runs back up to that man he once was, lives according to that man and is that man and gives what he gives to the body as to something other than himself; but someone else lives now this way and now the other; he has become a person mixed from the good self and the evil other. (VI.4.15.23–40)

Keep in mind that Plotinus holds that the goodness of soul is a harmony, order, beauty, and concordance (III.6.2) and that human justice is a well ordering of the soul, where one obeys Reason, which implies that Reason is in charge in a harmonious soul, given Plotinus' psychology.

Lastly, Plotinus claims that if two wise men possessing (or not) naturally good things are equally happy, then the Sage will reason (or threaten) away any involuntary fear if it arises unexpectedly:

> But suppose there were two wise [*sophia*] men, one of whom had all of what are called natural goods and the other their opposites, shall we say that they both have happiness equally? Yes, if they are equally wise.... If sometimes when he is concerned with other things an involuntary fear comes upon him before he has time to reflect, the wise man [in him] will come and drive it away and quiet the child in him which is stirred to a sort of distress, by threatening or reasoning; the threatening will be unemotional, as if the child was shocked into quietness just by a severe look. (I.4.15.1–3, 16–21; adapted from A.H. Armstrong)

So Plotinus agrees with Plato that human happiness implies the consistent, effective guidance of Reason in actions and decisions.

Happiness is a state, disposition, or possession as opposed to a process or action

Both philosophers believe that happiness is a state as opposed to a process (that is, a series of actions, or *praxeis*). They both hold that if one is happy (due to one's knowing the Good), then nothing can shake that happiness such that they become unhappy, no matter what may happen thereafter.

Plato:

> Each of us will be trying to prove some possession (*hexin*) or state (*diathesin*) of the soul to be the one that can render life happy for all human beings. Isn't that so?
>
> Quite so. (*Philebus* 11d4–7[23])

Note that A.H. Armstrong translates Plotinus' *diathesin* (or its variants) as "disposition," although Frede translates Plato's as "state." This explains the three words in this section's title, depending on one's translations of these words.

In addition, Plato explicitly raises the possibility of a just/virtuous person's body[24] acquiring a disease or being murdered, and maintains that it does not affect his soul's justice or virtue (or happiness, implied) (*Republic* X 609e1–10d4). Conversely, a happy person might do certain actions that are similar to other happy persons (for instance, perform just, generous, or temperate actions in the appropriate situations), but even if they are unable to perform these actions, Plato argues that they are nonetheless happy.

Plotinus: For Plotinus, first I can connect Plato's Greek in the *Philebus* with that of Plotinus: Plotinus asserts that they will investigate which states (*hexeis*) and dispositions (*diatheseis*) will be better and worse for the soul in general (I.1.2.5); he holds that happiness is a better state or disposition for the soul than unhappiness or vice.

Second, while Plotinus strongly urges against our believing that actions (*praxis*) cause or are necessary for one's continued happiness favoring instead our dispositions (*diatheseis*) and what we have (*exei*) as that which makes us happy (I.5.10.10–18), he also says that activity (*energeia*) of soul is the state of happiness, at, for example, I.5.10.20–3. Plato obviously does not use *energeia*, as Aristotle coined the word, but translating *energeia* as actuality (of soul) can imply a state of the soul, which is consistent with happiness' being a state. Alternatively, translating *energeia* as activity (of soul) can still be consistent with Plato's view, since the soul's intellectual activity (especially contemplating the Good, for example) entails and is entailed by one's being happy. And compare VI.8.5.34–7, where Plotinus implies that virtue is another sort of intellect, a state (*hexis*) that intellectualizes the soul in some way, keeping in mind that for Plotinus, being truly virtuous implies possessing happiness as well. Nonetheless, the latter interpretation of *energeia* as activity does not somehow negate what Plotinus says about happiness being a matter of dispositions and possessions, which we either presumably have or do not have (as opposed to certain actions we are or are not performing), which is the kind of view for which I argue.

Third, Plotinus states: "As regards happiness, it has a boundary and a limit and is always the same" (I.5.6.18–9; adapted from A.H. Armstrong),[25] though he also says that happiness is a definite condition (I.5.1) that does not increase or decrease with time (nor does unhappiness; I.5.6), and that a good person is happy though she may be unconscious or sleeping (I.4.9).

Misfortunes do not affect the happy, good man (or the Sage)

Plato and Plotinus both agree that happiness is a state, possession, or disposition, and not a process or a series of actions one performs. So either one is in the state of happiness (happy) or not in the state of happiness (unhappy). But what if one is happy and "bad things happen to good people"? This does not affect one's happiness.

Plato: Socrates seemed to have been a living example of this principle:[26] "of all those we have known the best, and also the wisest and the most upright" (*Phaedo* 118b16–7), even though Socrates never claimed to possess knowledge (and indeed quite the opposite). However, since one's possessing wisdom and being virtuous, on Plato's view, entails that one is also happy, we can infer that Socrates was happy. From the *Apology* (28e–9a, 29c–d, 32a–d, 40b–1a) and *Crito* (43b–c), we learn that Socrates is neither afraid nor resentful of death, respectively. Nonetheless, I realize that this claim about Socrates' being happy might be controversial and rejected, again, because Socrates states that he has no knowledge in several places in the aporetic dialogues, taken together with the claim that virtue is knowledge and entails happiness. So I will move on to other statements in the dialogues.

Plato states that those who are truly brave bear their misfortunes well, and shortly thereafter states:

> For that man's life is best arranged for whom all, or nearly all, the things that promote happiness depend on himself. Such a man does not hang from other men and necessarily rise or fall in fortune as they fare well or badly; he is the temperate, he is the brave and wise man. He above all, when wealth and children come and when they go, will pay heed to the adage: because he relies on himself, he will be seen neither to rejoice nor to grieve *too much.* (*Menexenus* 247e6–8a7[27])

A brief survey of the *Phaedo* and *Republic* cements my case. First, in the *Phaedo*, Plato makes these claims about misfortunes:

(1) True philosophers make dying their profession, thoroughly dissatisfied with the body, so it would be unreasonable for them to be frightened or distressed about death, especially because they might attain wisdom—their incarnated lifelong quest—after death; (*Phaedo* 67e5–8b6)
(2) Everyone except the philosopher regards death as a great evil; (*Phaedo* 68d5–12)[28] and:
(3) The true philosopher "keeps away from pleasures and desires and pains as far as he can" because they do not cause the mere expected evils of disease or the result of satisfying extravagant desires, but the "greatest and most extreme evil" of believing "that what causes such feelings must be very clear and true, which it is not." (*Phaedo* 83b4–c8)

So the true philosophers—the best human candidates for happiness—do not regard death, illness, or losing money as great evils, as do the multitude.

Second, in *Republic* X, Plato makes these relevant claims concerning the effect misfortunes have or should have on us:

(1) A decent man bears the loss of a son or some other prized possession more easily than others; he will feel grief in a measured way; (603e3–5, 7–8)
(2) The "law" declares that it is best to keep quiet as possible in misfortunes—human affairs aren't worth taking very seriously;[29] grieving checks or prevents deliberation (which is a much more valuable practice and the best way to face misfortune); (604b9–d4)[30]

(3) An immortal soul, since it lives for all time, should not be worried about the small "nothing" amount of time of one incarnation; (608c5–d2) and
(4) A just person who falls into poverty or disease or some other apparent evil, namely, that this will end well for him, either during this lifetime or afterwards, for the gods never neglect anyone who eagerly wishes to become just and who makes himself as much like a god as a human can by adopting a virtuous way of life. (613a4–b1)

Plato adds that the good or just person should not overly grieve at the death of loved ones, or take anything at all in this mortal life so seriously but face misfortune bravely and rationally. Perhaps even more hyperbolically, Plato claims that we should not take poverty and disease as just *bad* things, because they will prove to be *good* for the good or just person because the gods will not neglect the good person.

Thus, Plato believes that misfortunes do not affect the wise (good and just) person.

Plotinus:[31]

> If he is virtuous, he has all he needs for happiness and the acquisition of good; for there is no good that he has not got. What he seeks he seeks as a necessity, not for himself but for something that belongs to him; that is, he seeks it for the body which is joined to him; and even granting that this is a living body, it lives its own life and not the life which is that of the good man. He knows its needs, and gives it what he gives it without taking away anything from his own life. His happiness will not be reduced even when fortune goes against him; the good life is still there even so. When his friends and relations die he knows what death is—as those who die do also if they are virtuous. Even if the death of friends and relations causes grief, it does not grieve him but only that in him which has no intelligence, and he will not allow the distresses of this to move him. (I.4.4.23–36; adapted from A.H. Armstrong[32])

Here are some other relevant Plotinian claims:

(1) Freedom from pain, sickness, misfortune, disaster are not prerequisites for happiness (because no one could be happy if that were true); happiness is fruition of the authentic Good; (I.4.6)
(2) More pleasant conditions cannot add any particle towards the Sage's felicity;[33] his happiness will not be truly affected by the death of a child, becoming a king, being offered as a sacrifice, being unburied; "he will not be dependent on the good or bad fortune of other people"; (I.4.7.46–7)
(3) The Sage asks for no pity in all his violent personal sufferings, even if he is tortured; ordinary experiences do not pierce the inner person; he aims at a virtue that is "something better than most people are capable of; and it is better not to give in to what ordinary nature normally finds terrible'; he has a soul that is 'hard to disturb or distress"; (I.4.8.21–4, 29–30)[34]
(4) A Sage can remain equally happy even though asleep or ill; (I.4.9)

(5) The Sage can remain happy even in the Bull of Phalaris;[35] (I.4.13) and
(6) Two wise persons possessing all that is naturally welcome or unwelcome, are equally happy; the Sage will reason or menace away involuntary fear. (I.4.15)

In conclusion, happiness is either *equivalent* to wisdom and knowledge of the Good and possessing virtue, or *the direct result from them*; happiness is possessing the good or the beautiful and the good are happy; one's being ruled by Reason entails one's happiness; happiness is a state, and misfortunes do not seriously affect the good or happy man.

3.3 On love

Not all commentators of Plato and Plotinus believe that these philosophers have the same view of love (*eros*). For example, Anton and A.H. Armstrong[36] mention Plotinus' statement: "He, that same self, is lovable and love and love of himself, in that he is beautiful only from himself and in himself" (VI.8.15.1–2), and conclude that this is not Plato's view. However, while I concede the point that Plato does not state that the Good is self-love or simply love,[37] I agree with Rist who claims that Plotinus follows Plato in believing that there is more to Eros than mere self-seeking and desire,[38] that they both have the same "contradictory" notions of love (simple desire versus giving/creation),[39] and that the One's love cannot imply any lack.[40]

I would add that Plotinus' VI.8.15.1–2 passage seems to say only that the One loves itself *because* "he" is beautiful only from himself and in himself, with which Plato would agree.[41] From the Platonic side of the issue, I add to Rist's view that while discussing God's creation of the Forms (keeping in mind that I interpret "God" only here as the Good, but the Demiurge elsewhere), Plato attributes willing and wishing to God/the Good as well (*Republic* X 597c–d). This is similarly anthropomorphic to Plotinus' statement, and certainly metaphorical, since Plato does not elsewhere claim that the Good wills or wishes anything.[42] This is similar to Plotinus, who typically does not attribute willing to the One, but does so in VI.8.

In what follows, I argue that Plato and Plotinus agree that Love is the child of Resource (*Poros*) and Poverty (*Penia*) and that Love is the child of Aphrodite; Love is midway between ignorance and wisdom; the lover of beauty wants beauty/good to be his own and gain happiness therefrom: the Ladder of Love in the *Symposium* details the way in which one may know beauty; and Love can be either an irrational desire pursuing enjoyment of bodily beauty or a manifestation of the desire for the Good.

Love is the child of Poros and Penia (and Love is the child of Aphrodite)

Plato: Interestingly, Plato gives two lineages of Love (*Eros*): First, he states that Love is the child of Aphrodite, where Socrates asks, "Don't you believe that Love is the son of Aphrodite?" and Phaedrus answers, "This is certainly what people say" (*Phaedrus* 242d9–10).

Second, Plato—via Diotima who asserts that she'll tell the truth about love, at 199a–b—claims that Love is the progeny of Resource [*Poros*] and Poverty [*Penia*]:

> When Aphrodite was born, the gods held a celebration. *Poros* [Resource], the son of *Metis* [Craft], was there among them. When they had feasted, *Penia* [Poverty] came begging, as poverty does when there's a party, and stayed by the gates. Now *Poros* got drunk on nectar (there was no wine yet, you see) and, feeling drowsy, went into the garden of Zeus, where he fell asleep. Then *Penia* schemed up a plan to relieve her lack of resources: she would get a child from *Poros*. So she lay beside him and got pregnant with Love. That is why Love was born to follow Aphrodite and serve her: because he was conceived on the day of her birth. And that's why he is also by nature a lover of beauty, because Aphrodite herself is especially beautiful.
>
> As the son of *Poros* and *Penia*, his lot in life is set to be like theirs. In the first place, he is always poor, and he's far from being delicate and beautiful (as ordinary people think he is); instead, he is tough and shriveled and shoeless and homeless, always lying on the dirt without a bed, sleeping at people's doorsteps and in roadsides under the sky, having his mother's nature, always living with Need. But on his father's side he is a schemer after the beautiful and the good; he is brave, impetuous, and intense, an awesome hunter, always weaving snares, resourceful in his pursuit of intelligence, a lover of wisdom through all his life, a genius with enchantments, potions, and clever pleadings. (*Symposium* 203b2–e8; my emphasis; brackets added[43])

Plotinus:[44] Plotinus verifies both of Love's lineages:

> The Love whom we ought to make the main object of our philosophical discourse is the one whom not only the rest of mankind but those also who give accounts of the gods, and especially Plato, make a god; Plato in many places speaks of "Love son of Aphrodite,"[45] and says that his work is to be "guardian of beautiful boys"[46] and mover of the soul towards the beauty of the higher world, or also to increase the impulse towards that world which is already there; we must also take into account all that is said in the *Symposium*,[47] in which he says that Love is not born of Aphrodite but "from Poverty [*Penia*] and Resource [*Poros*] at Aphrodite's birthday party."[48] (III.5.2.1–9; adapted from A.H. Armstrong)

Plotinus goes on to analyze the *Symposium* passage:

> In the story of the birth of Love Plato says that Resource [*Poros*] was drunk from "the heavenly nectar—for this was before the days of wine," meaning that Love came into existence before the world of sense, and that Poverty [*Penia*] had intercourse with an intelligible nature, not merely with an image of the intelligible or an imagination derived from it, but she was there in the intelligible and united with it, and bore the substance of Love made from form and indefiniteness, the indefiniteness which the soul had before it attained the Good, while it was divining

> that there was something there by an indefinite, unlimited imagination. Therefore, since a rational principle came to be in something which was not rational, but an indefinite impulse and an obscure expression, what it produced was something not complete or sufficient, but defective, since it came into being from an indefinite impulse and a sufficient rational principle. (III.5.7.1–12; adapted from A.H. Armstrong[49])

Plotinus' interpretation that Love came into existence before the world of sense is warranted in part because Plato states at *Phaedrus* 242d9–10 that Love is a god, the son of Aphrodite. It is also plausible to claim that Poverty[50] is indefiniteness and that Resource is an intelligible nature, because there is something about Love that is rational according to Plato; namely that it strives and longs for the Good and wisdom.[51]

Moreover, Plotinus claims at III.5.2 that Aphrodite is twofold: the heavenly Aphrodite (daughter of Kronos and Uranus) is Soul at its finest or what he calls the higher part of Soul; and the earthly Aphrodite (daughter of Zeus and Dione) presides over earthly unions. In making this claim, he seems to be taking Pausanias' speech about love in Plato's *Symposium* to be Plato's view. There, at 180d–e, Pausanias claims that there is a heavenly Aphrodite and an earthly one as well, with the same parentage as Plotinus claims at III.5.2.

Thus, Plato and Plotinus each hold that Love is the child of Aphrodite in some sense, but also the son of Resource and Poverty.

Love is midway between ignorance and wisdom

Plato:

> On his father's side he is a schemer after the beautiful and the good; he is brave, impetuous, and intense, an awesome hunter, always weaving snares, resourceful in his pursuit of intelligence, a lover of wisdom through all his life, a genius with enchantments, potions, and clever pleadings.
>
> He is by nature neither immortal nor mortal. But now he springs to life when he gets his way; now he dies—all in the very same day. Because he is his father's son, however, he keeps coming back to life, but then anything he finds his way to always slips away, and for this reason Love is never completely without resources, nor is he ever rich.
>
> He is in between wisdom and ignorance as well. (*Symposium* 203d4–e5[52])

Plotinus: Finding confirmation in Plotinus that Love both lacks something but also seeks the good is necessarily indirect, but nonetheless available by implication:

> [Love] is a mixed thing, having a part of need, in that he wishes to be filled, but not without a share of plenitude, in that he seeks what is wanting to that which he already has; for certainly that which is altogether without a share in the Good would not ever seek the Good. So he is said to be born of Resource [*Poros*] and

> Poverty [*Penia*], in that the lack and the aspiration and the memory of the rational principles coming together in the soul, produced the activity directed towards the Good, and this is Love. . . . A spirit produced from soul insofar as soul falls short of the Good but aspires to it. (III.5.9.42–8, 56–7; adapted from A.H. Armstrong[53])

On the one hand, Love lacks its good but yearns for it, so it cannot be completely destitute—implying that it is "above" ignorance; on the other hand, Love does not possess its Good but wishes to do so—implying that it is "below" wisdom. This implies that Love lies between ignorance and wisdom.

Therefore, Plato and Plotinus hold that Love is midway between ignorance and wisdom.

The lover of beauty wants beauty/good to be his own and gain happiness therefrom

Related to the claims that there is a connection between our love of beauty and our desire for happiness, Plato and Plotinus hold that the lover of beauty desires to possess beauty and good and gain happiness from that possession.

Plato:

> "It's clearer this way: 'The lover of beautiful things has a desire; what does he desire?'"
>
> "That they become his own," I said.
>
> . . . suppose someone asks us, "Tell me, Socrates, a lover of good things has a desire; what does he desire?"
>
> "That they become his own," I said.
>
> "And what will he have, when the good things he wants have become his own?"
>
> "This time it's easier to come up with the answer," I said. "He'll have happiness."
>
> "That's what makes happy people happy, isn't it—possessing good things. There's no need to ask further, 'What's the point of wanting happiness?' The answer you gave seems to be final." (*Symposium* 204d5–7, e2–205a3[54])

So Plato believes that the lover of beauty (and good) longs to make the beautiful (or good) his own, gaining happiness along the way.

Plotinus:[55]

> It[56] has the good sense, then, to remain in itself, and would not come to be in another; but those other things hang from it as if by their longing they had found where it is. And this is "Love camping on the doorstep," even coming from outside into the presence of beauty and longing for it, and satisfied if in this way he can have a part in it; since the lover here below also has beauty in this way, not by receiving it [into himself] but by lying with it. But that [one beauty] remains by

> itself, and the many lovers of the one love the whole and have the whole like this, when they have it: for it was the whole that they loved. (VI.5.10.1–9[57])

I have shown that Plato and Plotinus have the same view of happiness; I will confirm that they both hold the related claim that all souls desire the Good. This should suffice for showing that they each believe that the lover of beauty wants beauty/good to be his own and gain happiness therefrom.

The Ladder of Love details the way in which one may know beauty

It is necessary to detail the steps on the Ladder and show them in both philosophers' writings, because commentators including Friedländer and Hadot have disputed the similarity.

Plato: To prepare the reader for the Ladder of Love, Plato (via Diotima at 210a4) states that Socrates must try his best to follow along; implying that what emerges is not something with which Socrates is familiar (especially given that they have just reviewed procreative love):[58]

> A lover who goes about this matter correctly must begin in his youth to devote himself to beautiful bodies. First, if the leader leads aright, he should love one body and beget beautiful ideas there; then he should realize that the beauty of any one body is brother to the beauty of any other and that if he is to pursue beauty of form he'd be very foolish not to think that the beauty of all bodies is one and the same. When he grasps this, he must become a lover of all beautiful bodies, and he must think that this wild gaping after just one body is a small thing, and despise it.
>
> After this he must think that the beauty of people's souls is more valuable than the beauty of their bodies, so that if someone is decent in his soul, even though he is scarcely blooming in his body, our lover must be content to love and care for him and to seek to give birth to such ideas as will make young men better. The result is that our lover will be forced to gaze at the beauty of activities and laws and to see that all this is akin to itself, with the result that he will think that the beauty of bodies is a thing of no importance. After customs he must move on to various kinds of knowledge. The result is that he will see the beauty of knowledge and be looking mainly not at beauty in a single example—as a servant would who favored the beauty of a little boy or a man or a single custom (being a slave, of course, he's low and small-minded)—but the lover is turned to the great sea of beauty, and, gazing upon this, he gives birth to many gloriously beautiful ideas and theories, in unstinting love of wisdom, until, having grown and been strengthened there, he catches sight of such knowledge, and it is the knowledge of such beauty. (*Symposium* 210a4–e1)

I see the steps of the ladder as follows: (1) Love of one beautiful body; (2) Love of every beautiful body; (3) Love of beautiful souls; (4) Love of beautiful laws and customs; (5) Love of beautiful ideas and theories, and the beauty of knowledge in general; and (6) the knowledge of Beauty. Plato also refers to a vision of Beauty and not only knowledge:

> So when someone rises by these stages, through loving boys correctly, and begins to see this beauty, he has almost grasped his goal. This is what it is to go aright, or be led by another, into the mystery of Love: one goes always upwards for the sake of this Beauty, starting out from beautiful things and using them like rising stairs: from one body to two and from two to all beautiful bodies, then from beautiful bodies to beautiful customs, and from customs to learning beautiful things, and from these lessons he arrives in the end at this lesson, which is learning of this very Beauty, so that in the end he comes to know just what it is to be beautiful. (*Symposium* 211b5–d1)

Plotinus:[59]

> The man could reach ["the true region" which contains "the glory above" from V.9.1] who is by nature a lover and truly disposed to philosophy from the beginning, in travail over beauty, since he is a lover, not enduring the "beauty of body" but escaping from it up to the "beauties of soul, virtues and kinds of knowledge and ways of life and laws"; and again he ascends to the cause of the beauties in soul, and again to anything there may be beyond this, till he comes to the ultimate which is the first, which is beautiful of itself. When he has arrived there he ceases from his travail [*ōdinos*], but not before. (V.9.2.2–10; my brackets[60])

Plotinus not only demonstrates that he agrees with the basic rungs of Plato's Ladder of Love, but that it is the authentic philosopher who will be the one to make this ascent. In claiming that the First is the self-springing beauty, Plotinus implies that Beauty is the Good. I argue that, ultimately, Beauty is not identical with the Good for either philosopher.[61]

Thus, Plato and Plotinus both believe that the Ladder of Love is a good procedure for the lover of wisdom to use in order to gain knowledge of Beauty.

Love can be either an irrational desire pursuing enjoyment of bodily beauty or a manifestation of the desire for the Good

Plato: Plato discusses the irrational as well as the rational aspects of love in the *Phaedrus*. Here he defines love for bodily beauty as a strong irrational desire or passion:

> Now, as everyone plainly knows, love is some kind of desire; but we also know that even men who are not in love have a desire for what is beautiful. So how shall we distinguish between a man who is in love and one who is not? We must realize that each of us is ruled by two principles which we follow wherever they lead: one is our inborn desire for pleasures, the other is our acquired judgment that pursues what is best. Sometimes these two are in agreement; but there are times when they quarrel inside us, and then sometimes one of them gains control, sometimes the

> other. Now when judgment is in control and leads us by reasoning toward what is best, that sort of self-control is called "being in your right mind"; but when desire takes command in us and drags us without reasoning toward pleasure, then its command is known as "outrageousness." . . . The unreasoning desire that overpowers a person's considered impulse to do right and is driven to take pleasure in beauty, its force reinforced by its kindred desires for beauty in human bodies—this desire, all-conquering in its forceful drive, takes its name from the word for force (*rhōmē*) and is called *erōs*. (*Phaedrus* 237d3–8a2, b7–c4; adapted from Nehamas/Woodruff)

In short, if one is merely physically attracted to someone and this attraction overpowers one's Reason, then this is love. Plato then writes about the "wrong" lover who seeks maximum pleasure for himself and maximum damage to the beloved's property, body, and spirit (238e–41d). Plato denies that this account is accurate about real Love, since Love is a god (as claimed at 242d), and a divine being cannot be an evil thing, as that speech implied (242e–3a). Plato continues his account of love by describing a soul that has only recently been reincarnated and had shortly before been in closer contact with the Forms; when this soul gets excited by true physical beauty, and its wings (painfully) grow, it fails to care about anything else if it can only have its beloved (251a–2b), and this is an accurate account of love (252b–c). Later, Plato claims that there are four kinds of madness, and attributes the fourth and highest kind to be that of "Aphrodite and to Love, [and] we said that the madness of love is the best" (265b4–5), which is compatible with the irrational aspect of love.

After describing the lover, Plato moves on to describe the beloved, and states that he will "secure a consummation" (253c3), and "the stream Zeus named 'Desire' when he was in love with Ganymede begins to flow mightily in the lover and is partly absorbed by him, and when he is filled it overflows and runs away outside him" (255c1–4) and "is in love, but has no idea what he loves" (255d3).

Plato summarizes the benefits of being a lover:[62]

> These are the rewards you will have from a lover's friendship, my boy, and they are as great as divine gifts should be. A non-lover's companionship, on the other hand, is diluted by human self-control; all it pays are cheap, human dividends, and though the slavish attitude it engenders in a friend's soul is widely praised as virtue, it tosses the soul around for nine thousand years on the earth and leads it, mindless, beneath it.
>
> So now, dear Love, this is the best and most beautiful palinode we could offer as payment for our debt, especially in view of the rather poetical choice of words Phaedrus made me use. . . . If Phaedrus and I said anything that shocked you in our earlier speech, blame it on Lysias, who was its father, and put a stop to his making speeches of this sort; convert him to philosophy like his brother Polemarchus so that his lover here may no longer play both sides as he does now, but simply devote his life to Love through philosophical discussions. (*Phaedrus* 256e3–7a6, b1–6)

Here Plato urges us to live for Love in singleness of purpose—to philosophize (love wisdom)—with the aid of philosophical discourse, thus claiming that Love plays a role in fulfilling our desire for the Good. Love is of beauty and goodness, that we long to make the good and beautiful our own, and that these loves link up to our happiness (*Symposium* 204d5–7, e2–205a3). These passages also demonstrate that for Plato, Love certainly has a positive side and not merely an irrational side.

Plotinus: Plotinus confirms the heart of the thesis, that love can be both a noble pursuit of God and an irrational pursuit of bodily beauty:

> The soul then in her natural state is in love with God and wants to be united with him; it is like the noble love of a girl for her noble father. But when the soul has come into the world of becoming and is deceived, so to say, by the blandishments of her suitors, she changes, bereft of her father, to a mortal love and is shamed; but again she comes to hate her shames here below, and purifies herself of the things of this world and sets herself on the way to her father and fares well. And if anyone does not know this experience, let him think of it in terms of our loves here below, and what it is like to attain what one is most in love with, and that these earthly loves are mortal and harmful and loves only of images, and that they change because it was not what is really and truly loved nor our good nor what we seek. But there is our true love, with whom also we can be united, having a part in him and truly possessing him, not embracing him in the flesh from outside. (VI.9.9.33–46[63])

Moreover, Plotinus makes reference to the drunkenness of Resource (Love's father), implying that Love is not entirely rational.[64] Plotinus also picks up Plato's metaphor of the winged soul in several passages.[65]

Plotinus holds that Love can also be related to our desire for the Good:[66]

> If someone assumed that the origin of love was the longing for Beauty Itself which was there before in men's souls, and their recognition of it and kinship with it and unreasoned awareness that it is something of their own, he would hit, I think, on the truth about its cause. For the ugly is opposed to nature and to God. For nature when it creates looks towards Beauty, and it looks towards the definite, which is "in the column of the good"; but the indefinite is ugly and belongs to the other column. And nature has its origin from above, from the Good and, obviously, from Beauty. But if anyone delights in something and is akin to it, he has an affinity also with its images. (III.5.1.16–26; adapted from A.H. Armstrong[67])

By being a part of nature, the human soul looks to the Good, and the primal source of Love is a soul's tendency toward pure beauty.[68]

Rist[69] argues that, for Plotinus—and not for Plato—the love of Beauty and the love of the Good may not be compatible, and: "Love of Beauty may even prevent the aspirant to philosophy from attaining the Good." *Both* philosophers hold that Beauty is similar to but not identical to the Good, so we should not believe that Plotinus has a different view of love of Beauty or the Good. We also have indications from Plato's *Symposium* that one can indeed be stuck on the first rung of the Ladder of Love (witness too the lovers of sounds and sights in *Republic* V); for instance, love of procreation does not entail that one will move on to the next rung.

Second, Wallis[70] claims that Plotinus takes over Plato's love theme but with drastic tacit corrections; namely, (1) he abandons homosexual associations of Platonic Eros; and (2) he claims that heterosexual love is a falling-short of the best, and that love is more perfect when it does not aim at procreation. Re: (1), however, Plotinus does not ignore homosexual love—see, for example, III.5.1.50–5, where Plotinus argues that what these lovers lack is the failure to recognize where love was leading them, the impulse of generating, the right use of the image of beauty, or what absolute beauty is. These failures, as I see it, are equally ascribed to heterosexuals, and basically amount to the charge of not rising beyond the first rung of the Ladder of Love, a failing which is entirely Platonic. Re: (2), similarly, Plato does not proclaim that heterosexual love is the epitome of love, beyond which one need not progress, if one wishes to be a philosopher, and by his description of the Ladder of Love, he demonstrates that love is more perfect when it does not aim at procreation—it is more perfect when aimed at achieving a vision of Beauty Itself. Thus, these Plotinian statements are neither drastic nor corrections of Plato's view of love.

Plato and Plotinus believe that noble love is a love for Beauty, and love of bodily beauty is a reflection of Love and Beauty, but is irrational and can lead to unhappiness if practiced poorly.

In conclusion, both philosophers are of the same mind concerning Love's lineage; its being situated between ignorance and wisdom; love's desire to possess goodness and beauty in order to be happy; the Ladder of Love's method to know/see Beauty; and that Love can be either irrational, selfish, and bodily, or noble and a true manifestation of the Good.

3.4 On purification and reverence

The main agreements here are that purification of the soul is an important requirement for one to advance on the philosophical path: namely, to achieve knowledge of the Forms; and reverence and/or piety are important characteristics for us to possess.

Purification of the soul is an important requirement for one to advance on the philosophical path

Plato: Plato states that purification is a primary requirement for one's gaining knowledge of the Forms:

> While we live, we shall be closest to knowledge if we refrain as much as possible from association with the body and do not join with it more than we must, if we are not infected with its nature but purify ourselves from it until the god himself frees us. In this way we shall escape the contamination of the body's folly; we shall be likely to be in the company of people of the same kind, and by our own efforts we shall know all that is pure, which is presumably the truth, for it is not permitted to the impure to attain the pure. . . .

> The journey that is now ordered for me is full of good hope, as it is also for any other man who believes that his mind has been prepared and, as it were, purified.
>
> It certainly is, said Simmias.
>
> And does purification not turn out to be what we mentioned in our argument some time ago, namely, to separate the soul as far as possible from the body and accustom it to gather itself and collect itself out of every part of the body and to dwell by itself as far as it can both now and in the future, freed, as it were, from the bonds of the body?
>
> Certainly, he said. (*Phaedo* 67a2–b2, b10–d3[71])

The inference is clear: The body is impure and contaminated; the Forms are pure and uncontaminated; one's soul can either be focused on—and therefore become—impure or pure; if one wants to know the pure Forms, the soul should become pure. Purification is the separation of the soul from the body as much as possible, concentrating the soul itself upon itself. Plato and Plotinus both seem to reference meditation or something closely resembling it.

Plato states that there are two kinds of purifications: bodily and intellectual (*Sophist* 226e–7c), and that the best way in which to purify the body is gymnastics, the next best is a non-fatiguing surging motion (sailing, for instance), and lastly the purgative treatment of physicians—but only when necessary (*Timaeus* 89a–b).

Thus, purification is an important requirement for advancement toward knowledge (of the Good, presumably).

Plotinus: Plotinus says much about purification, but I will confirm the main claim made in the *Phaedo*, that withdrawing from the body to become pure in soul is necessary for knowing the Forms:[72]

> For, as was said in old times, temperance, and courage and every virtue, is a purification, and so is even wisdom itself. (I.6.6.1–3; adapted from A.H. Armstrong[73])

This shows that purification is equated with wisdom (and all virtues), which is effectively equivalent to one's knowing the Good or One for both philosophers. Further:

> So the soul when it is purified becomes form and formative power, altogether bodiless and intellectual and entirely belonging to the divine. (I.6.6.13–4[74])

This links the idea of a cleansed soul's being one that is wholly free of the body, which was stated in the *Phaedo*—the separation of all that is body from the soul. Lastly, Plotinus believes that purification is necessary for knowledge of the Forms and of the "best":[75]

> But if purification causes us to be in a state of knowledge of the best, then the sciences which lie within become apparent, the ones which really are sciences. For it is certainly not by running around outside that the soul "sees self-control and justice,"

> but itself by itself in its understanding of itself and what it formerly was, seeing them standing in itself like splendid statues all rusted with time which it has cleaned: as if gold had a soul, and knocked off all that was earthy in it; it was before in ignorance of itself, because it did not see the gold, but then, seeing itself isolated, it wondered at its worth, and thought that it needed no beauty brought in from outside, being supreme itself, if only one would leave it alone by itself. (IV.7.10.40–52[76])

Plotinus says that the soul should not run around outside of itself, but be in contact with itself, which is parallel to Plato's concentration of the soul itself by itself.

Confirming that Plotinus believes in bodily purification is difficult, because he focused almost exclusively on the purity of the soul; however, he does refer to the medical technique of purging:

> The cure of diseases make this clear too. With a vigorous motion of the bowels or the giving of a drug the illness goes through the downward passage and out, and it goes out too with blood-letting; and fasting also heals. Does the evil spirit starve, and does the drug make it waste away, and does it sometimes come out all at once, or stay inside? (II.9.14.21–5[77])

This parallel is admittedly weak, but note that both philosophers obviously believe that purification of the soul is much more important than purification of the body, since they both dictate that we should ignore the body and withdraw the soul from it as much as possible. Plotinus makes other Platonic claims concerning purification,[78] but I will now conclude.

Therefore, Plato and Plotinus both hold that purification is an important requirement for one's soul to advance on the philosophical path.

Reverence and piety are important characteristics for us to possess

Plato:[79] In the *Euthyphro*, Plato makes several claims about piety that Plotinus does not explicitly confirm: the gods love piety because it is pious (10a–1b), and piety is a part of justice but not the whole of justice[80] (11e–2d). However, there is no evidence in Plotinus that he would deny the first claim but in fact reason to believe that he would endorse it, given his acceptance of the existence of gods and Forms. As for the second claim, Plotinus believes that the pure soul is just (and thereby ruled by Reason) (I.2.5; cf. II.1.9), so we have reason to believe that, since a pure soul is a godlike soul for Plotinus, and a pure soul is just, piety is certainly at the very least involved in one's being just, or a part of what it means for one to be just.

Plato claims that we should show reverence to the most divine part of us, the soul (*Laws* V 726a6–8b2); and the citizens of Kallipolis should "avoid blasphemy, and to use reverent language whenever they sacrifice and offer up their pious prayers" (VII 821d2–4)[81] and not to "venture any impiety where gods are concerned" (X 888d2–3).[82]

Plotinus:[83] Interestingly, Plotinus most mentions reverence when he is arguing against the Gnostics in II.9: he apparently thought that their views were irreverent. Plotinus argues that one's recollection of Beauty and harmony of the Intellectual realm should grip one with a reverent awe:

> For how could there be a musician who sees the melody in the intelligible world and will not be stirred when he hears the melody in sensible sounds? Or how could there be anyone skilled in geometry and numbers who will not be pleased when he sees right relation, proportion and order with his eyes? For, indeed, even in pictures those who look at the works of art with their eyes do not see the same things in the same way, but when they recognize an imitation on the level of sense of someone who has a place in their thought they feel a kind of disturbance and come to a recollection of the truth; this is the experience from which passionate loves arise. But if someone who sees beauty excellently represented in a face is carried to that higher world, *will anyone be so sluggish in mind and so immovable that, when he sees all the beauties in the world of sense, all its good proportion and the mighty excellence of its order, and the splendor of form which is manifested in the stars, for all their remoteness, he will not thereupon think, seized with reverence, "What wonders, and from what a source?"* If he did not, he would neither have understood this world here nor seen that higher world. (II.9.16.39–56; emphasis added[84])

In the second passage, Plotinus upbraids the Gnostics: To compare the mind of any human to the mind of the well-ordered and intelligent "All"—universe—is impious:

> For providential care is much more of wholes than of parts, and the participation in God of that universal soul, too, is much greater. Its existence, and its intelligent existence, make this clear. For who of those who are so mindlessly high-minded in looking down on it is as well ordered or has as intelligent a mind as the All? The comparison is ridiculous and very much out of place; anyone who made it except for the sake of argument would not be able to avoid impiety. (II.9.16.30–6[85])

Lastly, Plotinus claims that virtues and qualities such as modesty and gravity should be reverenced (I.6.6); a seer of Beauty Itself must reverence It (I.6.7); and he declares that the *Enneads*' reader will view Plotinus' doctrine as cultivating reverence, if viewed as a whole (II.9.14). As for Plato's claims in the *Laws* that we should revere our souls, have reverent language in prayers, and beware of all impiety towards the gods, these statements are all obviously Plotinian, given what Plotinus state about the value of the soul, prayer, God and gods, and his recently reviewed upbraiding of the Gnostics.

To summarize, purification is an important requirement for knowledge and reverence and piety both play a significant role in Platonic and Plotinian ethics.

3.5 How to live

I will more precisely go through what Plato and Plotinus urge us to do in our lives, keeping in mind my earlier claims related to ethics.

Plotinus: Plotinus discusses how we should live and may seem a bit out of step with what Plato seems to say; I will argue however, that this quotation relates to us nothing that we have not already seen in Plato's view:

> In proportion as the soul goes towards the formless, since it is utterly unable to comprehend it because it is not delimited and, so to speak, stamped by a richly varied stamp, it slides away and is afraid that it may have nothing at all. Therefore it gets tired of this sort of thing, and often gladly comes down and falls away from all this, till it comes to the perceptible and rests there as if on solid ground; just as sight when it gets tired of small objects is glad to come upon big ones.
>
> But when the soul wants to see by itself, seeing only by being with it and being one by being one with it, it does not think it yet has what it seeks, because it is not different from what is being thought. But all the same this is what one must do if one is going to philosophize about the One.
>
> Since, then, that which we seek is one and we are considering the principle of all things, the Good and the First, one must not go far away from the things around the primary by falling down to the last things of all, but as one goes to the primary one must lift oneself up from the things of sense which are the last and lowest, and become freed from all evil since one is hastening to the Good, and ascend to the principle in oneself and become one from many, when one is going to behold the Principle and the One. Therefore one must become Intellect and entrust one's soul to and set it firmly under Intellect, that it may be awake to receive what that sees, and may by this Intellect behold the One, without adding any sense-perception or receiving anything from sense-perception into that Intellect, but beholding the most pure with the pure Intellect, and the primary part of Intellect. (VI.9.3.4–27; my paragraphs[86])

When Plotinus says that the soul can fear that it may have nothing at all as it goes towards the formless, I believe he is saying that the soul can fear uniting with the beyond being of the Good or One. When he discusses the fatigue and states that the soul wants to retreat to the region of sense, gladly coming down, this passage is perfectly parallel with Plato's description in the Cave Allegory, when he describes the pain of seeing the fire in the cave, and that the just-released prisoner would believe that the shadows were more real when asked questions about the passing objects (*Republic* VII 515c–d). In fact, Plato also discusses how pained the prisoner's eyes are once outside the Cave as well (515e–6a), which can be interpreted as alluding to the pain that Plotinus describes as fearing the nothingness of the beyond-being Good.

In the second paragraph, Plotinus requires that the soul is one by being one with the Good/First/One. Admittedly, Plotinus holds that the ultimate experience is a non-dual experience, where there is no distinguishable soul and One, but only one thing; I can find no parallel Platonic passage.[87] However, Plato implies in the Sun Simile, a significant passage, that the soul must be sunlike—good—in order to see the sun: the Good (*Republic* VI 508b; see also *Sophist* 254a), and the Good is interpretively equivalent to the One,[88] so this implies that the soul also must be as unified as possible in order to know the One. I can arrive at this conclusion from another route too;

namely that a just soul—like a just state—is one and has nothing to divide it (*Republic* V 462a2–c2) and so is well harmonized, which again implies that a soul fit to see or know the Good or One is unified.

In the third paragraph, Plotinus is urging us to ascend to behold the One or Good; we must recollect who and what we truly are and where we came from; become unified; become Intellect in order to see the One with our pure intellect, Reason; and we must not use our senses to have this vision.

First, Plato obviously agrees with the recollection command and that we must know who we are in order to progress towards knowledge. Second, we have just seen that Plato agrees with unifying oneself in partial fulfillment of the requirements of the ultimate experience. Third, Plato concurs that to know the Good, we should become like Reason—and that we are more our Reason as well as that Nous is the highest faculty in the Divided Line—by downplaying the influences of passions, love, desires, and appetites, which is what we take on in being incarnated. Fourth, Plato certainly agrees that we should not use our senses more than our reason in trying to arrive at the truth of something.[89]

Lastly, both Plato and Plotinus endorse the view that we should honor our soul above all else.[90]

I will show many parallels between the two philosophers on the urging that we should practice philosophy; possess virtue; be just; and be temperate.

The philosopher and practicing philosophy

Perhaps the most significant ethical injunction that Plato and Plotinus issue is for one to become a philosopher. Plotinus actually assumes that his reader *is* a philosopher, and infrequently even uses the word philosopher.

Anton provides an excellent starting point to this section:[91]

> Plotinus made Plato peripheral to his own philosophy, a move that justifies my saying that he was not a Platonist. A most serious consequence of Plotinus' stance is his novel casting of the role and function of *philosophia*.
>
> I will try to support my position by bringing up three fundamental items: Political Theory, Cosmology, and the recasting of the role of Nous, all comprising a radical outlook on the principles on which Plotinus built his metaphysics of hypostatic being.
>
> Plotinus' ethics of escape to contemplation leaves hardly any room for political *eros*. As one interpreter has put it, "Plotinus is Plato diminished," and in effect, "a Plato without politics."[92]

Thus, Anton holds that the main reason that Plotinus differs from Plato is in the role and function of philosophy; I deny that they differ on cosmology and Nous,[93] so the only issues remaining are the notion that Plotinus but not Plato has an "ethics of escape" (see ascetism below) and political theory (see the best rulers below).

Plato and Plotinus hold the following claims in common about philosophers; namely, philosophers: are the best and happiest people; are or attempt to be godlike; are the best rulers; have knowledge and virtue; contemplate the Forms; follow their Reason; love learning and truth; practice asceticism and withdraw from the body; experience the best pleasure; care the least for wealth and reputation; are rare; practice dialectic and the Method of Division; and practice pure (as opposed to merely applied) mathematics.

Philosophers are the best and happiest people

Plato:[94] Socrates discusses the aristocratic government, which is run by philosopher-kings:

> Shall we, then, hire a herald, or shall I myself announce that the son of Ariston has given as his verdict that the best, the most just, and the most happy is the most kingly, who rules like a king over himself, and that the worst, the most unjust, and the most wretched is the most tyrannical, who most tyrannizes himself and the city he rules?
>
> Let it be so announced. (*Republic* IX 580b8–c5[95])

Of course, if one is most kingly over oneself, one is also just and temperate, on Plato's view.

Plotinus: Plotinus holds with Plato that philosophers are the best and happiest:[96] the Sage—the wise person or the philosopher—is happy, possesses every good, and adverse fortune does not affect him:

> He is what he has, his own good. The Transcendent Good is Cause of the good in him; the fact that It is good is different from the fact that It is present to him. There is evidence for this in the fact that the man in this state does not seek for anything else; for what could he seek? Certainly not anything worse, and he has the best with him. The man who has a life like this has all he needs in life. If he is virtuous, he has all he needs for happiness and the acquisition of good; for there is no good that he has not got. What he seeks he seeks as a necessity, not for himself but for something that belongs to him; that is, he seeks it for the body which is joined to him; and even granting that this is a living body, it lives its own life and not the life which is that of the good man. He knows its needs, and gives it what he gives it without taking away anything from his own life. His happiness will not be reduced even when fortune goes against him; the good life is still there even so. When his friends and relations die he knows what death is—as those who die do also if they are virtuous. Even if the death of friends and relations causes grief, it does not grieve him but only that in him which has no intelligence, and he will not allow the distresses of this to move him. (I.4.4.18–36; adapted from A.H. Armstrong[97])

The quotation begins by stating that the *means* to happiness and goodness lie within the Sage, but further into the paragraph Plotinus states that the Sage actually *has* happiness, come what may.

Therefore, Plato and Plotinus agree that the philosopher is the best and happiest of all people.

Philosophers are or attempt to be godlike

Plato:

> But it is not possible, Theodorus, that evil should be destroyed—for there must always be something opposed to the good; nor is it possible that it should have its seat in heaven. But it must inevitably haunt human life, and prowl about this earth. That is why a man should make all haste to escape from earth to heaven; and escape means becoming as like God as possible; and a man becomes like God when he becomes just and pure, with understanding [*phronēseōs*]. (*Theaetetus* 176a5–b2; my brackets)

Plato believed that the godlike ones are philosophers per se: "The philosopher, by consorting with what is ordered and divine and despite all the slanders around that say otherwise, himself becomes as divine and ordered as a human being can." (*Republic* VI 500c9–d2)[98]

Plotinus: Plotinus argues not only that there are godlike men, but hyperbolically that we should strive to be God.[99] Plotinus describes a third way of life:[100]

> But there is a third kind of godlike men who by their greater power and the sharpness of their eyes as if by a special keen-sightedness see the glory above and are raised to it as if above the clouds and the mist of this lower world and remain there, overlooking all things here below and delighting in the true region which is their own, like a man who has come home after long wandering to his own well-ordered country. (V.9.1.16–21[101])

Plotinus claims that we should be "god," as opposed to become godlike: "There is no sin in anything of this sort for a man, but only right action. Our concern, though, is not to be sinless, but to be god" (I.2.6.1–3). There are, however, two other quotations that show us that Plotinus cannot be literally urging us to be God, versus godlike: "You must become first all godlike and beautiful if you intend to see God and beauty" (I.6.9.32–34; adapted from A.H. Armstrong). He connects the ideas of becoming godlike with seeing, not being God. Secondly:

> [The good man will] choose . . . the life of the gods: for it is to them, not to good men, that we are to be made like. Likeness to good men is the likeness of two pictures of the same subject to each other; but likeness to the gods is likeness to the model, a being of a different kind to ourselves. (I.2.7.26–30)

If our likeness must look to the gods, and theirs is of a different kind than to ourselves, then Plotinus cannot mean that we should literally be God.

Therefore, both philosophers believe that philosophers are or should become godlike as humanly possible.

Philosophers are the best rulers

This is a controversial issue because many commentators (including Anton, quoted above) claim that Plotinus is not at all interested in politics; this is one of the major differences cited in the English literature between these two thinkers.

Plato: Before laying out his regimen and educational plan for the rulers,[102] Plato famously tells us that philosophers are the best rulers[103] in his "third wave," while discussing features of his ideal state:

> Until philosophers rule as kings or those who are now called kings and leading men genuinely and adequately philosophize, that is, until political power and philosophy entirely coincide, while the many natures who at present pursue either one exclusively are forcibly prevented from doing so, cities will have no rest from evils, Glaucon, nor, I think, will the human race.... There can be no happiness, either public or private, in any other city. (*Republic* V 473c11–d6, e5[104])

Plotinus: It is more controversial to show that Plotinus is committed to philosophers making the best rulers.[105] Beginning with Theiler,[106] scholars have accused Plotinus of being a "Plato *dimidiatus*"—a Plato by half—because he ignores or does not pay attention to politics.[107] I adduce biographical evidence, a passage in the *Enneads*, and an argument from inference, given other claims I have shown thus far.

First, in his *Life of Plotinus*, Porphyry relates:

> The Emperor Gallienus and his wife Salonina greatly honored and venerated Plotinus. He tried to make full use of their friendship: there was said to have been in Campania a city of philosophers which had fallen into ruin; this he asked them to revive, and to present the surrounding territory to the city when they had founded it. Those who settled there were to live according to the laws of Plato, and it was to be called Platonopolis; and he undertook to move there with his companions. The philosopher would easily have gained his wish if some of the courtiers, moved by jealousy, spite, or some other such mean motive, had not prevented it.[108]

Thus, though several commentators have asked exactly what it is that Plotinus is committed to from this description,[109] Plotinus implicitly endorses the laws of Plato, which are the laws of the ideal state, so we can infer that he endorses the *Republic* model or something close to it; for we have seen that he endorses dialectic as Plato does and, as we'll see below, he endorses mathematical education for philosophers.[110]

Second, Plotinus claims that Minos may have been a philosopher-king, legislating on the basis of his experience of the One, and he mentions the possibility of Minos' not wishing to involve himself in civic matters:

> Perhaps also it was because Minos attained this kind of union [with the One] that he was said in the story to be"the familiar friend of Zeus," and it was in remembering this that he laid down laws in its image, being filled full of lawgiving by the divine touch. Or, also, he may think civic matters unworthy of him and want to remain always above; this is liable to happen to one who has seen much. (VI.9.7.23–8; my brackets)

I agree with O'Meara[111] that this passage is parallel to Plato's passages at *Minos* 319b–20b, *Laws* I 624a, and *Republic* VI 500d–e. I also agree that—generalizing from Plotinus' statement about Minos—philosopher-kings do not have to get involved in the state[112] and the founding of Platonopolis are not at odds with Plotinus' other-worldly philosophy.

Third, Plotinus believes philosophers are the best and happiest people. It is plausible to suggest, then, that the best people (the most just, temperate, courageous, pious, and knowledgeable) would be the best rulers.[113]

Therefore, Plato and Plotinus both hold that philosophers make the best rulers.

Philosophers have knowledge and virtue

Plato:[114]

> Should we, then, make these blind people our guardians or rather those who know each thing that is and who are not inferior to the others, either in experience or in any other part of virtue?
>
> It would be absurd to choose anyone but philosophers, if indeed they're not inferior in these ways, for the respect in which they are superior is pretty well the most important one. (*Republic* VI 484d5–10)

This statement is made in the context of arguing that the philosophers should be rulers, but claims that the philosophers should be chosen to rule precisely because they possess knowledge and virtue.

Plotinus: Plotinus obviously agrees with Plato on this point;[115] for instance, philosophers are awake and others are dreaming. Also, given that philosophers are happy according to Plotinus, they have to possess knowledge and be virtuous. Plotinus implies that the "nobly good man" (*spoudaios*) acts by Reason and has an active intellect:

> What, then, is the nobly good man? He is the man who acts by his better part. He would not have been a good man if he had the guardian spirit as a partner in his own activity. For intellect is active in the good man. He is, then, himself a spirit or on the level of a spirit, and his guardian spirit is God. (III.4.6.1–4)

Plotinus believes that philosophers have knowledge:

> The knowledge or touching of the Good is the greatest thing, and Plato says it is the "greatest study," not calling the looking at it a "study," but learning about it

> beforehand. We are taught about it by comparisons and negations and knowledge of the things which come from it and certain methods of ascent by degrees, but we are put on the way to it by purifications and virtues and adornings and by gaining footholds in the intelligible and settling ourselves firmly there and feasting on its contents. (VI.7.36.3–10; adapted from A.H. Armstrong[116])

Admittedly, Plotinus does not directly claim that *philosophers* have knowledge, but the inference is clear by his statements: "we are taught about it," his mention of one's contemplating oneself, and even more importantly, his agreement that happiness is a direct result of, or nothing other than, possessing knowledge/wisdom and virtue(s). As they both agree that philosophers are the best and happiest, they both agree that philosophers have knowledge and virtue.

Philosophers contemplate the Forms

Plato:

> Since those who are able to grasp what is always the same in all respects are philosophers, while those who are not able to do so and who wander among the many things that vary in every sort of way are not philosophers. (*Republic* VI 484b3–6[117])

Plotinus: I can confirm a similar view in Plotinus, taking "the contemplation of that which intellect contains" to be interpretively equivalent to the Forms:

> What, then, is each particular virtue when a man is in this state? Wisdom, theoretical and practical, consists in the contemplation of that which intellect contains; but intellect has it by immediate contact. (I.2.6.11–3[118])

"This state" refers to the person who makes the best of the powers of his real nature like Intellect, implying someone who knows the Forms and is truly virtuous. If philosophers are wise (or at least seeking wisdom) and virtuous, then they must be contemplating the Forms.

Philosophers follow their Reason

Plato:[119]

> This is how the soul of the philosopher would reason: it would not think that while philosophy must free it, it should while being freed surrender itself to pleasures and pains and imprison itself again, thus laboring in vain like Penelope at her web. The soul of the philosopher achieves a calm from such emotions; it follows reason and ever stays with it contemplating the true, the divine, which is not the object of opinion. Nurtured by this, it believes that one should live in this manner as long as one is alive and, after death, arrive at what is akin and of the same kind, and escape from human evils. (*Phaedo* 84a2–b3[120])

Plotinus:[121]

> For when the desiring part of the soul is moved, the mental image of its object comes like a perception announcing and informing us of the experience, and demanding that we should follow along with it and obtain the desired object for it; but our other part necessarily falls into perplexity, whether it goes along and obtains the object or resists. And the spirited part when it summons us to repel something does the same when it is moved, and the needs of the body and the passions make us have continually different opinions. Then there is ignorance of the [true] good, and the soul's not knowing what to say when it is dragged in every direction, and still other results from the mixture of all these. But is it actually our best part which has different opinions? No, perplexity and variety of opinions belong to the gathering [of our various parts and passions]: from our best part the right account of the matter is given to the common gathering, and is weak because it is in the mixture, not by its own nature. But it is as if in the great clamour of an assembly the best of the advisors does not prevail when he speaks, but the worse of those who clamour and shout, but he sits quietly unable to do anything, defeated by the clamour of the worse. And in the worst kind of man there is the common gathering and his human nature is composed of everything in the manner of a bad political constitution; in the middling man it is as it is in the city in which some good can prevail as the democratic constitution is not entirely out of control; but in the better kind of man the style of life is aristocratic; his human nature is already escaping from the common gathering and giving itself over to the better sort. But in the best man, the man who separates himself, the ruling principle is one, and the order comes from this to the rest. It is as if there was a double city, one above and one composed of the lower elements set in order by the powers above. (IV.4.17.11–35[122])

Plotinus states that the aristocratic life, the philosophical life, is one wherein desires and passions are in check; that is, this man of good counsel does not remain ineffectual and overwhelmed by desires and passions.

Thus, Plato and Plotinus each claim that the philosopher follows Reason in her deliberations and actions.

Philosophers love learning and the truth

Plato:

> The one who readily and willingly tries all kinds of learning, who turns gladly to learning and is insatiable for it, is rightly called a philosopher, isn't he? (*Republic* V 475c6–8)

Glaucon does answer that Socrates makes lovers of sounds and sights into philosophers by this criteria, but Socrates clarifies that philosophers truly learn about real existents and the truth, as opposed to those—the lovers of sounds and sights—who believe that beauty and justice are many (*Republic* V 475c–6b).

And:

> And who are the true philosophers?
>
> Those who love the sight of truth. (*Republic* V 475e3–4[123])

Plotinus:

> What else could calculation be but the effort to find intelligence and reason which is true and attains to the truly existent? For the man who calculates is like one who is playing the lyre to acquire the art of lyre-playing or who is praticing to acquire habitual proficiency, or in general like one who is learning in order to know. For the man who is calculating seeks to learn that which if someone already possesses, he is intelligent: so that intelligence is in one who has come to rest. The man who has been calculating is himself a witness to this; for when he finds what is needed, he stops calculating; and he comes to rest because he has entered into intelligence. (IV.4.12.5–13[124])

As Plotinus agrees with Plato that the philosopher (good man) uses his Reason, we can infer from that claim and the first sentence of this passage that a philosopher seeks the truth.

Philosophers practice asceticism and withdraw from the body

Plato:[125,126]

> The soul reasons best when none of these senses troubles it, neither hearing nor sight, nor pain nor pleasure, but when it is most by itself, taking leave of the body and as far as possible having no contact or association with it in its search for reality.
>
> That is so.
>
> And it is then that the soul of the philosopher most disdains the body, flees from it and seeks to be by itself?
>
> It appears so. (*Phaedo* 65c5–d3)

The philosopher is the one who best ignores and disdains the body, becoming independent and avoiding it as much as possible, with a view to attaining the truth.

Plotinus:[127]

> So we must "fly from here" and "separate" ourselves from what has been added to us, and not be the composite thing, the ensouled body in which the nature of body (which has some trace of soul) has the greater power, so that the common life belongs more to the body; for everything that pertains to this common life is bodily. But to the other soul, which is outside the body, belongs the ascent to the higher world, to the fair and divine which no one masters, but either makes use of

> it that he may be it and live by it, withdrawing himself; or else he is bereft of this higher soul and lives under destiny. (II.3.9.19–28)

Obviously when Plotinus refers to this task, he believes he is talking to philosophers. While we technically do not find the phrase "true philosopher" in Plotinus' work as in Plato's, Plotinus explains himself:

> For existing is not one thing and always existing another, just as a philosopher is not one thing and the true philosopher another, but because there was such a thing as putting on a pretense of philosophy, the addition of "true" was made. (III.7.6.29–32[128])

That said, Plato and Plotinus aver that (true) philosophers practice asceticism and withdraw from the body.

Philosophers experience the best pleasure

Plato: John Stuart Mill discusses competent judges in his *Utilitarianism* as those who have experienced both noble and vulgar pleasures.[129] Plato anticipated this kind of claim:

> Since there's a dispute between the different forms of pleasure and between the lives themselves, not about which way of living is finer or more shameful or better or worse, but about which is more pleasant and less painful, how are we to know which of them is speaking most truly? (*Republic* IX 581e6–2a2)

He then compares the life of the lover of money, honor, and wisdom, and states that the latter is the most experienced and therefore the most competent judge of true pleasure:

> The pleasure of studying the things that are cannot be tasted by anyone except a philosopher.
>
> Then, as far as experience goes, he is the finest judge of the three.
>
> By far. (*Republic* IX 582c7–d3)

Plotinus:

> When they demand to be shown what is pleasant in a life of this kind, they will not be requiring the presence of the pleasures of debauchees, or of bodily pleasures at all—these could not be there and would abolish happiness—or of violent emotions of pleasure—why should the good man have any?—but only those pleasures which accompany the presence of goods, pleasures not consisting in movements, which are not the results of any process: for the goods are there already, and the good man is present to himself; his pleasure and happiness are at rest. . . . If anyone looks for another kind of pleasure in life it is not the life of virtue he is looking for. (I.4.12.1–8, 10–2; adapted from A.H. Armstrong[130])

Plotinus argues that the Sage is the one who has experienced true pleasure of the Good, and is immovable regarding the remaining pleasures, and therefore would be the best judge of true pleasure.

Thus, Plato and Plotinus claim that the philosopher experiences true pleasure and is the best judge thereof.

Philosophers care the least for wealth and reputation

Plato:

> Now, it is clear to everyone that the part with which we learn is always wholly straining to know where the truth lies and that, of the three parts, it cares least for money and reputation.
>
> By far the least.
>
> Then wouldn't it be appropriate for us to call it learning-loving and philosophical?
>
> Of course. (*Republic* IX 581b5–11[131])

Plotinus:

> But if anyone objects to wealth and poverty and the fact that all have not an equal share in things of this kind, first, he is ignorant that the good and wise man does not look for equality in these things, and does not think that people who have acquired a great deal of them have any kind of advantage, or that those who hold power have the advantage over private persons; he leaves concern of this kind to others. He has learnt that there are two kinds of life here below, one for the good and wise and one for the mass of men, that for the good and wise being directed to the highest point and the upper region, and that for the more human sort being of two kinds again; one is mindful of virtue and has a share in some sort of good, but the common crowd is there, so to speak, to do manual work to provide for the necessities of the better sort. (II.9.9.1–11[132])

The Sage cares not a whit about wealth and poverty, and Plotinus implies that the Sage is not concerned with his reputation.[133]

Therefore, Plato and Plotinus believe that the philosopher is not concerned with wealth and reputation.

Philosophers are rare

Plato and Plotinus claim that the philosopher, who believes in the existence of the Forms and then who actually has the experience of knowing the Good, is a rarity. Certainly this claim should not be construed as stating that almost no one loves wisdom or really wants to know anything. In the poetic words of More: "As it was said in the ancient mysteries: many carry the wand, the visionaries are few."[134]

Plato:[135]

> ... only a few natures possess all the qualities ["courage, high-mindedness, ease in learning, and a good memory" at 490c10–1] that we just now said were essential to becoming a complete philosopher and that seldom occur naturally among human beings. Or don't you think so?
>
> I certainly do. (*Republic* VI 491a8–b3; my brackets[136])

Thus Plato believes that the perfect philosopher is rare.

Plotinus: Plotinus agrees[137]:

> Shut your eyes, and change to and wake another way of seeing, which everyone has but few use.[138] (I.6.8.25–7)

Thus, both Plato and Plotinus believe that the (true) philosopher is rare.

Philosophers practice the Method of Division

Plato and Plotinus affirm that a philosopher practices the Method of Division, which is to intellectually gather Forms into their natural groups and comprehend them. Dialectic is related to this practice, and is sometimes known as Collection and Division.

Plato:

> But because of [many sophisticated people's] not being accustomed to carrying on their investigations by dividing according to real classes, the people in question throw these things together at once, despite the degree of difference between them, thinking them alike—and then again they also do the opposite of this by dividing other things not according to parts, when the rule is that when one perceives first the community between the members of a group of many things, one should not desist until one sees in it all those differences that are located in classes, and conversely, with the various unlikenesses, when they are seen in multitudes, one should be incapable of pulling a face and stopping before one has penned all the related things within one likeness and actually surrounded them in some real class. (*Statesman* 285a4–b6; my brackets[139])

Admittedly, Plato does not use the word philosopher, but he is clearly denigrating the "sophisticated people" who suppose "themselves to be expressing something clever" because they do not practice the Method of Division, where the inference is clear that the philosopher is the person who does pursue this practice.

Plotinus: Plotinus relates dialectic to the Method of Division:

> What then is dialectic, which the former kinds of men as well as philosophers must be given? It is the science which can speak about everything in a reasoned and

> orderly way, and say what it is and how it differs from other things and what it has in common with those among which it is and where each of these stands, and if it really is what it is, and how many really existing things there are, and again how many non-existing things, different from real beings. It discusses good and not good, and the things that are classed under good and its opposite, and what is the eternal and what not eternal, with certain knowledge about everything and not mere opinion. It stops wandering about the world of sense and settles down in the world of intellect, and there it occupies itself, casting off falsehood and feeding the soul in what *Plato calls "the plain of truth," using his method of division to distinguish the Forms, and to determine the essential nature of each thing, and to find the primary kinds, and weaving together by the intellect all that issues from these primary kinds*, till it has traversed the whole intelligible world; then it resolves again the structure of that world into its parts, and comes back to its starting-point; and then, keeping quiet (for it is quiet insofar as it is present There) it busies itself no more, but contemplates, having arrived at unity. It leaves what is called logical activity, about propositions and syllogisms, to another art, as it might leave knowing how to write. Some of the matter of logic it considers necessary, as a preliminary, but it makes itself the judge of this, as of everything else, and considers some of it useful and some superfluous, and belonging to the discipline which wants it. (I.3.4.1–23; my emphasis[140])

Admittedly, Plotinus does not claim that the philosopher practices the Method of Division, but it is difficult to imagine to whom else he could be referring, especially given that he states that dialectic is the best part of philosophy.

Therefore, Plotinus holds that philosophers practice the Method of Division, and Plato agrees.

Philosophers practice pure (as opposed to merely applied) mathematics

We find evidence that Plato and Plotinus both hold that philosophers study mathematics using pure units, not necessarily with a view to completing a practical project (construction or trading), but only for the sake of knowing the numbers and their relations.

Plato: Plato makes the claim that philosophers practice pure or theoretical mathematics[141] in several places; here is one such passage:

> Don't we have to agree, first, that the arithmetic of the many is one thing, and the philosopher's arithmetic is quite another?
>
> How could anyone distinguish these two kinds of arithmetic?
>
> The difference is by no means small, Protarchus. First these are those who compute sums of quite unequal units, such as two armies or two herds of cattle, regardless whether they are tiny or huge. But then there are the others who would not follow their example, unless it were guaranteed that none of those infinitely many units differed in the least from any of the others.

> You explain very well the notable difference among those who make numbers their concern, so it stands to reason that there are those two difference kinds of arithmetic. (*Philebus* 56d4–e6[142])

Plato does state that the guardians will be practical as well as theoretical, having to know arithmetic for the sake of winning wars, for instance, but he also emphasizes the ability of pure math to be able to convert the soul from becoming to being, and that the guardians will pursue arithmetic for the sake of knowledge (*Republic* VII 525b11–d3).

Plotinus: Plotinus confirms this use of mathematics,[143] first by confirming that there is pure versus applied math:

> But we suppose that geometry and arithmetic are double, and should rank one kind of them here in this qualitative, but the works of the soul itself directed to the intelligible should be ranked there. And indeed Plato says the same about music and astronomy. (VI.3.16.20–4[144])

Plotinus notes the similarity between geometry, arithmetic, music and astronomy's effects on the soul. The second passage prescribes the study of math by the philosopher:

> But the philosopher—he is the one who is by nature ready to respond and "winged," we may say, and in no need of separation like the others. He has begun to move to the higher world, and is only at a loss for someone to show him the way. So he must be shown and set free, with his own good will, he who has long been free by nature. He must be given mathematical studies to train him in philosophical thought and accustom him to firm confidence in the existence of the immaterial—he will take to them easily, being naturally disposed to learning; he is by nature virtuous, and must be brought to perfect his virtues, and after his mathematical studies instructed in dialectic, and made a complete dialectician. (I.3.3.1–10)

So Plotinus agrees with Plato that a philosopher should primarily use math as a way to convert his soul to the immaterial's existence and perfect his virtue.

Plato and Plotinus hold thirteen major claims about philosophy and philosophers, averring that philosophy is the best study in which people can engage, and that philosophers: are the best and happiest people; are or attempt to be godlike; are the best rulers; have knowledge and virtue; contemplate the Forms; follow their Reason; love learning and truth; practice asceticism and withdraw from the body; experience the best pleasure; care the least for wealth and reputation; are rare; practice dialectic and the Method of Division; and practice pure (as opposed to merely applied) mathematics.

Virtue

Plato and Plotinus agree that: virtue is one; to be truly virtuous, one must possess full virtue (possess all virtues); virtue is ultimately knowledge; virtue is a good condition of the soul; virtue is rare; philosophic virtue is more valuable than civic virtue; virtue is godlike; the virtuous are happy; and we should pursue virtue.

Virtue is one

Plato and Plotinus each claim that virtue is ultimately one thing, even though they each refer to different virtues (justice, temperance, courage, piety); additionally, from another perspective, virtue is one in the sense of being a Form.

Plato: Plato claims in the *Protagoras* (unanimously taken to be an earlier dialogue) and in the *Laws* (his latest dialogue) that virtue is one.[145] In the *Protagoras*, Socrates and Protagoras discuss this issue at 329b–34c and 349a–61c. They agree that virtue is one, analogous to the parts of a face, and not analogous to parts of gold:

> Is virtue a single thing, with justice and temperance and piety its parts, or are the things I have just listed all names for a single entity? This is what still intrigues me.
>
> "This is an easy question to answer, Socrates," he replied. "Virtue is a single entity, and the things you are asking about are its parts."
>
> Parts as in the parts of a face: mouth, nose, eyes, and ears? Or parts as in the parts of gold, where there is no difference, except for size, between parts or between the parts and the whole?
>
> In the former sense, I would think, Socrates: as the parts of the face are to the whole face. (*Protagoras* 329c7–e2[146])

Note that virtue is said to be a single whole, but there are other names for its parts; namely, justice, self-control, and holiness (others are mentioned in later passages). Protagoras actually gives up his position and states that, while the virtue parts of justice, temperance, piety, and wisdom closely resemble each other, courage is different, since many men possess courage but none of the other four virtues (349d–e). Socrates, however, spends the rest of the dialogue convincing Protagoras that he is not correct in this latter claim, since courage is the knowledge of what is and is not to be feared, and so is closely related to the other virtues as well. Ultimately, Socrates identifies wisdom with courage (360d), so that the dialogue concludes with virtue's being one in some sense.

Interestingly, Plato makes the same kind of argument in the *Laws*, which implies—assuming the principle of charity—that Plato did not significantly change his mind on this point. The passage begins with the Athenian:

> Well, when we said there were four species [*eidē*] of virtue, obviously the very fact that there were four meant that each had to be thought of as somehow distinct from the others.
>
> Surely.
>
> Yet in fact we call them all by a single name. We say courage is virtue, wisdom is virtue, and the other two similarly, on the ground that really they are not several things but just one—virtue.

> Very true.
>
> It's not hard to explain how these two "virtues" and the rest *differ* from each other and how each has acquired a different name. The real problem is this: why, precisely, have we described both of them (as well as the others) by this *common* term "virtue"?
>
> What do you mean?
>
> My point is perfectly easy to explain. Shall we let one of us ask the questions, and the other answer them?
>
> Again, what do you mean?
>
> Here's the question for you to put to me: "Why is it that after calling both by the single term 'virtue,' in the next breath we speak of two 'virtues,' courage and wisdom?" I'll tell you why. One of them, courage, copes with fear, and is found in wild animals as well as human beings, notably in the characters of very young children. The soul, you see, becomes courageous by a purely natural process, without the aid of reason. By contrast, in this absence of reason a wise and sensible soul is out of the question. That is true now, has always been true, and always will be true; the two processes are fundamentally different. (*Laws* XII 963c5–4a8)

The Athenian introduces the puzzle that we say that there are four types of virtue, but really they are just one thing, virtue. Courage might exist in a wild animal or an infant as a purely natural process attained without reason, but a soul cannot be wise without this reason.[147] He then states that a consummate guardian will need to be able to advance from regarding the many to the recognition of the one (XII 965b7–10), and then gives a constraint for the guardians:

> We have to compel the guardians of our divine foundation to get an exact idea of the common element in all the four virtues—that factor which, though single, is to be found in courage, temperance, justice and wisdom, and thus in our view deserves the general title "virtue." (*Laws* XII 965c9–d3; adapted from Saunders[148])

This implies that there is indeed a single common element that entitles courage, temperance, justice, and wisdom to be called one thing, virtue.[149]

Plotinus:

> So we shall be right in saying that the soul becomes ugly by mixture and dilution and inclination towards the body and matter. This is the soul's ugliness, not being pure and unmixed, like gold, but full of earthiness; if anyone takes the earthy stuff away the gold is left, and is beautiful, when it is singled out from other things and is alone by itself. In the same way the soul too, when it is separated from the lusts which it has through the body with which it consorted too much, and freed from its other affections, purged of what it gets from being embodied, when it abides alone has put away all the ugliness which came from the other nature. (I.6.5.48–58)

> For, as was said in old times, temperance, and courage and every virtue, is a purification, and so is even wisdom itself. (I.6.6.1–3; adapted from A.H. Armstrong)

Plotinus clearly states that virtue involves purification of the soul, stripping away bodily concerns, and concludes that every virtue—temperance, courage, wisdom, justice, and the rest—is a kind of purification. Of course, Plotinus uses the terms "every virtue" here, and he also refers to the need for us to have the "virtues" elsewhere.[150] One might then read Plotinus as differing with Plato that virtue is one. By itself, however, Plotinus' reference to "virtues" should not concern us, since Plato clearly refers to the "virtues" in many places as well,[151] despite his arguments that virtue is one. Plotinus also refers to singular perfected virtue that arises from one's possessing lower, natural virtues beforehand:

> Can one be a wise man and a dialectician without these lower virtues? It would not happen; they must either precede or grow along with wisdom. One might perhaps have natural virtues, from which the perfect ones develop with the coming of wisdom. So wisdom comes after the natural virtue, and then perfects the character; or rather when the natural virtues exist both increase and come to perfection together: as the one progresses it perfects the other; for in general natural virtue is imperfect both in vision and character, and the principles from which we derive them are the most important thing both in natural virtue and wisdom. (I.3.6.16–24)

Moreover, Plotinus and Plato agree that being a good person entails that one knows or has had a vision of the Good or the One.[152]

In addition, I can infer that virtue is one, but in another sense: Virtue is a Form according to both philosophers[153] and they also both agree that each Form is one; thus Virtue is one.[154]

Therefore, for a consistent overall reading of Plato and Plotinus, we should interpret them as holding that virtue is one.

Full virtue

The idea of full virtue is to delineate between those who are, for instance, relatively courageous but intemperate and unjust on one hand, and those who possess all virtues or who are perfectly virtuous on the other.[155]

Plato:

> Such a man ["those who display conspicuous gallantry in *total* war are very much more courageous" at 630a2–3], in our view, who fights in a tougher war, is far superior to the other—to just about the same degree as the combination of justice, self-control and good judgment, reinforced by courage, is superior to courage alone. In civil war a man will never prove sound and loyal *unless he has every virtue* [*aneu sympasēs aretēs*]; but in the war Tyrtaeus mentions there are hordes of mercenaries who are ready to dig their heels in and die fighting, most of whom,

> apart from a very small minority, are reckless and insolent rogues, and just about the most witless people you could find. (*Laws* I 630a7–b8; emphasis and brackets added[156])

Full virtue is related to virtue's being one, because if virtue is truly one, an agent cannot truly possess courage, for example, and not possess justice, wisdom, and the rest. Thus we must read Plato, when he uses words such as "far superior" and "sound and loyal," to imply that the best person will possess every virtue, and not merely be strong in certain areas and weak in others.

Thus, Plato believes that we must possess full virtue in order to be truly virtuous.

Plotinus:[157] Plotinus claims that the purification of the soul implies the production of all the virtues, and if any are lacking, then none of them is perfect:

> These virtues in the soul, too, imply one another reciprocally, in the same way as the exemplars (so to call them) There in intellect which are prior to virtue. . . . In the soul, sight directed towards intellect is wisdom, theoretical and practical; these are virtues belonging to soul; for it is not itself they, as is the case There, and the others follow in the same way. And if all virtues are purifications, in the sense that they are the result of a completed process of purification, that process must produce them all, otherwise, [if they are not all present], no single one of them will be perfect. Whoever has the greater virtues must necessarily have the lesser ones potentially, but it is not necessary for the possessor of the lesser virtues to have the greater ones. Here, then, we have described the life of the good man in its principal features. (I.2.7.1–13[158])

We can be sure that Plotinus is referring to the human soul as opposed to the World-Soul, because he clearly states that he is describing the life of the good man in the last sentence.

Therefore, Plato and Plotinus both think that full or perfect virtue is possible, and more preferable than a life wherein one is strong in one virtue but lacking others.

Virtue and knowledge

Plato: Plato states that virtue is knowledge—in the *Protagoras*, *Charmides*, and *Laches*, according to Irwin,[159] and additionally in the *Republic*, *Theaetetus*, and *Laws*, according to me[160]—and that virtue is *not* knowledge but instead a gift from the gods (in the *Meno*).[161] I aim to resolve this apparent contradiction.

Socrates argues that since there are no teachers of virtue, it is not knowledge—though virtue *is* good and useful:[162]

> As goodness does not come by nature, we inquired next whether it could be taught.
>
> Yes.
>
> We thought it could be taught, if it was knowledge?
>
> Yes.
>
> And that it was knowledge if it could be taught?

> Quite so.
>
> And that if there were teachers of it, it could be taught, but if there were not, it was not teachable?
>
> That is so.
>
> And then we agreed that there were no teachers of it?
>
> We did.
>
> So we agreed that it was neither teachable nor knowledge?
>
> Quite so.
>
> But we certainly agree that virtue is a good thing?
>
> Yes.
>
> And that which guides correctly is both useful and good?
>
> Certainly. (*Meno* 98d7–e13[163])

Further, Socrates states that virtue is a gift of the gods:

> If we were right in the way in which we spoke and investigated in this whole discussion, virtue would be neither an inborn quality nor taught, but comes to those who possess it as a gift from the gods which is not accompanied by understanding, unless there is someone among our statesmen who can make another into a statesman. If there were one, he could be said to be among the living as Homer said Tiresias was among the dead, namely, that "he alone retained his wits while the others flitted about like shadows."[164] In the same manner such a man would, as far as virtue is concerned, here also be the only true reality compared, as it were, with shadows.
>
> I think that is an excellent way to put it, Socrates.
>
> It follows from this reasoning, Meno, that virtue appears to be present in those of us who may possess it as a gift from the gods. We shall have clear knowledge of this when, before we investigate how it comes to be present in men, we first try to find out what virtue in itself is. (*Meno* 99e4–100b6)

Note the disclaimer at the end of the passage: we will not know virtue's true nature by only understanding where it comes from. Of course Plato holds elsewhere that wisdom is virtue, that the wise person is the best and happiest person, and that one's possessing wisdom implies that one is just, temperate, and courageous.

I submit that when Meno and Socrates in the *Meno* agree that virtue is a gift from the gods, Plato is emphasizing the nature of coming to know the Form of the Good: It is not as if someone can teach anyone else to come to know the Form of the Good, in the sense that such a knower could teach a non-knower and guarantee the result of the non-knower's coming to have knowledge of the Form of the Good.[165] Plato does not claim that every incarnated human *will* see or know the Form of the Good. Rather, after one has prepared oneself as much as possible, knowing the Form of the Good seems rather to be left up to chance in a sense. Here I follow A.E. Taylor (*mutatis mutandis* of course, since he was referring to Plotinus):

> We find Plotinus refusing to take any part in the revived Hellenic worship which carried some of his friends off their feet. He refused to visit the temples on the

> ground that "it is for the gods to come to me, not for me to go to them." [Porphyry, *Life*, ch. 10.] That is, the true temple of God is a soul made fit for His habitation. When a man has done all that is in him to make his own mind fit for the heavenly visitation, it must be left for Deity to choose when and how He will come to His temple; it is not for us to control His movements.[166]

As for Plato, *Republic* 517b–c tells us that we need the knowledge of the Form of the Good if we are to act wisely in private and public, so there *is* a connection between virtue and knowledge. On one hand, Plato claims that virtue is not teachable, because one cannot guarantee that a specific training—though dialectic would be the best—will in fact bring about knowledge of the Good.[167] On the other hand, it is correct to claim that if one possesses virtue, one also has knowledge, because to possess virtue fully, one must know the Good.

Thus, Plato ultimately believes that virtue is knowledge.[168]

Plotinus:[169] Though he does not explicitly discuss whether virtue is teachable,[170] Plotinus addresses the connection between knowledge and virtue, alluding to the *Phaedrus* and *Republic* X's sea god Glaucus passages:

> But if purification causes us to be in a state of knowledge of the best, then the sciences which lie within become apparent, the ones which really are sciences. For it is certainly not by running around outside that the soul "sees self-control and justice," but itself by itself in its understanding of itself and what it formerly was, seeing them standing in itself like splendid statues all rusted with time which it has cleaned: as if gold had a soul, and knocked off all that was earthy in it; it was before in ignorance of itself, because it did not see the gold, but then, seeing itself isolated, it wondered at its worth, and thought that it needed no beauty brought in from outside, being supreme itself, if only one would leave it alone by itself. (IV.7.10.40–52)

Plotinus says *if* the purification leads to knowledge—which is consistent with Plato's notion that one cannot guarantee that if one is a "good person" (a requirement for the ultimate experience)—then one will know or see the Good. Plotinus states (especially with the help of the "purified gold" metaphor) that self-knowledge leads to understanding of morality and right conduct.

Plotinus also claims that virtue is not the highest Good or Beauty: "We said that virtue was not Absolute Beauty or Absolute Good because Absolute Beauty and Absolute Good are prior to it and transcend it; it is good and beautiful by some kind of participation" (I.8.13.9–12). This is entirely consistent with Plato's view, given that Plato also argues that the Good is the source of everything else that is good, as well as of all Beings/Forms, of which Virtue is one.

Lastly, I agree with A.E. Taylor regarding Plotinus and his refusal to participate in Hellenic worship, that though one might prepare oneself thoroughly (via practicing philosophy, purifying oneself, practicing dialectic), one is not guaranteed to know the Good.[171]

Therefore, Plato and Plotinus agree that virtue is connected to knowledge in the sense that if one has knowledge, one is virtuous; however, virtue is not something that a knower can simply tell to another, or train someone else in some way that will necessarily lead to one's either being virtuous or gaining knowledge.

Virtue is a good condition of the soul

Plato:

> Virtue seems, then, to be a kind of health, fine condition, and well-being of the soul, while vice is disease, shameful condition, and weakness.
>
> That's true.
>
> And don't fine ways of living lead one to the possession of virtue, shameful ones to vice?
>
> Necessarily. (*Republic* IV 444d11–e6[172])

Plotinus: Plotinus states that harmony (analogous to Plato's justice of the soul) and virtue are phases of the soul:

> First we must explain about virtue and vice, what happens at any time when vice is said to be present; for we assert that one must "take away," as if there was some evil in the soul, and "put in" virtue, and set the soul in order and produce beauty in it instead of the ugliness which was there before. Now if we say that "virtue is harmony" and vice lack of harmony, should we be expressing an opinion that accords with the views of the ancients, and would the statement contribute something of no small value to our investigation? For if the natural harmony of the parts of the soul with each other is virtue, and their disharmony, vice, then there would be nothing brought in from outside, or from another source, but each part would enter into the harmony just as it is, or would not enter in, and remain in disharmony, because it was the sort of thing it was; just as dancers dance, and sing in accord with each other, even if it is not [always] the same ones who sing, and [sometimes] one sings when the others do not, and each sings in his own way, for they must not only sing together but each one, as they sing together, must also sing his own part beautifully by his own personal art of music; so there, too, in the soul there is a harmony when each part does what is proper to it. (III.6.2.1–18[173])

So virtue is a harmony of the soul, and as such is a good condition of the soul, for Plotinus and Plato.

Virtue is rare

Plato: One of Plato's claims occurs in the *Phaedo*: "The very good and the very wicked are both quite rare, and that most men are between those extremes" (90a1–2),[174] and this "is in fact true" (89e8–90a1).

Plotinus: Plotinus affirms this view in a similar way: "The fact is that man has the middle place between gods and beasts, and inclines now one way, now the other, and some men become like gods and others like beasts, and some, the majority, are in between" (III.2.8.9–11).[175]

Philosophic virtue versus civic virtue

Civic virtues are the virtues that people who obey the law and do not cause any trouble have, but according to both philosophers, these people have not practiced dialectic and do not know the Good: civic virtue is inferior to philosophic virtue.

Plato: Plato makes his degradation of civic virtue[176] first known in the *Phaedo*:

> The happiest of these, who will also have the best destination, are those who have practiced *popular and social virtue*, which they call moderation and justice and which was developed by habit and practice, without philosophy or understanding?
>
> How are they the happiest?
>
> Because is it likely that they will again join a social and gentle group, either of bees or wasps or ants, and then again the same kind of human group, and so be moderate men.
>
> That is likely.
>
> No one may join the company of the gods who has not practiced philosophy and is not completely pure when he departs from life, no one but the lover of learning. (*Phaedo* 82a11–c1; my emphasis[177])

To be certain, Plato certainly lauds those who practice civic virtue and thinks they will have good lives (which are happy in some sense), but he thinks more highly of the philosophers, who practice virtue with the help of philosophy.

Plotinus:[178]

> Plato, when he speaks of "likeness" as a "flight to God" from existence here below, and does not call the virtues which come into play in civic life just "virtues," but adds the qualification "civic," and elsewhere calls all the virtues "purifications," makes clear that he postulates two kinds of virtues and does not regard the civic ones as producing likeness. (I.2.3.5–10[179])

All of this is consistent with what we read in Plato, where Plotinus is referring to *Theaetetus* 176a–b to make his point. Plotinus confirms that philosophic virtue is of a higher order than civic virtue:

> Perhaps the possessor of the virtues will know them, and how much he can get from them, and will act according to some of them as circumstances require. But when he reaches higher principles and different measures he will act according to these. For instance, he will not make self-control consist in that former observance

> of measure and limit, but will altogether separate himself, as far as possible, from his lower nature and will not live the life of the good man which civic virtue requires. He will leave that behind, and choose another, the life of the gods: for it is to them, not to good men, that we are to be made like. Likeness to good men is the likeness of two pictures of the same subject to each other; but likeness to the gods is likeness to the model, a being of a different kind to ourselves. (I.2.7.19–30[180])

Thus, Plotinus agrees with Plato that although civic virtue is certainly commendable, philosophic virtue is even more godlike and therefore superior.

Virtue is godlike

Plato: Plotinus mentions *Theaetetus* 176a–d often,[181] which contains the claim that to be just is to be godlike, and to know this is to be virtuous:[182]

> In God there is no sort of wrong whatsoever; he is supremely just, and the thing most like him is the man who has become as just as it lies in human nature to be. And it is here that we see whether a man is truly able, or truly a weakling and a nonentity; for it is the realization of this that is genuine wisdom and goodness, while the failure to realize it is manifest folly and wickedness. (*Theaetetus* 176b8–c5[183])

Thus Plato believes that being just (as God is) and realizing justice is genuine wisdom and goodness, implying that being virtuous is godlike.

Plotinus:[184]

> Since it is here that evils are, and "they must necessarily haunt this region," and the soul wants to escape from evils, we must escape from here. What, then, is this escape? "Being made like god," Plato says. And we become godlike "if we become righteous and holy with the help of wisdom," and are altogether in virtue. If then it is virtue which makes us like, it presumably makes us like a being possessing virtue. Then what god would that be? Would it be the one that appears to be particularly characterized by the possession of virtue, that is, the soul of the universe and its ruling principle, in which there is a wonderful wisdom? It is reasonable to suppose that we should become like this principle, as we are here in its universe. (I.2.1.1–10[185])

Therefore, Plotinus is in agreement with Plato that to be virtuous is to be godlike.

The virtuous are happy

Plato:[186]

> What we want when we choose between lives is not a predominance of pain: we have chosen as the pleasanter life the one where pain is the weaker element. And so

> we can say that the self-controlled, the wise and the courageous, experience pleasure and pain with less intensity and on a smaller and more restricted scale than the profligate, the fool and the coward. The first category beats the second on the score of pleasure, while the second beats the other when it comes to pain. The courageous man does better than the coward, the wise man than the fool; so that, life for life, the former kind—the temperate, the courageous, the wise and the healthy—is pleasanter than the cowardly, the foolish, the licentious and the unhealthy.
>
> To sum up, the life of physical fitness, and spiritual virtue too, is not only pleasanter than the life of depravity but superior in other ways as well: it makes for beauty, an upright posture, efficiency and a good reputation, so that if a man lives a life like that it will make his whole existence infinitely happier than his opposite number's. (Laws V 734c1–e2; adapted from Saunders)

The temperate, wise, courageous, just, virtuous life is thus unreservedly happier than the opposite life for Plato.

Plotinus: Plotinus discusses the Ladder of Love and states that virtue is required to reach the First Principle, which entails the end of suffering:

> What, then, is this region? And how could one reach it? The man could reach ["the true region" which contains "the glory above" from V.9.1] who is by nature a lover and truly disposed to philosophy from the beginning, in travail over beauty, since he is a lover, not enduring the "beauty of body" but escaping from it up to the "beauties of soul, virtues and kinds of knowledge and ways of life and laws"; and again he ascends to the cause of the beauties in soul, and again to anything there may be beyond this, till he comes to the ultimate which is the first, which is beautiful of itself. When he has arrived there he ceases from his travail, but not before. (V.9.2.1–10; my brackets)

Plotinus (and Plato) hold that knowledge of the Good causes virtue, and that virtue is a direct result of happiness;[187] we may therefore safely conclude that Plotinus and Plato both believe that the virtuous are happy.

We should pursue virtue

Plato: Socrates states at his trial that he has done nothing in his life with the Athenians but exhort them to give attention to virtue and the perfection of their souls, and not to be concerned with money, reputation, and/or honor (*Apology* 29d7–30b4). There is nothing that Plato writes after the *Apology* that conflicts with Socrates' exhortation. For instance, even in the *Laws*, Plato writes:

> Body must possess virtue in all its completeness, which means above all that it will *not* take erratic aim at one target after another but keep its eye on one single target and shoot all its arrows at that.
>
> Certainly. (*Laws* XII 962d2–6[188])

Plotinus:

> Here the greatest, the ultimate contest is set before our souls; all our toil and trouble is for this, not to be left without a share in the best of visions. The man who attains this is blessed in seeing that "blessed sight," and he who fails to attain it has failed utterly. A man has not failed if he fails to win beauty of colors or bodies, or power or office or kingship even, but if he fails to win this and only this. For this he should give up the attainment of kingship and of rule over all earth and sea and sky, if only by leaving and overlooking them he can turn to That and see. (I.6.7.30–9[189])

Admittedly, this passage does not contain the word virtue, but by implication from other claims—the vision of the Good implies that one is virtuous, and we should become inwardly beautiful so that we can experience true Beauty (I.6.7)—I can be assured of my inference that Plotinus is urging us toward the virtuous life. This passage also confirms Plotinus' agreement with Socrates' exhortation not to be concerned with honor or reputation, but to have the ultimate vision.[190]

Both philosophers hold these nine statements to be true about virtue: virtue is ultimately one, though there are different names for different aspects of virtue; to be truly virtuous, one must possess full virtue; virtue is ultimately related to knowledge but is not itself knowledge; virtue is a good condition of the soul; possession of virtue is rare; philosophic virtue is more valuable than civic virtue; virtue is godlike; the virtuous are happy; and we should pursue virtue.

Justice and being just

As justice is part of virtue for both philosophers,[191] I will not review that aspect of justice here. I will focus instead on the following seven characteristics of justice and the just person:

(1) Justice is a Form;
(2) Divine and earthly providence is just;
(3) The just are godlike;
(4) Justice is a well ordering of the soul, where one obeys Reason;
(5) We should be just;
(6) It is just for an offender to be punished; and
(7) So-called bad things (poverty and disease) are good for the just person.

Justice is a Form

Plato:

> Do we say that there is such a thing as the Just itself, or not?
> We do say so, by Zeus.
> And the Beautiful, and the Good?
> Of course.

And have you ever seen any of these things with your eyes?
In no way, he said. (*Phaedo* 65d4–10[192])

Assuming that Beauty and Good are Forms, Justice is equated with them. Plato also claims that justice is just[193] and analyzes those words.[194]

Plotinus:[195]

> Since, then, it is the primary living being, and for this reason the Absolute Living Being, and is Intellect and substance (*ousia*), real substance, and we claim that it contains all living things and the whole of number, and the Absolutely Just and Beautiful and all other such things—we speak in a different way of Absolute Man and Absolute Number and Absolute Justice. (VI.6.8.1–5; adapted from A.H. Armstrong[196])

Plotinus holds with Plato that things that are just, are so by Justice (VI.6.14).

Divine and earthly providence is just

Plato: Platonic evidence can be inferred from various claims concerning the gods and their relation to humans. For instance, Plato states that the gods are just (implied at *Laws* X 907b1–4), that humans are playthings of the gods,[197] that we should play our role well (*Laws* VII 803c6–8), and that punishment in the afterlife is necessary and justified, all of which imply that whatever happens to us is something that the gods have justly planned for us so we should at least stoically deal with it.

Plotinus:[198] First, it is just for us to be seen as actors in a play, with changing roles as dictated by the "author" or God:

> Just as the actors here ["in human plays" from III.2.17.28–9] get their parts and their costumes, the saffron robes and the rags, so the soul, too, itself gets its fortunes, and not by random chance; these fortunes, too, are according to the rational principle; and by fitting these into the pattern it becomes in tune itself and puts itself into its proper place in the play and the universal rational pattern; then it makes its actions sound out, we may say, and everything else that a soul might produce according to its character, like a song. And as the sound of the voice and the gestures of the actor are beautiful or ugly as he makes them, and either adorn the poet's creation further, as one might think, or by adding the badness of the actor's own voice, do not make the play other than what it was, but the actor makes a grotesque exhibition of himself, and the author of the play sends him off in deserved disgrace, behaving in this like a good judge of acting, but promotes the good actor to higher rank. (III.2.17.35–47; my brackets[199])

For Plotinus it is perfectly just for the dramatist (that is, God or the gods) to give different roles to the actors (us).

For argument's sake, let us assume that earthly providence includes whether it is just for moral weaklings (who are physically strong) to triumph over the physically weak (but financially strong). Plotinus argues that it is just for bad men to rule by the weakness of the ruled, in successive treatises:

> But the wicked rule by the cowardice of the ruled; for this is just, and the opposite is not. (III.2.8.50–2)

> Providence ought not to exist in such a way as to make us nothing. If everything was providence and nothing but providence, then providence would not exist; for what would it have to provide for? There would be nothing but the divine. (III.2.9.1–4)

The context of these quotations is one where Plotinus has mentioned a gang of morally lax, buff boys who take the food and clothes from morally lax, wimpy people, and says that this situation is nothing other than a joke (III.2.8.16–21). Plotinus' analysis immediately follows:

> Or would it not be right for even the lawgiver to allow them to suffer this as a penalty for their laziness and luxury, these boys, who, though they were assigned gymnasiums, because of laziness and soft and slack living allowed themselves to become fattened lambs, the prey of wolves? (III.2.8.21–6; adapted from A.H. Armstrong)

Thus, Plotinus believes it is just for moral weaklings (who are physically strong) to triumph over the physically weak (but financially strong).

Plato: Plato seems to agree, and even to have used the fattened sheep metaphor first, in the *Republic*. Socrates asks Adeimantus:

> Don't you think that one boxer who has had the best possible training could easily fight two rich and fat non-boxers? (*Republic* IV 422b6–8)

Adeimantus questions this but thinks it might be possible. Socrates suggests that the guardians make a proposal to another city as follows:

> What if they sent envoys to another city and told them the following truth: "We have no use for gold or silver, and it isn't lawful for us to possess them, so join us in this war, and you can take the property of those who oppose us for yourselves." Do you think that anyone hearing this would choose to fight hard, lean dogs, rather than to join them in fighting fat and tender sheep? (*Republic* IV 422d1–7)

Plato implies that whatever happens is a matter of one's training, just as Plotinus states.

Therefore, both thinkers hold that divine and earthly providence are just.

The just are godlike

It stands to reason that if Plato and Plotinus state that the gods are just, then they will agree that just persons are godlike.

Plato:[200]

> In God there is no sort of wrong whatsoever; he is supremely just, and the thing most like him is the man who has become as just as it lies in human nature to be. And it is here that we see whether a man is truly able, or truly a weakling and a nonentity; for it is the realization of this that is genuine wisdom and goodness, while the failure to realize it is manifest folly and wickedness. (*Theaetetus* 176b8–c5[201])

Plotinus: Plotinus explicitly supports this very point:

> Since it is here that evils are, and "they must necessarily haunt this region," and the soul wants to escape from evils, we must escape from here. What, then, is this escape? "Being made like god," Plato says. And we become godlike "if we become righteous and holy with the help of wisdom," and are altogether in virtue. (I.2.1.1–5[202])

Therefore, I have shown that Plato and Plotinus both believe that being just is to be godlike.

Justice is a well ordering of the soul, where one obeys Reason

Plato and Plotinus both assert that justice is a kind of good ordering of the soul, where Appetite and Spirit do not overwhelm but are instead controlled by one's Reason. They also put this concept in another way; namely that justice occurs when each part (of the soul or of the city) does its own work.

Plato: Plato believes that justice is a well ordering of the soul, where the just person obeys her Reason—her "philosophic part":[203]

> Therefore, when the entire soul follows the philosophic part, and there is no civil war in it, each part of it does its own work exclusively and is just, and in particular it enjoys its own pleasures, the best and truest pleasures possible for it.
>
> Absolutely. (*Republic* IX 586e4–7a2[204,205])

Plato also claims that justice is exclusively doing one's own work,[206] and that if justice is present in a soul, then that soul is temperate as well (temperance implies justice),[207] which is consistent with Plato's claim that if one is truly virtuous, one possesses all virtues.

Thus, Plato believes that Justice is a soul's well ordering, where Reason is obeyed.

Plotinus: First, I can verify that Plotinus believes that a just soul is one where Reason rules the soul:

> Since the soul is evil when it is thoroughly mixed with the body and shares its experiences and has all the same opinions, it will be good and possess virtue when it no longer has the same opinions but acts alone—this is intelligence and wisdom—and does not share the body's experiences—this is self-control—and is not afraid of departing from the body—this is courage—and *is ruled by reason and intellect, without opposition—and this is justice.* One would not be wrong in calling this state of the soul likeness to God, in which its activity is intellectual, and it is free in this way from bodily affections. (I.2.3.11–21; adapted from A.H. Armstrong; emphasis added[208])

Plotinus further agrees with Plato that it is good for one to perform one's own work, equating this with virtue: when each part performs its proper function, this is a harmony:[209]

> Now if we say that "virtue is harmony" and vice lack of harmony, should we be expressing an opinion that accords with the views of the ancients, and would the statement contribute something of no small value to our investigation? For if the natural harmony of the parts of the soul with each other is virtue, and their disharmony, vice, then there would be nothing brought in from outside, or from another source, but each part would enter into the harmony just as it is, or would not enter in, and remain in disharmony, because it was the sort of thing it was; *just as dancers dance, and sing in accord with each other, even if it is not [always] the same ones who sing, and* [sometimes] *one sings when the others do not, and each sings in his own way, for they must not only sing together but each one, as they sing together, must also sing his own part beautifully by his own personal art of music; so there, too, in the soul there is a harmony when each part does what is proper to it.* (III.6.2.5–18; emphasis added[210])

Thus, Plotinus believes with Plato that it is virtuous (and by implication just) for each faculty of the soul to perform its appropriate part.

Therefore, both philosophers declare that justice is a well ordering of the soul, where each faculty performs its function well, and obeys Reason.

We should be just

Plato: Plato makes several strong statements in the dialogues urging us to be just, but let us examine this quotation from the *Republic*:

> Each of us must neglect all other subjects and be most concerned to seek out and learn those that will enable him to distinguish the good life from the bad and always to make the best choice possible in every situation. He should think over all the things we have mentioned and how they jointly and severally determine what

> the virtuous life is like. That way he will know what the good and bad effects of beauty are when it is mixed with wealth, poverty, and a particular state of the soul. He will know the effects of high or low birth, private life or ruling office, physical strength or weakness, ease or difficulty in learning, and all the things that are either naturally part of the soul or are acquired, and he will know what they achieve when mixed with one another. And from all this he will be able, by considering the nature of the soul, to reason out which life is better and which worse and to choose accordingly, calling a life worse if it leads the soul to become more unjust, better if it leads the soul to become more just, and ignoring everything else: We have seen that this is the best way to choose, whether in life or death. (*Republic* X 618b7–e4[211])

Plato adds that this subject with which we must "be most concerned": namely, pursuing knowledge and justice is the "way that a human being becomes happiest" (619a7–b1).

Plotinus: Plotinus urges us to be godlike, and in order to be godlike, we must be just (I.2.1); this is merely a rehashing of Plato's *Theaetetus* 176a passage, but he also indirectly tells us that we should pursue the vision of beauties beyond (rather than the beauties of sense), one of which is the face of Justice:

> But about the beauties beyond, which it is no more the part of sense to see, but the soul sees them and speaks of them without instruments—we must go up to them and contemplate them and leave sense to stay down below. Just as in the case of the beauties of sense it is impossible for those who have not seen them or grasped their beauty—those born blind, for instance—to speak about them, in the same way only those can speak about the beauty of ways of life who have accepted the beauty of ways of life and kinds of knowledge and everything else of the sort; and people cannot speak about the splendor of virtue who have never even imagined how fair is the face of Justice and Temperance. (I.6.4.1–11; adapted from A.H. Armstrong)

It is just for an offender to be punished

Plato: Plato, for instance, has Socrates state:

> Now, wasn't paying what's due getting rid of the worst thing there is, corruption?
>
> It was.
>
> Yes, because such justice makes people self-controlled, I take it, and more just. It proves to be a treatment against corruption.
>
> Yes. (*Gorgias* 478d4–7[212])

Plotinus:[213]

> Since there are many places for each as well [as many bodies], the difference between them must come from the disposition of the soul, and must come

> also from the justice in the nature of things. For no one can ever evade what he ought to suffer for his unrighteous doings: for the divine law is inescapable and has in itself together with the judgment already pronounced its execution. He too who is to suffer punishment is carried unknowing to what he has to suffer; on his unsteady course he is tossed about everywhere in his wanderings, and in the end, as if utterly weary, by his very efforts at resistance he falls into the place which suits him, having that which he did not will for his punishment as a result of the course which he willed. But it is stated in the law how much and how long he must suffer, and again there come together the release from punishment and the ability to escape up from these regions by the power of the harmony which holds the universe together. (IV.3.24.6–21[214])

Therefore, both philosophers advance the view that it is just for offenders to be punished.

So-called bad things (poverty and disease) are good for the just person

Plato and Plotinus make several interesting, perhaps even shocking, statements concerning the just person. They hold that for the just person, even if what most people would consider to be bad fortune (poverty, sickness, bad reputation) happens, these conditions will not turn out to be bad, but good.

Plato:

> And won't we also agree that everything that comes to someone who is loved by gods, insofar as it comes from the gods themselves, is the best possible, unless it is the inevitable punishment for some mistake he made in a former life?
>
> Certainly.
>
> Then we must suppose that the same is true of a just person who falls into poverty or disease or some other apparent evil, namely, that this will end well for him, either during his lifetime or afterwards, for the gods never neglect anyone who eagerly wishes to become just and who makes himself as much like a god as a human can by adopting a virtuous way of life. (*Republic* X 612e8–3b1[215])

So because the gods watch over just and virtuous persons, and apparent evils are no threat to their happiness in this life or thereafter, they have nothing that can truly harm them.

Plotinus: Plotinus states that if the sufferer of wrong-doing is a good person (and the good person is a just person for Plotinus), then the issue will be to his gain:

> And the injustice which one man does to another is certainly an injustice from the point of view of the doer, and the man who perpetrates it is not free from guilt, but as contained in the universal order it is not unjust in that order, or in relation to the sufferer, but it was ordained that he should so suffer. But *if the sufferer is a good man, this will turn out for his good.* For one must not think that the order is godless or

unjust, but that it is accurate in the distribution of what is appropriate, but it keeps its reasons hidden and gives grounds for blame to those who do not know them. (IV.3.16.17–25; emphasis added[216])

We can also make the inference in the following way: First, Plato and Plotinus clearly agree that the knower of the One or Good is happy, wise, just, and temperate; so if she is unhealthy and has no money, it will not decrease the goodness of her life; likewise, if she is wealthy and healthy, it will not increase the goodness of her life. After all, happiness is a state or a disposition for both philosophers, and, unlike Aristotle, Plato, and Plotinus do not hold that happiness depends on external goods, so their presence or absence makes no difference to the happy person.

Thus, both philosophers believe that justice is a Form, divine (and earthly providence) is just, the just are godlike, justice is a well ordering of the soul, where the just person obeys Reason; we should be just; it is just for the offender to be punished, and things popularly thought to be bad are good for the just person.

Temperance/moderation/self-mastery

Plato and Plotinus claim that temperance is a mastering of oneself, which is essentially not being overcome by passions and pleasures, that temperance is self-knowledge, and the temperate are happy.

Temperance is a mastering of oneself; that is, not being overcome by passions and pleasures

Plato and Plotinus advance the view that temperance is mastering oneself, by which they denote one's (Reason) not being overcome by passions and pleasures.

Plato: Plato discusses temperance in many dialogues, most notably in the *Charmides*, *Protagoras*, *Gorgias*, *Phaedo*, *Republic*, and *Laws*.

In the *Gorgias*, for instance, Callicles has just asked Socrates what he means by his question (are the leaders rulers in relation to themselves, or their subjects?), and Socrates answers:

> I mean each individual ruling himself. Or is there no need at all for him to rule himself, but only to rule others?
>
> What do you mean, rule himself?
>
> Nothing very subtle. Just what the many mean: being temperate and master of oneself, ruling the pleasures and appetites within oneself. (*Gorgias* 491d7–e1; adapted from Zeyl)

Temperance deals with pleasures and appetites, and not letting them rule over a person—presumably over one's Reason. Plato makes essentially the same claim—temperance is one's not being carried away by one's desires—but then adds that when one is temperate, one is actually *indifferent* toward pleasures, not merely their master:

> And the quality of temperance which even the majority call by that name, that is, not to get swept off one's feet by one's passions, but to treat them with disdain and orderliness, is this not suited only to those who most of all despise the body and live the life of philosophy?
>
> Necessarily so, he said. (*Phaedo* 68c8–d1; adapted from Grube[217])

Plato also infrequently associates temperance with one's being in control of one's passions.[218] Plato discusses the absurdity of the phrase "master of himself":

> Temperance is surely a kind of order, the mastery of certain kinds of pleasures and desires. People indicate as much when they use the phrase "self-control" and other similar phrases. I don't know just what they mean by them, but they are, so to speak, like tracks or clues that moderation has left behind in language. Isn't that so?
>
> Absolutely.
>
> Yet isn't the expression "self-control" ridiculous? The stronger self that does the controlling is the same as the weaker self that gets controlled, so that only one person is referred to in all such expressions.
>
> Of course.
>
> Nonetheless, the expression is apparently trying to indicate that, in the soul of that very person, there is a better part and a worse one and that, whenever the naturally better part is in control of the worse, this is expressed by saying that the person is self-controlled or master of himself. At any rate, one praises someone by calling him self-controlled. But when, on the other hand, the smaller and better part is overpowered by the larger, because of bad upbringing or bad company, this is called being self-defeated or licentious and is a reproach.
>
> Appropriately so. (*Republic* IV 430e6–1b3; adapted from Grube/Reeve)

Plato says that the phrase "master of himself" is absurd because it implies that one person is actually two—the master and the mastered—which in turn implies that if Socrates is temperate, then Socrates is one or unified, and not two or dual. Moreover, though, Plato holds that temperance implies that the better part (Reason) is governing a worse part (either Appetite or Spirit).[219] Lastly and not surprisingly, Plato states that the victory over self is the primal and subtlest victory in the *Laws*.[220]

Plotinus:[221] First, Plotinus believes that temperance is self-mastery over pleasures and agrees with Plato that temperance implies one's indifference toward pleasures:

> For what can true temperance be except not keeping company with bodily pleasures, but avoiding them as impure and belonging to something impure? (I.6.6.6–8; adapted from A.H. Armstrong)

Actually, Plotinus says the truly temperate person will not take any part in bodily pleasures, but Plato agrees with this as well.[222]

Second, Plotinus agrees with Plato that self-mastery implies a unity as opposed to a duality of oneself:

For, again, it has been let go into self-mastery in that it is what is primarily related to substance. That, then, which has made substance free, which is clearly of a nature to liberate and can be called liberator—to what could it be a slave, if it is even in any way permitted to utter this word? To its own substance? But this substance gets its freedom from it and comes after it, and it is not in possession of substance. If then there is an active actuality in him, and we are going to locate him himself in the active actuality, he would not because of this be something else than himself and not himself master of himself, he from whom the active actuality comes, because active actuality and he himself are not different. (VI.8.12.16–25[223])

Plotinus also agrees with Plato that temperance can constitute one's being in control of one's passions.[224] Both philosophers chiefly seem to think of temperance as involving mastery over pleasures and desires, but they each also mention being master of oneself over one's passions. This agreement might be entailed by, for instance, Plato's claim that Spirit is usually an ally with Reason. (*Republic* IV 440e)

Temperance is self-knowledge

According to each philosopher, if one has knowledge of the Good, then one is (fully) virtuous, which implies that one is just, temperate, courageous, pious, and so on, and that one would know oneself.

Plato:[225] Socrates asks whether self-knowledge is a difficult thing, which few are able to attain (*Alcibiades* I 129a2–10), and he agrees with Alcibiades that self-knowledge is wisdom (133c4–d7).

Plato also discusses self-knowledge in the *Charmides*, where it is proposed by Charmides but not ultimately agreed upon that self-knowledge is temperance (164d–5b). Socrates asks: "Is it any more possible to know what one knows and does not know? We did say, I think, that knowing oneself and being temperate consisted in this? … It is not this point … on which I am confused, that whenever someone possesses this thing which knows itself he will know himself' (169d6–e7).[226]

Lastly, Plato ties not knowing oneself with ignorance in general:

> [Ignorance] is, in sum, a kind of vice that derives its name from a special disposition; it is, among all the vices, the one with a character that stands in direct opposition to the one recommended by the famous inscription in Delphi.
>
> You mean the one that says "Know thyself," Socrates?
>
> I do. The opposite recommendation would obviously be that we do not know ourselves at all.
>
> No doubt. (*Philebus* 48c6–d3)

He also implies that knowledge of ourselves is possible and necessary for happiness:

> We would prefer to live side by side with that best kind of knowledge, the kind that understands not only all other things but also each one of us, as far as that is possible. (*Philebus* 63c1–3)

Thus, Plato believes that temperance is self-knowledge.

Plotinus:[227] As Plato did before him, Plotinus connects self-knowledge with (the opposite of) ignorance:

> Since also "Know yourself" is said to those who because of their selves' multiplicity have the business of counting themselves up and learning that they do not know all of the number and kind of things they are, or do not know any one of them, not what their ruling principle is or by what they are themselves. (VI.7.41.22–5[228])

Not only does Plotinus connect self-knowledge with wisdom, as Plato did; he also connects self-knowledge with beauty:

> For when we ourselves are beautiful, it is by belonging to ourselves, but we are ugly when we change to another nature: when we know ourselves we are beautiful, but ugly when we are ignorant of ourselves. (V.8.13.19–22)

Therefore, Plato and Plotinus both believe that temperance is self-knowledge, value self-knowledge, and believe it to be wisdom (or the lack of self-ignorance).

The temperate are happy

Since this issue is uncontroversial, I can briefly state without argument that both philosophers hold that the temperate are happy.[229] This seems reasonable, given what Plato and Plotinus write about true happiness' being a matter of one's having knowledge of the Good, and in turn one's being virtuous.

Both thinkers believe that temperance is self-mastery, where one is not overcome by one's pleasures (and passions), temperance is self-knowledge, and the temperate are happy.

Therefore, to have the best life, we should become philosophers and practice asceticism and dialectic in order to be virtuous, just, and temperate.

3.6 How not to live: On the way in which the soul errs

Both Plato and Plotinus describe ways in which we should not live, describing some of the diseases of the soul: the nature of vice (injustice, intemperance, and so on) and its effects (unhappiness, and its ability to corrupt positive qualities); ignorance (either the lack of knowledge or wisdom); paying attention to one's honor, possessions, body, food, sex, or money more than virtue and/or knowledge; allowing emotions or appetites to rule reason when reason should in fact be in charge; impiety; and attachment to the self or over-concern for the body.

Note that both philosophers agree that suicide is not to be chosen in general,[230] except when it is futile to keep oneself alive, such as the use of extraordinary means in medical care.[231] Second, they agree that we should not take mortal life too seriously.[232]

Vice

Plato and Plotinus agree on three main claims about the nature of vice: vice is a corrupt condition of the soul, caused by ignorance and/or a lack of virtue (injustice, intemperance, impiety, and so on); being vicious leads to one's unhappiness; and positive qualities may be corrupted or misused by the vicious soul.

Vice is a corrupt condition of the soul (a vicious soul is ignorant, seeks bodily pleasure, and lacks virtue)

I will assume that if ignorance is a lack of the knowledge of the Good, and if one is ignorant, then it is highly likely—if not necessary—that one will be unjust, intemperate, impious, or cowardly, at least to some degree, if not fully. Moreover, if one is unjust and intemperate, for instance, then one would probably pursue bodily pleasures or overly indulge one's emotions. Lastly, I will assume that if one is vicious, one is bad or evil.

Plato: Glaucon states, and Socrates agrees, that injustice, intemperance, cowardice and ignorance make the soul evil:[233]

> Well, what about the soul? Isn't there something that makes it bad?
>
> Certainly, all the things we were mentioning: Injustice, licentiousness, cowardice, and ignorance. (*Republic* X 609b9–c1; adapted from Grube/Reeve)

Plato describes the bad soul as teeming with evils, marred by its communion with the body in a metaphor about the sea god Glaucus (which Plotinus makes as well):

> Yet our recent argument and others as well compel us to believe that the soul *is* immortal. But to see the soul as it is in truth, we must not study it as it is while it is maimed by its association with the body and other evils—which is what we were doing earlier—but as it is in its pure state, that's how we should study the soul, thoroughly and by means of logical reasoning. . . . But the condition in which we've studied it is like that of the sea god Glaucus, whose primary nature can't easily be made out by those who catch glimpses of him. Some of the original parts have been broken off, others have been crushed, and his whole body has been maimed by the waves and by the shells, seaweeds, and stones that have attached themselves to him, so that he looks more like a wild animal than his natural self. The soul, too, is in a similar condition when we study it, beset by many evils. . . .
>
> We must realize what it would become if it followed this longing with its whole being, and if the resulting effort lifted it out of the sea in which it now dwells, and if the many stones and shells (those which have grown all over it in a wild, earthy, and stony profusion because it feasts at those so-called happy feastings on earth) were hammered off it. . . . But we've already given a decent account, I think, of what its condition is and what parts it has when it is immersed in human life.
>
> We certainly have. (*Republic* X 611b9–d7, 611e3–2a3, 612a5–7)

Plato describes the bad soul as one whose wings have failed:

> All soul [*psychē pasa*] looks after all that lacks a soul, and patrols all of heaven, taking different shapes at different times. So long as its wings are in perfect condition it flies high, and the entire universe is its dominion; but a soul that sheds its wings wanders until it lights on something solid, where it settles and takes on an earthly body, which then, owing to the power of this soul, seems to move itself. The whole combination of soul and body is called a living thing, or animal, and has the designation "mortal" as well. (*Phaedrus* 246b6–c6)

Plato also discusses souls that are in poor condition:

> Don't we see that there's dissension in the souls of people in poor condition, between beliefs and desires, anger and pleasures, reason and pains, and all of those things with each other?
>
> Absolutely. (*Sophist* 228b2–5[234])

In a bad person, the soul's elements (Reason, Spirit, and Appetite) are opposed to one another, implied by what Plato states about the just soul.

Plotinus: Plotinus makes three claims: Ignorance is the main cause of vice; an "ugly" soul—which I take to be equivalent to a vicious soul—is teeming with conflicts (as in Plato's sea god Glaucus passage in *Republic* X);[235] bad souls have failed wings; and the soul's elements of Reason, Spirit and Appetite do not work together in the bad or vicious soul.

First, then, Plotinus claims that ignorance is the main cause of vice:

> Perhaps one might say that the vice of the reasoning part was unintelligence [*anoian*], and unintelligence in the negative sense, and would not be asserting the presence of anything. But when false opinions are there in the soul (and this is what most of all produces vice), how will one be able to assert that they have not come in and that this part of the soul has not in this way become different? (III.6.2.22–5; my brackets[236])

Second, Plotinus claims that an ugly soul is dissolute, unrighteous, teeming with lusts, torn by discord, beset by fears, pleasure-seeking, and that this is a foreign bane added to the soul:

> Suppose, then, an ugly soul, dissolute and unjust, full of all lusts, and all disturbance, sunk in fears by its cowardice and jealousies by its pettiness, thinking mean and mortal thoughts as far as it thinks at all, altogether distorted, loving impure pleasures, living a life which consists of bodily sensations and finding delight in its ugliness. Shall we not say that its ugliness came to it as a "beauty" brought in from outside, injuring it and making it impure and "mixed with a great deal of evil," with its life and perceptions no longer pure, but by the admixture of evil living a dim life and diluted

> with a great deal of death, no longer seeing what a soul ought to see, no longer left in peace in itself because it keeps on being dragged out, and down, and to the dark? Impure, I think, and dragged in every direction towards the objects of sense, with a great deal of bodily stuff mixed into it, consorting much with matter and receiving a form other than its own it has changed by a mixture which makes it worse. (I.6.5.25–43[237])

This passage is entirely parallel with Plato's view, since it mentions internal discord, desires and emotions as being additions to the soul as opposed to being part of its essential nature, and the marring of the soul in its delight with bodily taints.

Third, Plotinus believes that what Plato referred to as "mortal souls," namely human, incarnated souls (and animal and plant souls), have failed in maintaining their wings: "For what it is here and among the things of this world is a falling away and an exile and a 'shedding of wings'" (VI.9.9.22–4).[238,239]

Fourth, Plotinus holds that in a vicious soul, Reason is not in charge, and there is conflict between the three main parts of the soul:

> It is like when in an assembly the elders of the people sit in quiet consideration, and the disorderly populace, demanding food and complaining of other sufferings, throws the whole assembly into an ugly tumult. Now if people like this keep quiet and a speech from a sensible man gets through to them, the multitude settles to a decent order and the worse has not gained the mastery; but if not, the worse is master and the better keeps quiet, because the tumultuous mob could not receive the word from above, and this is the vice of city and assembly. But this is also the vice of man; he too has in himself a populace of pleasures and lusts and fears, which gain the mastery when a man of this kind surrenders himself to a populace of this kind. (VI.4.15.23–35[240])

Plotinus' use of the "Assembly Elders" metaphor is not only indicative of the evil state and council, but of the evil/vicious man as well.

As for the number of vicious human souls, Plotinus says there aren't many truly vicious souls, as there are not many virtuous souls, but that the majority fall somewhere in between (III.2.8; cf. III.3.4).

Lastly, Plotinus claims that the soul cannot descend to utter nothingness, even if it is evil:

> For the nature of the soul will certainly not arrive at absolute non-existence, but when it goes down it will arrive at evil and in this way at non-existence, not at absolute non-existence. (VI.9.11.36–8)

Of course, this Plotinian claim is parallel with *Republic* X 609a–11a, where Plato argues that the soul is immortal, and nothing, including injustice, intemperance, cowardice, or ignorance, can destroy the soul.

Therefore, I have confirmed that Plotinus looks at vice in the same way as Plato.

Being vicious leads to unhappiness

Plato:[241]

> My friend, there are two patterns set up in reality. One is divine and supremely happy; the other has nothing of God in it, and is the pattern of the deepest unhappiness. This truth the evildoer does not see; blinded by folly and utter lack of understanding, he fails to perceive that the effect of his unjust practices is to make him grow more and more like the one, and less and less like the other. For this he pays the penalty of living the life that corresponds to the pattern he is coming to resemble. And if we tell him that, unless he is delivered from this "ability" of his, when he dies the place that is pure of all evil will not receive him; that he will forever go on living in this world a life after his own likeness—a bad man tied to bad company. (*Theaetetus* 176e3–7a7[242])

Evil (and unjust) men associated with evils lead supremely unhappy lives and will continue to do so, until they use their Reason (via dialectic) and come to know the Good.

Plotinus:

> The cause of the wrongs men do to one another might be their effort towards the Good; when they fail through their impotence to attain it, they turn against other men. But the wrongdoers pay the penalty, being corrupted in their souls by their works of wickedness, and are set in a lower place; for nothing can ever escape that which is ordained in the law of the All. (III.2.4.20–6)

It is a decreed law of the Universe that if one soul harms another, it will pay a price in the form of degradation in its next incarnation.

Therefore, Plotinus and Plato believe that those with vicious souls are unhappy.

Positive qualities may be corrupted or misused by the vicious soul

I can confirm that what most would consider positive qualities—intelligence, wealth, strength—may be corrupted or misused by the vicious soul.

Plato:

> What will surprise you most, when you hear it, is that each of the things we praised in that nature tends to corrupt the soul that has it and to drag it away from philosophy. I mean courage, moderation, and the other things we mentioned.
>
> That does sound strange.
>
> Furthermore, all the things that are said to be good also corrupt it and drag it away—beauty, wealth, physical strength, relatives who are powerful in the city, and all that goes with these. (*Republic* VI 491b7–c4[243])

So gifts of nature—courage and moderation—and beauty, wealth, strength, and powerful family connections can all corrupt one's soul, because, as Plato implies, these things can divert one's attention from philosophy and make one believe that one does not need philosophy. Plato also argues that excellence of thought—which I take to be equivalent to intelligence or practical wisdom—can be used in the service of evil (*Republic* VII 518d9–9a6),[244] and that the unjust, arrogant person with lifelong health, wealth, absolute power, strength, immunity from death, and the exemption from other so-called evils is miserable and unhappy (*Laws* II 661d6–e4).

Thus, Plato believes that what are usually construed as positive qualities and/or goods may be misused by one's soul.

Plotinus:

> But if their property is taken away while they are still alive, they may recognize that it was not theirs before either, and that its possession is a mockery to the robbers themselves when others take it away from them; for even to those who do not have it taken away, to have it is worse than being deprived of it. (III.2.15.39–43)

So an unjust robber who retains property loses more than if he forfeits the property. Plotinus also mentions that an unjust soul who is attached to the body will be overbearing in wealth and arbitrary in power, implying that his possession of either will not be a boon (III.1.8).[245] Intelligence can be misused as well: "The efflux of intellect produces knavery; for knavery wants to be intellect, only it is unable to attain what it aims at" (II.3.11.8–10).[246] Plotinus also implies that strength can be misused: "But the wicked rule by the cowardice of the ruled; for this is just, and the opposite is not" (III.2.8.50–2), and his other passages in III.2.8 about the gymnasiums lying before everyone: if one is not fit, it is one's own fault that an unjust but strong person can overtake the other.

Therefore, Plotinus agrees with Plato that so-called goods or qualities are not good for the vicious person, and are, in fact, bad for such a person.

Ignorance is a bad condition of the soul; ignorance is being ruled/mastered by passion, pleasure, love and/or fear

Ignorance is associated with one's lack of knowledge of the Forms (especially the Good) and/or one's having false opinions, especially the opinion that one believes one has knowledge when one does not. Possessing ignorance is closely related—if not identical—to one's being unjust or intemperate, for instance, because one does not know which beliefs are true and which are false.

Plato:[247]

> Do you believe that there's also some corrupt [*ponērian*] condition of the soul?
>
> Of course.
>
> And don't you call this condition injustice, ignorance, cowardice, and the like?
>
> Certainly. (*Gorgias* 477b5–8; my brackets[248])

Socrates describes ignorance:

> You asked it, if you remember, when we were agreeing that nothing was stronger or better than knowledge, which always prevails, whenever it is present, over pleasure and everything else. At that point you said that pleasure often rules even the man who knows; since we disagreed, you went on to ask us this: "Protagoras and Socrates, if this experience is not being overcome by pleasure, what is it then; what do you say it is? Tell us." If immediately we had said to you "ignorance," you might have laughed at us, but if you laugh at us now, you will be laughing at yourselves. For you agreed with us that *those who make mistakes with regard to the choice of pleasure and pain, in other words, with regard to good and bad, do so because of a lack of knowledge*, and not merely a lack of knowledge but a lack of that knowledge you agreed was measurement. And *the mistaken act done without knowledge you must know is one done from ignorance. So this is what "being overcome by pleasure" is—ignorance in the highest degree.* (*Protagoras* 357c1–e2; emphasis added)

It might appear that Socrates is only referring to the mastery of pleasure here, but he reminds Protagoras that he is also discussing the mastery of "everything else": "sometimes desire, sometimes pleasure, sometimes pain, at other times love, often fear" (*Protagoras* 352b7–8). Thus, Socrates is claiming that ignorance is a lack of mastery of one's soul over passion, pleasure/pain, love, and fear. Lastly in the *Protagoras*, Plato states: "To give into oneself is nothing other than ignorance" (358c1–2) and: "Ignorance is to have a false belief and to be deceived about matters of importance" (358c4–5).

Elsewhere, Plato states that injustice is effectively the equivalent of ignorance (as is intemperance, cowardice, and the rest). This is equivalent to the *Protagoras* passages, because temperance is a mastery of pleasures; justice is when each part of the soul does its own and allows Reason to rule; and courage is the mastery of fear.[249] Here the question raised concerns injustice:

> We must look for injustice.
>
> Clearly.
>
> Surely, it must be a kind of civil war between the three parts, a meddling and doing of another's work, a rebellion by some part against the whole soul in order to rule it inappropriately. The rebellious part is by nature suited to be a slave, while the other part is not a slave but belongs to the ruling class. We'll say something like that, I suppose, and that the turmoil and straying of these parts are injustice, licentiousness [*akolasian*], cowardice, ignorance [*amathian*], and, in a word, the whole of vice.
>
> That's what they are. (*Republic* IV 444a10–b9; my brackets[250])

At *Republic* I 351a, Plato claims that injustice is ignorance,[251] so this passage only demonstrates his consistency with his earlier claims in the *Republic* (and with the *Protagoras*).

Plato discusses ignorance qua perverted process of understanding:

> Ignorance [*agnoein*] occurs precisely when a soul tries for the truth, but swerves aside from understanding and so is beside itself.
> Of course. (*Sophist* 228c10–d3; my brackets)

He also claims that the large, difficult kind of ignorance is 'not knowing, but thinking that you know' (229c5).[252]

Thus, Plato believes that ignorance is an evil condition of the soul and that ignorance is being ruled/mastered by passion, pleasure, love and/or fear.

Plotinus: First, for Plotinus ignorance is an evil condition of the soul:[253] "Vice ... is ignorance and unmeasuredness in the soul" (I.8.8.41–2).[254]

Second, ignorance is related to passions, desires, and so forth overcoming one's Reason.[255] Plotinus discusses what can happen when desires and passions pull the soul in every direction, referring to such pulling as an ignorance of what is good. Like the best advisor at a community meeting who cannot be heard because he is overwhelmed by the tumult, we will not listen to Reason because of our desires and passions:

> For when the desiring part of the soul is moved, the mental image of its object comes like a perception announcing and informing us of the experience, and demanding that we should follow along with it and obtain the desired object for it; but our other part necessarily falls into perplexity, whether it goes along and obtains the object or resists. And the spirited part when it summons us to repel something does the same when it is moved, and the needs of the body and the passions make us have continually different opinions. Then there is ignorance of the [true] good, and the soul's not knowing what to say when it is dragged in every direction, and still other results from the mixture of all these. But is it actually our best part which has different opinions? No, perplexity and variety of opinions belong to the gathering [of our various parts and passions]: from our best part the right account of the matter is given to the common gathering, and is weak because it is in the mixture, not by its own nature. But it is as if in the great clamor of an assembly the best of the advisors does not prevail when he speaks, but the worse of those who clamor and shout, but he sits quietly unable to do anything, defeated by the clamor of the worse. And in the worst kind of man there is the common gathering and his human nature is composed of everything in the manner of a bad political constitution; in the middling man it is as it is in the city in which some good can prevail as the democratic constitution is not entirely out of control. (IV.4.17.11–30[256])

Thus, Plotinus agrees with Plato that ignorance of the Good leads to the submission of one's Reason to desires and passions.

Lastly, Plotinus believes that ignorance involves a defective reasoning process (as we saw in Plato's *Sophist*):

> What is it then, by the presence of which each part is evil? Vice. . . . Now perhaps one might say that the vice of the reasoning part was unintelligence [*anoian*], and

> unintelligence in the negative sense, and would not be asserting the presence of anything. But when false opinions are there in the soul (and this is what most of all produces vice), how will one be able to assert that they have not come in and that this part of the soul has not in this way become different? And is not the spirited part in one state when it is cowardly and in another when it is brave? And is not the desiring part when it is unrestrainedly lustful in one state, and in another when it is under control? Well, then, it has been affected. (III.6.2.22–9; my brackets[257])

Here Plotinus implies that ignorance[258] leads to false judgments, which are the main cause of vice. He states that ignorance is not something positive in the soul, and questions whether some other thing is positively perverting the reasoning, but in the rest of the explanation, he implies that ignorance is what makes one have false judgments, which is precisely what makes one not follow one's Reason.

Plotinus agrees with Plato that love can be an irrational desire pursuing enjoyment of bodily beauty, so there is good reason to believe that Plotinus concurs with Plato that love may be a hindrance to virtue, depending on how it manifests in one's soul.

This leaves fear, and—assuming that, for Plotinus, an ugly, dissolute, unjust soul is an ignorant one—Plotinus agrees with Plato that fear is a mastering of Reason as a result of ignorance:

> Suppose, then, an ugly soul, dissolute and unjust, full of all lusts, and all disturbance, sunk in fears by its cowardice and jealousies by its pettiness, thinking mean and mortal thoughts as far as it thinks at all, altogether distorted, loving impure pleasures, living a life which consists of bodily sensations and finding delight in its ugliness. (I.6.5.25–31[259])

Thus, Plotinus believes with Plato that ignorance is an evil condition of the soul and that ignorance is being ruled by passion, pleasure, love and/or fear, when Reason should really be in control.

Impiety

Plato: Plato admonishes the poets (especially Homer), for writing that the gods do impious deeds and, more importantly, cause evil to humans:

> Nor will we allow it to be said that Theseus, the son of Posidon, and Pirithous, the son of Zeus, engaged in terrible kidnappings, or that any other hero and son of a god dared to do any of the terrible and impious deeds that they are now falsely said to have done. We'll compel the poets either to deny that the heroes did such things or else to deny that they were children of the gods. They mustn't say both or attempt to persuade our young people that the gods bring about evil or that heroes are no better than humans. As we said earlier, these things are both impious and untrue, for we demonstrated that it is impossible for the gods to produce bad things.
>
> Of course. (*Republic* III 391c8–e3[260])

Plotinus: Plotinus attacks the Gnostics' view that there is only providence for Gnostics:

> What piety is there in denying that providence extends to this world and to anything and everything? And how are they consistent with themselves in this denial? For they say that God does care providentially for them, and them alone. . . . For providential care is much more of wholes than of parts, and the participation in God of that universal soul, too, is much greater. Its existence, and its intelligent existence, make this clear. For who of those who are so mindlessly high-minded in looking down on it is as well ordered or has as intelligent a mind as the All? The comparison is ridiculous and very much out of place; anyone who made it except for the sake of argument would not be able to avoid impiety. (II.9.16.14–7, 30–6[261])

Thus, Plotinus agrees that for one to think that providence is only for some and not for all is impious. Plotinus also implies that the gods do not cause evil for us, as murders and other bad things are changing scenes in a play, made on stages of our own construction (III.2.15). Since we construct the stage, it is our mindsets, reason (or lack thereof), desires, and passions that cause the bad actions that happen.

Therefore, Plato and Plotinus agree that we should not make impious claims (or have impious thoughts) concerning the gods.

Attachment to self or over-concern for the body

Besides advocating asceticism, Plato and Plotinus also submit that the attachment to self or the over-concern for the body is not a proper way to live.

Plato:

> The most serious vice innate in most men's souls is one for which everybody forgives himself and so never tries to find a way of escaping. You can get some idea of this vice from the saying that a man is in the nature of the case "his own best friend," and that it is perfectly proper for him to have to play this role. It is truer to say that the cause of each and every crime we commit is precisely this excessive love of ourselves, a love which blinds us to the faults of the beloved and makes us bad judges of goodness and beauty and justice, because we believe we should honor our own ego rather than the truth. Anyone with aspirations to greatness must admire not himself and his own possessions, but acts of justice, not only when they are his own, but especially when they happen to be done by someone else. It's because of this same vice of selfishness that stupid people are always convinced of their own shrewdness, which is why we think we know everything when we are almost totally ignorant, so that thanks to not leaving to others what we don't know how to handle, we inevitably come to grief when we try to tackle it ourselves. For these reasons, then, every man must steer clear of extreme love of himself, and be loyal to his superior instead; and he mustn't be put off by shame at the thought of abandoning that "best friend." (*Laws* V 731d6–2b4[262])

Plato's passion is clear here, as he states that excessive self-love is a major hindrance to one's becoming a good person. It is evident from the context that attachment to the self is meant to refer to attachment to bodily concerns, reputation, and/or love, for instance.

Plotinus:[263] Plotinus claims that the soul's association with the body is its evil, its release its good:

> "Descent" means coming to be in body as we say soul comes to be in body, the giving to this body of something from itself, not coming to belong to it, and "departure" means that body in no way has any community with it; and there is an order of this kind of communion for the parts of this All, but soul, which is as it were on the edge of the intelligible region, often gives them something of itself since it is close to them by its power and the distances are shorter by the law of a nature of this kind; but communion of this kind is an evil [for soul] and release from it a good. Why? Because, even if it does not belong to this particular body, yet when it is said to belong to this body, it in some way or other comes out of its All to be partial. (VI.4.16.13–24[264])

Plotinus goes so far as to say: "Weakness of the soul must be found either in those souls which are completely separate or in those which are in matter or in both" (I.8.14.17–9).[265]

Therefore, Plato and Plotinus both claim that over-attachment to one's body is yet another example of the way in which we should not live.

To conclude, Plato and Plotinus share the following beliefs about how we should not live: vice is a corrupt condition of the soul, caused by ignorance and/or a lack of virtue (injustice, intemperance, impiety); being vicious leads to one's unhappiness; positive qualities may be corrupted or misused by the vicious soul; ignorance is an evil condition of the soul; ignorance is being mastered by passion, pleasure, love and/or fear; it is impious to question the gods' providence; and we should not be attached to ourselves or over-concerned with our body.

3.7 Music and musicians

Plato and Plotinus view music and true musicians to be those who are concerned with the Form of Harmony and its ability to influence the soul to appreciate the existence of immaterial beings, as well as being a stepping stone to gaining knowledge of the Good.

Plato: I will pass over the ideal modes and rhythms that Plato prescribes for the training of the Kallipolis' citizens,[266] but note that Plotinus implicitly accepts Plato's outline of the ideal state, since he wanted to found Platonopolis based on Plato's *Republic* and *Laws* (*Life*, ch. 12). Plato states that the true musician is basically a philosopher, who should learn to recognize the forms of temperance, courage, and other Forms, since these virtues are harmonies of the soul, related to the harmonies in music:

> Then, by the gods, am I not right in saying that neither we, nor the guardians we are raising, will be educated in music and poetry until we know the different forms of moderation, courage, frankness, high-mindedness, and all their kindred, and their opposites too, which are moving around everywhere, and see them in the things in which they are, both themselves and their images, and do not disregard them, whether they are written on small things or large, but accept that the knowledge of both large and small letters is part of the same craft and discipline?
>
> That's absolutely essential.
>
> Therefore, if someone's soul has a fine and beautiful character and his body matches it in beauty and is thus in harmony with it, so that both share in the same pattern, wouldn't that be the most beautiful sight for anyone who has eyes to see?
>
> It certainly would.
>
> And isn't what is most beautiful also most loveable?
>
> Of course.
>
> And a musical person would love such people most of all, but he wouldn't love anyone who lacked harmony?
>
> No, he wouldn't, at least not if the defect was in the soul, but if it was only in the body, he'd put up with it and be willing to embrace the boy who had it. (*Republic* III 402b9–e1)

So the proper study of music for Plato is effectively the proper study of philosophy, perhaps with an emphasis on harmony and rhythm.

Plato claims that the gods gave humans music (and gymnastics) for the service of the soul's high-spirited principle and the love of wisdom; and the most perfect/harmonious musician is the best combination of gymnastics and music applied to the soul:

> It seems, then, that a god has given music and physical training to human beings not, except incidentally, for the body and the soul but for the spirited and wisdom-loving parts of the soul itself, in order that these might be in harmony with one another, each being stretched and relaxed to the appropriate degree.
>
> It seems so.
>
> Then the person who achieves the finest blend of music and physical training and impresses it on his soul in the most measured way is the one we'd most correctly call completely harmonious and trained in music, much more so than the one who merely harmonizes the strings of his instrument.
>
> That's certainly so, Socrates. (*Republic* III 411e4–2a8[267])

Thus, Plato believes that the true musician studies harmony in the abstract with a view to harmonizing the soul, in its pursuit of wisdom—knowledge of the Good.

Plotinus: Plotinus confirms that he has the same view as Plato in several places, but it is especially apparent in his claim that the musician must be made to see that perceptible harmonies and beauty of music are caused by Harmony Itself and Beauty Itself of the Intelligible Region, and that he must have the truths of philosophy implanted in him (perhaps implying recollection):

> We will begin by describing the nature of the musician. We must consider him as easily moved and excited by beauty, but not quite capable of being moved by absolute beauty; he is however quick to respond to its images when he comes upon them, and just as nervous people react readily to noises, so does he to articulate sounds and the beauty in them; and he always avoids what is inharmonious and not a unity in songs and verses and seeks eagerly after what is rhythmical and shapely. So in leading him on, these sounds and rhythms and forms perceived by the senses must be made the starting-point. He must be led and taught to make abstraction of the material element in them and come to the principles from which their proportions and ordering forces derive and to the beauty which is in these principles, and learn that this was what excited him, the intelligible harmony and the beauty in it, and beauty universal, not just some particular beauty, and he must have the doctrines of philosophy implanted in him; by these he must be brought to firm confidence in what he possesses without knowing it. (I.3.1.19–34[268])

Thus, Plotinus also believes with Plato that music's value is to lead one to see the Form of Harmony, as part of the larger philosophical program of knowing the Good.

3.8 Arts and artisans

Plato is especially notorious for his judgments and admonitions concerning poets and artists, but Plotinus also has a similar view of the arts and artists.

Plato: Poets and painters are imitators, three removes (on Greek counting that is, where we would count it as two removes) away from the real nature of what they are imitating:

> Wouldn't you call someone whose product is third from the natural one an imitator?
>
> I most certainly would.
>
> Then this will also be true of a tragedian, if indeed he is an imitator. He is by nature third from the king and the truth, as are all other imitators.
>
> It looks that way.
>
> We're agreed about imitators, then. Now, tell me this about a painter. Do you think he tries in each case to imitate the thing itself in nature or the works of craftsmen?
>
> The works of craftsmen.
>
> As they are or as they appear? You must be clear about that.
>
> How do you mean?
>
> Like this. If you look at a bed from the side or the front or from anywhere else is it a different bed each time? Or does it only appear different, without being at all different? And is that also the case with other things?
>
> That's the way it is—it appears different without being so.

> Then consider this very point: What does painting do in each case? Does it imitate that which is as it is, or does it imitate that which appears as it appears? Is it an imitation of appearances or of truth?
>
> Of appearances.
>
> Then imitation is far removed from the truth, for it touches only a small part of each thing and a part that is itself only an image. And that, it seems, is why it can produce everything. For example, we say that a painter can paint a cobbler, a carpenter, or any other craftsman, even though he knows nothing about these crafts. Nevertheless, if he is a good painter and displays his painting of a carpenter at a distance, he can deceive children and foolish people into thinking that it is truly a carpenter.
>
> Of course. (*Republic* X 597e3–8c5[269])

Second, Plato discusses the banishment of poetry:

> And so, Glaucon, when you happen to meet those who praise Homer and say that he's the poet who educated Greece, that it's worth taking up his works in order to learn how to manage and educate people, and that one should arrange one's whole life in accordance with his teachings, you should welcome these people and treat them as friends, since they're as good as they're capable of being, and you should agree that Homer is the most poetic of the tragedians and the first among them. But you should also know that *hymns to the gods and eulogies to good people are the only poetry we can admit into our city.* (*Republic* X 606e1–7a8; emphasis added)

Plato does not ban all kinds of poetry from the state, but admits hymns to the gods and the praises of good men.[270] Moreover, as P. Murray points out, the Athenian refers to making children learn large amounts of poetry by heart so they may grow to be good and wise (*Laws* VII 810e–1a), which is more evidence that Plato has not entirely banned poetry from the ideal state.[271]

Can or does the artist look to the Form in order to do her work?[272] This is said to be a major point of difference between Plato and Plotinus' views on art. In Book X, it certainly seems to be that the artist only looks to the sensible instance (bed) to paint something. However, Plato makes an analogy from a painter to the philosopher-king, both of whom look to the Forms:

> Do you think, then, that there's any difference between the blind and those who are really deprived of the knowledge of each thing that is? The latter have no clear model in their souls, and so they cannot—in the manner of painters—look to what is most true, make constant reference to it, and study it as exactly as possible. Hence they cannot establish here on earth conventions about what is fine or just or good, when they need to be established, or guard and preserve them, once they have been established. (*Republic* VI 484c6–d3[273])

One can read this passage as saying that the artist, like the philosopher-king, can look to the relevant Forms to create their art or state, respectively. Also, we should keep in mind that Plato is said to be a poet by some,[274] and it seems clear that Plato was looking to the Forms in order to write his dialogues. Lastly, Plato states more than once that poets are divinely inspired (see *Apology* 22a–c and *Phaedrus* 245a), which implies that they get some of their ideas straight from the Muses or the gods, both of whom are not sensible instances that are merely being imitated. So the suggestion that artists can look to Forms in doing their art is plausible on Plato's view.

Thus, for Plato, poetry is an imitation that should be understood as such and not revered as the ultimate human endeavor (philosophy), but is admissible in the ideal state, and Plato believes that artists may look to Forms in order to create their art.

Plotinus:[275,276] Plotinus generally lists the imitative arts:

> As for all the imitative arts, painting and sculpture, dancing and mime, which are in some way composed of elements from this world and use a model perceived by sense and imitate the forms and movements and transpose into their own terms the proportions which they see, it would not be reasonable to trace them back to the intelligible world except as included in the forming principle of man. (V.9.11.1–6[277])

Plotinus explicitly states that painters "use a model perceived by sense."[278] He then claims that art, depending on its nature and content, can be beautiful in a far higher and purer degree, similar to his and Plato's claims about the true musician:

> If art makes its work like what it is and has—and it makes it beautiful according to the forming principle of what it is making—it is itself more, and more truly, beautiful since it has the beauty of art which is greater and more beautiful than anything in the external object. For a thing is weaker than that which abides in unity in proportion as it expands in its advance towards matter. Everything which is extended departs from itself: if it is bodily strength, it grows less strong, if heat, less hot, if power in general, less powerful, if beauty, less beautiful. (V.8.1.22–30)

In a Platonic way, Plotinus states that the more an art uses or involves matter, the less beautiful it is and can be.

Lastly, Plotinus also states that playwrights are imitators:

> Now in human plays the author provides the words, but the actors, each and every one of them, are responsible by themselves and from themselves for the good or bad acting of their parts—for there is action, too, which is their business, following from the speeches written by the author. (III.2.17.28–32)

I should note that the context of this passage is a larger discussion about providence and the human condition as being like that of actors in a play written by a good poet or playwright. Nonetheless, Plotinus states that poets or playwrights are imitators, which is all that my argument requires.

However, it also must be admitted that Plotinus does not explicitly argue that poets encourage the emotions when they should be drying them up, as Plato states at *Republic* X 606d. He does say that poetry is an imitation, and he certainly holds that we should not pursue imitations or follow our Appetite or Spirit over our Reason, for instance, but instead seek knowledge of Forms.[279]

Therefore, Plotinus and Plato both hold that artists are imitators whose pieces of art are several removes away from Beauty Itself.

3.9 Desire for the Good

Plato and Plotinus agree on the following claims: humans (within their Reason) desire the Good; humans do actions (neither good nor bad things and actions, or good actions) for the sake of the Good; and animals and plants desire the Good to the extent possible.

Humans (within their Reason) desire the Good

Plato and Plotinus believe that there are three parts of the human soul, and as Appetite desires food, drink, and sex, so Reason desires the Good.

Plato:[280]

> Were you not saying just now that virtue is to desire good things and have the power to secure them?
>
> Yes, I was.
>
> The desiring part of this statement is common to everybody, and one man is no better than another in this?
>
> So it appears.
>
> Clearly then, if one man is better than another, he must be better at securing them.
>
> Quite so. (*Meno* 78b3–8[281])

I take it that when Plato states that all men desire the power to secure good things, he means that they want to have knowledge of the Good, which is precisely what is required for one to secure good things. If I do not know what the Good is, how would I even know if any of my possessions or qualities were indeed good *simpliciter*, good for me, or *would* be good for me to acquire?[282]

Plato states more explicitly that everything that the soul does and pursues is for the sake of the Good (what is really best for itself), and *not* the semblance of the Good (what it *thinks* really best for itself):

> Nobody is satisfied to acquire things that are merely believed to be good, however, but everyone wants the things that really *are* good and disdains mere belief here.
>
> That's right.

> Every soul pursues the good and does whatever it does for its sake. It divines that the good is something but it is perplexed and cannot adequately grasp what it is or acquire the sort of stable beliefs it has about other things, and so it misses the benefit, if any, that even those other things may give. (*Republic* VI 505d7–e4[283])

Lastly, as no one would desire to have only memory, intelligence, knowledge and true opinion without pleasure, and no one would desire pleasure without any intelligence, then "neither of the two can be the perfect thing that everyone desires, the Good Itself" (*Philebus* 61a1–2; adapted from Hackforth). Plato is referring to the Good Itself here and not the human good, since to set up the discussion at the beginning of the dialogue, Socrates asks if what ranks as the good must be perfect or imperfect, and Protarchus agrees that it must be perfect, as well as sufficient (20d1–6). In the Platonic corpus, the only entity that meets the criteria of being perfect is the best, or the Good: the highest principle of Plato's philosophy. Thus, Plato holds that humans desire the Good.

Plotinus:[284]

> So we must ascend again to the Good, which every soul desires. Anyone who has seen it knows what I mean when I say that it is beautiful. It is desired as good, and the desire for it is directed to Good, and the attainment of it is for those who go up to the higher world. . . . If anyone sees it, what passion will he feel, what longing in his desire to be united with it, what a shock of delight! The man who has not seen it may desire it as good, but he who has seen it glories in its beauty and is full of wonder and delight. (I.6.7.1–4, 12–6; adapted from A.H. Armstrong[285])

Plotinus also confirms that if one possesses the Good, it is sufficient, and no one wants the semblance of the Good:

> All men think that when they have attained the Good it is sufficient for them: for they have reached their end. . . . But they do not want to have the Good in seeming only. (V.5.12.19–20, 24)

Thus, Plotinus holds with Plato that humans desire the Good.

Humans do actions (neither good nor bad things and actions, or good actions) for the sake of the Good

Plato and Plotinus discuss more specific actions, such as doing neither good nor bad actions for the sake of the Good, as well as doing what might normally be considered bad actions such as murder, for the sake of the Good.

Plato: According to Plato, we perform "neither good nor bad" actions—sitting, walking, running, and sailing—and use "neither good nor bad" objects—stones or twigs—for the sake of the good if they benefit us, but do not will them if they harm us (*Gorgias* 467e–8d).[286] Plato also says that no one desires what is bad, but all men desire the good:

> It is clear then that those who do not know things to be bad do not desire what is bad, but they desire those things that they believe to be good but that are in fact bad. It follows that those who have no knowledge of these things and believe them to be good clearly desire good things. (*Meno* 77d7–e4)

For example, if I do not *know* that driving drunk is a bad thing, but I *believe* I can make it home safely, I do not desire to get into a car accident (or other bad consequences that might follow), but I do desire to get home safely without hitting anyone or anything (if that leads to my happiness). In this case, I would believe that driving home would be a good thing, and I desire that, and not a car accident (which is in fact bad).

Thus, Plato believes that humans do actions for the sake of the Good.

Plotinus: Plotinus actually refers to "indifferent" (*adiaphoros*) objects (I.4.2.13–5, VI.7.23.15–7; cf. V.5.13), individual living things (more hypothetically at V.7.3.6–10; cf. VI.7.10.16–17) and others,[287] but more relevantly, we act for the sake of goodness:

> They act for the sake of a good; but this means, not that the good arising from their action should be outside them, or that they should not have it, but that they should have it. But where do they have it? In their soul. (III.8.6.6–9[288])

This passage (along with his phrase "[the Good] . . . to which all look and are and *live and think*" at I.6.7.10–1; emphasis added) implies that we all act for the sake of some good, whenever we are walking or sitting (Plato's examples of neither good nor bad actions), or using stones and twigs (neither good nor bad objects), and so forth.

Moreover, confirming Plotinus' agreement with Plato that we do not desire what is in fact bad for us, Plotinus states that when one man wrongs another, this wrongdoing can be derived from an effort towards the Good:

> The cause of the wrongs men do to one another might be their effort towards the Good; when they fail through their impotence to attain it, they turn against other men. But the wrongdoers pay the penalty. (III.2.4.20–3[289])

Plotinus is careful here to note that the offender's true desire (that is foiled along the way) is not to harm others, and implies that they truly desire the Good but mistake what actions to perform in order to attain it. This notion of true desire in the face of wronging another is parallel with Plato's argument that the tyrant does not do what he wishes (though he does whatever he thinks best) when he burns or murders (*Gorgias* 466c–7b).

Therefore, I have confirmed that Plato and Plotinus both believe that when humans act or use objects, they do so for the sake of the Good.

Animals and plants desire the Good to the extent possible

Interestingly, Plato and Plotinus both make claims to the effect that animals and plants desire the Good, but they each also make statements that hedge that claim. They both state that "every soul" desires and pursues the Good.[290] If that were all they said with respect to this issue, we would need to go no further. However, as it is, they also make other statements that require more investigation.

Plato: In addition to the *Republic* VI passage stating that *every* soul desires the (real) Good, he states at *Philebus* 22a that neither intelligence nor pleasure is the perfect thing we seek, the Good Itself.[291] On the other hand, if we look at the *Timaeus*, *Sophist*, and *Philebus*, we get a muddier picture of what Plato's view really is concerning whether plants and animals desire the Good to the same extent as humans do.[292] Starting with the *Timaeus*, Plato there states that the gods made plants with no part in opinion, reason, or mind, but only the capability of experiencing pleasure, pain, and desires that accompany them; they also lack the power to observe and reflect upon any of their own concerns:

> [The gods] made another mixture and caused another nature to grow, one congenial to our human nature though endowed with other features and other sensations, so as to be a different living thing. These are now cultivated *trees, plants and seeds*, taught by the art of agriculture to be domesticated for our use. But at first the only kinds there were were wild ones, older than our cultivated kinds. We may call these plants "living things" on the ground that anything that partakes of life has an incontestable right to be called a "living thing." And in fact, what we are talking about now partakes of the third type of soul, the type that our account has situated between the midriff and the navel. *This type is totally devoid of opinion, reasoning or understanding, though it does share in sensation, pleasant and painful, and desires*. For throughout its existence it is completely passive, and *its formation has not entrusted it with a natural ability to discern and reflect upon any of its own characteristics*, by revolving within and about itself, repelling movement from without and exercising its own inherent movement. Hence it is alive, to be sure, and unmistakably a living thing, but it stays put, standing fixed and rooted, since it lacks self-motion. (*Timaeus* 77a3–c5; emphasis added[293])

Though this passage could stand on its own, see the *Sophist*, where Plato states via the Stranger, speaking to Theaetetus, that animals and plants were not caused by a spontaneous nature that has no intelligence, but one which is divine and does possess intelligence (with the Stranger first here):

> Take animals and everything mortal, including plants and everything on the earth that grows from seeds and roots, and also all lifeless bodies made up inside the earth, whether fusible or not. Are we going to say that anything besides *the craftsmanship of a god makes them come to be after previously not being*? Or shall we rely on the saying and the widespread belief that . . .?
>
> That what?
>
> Are we going to say that nature produces them by some spontaneous cause that generates them without any thought, or by *a cause that works by reason and divine knowledge derived from a god*? . . .

> Supposing that you think they come to be by the agency of a god, that's what I think too. (*Sophist* 265c1–d4; emphasis added)

Now, the *Timaeus* and the *Sophist* passages are not incompatible in principle, since we can interpret the *Sophist* as merely saying that animals and plants are caused by a divine intelligence, while still themselves not possessing intelligence.

The situation gets even more interesting, however, when we add the *Philebus*. Near the beginning, Plato seems to remain consistent with what he had said in the *Timaeus*, that plants (and perhaps animals) do not have reason or intelligence, but can experience pleasure and pain.

First, while laying out Socrates' contention at the start, that, for "all creatures" [*pasi zōiois*] (*Philebus* 11b4), intelligence proves better and more valuable than pleasure, he adds the qualification "to all who can attain them" (11b9–c1). Again, I suppose we can interpret these claims consistently by arguing that Plato still has not attributed intelligence to plants or animals, because the qualification can exempt those beings.

Second, he issues a similar (and consistent) caveat at *Philebus* 20d8–10, when he is discussing the perfect, sufficient good: "*Everything that has any notion of it* hunts for it and desires to get hold of it and secure it for its very own, caring nothing for anything else except for what is connected with the acquisition of some good" (emphasis added).

Third, when Plato is discussing the two lives, of intelligence and of pleasure, he explicitly *includes* some animals and plants, and implies that plants and animals have desires and are candidates for the intelligence/pleasure contest:

> As far as they [the life of pleasure and the life of intellect] are concerned, is it then not clear at least, that neither the one nor the other contained the good, since otherwise it would be sufficient, perfect, and worthy of choice for any of *the plants and animals that can sustain them*, throughout their lifetime? And if anyone among us should choose otherwise, then he would do so involuntarily, in opposition to what is by nature truly choiceworthy, from ignorance or some unfortunate necessity.
>
> It certainly looks that way. (*Philebus* 22b3–9; emphasis added; my brackets)

The italicized phrase indeed qualifies the claim about animals and plants, but if they were not even candidates or starters from the beginning (due to their lack of any intelligence), why would Plato have put them into this passage, as relevant to the search for the desirable, complete, and sufficient Good? We can only return to what Plato says in the *Republic* VI: namely, that every soul desires the Good, no matter what their exact capacities may be.

Thus, Plato believes that animals and plants desire the Good to the extent that they are capable of doing so.

Plotinus: Plotinus claims that every soul desires the Good (I.6.7),[294] so if he says either that animals or plants do or do not have some intelligence, we can find compatible Platonic passages. Interestingly, we can find Plotinus' agreement with the claims in the *Timaeus*, *Sophist*, and *Philebus*. For instance, Plotinus affirms the *Sophist* claim that divine intelligence is the cause of plants:

> *For the plant here is a rational forming principle resting in life.* If then indeed the forming principle in matter, that of the plant, by which the plant exists, is a particular life and a soul, and the forming principle is some one thing, then this principle is either the first plant or it is not, but the first plant is before it, and this plant here derives from it. For that first plant is certainly one, and these plants here are many, and necessarily come from one. If this is really so, that plant must be much more primarily alive and be this very thing, plant, and these here must live from it in the second and third degree and from its traces. (VI.7.11.9–17; emphasis added)

Plotinus is not only claiming that vegetal life is a Reason-Principle established in life, but also that plants are copies of the Form, Plant Itself. Admittedly, Plato does not explicitly state that Plant Itself exists (but see *Republic* X 596c6). However, it stands to reason that if both Plato and Plotinus believe that the perceptible region is nothing but becomers that resemble many and various Forms, then plants would have to resemble Forms as well.

In Plotinus' treatise on happiness (I.4), he argues that animals and plants can be happy. However, he issues a caveat:

> If anyone dislikes the idea of *extending some degree of happiness down to the other living things—which would involve giving a share in it even to the meanest; one would have to give a share to plants*, because they too are alive and have a life which unfolds to its end; first of all, why will it not seem absurd of him to deny that other living things live well just because he does not think them important? Then, *one is not compelled to allow to plants what one allows to all other living beings; for plants have no sensations.* But there might perhaps be someone who would allow happiness to plants just because they have life; one life can be good, another the opposite, as plants too can be well or badly off, and bear fruit or not bear fruit. *If pleasure is the end and the good life is determined by pleasure, it is absurd of anyone to deny the good life to other living things*; the same applies to tranquility, and also if the life according to nature is stated to be the good life. (I.4.1.15–30; adapted from A.H. Armstrong; emphasis added[295])

First, Plotinus is claiming that plants and animals might be happy, which is implied by Plato in the *Philebus*, and less explicitly at *Republic* VI, since Plato had included animals and plants in the discussion about whether intelligence or pleasure were also the complete good for them.

Second, Plotinus issues the caveat that plants may not possess certain functions of the soul, and in particular, feeling. This is consistent with what Plato said about plants in the *Timaeus*, since he only attributed the ability of them to experience pleasure, pain, and accompanying desires.

Third, Plotinus implies that plants can experience pleasure, which as just noted, is precisely what Plato claimed in the *Timaeus*.

Lastly, Plotinus asks whether his argument (not relevant here) so far has implied that divine power reaches the earth, and answers that it does, and that this is sufficiently established: "That the other things happen in a rational pattern is evidence that it reaches the earth too; for animals and plants share in reason and soul and life" (III.2.7.33–6). Thus, Plotinus implies that animals and plants have some share in reason, which I can deduce in Plato's works from the *Philebus*, even though the *Timaeus* seemingly contradicts that claim.

Therefore, Plotinus agrees with Plato that animals and plants desire the Good, even though, within their works, their precise views may be inconsistent.

In sum, humans desire the Good, and do all of their actions and use any objects for the sake of the Good; and that animals and plants desire and pursue the Good to the extent that they are able.

3.10 That no one errs willingly

Plato and Plotinus both believe that we have free will[296] and are responsible for our actions, but they also agree that no one errs willingly: no one willingly does actions that will lead to their unhappiness.

Plato: Plato states in various ways that no one errs willingly.[297] Socrates argues that those who harm voluntarily—hurt or injure mankind, speak falsely, deceive, and err voluntarily—are far better than those who harm involuntarily (*Lesser Hippias* 372d–3a), but with a qualification:

> Therefore, it's up to the good man to do injustice voluntarily, and the bad man to do it involuntarily; that is, if the good man has a good soul.
>
> But surely he has.
>
> So *the one who voluntarily misses the mark and does what is shameful and unjust, Hippias—that is, if there is such a person—would be no other than the good man.* (*Lesser Hippias* 376b2–6; emphasis added)

Socrates concludes that the bad man does wrong involuntarily (or unwillingly), but that it is the good man who errs voluntarily, because the good—as opposed to the bad—man would possess knowledge of good and bad actions. However, he qualifies his statement that good men voluntarily do wrong with "if there is such a person," which we should take as hyperbole, since nowhere else in the dialogues does Plato claim that a good person (who knows the good) can or will do wrong.[298]

While analyzing Simonides' poem in the *Protagoras*, Socrates is fairly certain that no wise man believes that anyone errs willingly or willingly perpetrates any evil or base act, and that all evil or base action is involuntary (345d–e). He summarizes his argument: "Then if the pleasant is the good, no one who knows or believes there is something else better than what he is doing, something possible, will go on doing what he had been doing when he could be doing what is better" (358b6–c1); and: "No one goes willingly toward the bad or what he believes to be bad; neither is it in human nature, so it seems, to want to go toward what one believes to be bad instead of to the good. And when he is forced to choose between one of two bad things, no one will choose the greater if he is able to choose the lesser" (358c6–d4).

Regarding 358b6–c1, note the antecedent "if the pleasant is the good": taking the dialogues as a whole, Plato argues that seeking bodily pleasures is not the good (*Gorgias*, *Republic*, *Philebus*, and others), that knowledge is true pleasure (*Republic* and *Philebus*), and that pleasure by itself is not sufficient or complete because intellect is needed as well (*Philebus*). The principle of charity urges us to be careful not to assume that the pleasant is the good, given the other dialogues' claims concerning pleasure. Regardless of this point, Plato still states that no one errs willingly in many other places in the dialogues, up to and including his *Laws*.

Plato states: "No one does what's unjust because he wants to, but . . . all who do so do it unwillingly" (*Gorgias* 509e5–7).[299]

Plato concludes an argument between Meno and Socrates with this exchange:

> No one then wants what is bad, Meno, unless he wants to be such. For what else is being miserable but to desire bad things and secure them?
>
> You are probably right, Socrates, and no one wants what is bad.
>
> Were you not saying just now that virtue is to desire good things and have the power to secure them?
>
> Yes, I was.
>
> The desiring part of this statement is common to everybody, and one man is no better than another in this?
>
> So it appears. (*Meno* 78a6–b6)

Nobody desires what is bad, and everyone wishes for good things, so when someone does something wrong, it cannot be that she wanted to do something that would make her miserable. These claims are consistent with the other claims we've seen thus far in the *Lesser Hippias*, *Protagoras*, and *Gorgias*.

Plato states via Socrates that men are unwillingly deprived of good things, but willingly deprived of bad things (*Republic* III 413a4–10), and in Book VI, that every soul pursues the Good and does not want the semblance of goodness but wants what is in reality good.

Plato states:

> Just about every type of succumbing to pleasure is talked about as something reproachable, as though the evils are willfully done. But it is not right to reproach people for them, for no one is willfully evil. A man becomes evil, rather, as a result of one or another corrupt condition of his body and an uneducated upbringing. No one who incurs these pernicious conditions would will to have them. (*Timaeus* 86d5–e3[300])

Lastly, in the *Laws*, there are four related claims to highlight:

(1) "Every unjust man is unjust against his will. No man on earth would ever deliberately embrace any of the supreme evils, least of all in the most precious parts of himself . . . his soul. So no one will ever voluntarily accept the supreme evil into the most valuable part of himself and live with it throughout his life" (*Laws* V 731c2–7);

(2) "All wicked men are, in all respects, *unwillingly* wicked" (*Laws* IX 860d1);
(3) "The unjust man is doubtless wicked; but that the wicked man is in that state only against his will" (*Laws* IX 860d5);[301] and
(4) "A man who acts unjustly would seem to be doing so against his will. Here and now, that is the position *I* have to accept: I allow that no one acts unjustly except against his will. (If anyone with a disputatious disposition or a desire to attract favorable notice says that although there *are* those who are unjust against their will, even so many men do commit unjust acts voluntarily, I would reject his argument and stick to what I said)." (*Laws* IX 860d7–e3)[302]

Thus, there is abundant evidence that Plato holds that no one errs willingly.

Plotinus:[303] Plotinus asks and answers whether evil in men is involuntary:

> But if men are unwillingly wicked, and are the sort of people they are, not by their own free will, one could neither blame the wrongdoers nor those who suffer wrong because they suffer it by their agency.... But "unwilling" means that the error is unwilling; and this does not do away with the fact that it is men themselves who act of themselves but it is because they themselves do the deed that they themselves err; if they were not themselves the doers, they would not have erred at all. (III.2.10.1–3, 7–11[304])

So Plotinus asks how we can blame men if evil is in them unwillingly, and answers that when they err, they do not desire to err, and that wrongdoers choose as agents to perform their actions, and thus may be held accountable for their actions.

Interestingly, Plotinus also states, with Plato, that we do bad things when our baser parts take over:

> Evil is done when we are mastered by what is worse in us—for we are many—by desire or passion or an evil image. What we call thinking falsities is a making of mind-pictures which has not waited for the judgment of the reasoning faculty—we have acted under the influence of our worse parts, just as in sensation the perception of the joint entity may see falsely before our reasoning faculty has passed judgment on it. (I.1.9.6–12[305])

Lastly, Plotinus argues (as Plato did in the *Timaeus*) that ignorance is the having of false judgments and is the cause of evil:

> Perhaps one might say that the vice of the reasoning part was unintelligence [*anoian*], and unintelligence in the negative sense, and would not be asserting the presence of anything. But when false opinions are there in the soul (and this is what most of all produces vice), how will one be able to assert that they have not come in and that this part of the soul has not in this way become different? (III.6.2.22–5[306])

Therefore, I have shown that Plato and Plotinus both believe that no one errs willingly.

3.11 Pleasure and pain

Both philosophers agree: true pleasure is that pleasure (or happiness) which results from knowing the Good, and it is wrong to pursue bodily pleasures (bad pleasures) as the end of human life.

True pleasure is pleasure (or happiness) that results from knowing the Good

Plato and Plotinus believe that there is such a thing as true pleasure: pleasure that is equivalent to lifelong or true happiness that is a result of one's knowing the Good. The view that there are true or good pleasures implies that there are also false or bad ones. If one does not have the ability—more specifically, knowledge of the Good—to choose between the true and false pleasures, one cannot be truly happy (except perhaps by being incredibly lucky and just by happening to choose to perform or not perform every action needed to produce one's happiness). Thus, in order to experience true pleasure—the pleasure that comes from knowing the Good—for instance, one might have to perform actions (say eating or drinking) that will result in some bodily pleasure (which Plato and Plotinus both refer to as necessary pleasures), but one will have to avoid many bodily pleasures as well.

However, I cannot confirm that, for Plotinus: true pleasures occur when one can accurately anticipate one's future pleasure; false pleasures occur when one fails to accurately predict one's future pleasure;[307] pleasant smells—because they lack previous pain—are one type of true pleasure;[308] and pleasant colors are true pleasures.[309] However, this caveat does not imply that Plato and Plotinus necessarily disagreed on these issues.

Plato: Plato argues that pleasure qua pleasure is good, as opposed to bad pleasures (contracting AIDS from an impromptu, otherwise enjoyable, tryst) or good pains (undergoing surgery to fix a clogged artery) (*Protagoras* 351b–e). Plato questions whether living well is passing one's life not in pain and vexation, but living it out to the end with enjoyment, and whether living pleasurably is good (351b–c).[310]

In the context of Plato's corpus, the *Protagoras* passages add to the definition of what pleasure is and what knowledge of virtue is; true pleasure comes from having or gaining knowledge, and knowledge of virtue is identical with the knowledge of the Good, respectively. Thus, the only way for one to live pleasurably is to experience true pleasure and to gain knowledge of the Good.

The other relevant passage in the *Protagoras* discuss measuring art, which involves weighing immediate versus future pleasures and pains, and choosing the ones that will result in the most pleasure over a lifetime (355e–6c). This is consistent with the rest of the Platonic corpus: to be able to assess which pleasures or pains are truly the long-term ones, and which are better than the others, one must know what goodness is, or the Good. Let us suppose, however, that one is not convinced by this argument, and instead believes that Plato changes his mind about pleasure from the *Phaedo* and onward. Even if we assume that Plato does not have a consistent view of pleasure in the dialogues, as long as Plotinus agrees with Plato that there are true pleasures that we should pursue, then I achieve my interpretive goal.

In the *Phaedo*, Plato actually states that we should not exchange one degree of pleasure and pain or fear for another, but instead pursue wisdom as the true moral ideal:

> I fear this is not the right exchange to attain virtue, to exchange pleasures for pleasures, pains for pains and fears for fears, the greater for the less like coins, but that the only valid currency for which all these things should be exchanged is wisdom [*phronēsis*]. With this we have real courage and moderation and justice and, in a word, true virtue, with wisdom [*phronēsis*], whether pleasures and fears and all such things be present or absent. Exchanged for one another without wisdom [*phronēsis*] such virtue is only an illusory appearance of virtue; it is in fact fit for slaves, without soundness or truth, whereas, in truth, moderation and courage and justice are a purging away from all such things, and wisdom [*phronēsis*] itself is a kind of cleansing or purification. (*Phaedo* 69a6–c3; my brackets)

It can certainly be argued that Plato has changed his mind here from what he said in the *Protagoras*, but based on what Plato says in the *Republic*, *Symposium*, and other dialogues related to the ultimate experience, a virtuous person is one who has seen the Good and knows the Forms, which is equivalent to wisdom; she is not someone who indulges in bodily pleasures and tries to avoid bodily pains. This is compatible with the measuring art of the *Protagoras* because the purpose of that art is to choose those pleasures that will result in the most pleasure over a complete life. Based on all the dialogues, such a life for Plato is the one filled with wisdom, knowledge, dialectic, and similar actions and states, and not which five-star meal one has, nor with whom one goes on a date.

The second passage of the *Phaedo* discusses and endorses pleasures associated with acquiring knowledge, which also supports the preceding paragraph:

> A man should be of good cheer about his own soul, if during life he has ignored the pleasures of the body and its ornamentation as of no concern to him and doing him more harm than good, but has seriously concerned himself with the pleasures of learning, and adorned his soul not with alien but with its own ornaments, namely, moderation, righteousness, courage, freedom and truth, and in that state awaits his journey to the underworld. (*Phaedo* 114d8–5a3)

Thus, Plato endorses pleasures of knowledge, but urges us to abandon bodily pleasures, proclaimed throughout the rest of the dialogues in various ways.[311]

Plato claims that harmless pleasures are desired for their own sake, and not for their results (*Republic* II 357b–c). Pleasure is not the Good because there are bad pleasures, such as contracting food poisoning from apparently enjoyable food (VI 505b–c). At VI 509a, Glaucon says that Socrates is discussing an inconceivable beauty if it is the source of knowledge and truth but surpasses them in beauty, so Socrates cannot mean to be referring to pleasure. Socrates responds with "Hush" [*euphēmei*], as it is typically translated, but can be translated as the more appropriate "Avoid all unlucky words" or "Keep a religious silence!" Of course, this is equivalent to Plato's claim we saw in the *Phaedo* above (69a6–c3), that we should not pursue bodily pleasures as the end of our lives, but should instead pursue wisdom and the pleasures of knowledge.

Plato returns again to pleasure as a major theme in the *Republic* IX, linking true pleasure with one's soul being filled with more real or true things, and claims that to be filled with what befits nature is pleasure[312] (585b–e). Plato continues: those delighted with bodily pleasure—the multitude—who have no knowledge of the wisdom, virtue, or Nous, do not know true, stable, and pure pleasure. He adds that their pleasures are mixed with pains, the latter of which I cannot confirm in the writings of Plotinus. Here is the passage:

> Isn't it necessary for these people [the majority of people—at 586b5, who have no experience of reason or virtue—at 586a1] to live with pleasures that are mixed with pains, mere images and shadow-paintings of true pleasures? And doesn't the juxtaposition of these pleasures and pains make them appear intense, so that they give rise to mad erotic passions in the foolish, and are fought over in just the way that Stesichorus tells us the phantom of Helen was fought over at Troy by men ignorant of the truth?
>
> Something like that must be what happens. (*Republic* IX 586b7–c6; my brackets[313])

In addition, Plato states that when the non-rational parts of the soul (Appetite and Spirit) follow Reason (also referred to here as the just person and elsewhere as the temperate person), the person enjoys true and proper pleasure; when they do not, the soul pursues an alien pleasure and not true pleasure (IX 586d–7a).

In the *Phaedrus*, Plato refers to the pleasures of good poetry, and states that without these pleasures (as opposed to those which involve previous pleasure and pain—for example, bodily pleasures—which are rightly called slavish), life would hardly be worth living (258d–e).

Leaving aside Plato's claims in the *Philebus* about true pleasures' being ones wherein the agent has correctly anticipated one's future pleasure, whereas false pleasures are incorrectly anticipated future pleasures (36b–d), he also argues for the following:

(1) There is a difference between pleasure associated with right opinion (or knowledge) and pleasure with false opinion and ignorance (38a–b);
(2) The evil and good have false pleasures painted on their minds; the good delight in true pleasures; evil in false ones; and fear, anger and other feelings are sometimes false (40a–1b);
(3) Pleasures and pains can be incorrectly perceived as appearing more intense than they are, but should be compared to one another to discover the natural state with a view of establishing that within ourselves, which is pleasure (42a–d);
(4) Some pleasures are truer than others (analogous to knowledge) (61d–e);
(5) Pleasures should prefer to live together with every kind of knowledge as opposed to living without it entirely (63b–c); and
(6) Painless and pure pleasures are fifth on the scale of what humans should pursue [after the region of measure, the proportioned, beautiful, perfect, satisfying region, reason and intelligence, and sciences/arts, and true opinion] (66a–c).

In the *Laws*, Plato makes the following claims concerning pleasure and pain:

(1) If the rulers are not trained in the most intense pleasures, but are in such pains, they will be half free and half brave (not brave and free without qualification) (I 635b–d);[314]
(2) The happy draw from nature's twin fountainheads—pleasure and pain—at the right time, in the right way (and the unhappy the opposite) (I 636d–e);
(3) Pleasure and pain are unwise and conflicting counselors (I 644c);
(4) The following conditions drive us frantic with the intoxication of pleasure: anger, lust, pride, folly, greed, cowardice, wealth, beauty, and physical vigor, and we should take care not to shame ourselves with any of these (I 649d);
(5) Pleasure and pain is the domain wherein the soul first acquires virtue and vice; true education is the rightly disciplined state of pleasures and pains, abhorring what should be abhorred, and relishing what you should relish (II 653a–c);
(6) The noble life has a predominance of pleasure over pain (and pleasure, pain, and desire are most native to man) (V 732e–3a);
(7) We wish for and choose pleasure, not pain, unless we're ignorant and have defective experience (V 733b–d); and
(8) A pleasant life is not a profligate one; temperance is the pleasant life; and pleasure dominates in the life of health (V 733e–4c).

Lastly, in *Letter* III, Plato states that he would not bid a human being or a god to enjoy himself, because gods dwell far above the sphere of pleasure and pain, and for humans, in most cases pleasure and pain work harm and produce dullness, forgetfulness, folly and lawlessness in the soul (315c).

Thus, though Plato makes many additional claims related to pleasure, he believes that true pleasure is pleasure (or happiness) that results from knowing the Good.

Plotinus: Plotinus believes in pure pleasure and that the good person—the Good knower, the truly happy person—experiences pleasure.[315] First he assumes that pure pleasure exists:

> We must enquire how it is with intelligence, whether we are going to allow this to the soul; and also whether it experiences pure pleasure when it is alone. (I.1.2.28–30[316])

Plotinus asks whether pure pleasure exists in the soul in its solitary state, but assumes that it does exist. This is consistent with what he says later about the good person's possession of pleasure:

> When they demand to be shown what is pleasant in a life of this kind, they will not be requiring the presence of the pleasures of debauchees, or of bodily pleasures at all (these could not be there and would abolish happiness) or of violent emotions of pleasure—why should the good man have any?—but only those pleasures which accompany the presence of goods, pleasures not consisting in movements, which

> are not the results of any process: for the goods are there already, and the good man is present to himself; his pleasure and happiness are at rest. The good man is always happy; his state is tranquil, his disposition contented and undisturbed by any so-called evils—if he is really good. If anyone looks for another kind of pleasure in life it is not the life of virtue he is looking for. (I.4.12.1–12; adapted from A.H. Armstrong)

Plotinus agrees with Plato's argument against a life of profligate pleasure (*Phaedo* 114d–5a, *Republic* IX 586a–c and *Laws* V 733e–4c). He then states that the only kind of pleasure that would move a good person is the pleasure related to the state of the Good, which is equivalent to happiness. This is the pleasant life of the good person.

Parallel to *Phaedo* 69a6–c3, where Plato states that the presence or absence of pleasures, pains (and fears) do not matter when compared to wisdom, Plotinus states:

> [The wise man] will take care of his bodily health, but will not wish to be altogether without experience of illness, nor indeed also of pain. Rather, even if these do not come to him he will want to learn them when he is young, but when he is old he will not want either pains or pleasures to hinder him, or any earthly thing, pleasant or the reverse, so that he may not have to consider the body. When he finds himself in pain he will oppose to it the power which he has been given for the purpose; he will find no help to his happiness in pleasure and health and freedom from pain and trouble, nor will their opposites take it away or diminish it. (I.4.14.21–30)

Immediately preceding the passage, it must be admitted, Plotinus states that the young wise person will wish to know troubles, so he may familiarize himself with them and train himself; however, this is consistent with Plato's training of the guardians in pains and pleasures and fears (see, for example, *Republic* IV 429a–30c), so we can be assured that this is not an inconsistency between the philosophers.

In a telling passage, pleasure, when construed as the unhindered act of a good person (implied), just is happiness. In fact, we can name this construal true pleasure:

> "But the first man had a longer period of pleasure." But it is not right to count pleasure in reckoning happiness. But if someone says that pleasure is "unhindered activity," he is stating just the conclusion we are seeking. And anyhow this longer-lasting pleasure at any moment only has what is present; past pleasure is gone and done with. (I.5.4.1–5; adapted from A.H. Armstrong)

Thus, Plotinus has the notion of true pleasure, where it is equivalent to happiness, which also affirms Plato's view.

Moreover, Plotinus strongly alludes to necessary pleasures when he says that the purified soul makes itself aware of pleasures "when it has to," in the context of the soul's withdrawal from the sensible realm:

> We might say that the soul draws together to itself in a sort of place of its own away from the body, and is wholly unaffected, and only makes itself aware of pleasures

> when it has to, using them as remedies and reliefs to prevent its activity being impeded; it gets rid of pains or if it cannot, bears them quietly and makes them less by not suffering with the body. It gets rid of passion as completely as possible, altogether if it can, but if it cannot, at least it does not share its emotional excitement.... It does away with fear altogether, for it has nothing to be afraid of.... It will obviously not desire anything bad; it will not itself have the desire of food and drink for the relief of the body, and certainly not of sexual pleasures either. If it does have any of these desires they will, I think, be natural ones with no element of involuntary impulse in them; or if it does have other kinds, only as far as it is with the imagination, which is also prone to these. (I.2.5.5–13, 15, 17–21)

It is unnecessary to review this passage line by line, as all these claims are verifiably Platonic.

Lastly, recalling that Plato in *Letter* III claims that the gods live above the sphere of pleasure, Plotinus makes an interesting claim that God (and not necessarily gods) experiences pleasure:

> [The seer] reports that he has seen a god in labor with a beautiful offspring all of which he has brought to birth within him, and keeping the children of his painless birth-pangs within himself; for he is pleased with what he has borne and delighted with his offspring and so keeps all with him in his enjoyment of his and their glory. (V.8.12.3–7)

One might think that Plotinus has veered from Plato's view in stating that God experiences pleasure, when Plato states that the gods live above the sphere of pleasure. There are three replies to such a view.

First, Plotinus also says the following about the gods, and their inability to enjoy pleasures of earth, just as Plato stated at *Letter* III 315c:

> This is the life of gods and of godlike and blessed men, deliverance from the things of this world, a life which takes no delight in the things of this world, escape in solitude to the solitary. (VI.9.11.49–51)

This passage clearly confirms that Plato and Plotinus agree that the *gods*, at any rate (and we'll return to God in a moment), do not partake in bodily pleasures.

Second, if Plotinus states that the only kind of pleasure that a Sage is capable of having is basically wisdom, then pleasure is identical to happiness (as Plotinus himself *also* states). Now combine the claims that God and the gods are wise,[317] and are therefore happy, at least in the sense of their being in the state of knowing the Good, which also implies that they experience true pleasure.

Third, if this brief argument does not convince, then we have Plato's *Timaeus* to aid us:

> Now when the Father who had begotten the universe observed it set in motion and alive, a thing that had come to be as a shrine for the everlasting gods, he was well

> pleased, and in his delight he thought of making it more like its model still. So, as the model was itself an everlasting Living Thing, he set himself to bringing this universe to completion in such a way that it, too, would have that character to the extent that was possible. (*Timaeus* 37c6–d2)

Plato claims that God, the creator of the universe, rejoiced and experienced joy at his created image. Thus, Plotinus' claim that God can experience pleasure is not incompatible with the dialogues.

In sum, true pleasure is pleasure (or happiness) which results from knowing the Good (and not the enjoyment of bodily pleasures, or instance).

It is wrong to pursue bodily pleasures (bad pleasures) as the end of human life

Plato:[318] Plato assumes that the life of the philosopher is the best life, and then states that the philosopher should not concern herself with bodily pleasures:

> Do you think it is the part of a philosopher to be concerned with such so-called pleasures as those of food and drink?
>
> By no means.
>
> What about the pleasures of sex?
>
> Not at all.
>
> What of the other pleasures concerned with the service of the body? Do you think such a man prizes them greatly, the acquisition of distinguished clothes and shoes and the other bodily ornaments? Do you think he values these or despises them, except insofar as one cannot do without them?
>
> I think the true philosopher despises them . . . .
>
> So in the first place, such things show clearly that the philosopher more than other men frees the soul from association with the body as much as possible?
>
> Apparently.
>
> A man who finds no pleasure in such things and has no part in them is thought by the majority not to deserve to live and to be close to death; the man, that is, who does not care for the pleasures of the body.
>
> What you say is certainly true. (*Phaedo* 64d2–e3, 64e8–5a8)

Plato emphasizes that his view that we should not pursue bodily pleasures to get to the truth was not a popular one at the time.

Plato vehemently upbraids those who might think that pursuing and satisfying bodily pleasures is the end of human life:

> Those who have no experience of reason or virtue, but are always occupied with feasts and the like, are brought down and then back up to the middle, as it seems, and wander in this way throughout their lives, never reaching beyond this to what is truly higher up, never looking up at it or being brought up to it, and so they aren't filled with that which really is and never taste any stable or pure pleasure. Instead, they always look down at the ground like cattle, and, with their heads bent over the

> dinner table, they feed, fatten, and fornicate. To outdo others in these things, they kick and butt them with iron horns and hooves, killing each other, because their desires are insatiable. For the part that they're trying to fill is like a vessel full of holes, and neither it nor the things they are trying to fill it with are among the things that are.
>
> Socrates, you've exactly described the life of the majority of people, just like an oracle.
>
> Then isn't it necessary for these people to live with pleasures that are mixed with pains, mere images and shadow-paintings of true pleasures? And doesn't the juxtaposition of these pleasures and pains make them appear intense, so that they give rise to mad erotic passions in the foolish, and are fought over in just the way that Stesichorus tells us the phantom of Helen was fought over at Troy by men ignorant of the truth?
>
> Something like that must be what happens. (*Republic* IX 586a1–c6[319])

This passage is quite stunning—though completely consistent with what we see Plato say elsewhere in the dialogues—in the degree of its degradation of those who strive to experience bodily pleasures.

Even in the late *Timaeus*, Plato states: "Pleasure [is] evil's most powerful lure" and "Pains . . . make us run away from what is good" (69d1–2).

Thus, Plato holds that it is wrong to pursue bodily pleasures—bad pleasures—as the end of human life.

Plotinus: Plotinus agrees that we should not pursue bodily pleasures if we wish to be truly happy or pleased.[320] Pursuing pleasure is at least in part what constitutes vice:

> Each and every thing's desire and birth-pangs of longing bear witness that there is some good for each. For to things without soul the gift of the good comes from another, but for that which has soul it is the desire which brings about the pursuit, just as when bodies have become corpses they are tended and prepared for burial by the living, but the living take thought for themselves. But the attainment is confirmed when a thing becomes better and has no regrets, and fulfillment comes to it and it remains with the Good and does not seek something else. *This is why pleasure is not self-sufficient; for one is not satisfied with the same thing; for what pleasure is satisfied with again is not the same; for that which gives one pleasure is always something else.* Certainly the good which one chooses must be something which is not the feeling one has when one attains it; that is why the one who takes this for good remains empty, because he only has the feeling which one might get from the good. This is the reason why one would not find acceptable the feeling produced by something one has not got; for instance, one would not delight in a boy because he was present when he was not present; nor do I think that those who find the good in bodily satisfaction would feel pleasure as if they were eating when they were not eating or as if they were enjoying sex when they were not with the one they wanted to be with, or in general when they were not active. (VI.7.26.6–24, emphasis added[321])

To everything there is a good, but pleasure shows itself inadequate as a truly satiable option that is complete and perfect, as Plato claims in the *Philebus*.

Plotinus shows his agreement with the kind of stunning statements that Plato made in the *Republic* IX 586a1–c6 about those feasting humans who are like animals:

> Do not, then, seek to see with mortal eyes this as our account describes it, nor to see that it is in the way in which someone would expect it to be who assumes that all things are perceived by the senses, by which supposition he eliminates that which is most real of all. For the things which one thinks are most real, are least real; and the [materially] large has less genuine existence. But the First is the principle of existence and, again, more authentic than substantial reality. So reverse your way of thinking, or you will be left deprived of God, like the people at festivals who by their gluttony stuff themselves with things which it is not lawful for those going in to the gods to take, thinking that these are more obviously real than the vision of the god for whom they ought to be celebrating the festival, and take no part in the rites within. (V.5.11.5–16)

Note that Plotinus also mentions (as in *Republic* IX 586a1–c6) that those gluttons hold these physical goods to be more real than the truly real goods.

Plotinus argues that we should not pursue bodily pleasure even more clearly, noting the images of sense, which we can take to be equivalent to the images of pleasure that Plato referred to in the *Republic* IX passage:

> Therefore one must "escape" to the upper world, that we may not sink to the level of sense-perception by pursuing the images of sense, or to the level of the growth-principle by following the urge for generation and the "gluttonous love of good eating," but may rise to the intelligible and intellect and God. Those, then, who guarded the man in them, become men again. Those who lived by sense alone become animals; but if their sense-perceptions have been accompanied by passionate temper they become wild animals, and the difference in temper in them makes the differences between the animals of this kind; those whose sense-perceptions went with desires of the flesh and the delight of the desiring part of the soul become lustful and gluttonous animals. But if they did not even live by sense along with their desires but coupled them with dullness of perception, they even turn into plants; for it was this, the growth-principle which worked in them, alone or predominantly, and they were taking care to turn themselves into trees. (III.4.2.12–24)

In this equally stunning passage, Plotinus certainly shows that he agrees with Plato about those who satisfy their appetites believing that they are the most important ends of life.

Plotinus' last sentence (as the *Enneads* are arranged by Porphyry) also berates pleasure:

> This is the life of gods and of godlike and blessed men, deliverance from the things of this world, a life which takes no delight in the things of this world, escape in solitude to the solitary. (VI.9.11.49–51)

Thus, Plato and Plotinus both believe that true pleasure is pleasure (or happiness) which results from knowing the Good and that it is wrong to pursue bodily pleasures—bad pleasures—as the end of human life.

In conclusion, Plato and Plotinus agree on the following ethical points: the nature of happiness and the happy person; the nature of Love, its connection to Beauty, and its ability to manifest itself as either an irrational desire for bodily beauty or desire for the Good; the importance of purification and reverence or piety; the way in which we should live: we should be philosophers, virtuous, just, and temperate (among other things); the way in which we should not live: we should avoid being vicious, ignorant, impious, and over-concerned with our self or our body (among other things); the importance of music, when properly practiced/enjoyed; the imitative nature of arts and the acceptance of certain kinds of art; humans and other living things' desire for the Good; the doctrine that no one errs willingly; and pleasure and pain, where there is such a thing as true pleasure that should be pursued, and false pleasure that should not.

4

Conclusion

I have tried to show as conclusively as possible, while addressing my opponents' objections, that Plotinus followed Plato's philosophy closely, not essentially differing on eighty-seven separate major (and some minor) philosophical claims related to mysticism, epistemology, and ethics.

I have addressed the following criticisms elsewhere: (1) There are Aristotelian/Stoic elements in Plotinus so he is not a Platonist; (2) Plotinus endorses the existence of Forms of Individuals (such as the Form of Socrates), but Plato does not, so he fails to be a Platonist in this respect; (3) Plotinus will not be an original philosopher if he merely follows what Plato says; (4) Plotinus claims that the ultimate experience is a non-dual union, where one's soul somehow literally becomes one with the One, to the point where there are not two things, but only One; Plato never declares this, so Plotinus has a different view of the ultimate experience and fails to be a Platonist in this respect; and (5) Since Plotinus only mentions a handful of dialogues, he cannot be a full-fledged Platonist.[320]

Therefore, given my adducement of passages, my analysis, and my replies to my opponents in this work, I conclude that Plotinus does not essentially differ on the issues of mysticism, epistemology, or ethics. Adding the passages, analysis, and replies to opponents in my previous work, I hope we are warranted in concluding that Plotinus is indeed an exemplary Platonist, if not *the* Platonist.

Notes

Introduction

1 The following interpreters argue in favor of the Unwritten/Esotericist position: Findlay (1974, pp. xii, 29; 1978, pp. 106, 232–3); Gaiser (1980, p. 8); Miller (1995, pp. 226–7; see pp. 236–7, 239 with pp. 239n. 20, 242–3 for considerations in favor); Reale (1997, p. 24 and a point in favor at p. 45); Sayre (1983; see especially p. 283n. 4 for his list of those in favor as of 1983; 1987, p. 72); Tigerstedt (1977, p. 69); Brisson (1995, p. 117) adds Kramer, Szlezak, Robin, and Trendelenburg to the list. And against: Brisson (1995, p. 117; see p. 126 for an argument to that effect); and Cherniss (1945, pp. 1–31). Miller (1995, p. 240n. 21) finds the 'unwritten teachings' in *Parmenides*, *Philebus*, and *Statesman*. Reale (1997, p. 67) gives a list of topics that Plato does not cover in the dialogues because they are in the Unwritten Doctrines.

2 Gerson, 1997, pp. 295–6.

3 Tigerstedt, 1974, p. 5.

4 For views, theories, and comments on the Indefinite Dyad and/or the Great and Small, see: A.H. Armstrong (1940, p. 65); Atkinson (1983, p. 109); Bussanich (1996, pp. 51, 54); Findlay (1974, pp. 77, 218, 251; 1978, pp. 44–5); Inge (1929a, pp. 83–4); Rist (1962a, pp. 100, 102–3, 107; 1967a, p. 180); Slaveva-Griffin (2009, pp. 6–7, 14, 38, 56, 62, 68–9, 72); and de Vogel (1986, p. 83). I will not be addressing the issue in this book, except to say that I am convinced by Slaveva-Griffin's (2009) account that number originates from the Indefinite Dyad for Plato and Plotinus (p. 56).

5 Aristoxenus, *Elementa harmonica* II 30–31, adapted from Barnes (1984, p. 2397). The translations of all Aristotelian passages in this work are from Barnes (1984) unless otherwise noted.

6 *Republic* VI 506d–7c.

7 Cherniss 1944, 1945.

8 In spite of the fact that Plotinus sometimes took Aristotle's view as being compatible with Plato's, and assuming Plotinus accepted the unwritten doctrines, it is not necessary to review Cherniss' allegations of Aristotelian misinterpretations or to defend Aristotle's interpretation of Plato, for the following reasons: (1) Plotinus nowhere said that everything that Aristotle states about Plato's view is correct; (2) to the contrary, Plotinus disagreed with Aristotle on many points; and (3) Plotinus does not use Aristotle's words or accounts of Plato to describe or defend Plato's view. Thus, it is possible that Aristotle got Plato wrong in many ways, but that (a) there really were unwritten doctrines (even though my argument does not rely on their veracity per se), and (b) Plotinus was still free to investigate compatibilities between Plato and Aristotle and to use Aristotelian concepts such as *energeia*, without being accountable for all of Aristotle's interpretations of Plato's view.

9 Brisson, 1995, p. 126; my brackets.

10 For an argument where Tigerstedt speaks in favor of the Esotericist's view, see Tigerstedt (1977, p. 69).

11 Tigerstedt, 1974, p. 5. He claims to prove this thesis in Tigerstedt, 1977.
12 Ibid., 1974, p. 70. For some reason, Tigerstedt is not consistent on his spelling of "Esotericist," sometimes spelling it "Esoterist"; hence my brackets.
13 Yount, 2014, p. xx.
14 Tigerstedt, 1977, p. 64.
15 Ibid., 1974, p. 6.
16 Ibid., 1977, p. 64.
17 There is also, of course, room to investigate what Aristotle and others claim about the dialogues' contents and Plato's corpus; I focus on the dialogues here.
18 Tigerstedt, 1977, p. 65.
19 Ibid., pp. 65–6.
20 Ibid., p. 66.
21 Ibid.
22 Yount, 2014.
23 Findlay, 1974.
24 Besides Aristotle, Simplicius, Alexander, and Philoponous attribute unwritten doctrines to Plato.
25 See Findlay (1974, pp. 77, 210, 251, 374–5, 414–5, and 418–20; and 1978, pp. 44–5).

Chapter 1

1 Inge (1929a, p. 249) alludes to this kind of experience and terminology, but I myself had come to that term before reading this passage.
2 To my knowledge, no scholar's work in English claims that Plotinus is not a mystic, though it is certainly true that not every scholar claims positively that Plotinus *is* a mystic. However, Ullman and Reichenberg-Ullman (2001), in their *Mystics, Masters, Saints, and Sages: Stories of Enlightenment*, curiously neglect to mention Plotinus (and perhaps less curiously Plato) at all in their entire book.
3 Bowe (2003, p. 19); Bussanich (1999, pp. 48–9); Duncan (1940, p. 354); Edman (1925, p. 51); Findlay (1974, pp. x, 298; 1975b, p. 135; 1976, p. 24; 1978, pp. 15–6, 240); Garvie (1937, p. 425); Harvey (1996, pp. 111–35); Inge (1936, pp. 136-7, implied; 1948, p. 152); Kaplan (1958, p. 55); Laguna (1934, p. 469); Lamprecht (1927, pp. 714–5); Lodge (1966, p. 437), implied; Louth (1981, p. 1), implied; Marlow (1954, p. 39), implied; Mayhall (2004, pp. 85, 88); McEvilley (2002, pp. 186–7); Morrow (1929, pp. 345–6); Notopoulos (1944, p. 240); Raphael (1984, pp. 24, 93); Rawson (1996, p. 104): "Plato's claims about the causal and epistemic roles of the Good are certainly problematic, and mysticism may be entailed"; Rist (1964, p. 14; 1967b, pp. 414–5); Rogers (1936, pp. 76–7); Russell (1917, p. 8); Seeskin (1976, p. 574); Sheldon (1952, p. 140); Shrine of Wisdom (1936, pp. 11, 15); Sinnige (1999, p. 14); J. Stewart (1917, pp. 400, 404); Thorp (1994, pp. 3–4, 6); Underhill (1974, pp. 238, 262); Unger (1952, p. 239); Vlastos (1965, pp. 7–8; 1991, pp. 49, 78–80); and Wallis (1972, p. 3). The following commentators state that mysticism can be traced back to Plato, which does not necessarily imply that they believe that Plato is a mystic: Inge (1929a, p. 7); Pond (1856, p. 143): Platonism is a source of mysticism in general; and Whittaker (1961, p. 106). Merlan (1967, p. 356) and Shorey (1895, p. 28; 1938, pp. 49–51) claim that Plotinus takes Plato as a mystic; and T. Taylor (1816, p. 51) claims that Proclus took Plato as a mystic as well. Finally, A.E. Taylor (1934, p. 145) claims that the *Parmenides* is a "chief source of the whole Christian *theory* of mysticism."

4 Abhayananda (1994, p. 103): "Plato was not a mystic like his master; he was a thinker." See also Alexandrian Press (1985, p. 5): "The Immortal Plato is the Master Philosopher and Idealist, while the 'Divine' Plotinus is that Master of Philosophic Religious Mysticism. This is the distinction between them." See also Anderson (2004, p. 71); A.H. Armstrong (1945, p. 133); Boodin (1929, p. 495); Cornford (1939, p. 132); Dillon (1992, p. 189), implied; Gaiser (1980, p. 26); Hadot (1993, pp. 52–5); Hamilton and Cairns (1961, p. xv); Kahn (1996, pp. 390–2); Majercik (1995, p. 40): "Plato cannot with confidence be called a mystic"; More (1923, p. 184); Shorey (1895, pp. 34, 63; 1903a, pp. 3, 57; 1938, pp. 47–8); Stace (1967, p. 372); Turnbull (1948, p. xvii); Walker (1938, p. 489), implied; and Zeller (1931, pp. 290–291). Perhaps Fox (1957, p. 23) and Friedländer (1969 p. 59)—compare de Vogel (1986, p. 49)—belong in this camp as well, with their view that Socrates may be a mystic, but not necessarily Plato. Lastly, the following four commentators seem to give indications that Plato both is and is not a mystic: Carter (1975, p. 268), Plato is a mystic: "Plato shares with the traditional mystics many features," but see 1975, pp. 255, 258–60, 268, where Plato is not a mystic according to his definition thereof; according to Field, Plato is a mystic: (1934, p. 290), and not a mystic: (1934, p. 285); Friedländer, Plato is a mystic, implied (1969, p. 61, but see 1969, p. 64); and Penner, Plato is a mystic (1987): his *initial* reading of Plato: "Plato's rather extreme views seemed all too emotionally surcharged with mystical and ascetic longings brought on by epistemological and even political disappointments with the world of temporal flux" (p. viii): Plato has "semi-mystical purism" (p. 43; see also p. 127); Plato is not a mystic: (1987, p. 56, and 2003, p. 220): "There is thus no reason to be thinking here of some mystical power of the Form of the Good in another world beyond this world."

5 Abhayananda (1994, pp. 88–103; using the *Republic* as evidence that Socrates is a mystic) says, "Plato was not a mystic like his master; he was a thinker" (1994, p. 103). See also Sheldon (1952, p. 140); compare A.E. Taylor (1956, pp. 232–3), who interestingly states that Plato writes in a mystic way because Socrates in the *Symposium* has attained the vision for himself. Fox (1957, p. 23) and Friedländer (1969, p. 59); compare de Vogel (1986, p. 49) who says Socrates *may* be a mystic, but not necessarily Plato. I only count the first two commentators because they are more decisive.

6 See A.H. Armstrong (1945, p. 133); Cornford (1939, p. 132); and Vlastos (1991, p. 79).

7 Abhayananda (1994, p. 144); Alexandrian Press (1985, pp. 5–6); Allen (1983, pp. 190–1); Anderson (2004, p. 71); Anton (2000, pp. 161–2); A.H. Armstrong (1945, pp. 131–3, 137–8, 141–2; 1947, pp. 131, 154, 183; 1967b, p. 263; 1974, pp. 181, 193); Blumenthal (1996, p. 95); Boas (1921, p. 328); Bowe (2003, pp. vi–vii); Bréhier (1958, pp. 152–3); Bussanich (1988, pp. 190, 192–3; 1994, pp. 5300, 5305; 1997, pp. 339, 341–2, 364–5); Dillon (1988, p. 356; 1992, p. 189); Dodds (1928, p. 141), implied; Edman (1925, pp. 51, 54); Findlay (1975b, p. 135; 1976, p. 24); Friedländer (1969, p. 64; but see p. 61); Gerson (1994, p. 224); Hadley (1997, p. 453); Hadot (1993, pp. 6, 52–5, 72); Harris (1976, p. 6); Harvey (1996, pp. 111–35); Inge (1929a, pp. 113–4, 263; 1929b, p. 241, implied; 1936, p. 136; 1948, p. 152); Kaplan (1958, p. 55); Katz (1950a, pp. xii–xiii, depending on the definition of "mystic"; 1950b, pp. 17–8); Kenney (1997, pp. 317, 336); Lloyd (1990, p. 166); Lounibos (1984, p. 131, implied); Majercik (1995, pp. 40, 45, 48–9); Majumdar (2005, pp. 131–2); Marshall (1922, p. 464); Mayhall (2004, pp. 85, 88); McEvilley (2002, p. 649); Miles (1999, p. 169); More (1923, pp. 204–5, 243, 251, 253); Organ (1991, pp. 30, 35); Pistorius (1952, p. 161);

Rist (1964, pp. 91, 183; 1967a, pp. 221, 228; 1989, p. 188); Santayana (1913, pp. 595–6; 1936, p. 77); Sheldon (1952, p. 133); Shorey (1938, p. 40); Sinnige (1999, pp. 14–5); Snell (1944, p. 149); Stace (1967, p. 374); Turnbull (1948, pp. vii, xv); Underhill (1974, pp. 93, 263, 273, 455); Vlastos (1991, p. 78n. 158): Plotinus is the "purest" mystic in the Western world; Wallis (1972, p. 3): "Even those who know nothing else of Neoplatonism are aware that Plotinus was a mystic"; pp. 55, 88); and Zeller (1931, pp. 290–1).

8 As previous mentioned, Ullman and Reichenberg-Ullman (2001), in their *Mystics, Masters, Saints, and Sages: Stories of Enlightenment*, neglect to mention Plotinus in their entire book. Bréhier (1958) seriously questions whether Plotinus is a mystic at p. 133, but seems to assume so at pp. 147–8, and pp. 152–4.

9 It is curious not to see more mention of this in introductory philosophy textbooks because it is apparent that Plato is interpreted as a mystic in the majority opinion of scholars. In fact, in my survey of forty-eight introductory philosophy texts, forty mentioned nothing about Plato's being a mystic; five mentioned the concept of "enlightenment" in explaining the prisoner's ascent in the Cave Allegory, and only one author used the word "mysticism." However, that last author only mentioned that theologians and philosophers in the Middle Ages *interpreted* Plato that way, making it seem like this is not an accurate representation of Plato's view. In another text, the author had a section entitled "Mysticism and Religious Experience," and Plato was not mentioned there. Thus, judging from at least this survey, we have an odd way of showing or telling our students that Plato is a mystic. Perhaps this book will help to persuade differently.

10 Hamilton and Cairns, 1961, p. xv; see also Organ (1991, p. 22), who makes the claim: "Plato was perhaps more poet than philosopher."

11 Hamilton and Cairns, 1961, p. xv.

12 Ibid., p. xvi.

13 *Republic* X 595b–c, 598e, and 606e–7a.

14 I leave it open whether Philo of Alexandria may have misread or misunderstood Plato for another study and time.

15 Anderson, 2004, p. 71.

16 Boodin, 1929, p. 495.

17 Carter, 1975, p. 268.

18 Hadot, 1993, p. 54.

19 Shorey, 1938, pp. 47–8.

20 Zeller, 1931, pp. 290–1; compare Organ (1991, p. 45): "Plotinianism is the death spasm of Greek philosophy." And: G. Murray (1912, pp. 7–8): "The title of the third essay I owe to a conversation with Professor J.B. Bury. We were discussing the change that took place in Greek thought between, say, Plato and the Neo-Platonists, or even between Aristotle and Posidonius, and which is seen at its highest power in the Gnostics. I had been calling it a rise of asceticism, or mysticism, or religious passion, or the like, when my friend corrected me. "It is not a rise; it is a fall or failure of something, a sort of failure of nerve.""

21 For different definitions that commentators have created or considered, including the nature of mysticism, see, for example, A.H. Armstrong (1945, p. 131); Earle (1976, p. 520); Findlay (1975b, p. 135); Gale (1960, p. 479; mysticism is nonfalsifiable); Inge (1929a, pp. 5, 230; 1936, pp. 136–7; 1948, pp. 154–5, 157); Lamprecht (1927, p. 701); Rist (1967a, p. 214: Zaehner's definitions; 1989, p. 184); Russell (1917, pp. 8, 11); Shorey (1895, p. 28: quotes Emerson and Mill on mysticism); Sinnige (1999,

pp. 14–5); Thorp (1994, pp. 2–3: soft and hard mysticism); Underhill (1974, pp. xiv–xv); Unger (1952, p. 239); Vlastos (1991, p. 78: OED definition); and Wallis (1972, p. 3).

22 For example, uniting with nature, uniting with Soul, uniting with all there is (Being), and uniting with the source of all that is.

23 Bussanich, 1997, p. 351; see also p. 340.

24 Gale (1960, pp. 473–5) argues that Stace's view about mysticism is mistaken.

25 If it is not convincing to infer that Plato actually had a mystical experience, that is fine for my purposes—even though I personally take Plato and Plotinus to have had such an experience [agreeing with, for instance, McEvilley (2002, p. 188: "Plato, like Plotinus (and perhaps like Socrates), did in fact have that 'higher' experience of consciousness at some time or other and is in fact somewhat cryptically referring to it in such passages")]; then instead only think of my project as asserting that the claims found in Plato's dialogues and Plotinus' *Enneads* are mystical in nature.

26 I sympathize with anyone who finds this notion of a non-dual experience bewildering. Plotinus seems to refer to becoming one with the One (VI.9.3, 10, 11; VI.5.10; V.8.11; V.3.8, V.5.4, 8, 10; VI.7.34-7; and IV.4.2), but at least at VI.9.10.7–8, mentions one's ability to differentiate oneself from that moment and/or the One. For instance, Plotinus does not believe that each of us just *is* the One, the beyond being creator of the Forms, or that the One just is the Forms (see Yount 2014, pp. 8–18). For the non-dual experience possibly in Plato see Yount 2014 (pp. 127–8).

27 The only adaptations I will make to A.H. Armstrong's text is where he does not capitalize the Good, the One, or Forms, as is standard translation practice in Plato; I want to make it obvious when they are presumably referring to the same object.

28 This quotation about seeing the Good and then describing its impact on one's views concerning beautiful things occurs in Plotinus' treatise on Beauty; note that Porphyry gave the titles of the treatises, and that a charitable overall reading of Plotinus is that Beauty is not identical to the One or Good (see Yount, 2014, pp. 51–6).

29 Bussanich, 2004, p. 16.

30 Ibid., p. 15.

31 There are other similar Plotinian passages; compare IV.4.2, IV.4.5, and V.3.17.

32 *Life*, ch. 23.

33 The following commentators agree with me that the Good has all three features: Hitchcock (1985, p. 65) and Santas (1983, p. 256). Lachterman (1989–1990, pp. 139–40) argues that neither the view that the Good is chiefly an ethical principle, nor the view that it is chiefly a metaphysical principle are correct, but, to my knowledge, does not conclude that the Good is both. He also fails to mention the epistemological aspect of the Good. Luban (1978, p. 162) states: "The doctrine of the Good is best understood as an ontological, not a moral or axiological doctrine," again failing to mention the epistemological aspect of the Good. Shorey (1895, p. 74) seems to state that the Good is the summit of ethical contemplation and implies that it is the epistemological principle, and adds in the same work that the Good is primarily relevant to the logic of ethics for Plato, but is also an ontological principle that fulfills the treatment of "good" in the early dialogues (79). De Vogel (1986, pp. 52–3) mentions the supreme moral and metaphysical aspects of the Good but fails to mention its epistemological aspect. Compare Rawson (1996, p. 105): "Generally in Plato's work, and emphatically in *Republic*, metaphysics serves epistemology, and epistemology serves ethics." My view is that, at least as concerns the Good, these philosophical disciplines all meet there, at that summit.

34 Compare *Epinomis* 986c5–d4. In addition, Rist (1964, p. 91) fails to convince in his claim that "The philosophic goal of the historical Plato is to contemplate the Forms", because it is clear from this passage and others that Plato believes the goal is to know or have the vision of the Good, without which one cannot know—or benefit from the knowledge of—the Forms. Meredith's (1993, p. 52) comments about the sun in the Cave are also puzzling: "One thing we can say for certain. The 'sun' is either in the cave all the time, at least in the minds of the prisoners, or alternatively, has to be sought outside the cave and the world of sense for which it is a symbol. It can hardly be said to come into the cave." First, Plato tells us to "imagine human beings living in an underground, cavelike dwelling, with an entrance a long way up, which is both open to the light and as wide as the cave itself" (*Republic* VII 514a2–5), which implies that the light of the sun does indeed make it into the cave, even if the Good Itself does not make it into the cave. Second, Plato explicitly tells us to imagine that our visible sun is the fire in the cave, and that the sun outside the cave is the Good (*Republic* VII 517b). Third, from *Republic* VII 516b–c and 517b–c, Plato says that the Good is the cause of all things, the seasons, years, sun, and the earth, the cause of all that is right and beautiful, so this is consistent with his claim that the sun's light makes it into the cave to some extent. But to know the Good, one certainly needs to exit the cave via dialectic and other methods.

35 See the Sun Simile at *Republic* VI 508d–9a and 509b–c, the Cave Allegory at VII 517b–c, and the reprise of the Line Analogy and Cave Allegory at VII 532a–b.

36 Katz (1950b, p. 19) mentions the One/Good as the metaphysical summit of the experience, and the resulting enjoyment, but he fails to mention the epistemological or ethical components thereof; then he clarifies at p. 85n. 28: "It should also be emphasized that the Plotinic [sic] vision is ontological, not epistemological, in character. This means that it involves not only the enlightenment of the subject but also the disclosure of ontologically superior objects." Katz's comment confuses because it seems to suggest both that the experience is enlightening, but is not epistemological in nature. In the next Plotinian quotation, Plotinus believes that the experience of the Good issues knowledge, or that knowledge of the Good is possible.

37 Meredith (1993, p. 52) claims that the end of Plotinus' ascent is metaphysical and involves the contemplation of intellect and being, which implies its epistemological aspect; however, she also states that Plotinus uses Plato's metaphors (such as "the language of freedom and ascent") "which we can hardly suppose were intended by Plato to be taken anymore than as figures of the intellectual life," insinuating that Plotinus somehow is not referring to the same experience or using the same language in the same way. I believe he is doing so and we have no evidence that he is not.

38 Kenney (1997, p. 335) comes the closest to stating what I have in mind about the Plotinian ultimate experience, when he states that *contemplation* simpliciter "involves much more than 'mystical experience'" and "is a far richer notion, with moral, epistemic, ontological, and soteriological dimensions, all of which are essential to Plotinus's depiction of it." However, Kenney does not make this claim per se about the One or the Good, so we do not agree on this point.

39 Compare II.9.18.40–8 and VI.7.26.1–2. I agree with de Vogel (1986, p. 225) who states that Plotinus follows Plato very closely in what Plato says about the ascent in the Cave Allegory and the prisoners' ability to escape. However, Miles (1999, p. 170)

criticizes Bos for thinking that Plotinus' experience leads to knowledge: "From the perspective of Plotinus's philosophy, Bos's fantasy of unquestionable knowledge and absolute authority is exposed as a projection." She characterizes Plotinus' belief about the ultimate experience as being "that human access to the way the world is is only achieved by a fundamentally ineffable experience of vision/touch." We will see that Plato also describes the experience as being ineffable, as well as a vision or a touching. For now I only note the issues I take with Miles.

40 Compare VI.5.7.9–17 and V.8.10.

41 Plato also says that everything we do, we pursue for the sake of the Good (*Republic* VI 505d–6a).

42 Anton, 2010, p. 11.

43 For the Good as source of the Forms, Beauty, and knowledge, see Yount, 2014, pp. 2–18, 21–5, 56. I disagree with Anton's (2010, p. 11) view that Plotinus claims we must *climb above the Form of the Good* to touch the One. Instead, I concur with Fuller (1938, p. 286) here.

44 Sinnige (1999, p. 91) agrees and makes this point as well.

45 Compare the treatise immediately following the passage just quoted, at VI.7.35.1–19. More (1923, pp. 218–9) focuses on the negative aspect of the experience of the One: "For Plotinus the One, as the abyss into which contemplation plunges any kind of suicidal vertigo, must be lifted into the dark vacuity above both mind and being, which are relegated to a second place in a new triad." See Yount, 2014, pp. 3, 5–6, 10–11, 14–15, 43, 41, and 110, for the way in which both philosophers describe the Good as being the source of Being, and not the same as it.

46 Meijer, 1992, p. 263.

47 Mayhall, 2004, p. 9.

48 Compare *Letter* II 313b4–c1. Duncan (1940, p. 362) notes the leaping spark Plato refers to in *Letter* VII: "the highest truths could not be conveyed by the study of treatises or systems, but must pass by a spark of illumination from one soul to another."

49 To my knowledge, the *Symposium*'s authenticity has never been doubted. Cooper (1997) does not hint at any controversy as to the authenticity of the *Laws* in his introduction; however, see Nails and Thesleff (2003), who argue that Philip of Opus (qua general editor of the *Laws*) did not simply compile or arrange a collection of Platonic texts, but edited works by multiple Academicians, which they base on the *Laws*' inconsistent terminology; internal inconsistency (in doctrine or in explicit intentions never carried out, and in education requirements); and incompatibility of the philosophical underpinning of just action with other dialogues. However, since I do not *only* use the *Laws* as evidence of Plato's view in any given case (as is true here), their argument should not unduly affect my overall thesis.

50 Findlay (1975a, p. 673) notes that "Absolute Beauty is said to subsist by itself in eternal unity," but does not mention whether the experience is everlasting. Compare Rein'l (1956, p. 62), who mentions Plato, Plotinus and other Eastern writings and traditions, and then immediately thereafter states: 'What appears to be common to all of them is an element central and independent that, once grasped, illuminates the entire intelligible world.' For now I merely wish to argue that Rein'l is correct with respect to Plato and Plotinus.

51 Per Cicero (1903, pp. 39, 94, and p. 122; and see also: "The Bull of Phalaris," Livius (2015): Phalaris (c. 570–554 BCE), was a tyrant of Acragas in Sicily who became

renowned for his excessive cruelty. In his brazen bull, reportedly invented by Perillus of Athens, the tyrant's victims were shut up and, a fire being kindled beneath, were roasted alive, while their shrieks from small sounding pipes represented the bellowing of the bull. Perillus himself is said to have been the first victim. Very little of this is known for certain. For more on the bull, see McGroarty (2006, pp. 174–5).

52 The following commentators mention the difficulty in attaining the experience in Plato: Carone (2005, p. 7) and Rist (1964, p. 88). Rarity in Plato: J. Armstrong (2004, p. 179); Carone (2005, p. 7); Findlay (1978, p. 171); Robin (1928, pp. 370–2); and Thorp (1994, p. 6). Difficulty in Plotinus: Majercik (1995, p. 48); Rist (1964, p. 88); and Whittaker (1961, p. 100). Rarity in Plotinus: Majercik (1995, p. 48); Tinsley (1954, p. 48); and Turnbull (1948, pp. iii–iv); note that Robin (1928, pp. 370–2) highlights the rarity aspect in Plato, and in the next paragraph, while discussing Plotinus, fails to do so, apparently to move on to another point of difference such as the soul's fall, evil, and others. On the rarity of the experience in general, More's (1923, p. 240) comment is apropos: "As it was said in the ancient mysteries: many carry the wand, the visionaries are few."

53 I am citing different passages that show Plato's view of the difficulty of becoming virtuous, of having a vision of either the Good or Beauty. I do not intend to necessarily imply that these are identical experiences.

54 Plato also asserts the difficulty in discussing the maker and father of the universe at *Timaeus* 28c3–5; compare 40d6–9.

55 Compare *Protagoras* 344b6–c5. See also *Epinomis* 991b5–c1, *Republic* VI 509d–11e, 511c3–4, and 511d6.

56 See also *Phaedrus* 256b4–5, and compare *Gorgias* 526a2–b1.

57 Hesiod, *Works and Days*, 287. See also *Protagoras* 340b7–c2, c8–d5 and *Republic* II 364c7–d3. Compare *Republic* IV 435c, *Greater Hippias* 304e, and *Meno* 81d–e.

58 See also *Republic* VI 503e–4a.

59 See also *Letter* VII 340d6–1a1.

60 Compare VI.7.26.1–2, 6–12, and see III.2.5.1–5.

61 See also *Republic* VI 493e2–4a5.

62 Compare *Sophist* 254a–b.

63 It should be noted that Plato emphatically states in several places in the *Republic* that women are in principle just as qualified as men to know the Good and be guardians of the ideal state (see V 451d–2a, 455c–e, 456a–b, 456c–d, 456d–7a, 457a–d, and 459d–e).

64 Compare *Laws* XII 951b4–7 and *Epinomis* 992c4–d3; according to Plato, few people are happy and only a few can truly be happy in this lifetime, given their thoughts, abilities, and pursuits.

65 Compare III.3.4.13–8.

66 For literature on ineffability in general, see Appleby (1980); A.H. Armstrong (1945, p. 131); Gale (1960); Hick (2000, p. 35); Kellenberger (1979); O'Meara (1993, pp. 54–9); Sells (1994, pp. 3–4); and Yandell (1975, 1979). For arguments that the notion of ineffability is inconsistent or logically incoherent, see Appleby (1980) and Gale (1960, p. 473).

67 The first two of these quotations come from p. 308, the latter two from p. 309. Kellenberger (1979, p. 309) states that the fourth sense of ineffability is "the most pregnant category."

68 For ineffability in Plato, see Benitez (1995, p. 129); Dodds (1928, p. 141); Findlay (1974, pp. 298, 301; 1978, pp. 28, 171, 214–5); Friedländer (1969, pp. 60–3); Gadamer

(1986, p. 28); Gaiser (1980, pp. 14–15); Inge (1948, p. 157) implied; Jessop (1930, p. 47); Laguna (1934, p. 469); Luban (1978, p. 167); Miller (1995, p. 242); Reale (1997, pp. 192–6); Rist (1967a, p. 221); Runciman (1959, p. 117); Sells (1994, p. 5): "elements of apophasis existed" in Plato; and Shorey (1938, p. 41): "in some moods." This list totals sixteen. Ineffability in Plotinus: A.H. Armstrong (1945, pp. 138–9; 1974, p. 182); Bussanich (1996, p. 38); Dillon (1988, p. 356); Dodds (1928, p. 141); Findlay (1976, p. 28; 1978, pp. 214–5); Friedländer (1969, p. 63; 1991a, p. 72); Inge (1948, p. 157); Katz (1950b, pp. 20, 23–4, 47); Miles (1999, p. 170); O'Meara (1999, p. 281); Organ (1991, pp. 45–6); Rappe (2000, pp. ix, xi, 19–21) inferred from "Neo-Platonists"; Rist (1967a, pp. 183, 217, 221); Robin (1928, pp. 370–3); Sells (1994, pp. 5, 15); Shorey (1938, p. 41); Wallis (1972, pp. 88, 90); and Whittaker (1961, p. 102). This list totals eighteen. Ineffability in Socrates (from the trance passage in the *Symposium*): Friedländer (1969, p. 59).

69 A.E. Taylor, 1956, p. 232. I disagree with Taylor that Plato never refers to the Good as God; I believe he does just that in only one place, at *Republic* X 597b–d, where he claims that God creates the Forms, which is consistent with the Sun Simile of *Republic* VI.

70 Ibid., 1960, pp. 94–5.

71 See also *Timaeus* 40d6–9.

72 See also *Timaeus* 49a6–b4; compare 29b1–c7.

73 This feature seems to fit either category 1 or 2 of Kellenberger's criteria.

74 See also VI.9.7.16–23.

75 For more passages on ineffability in Plotinus, see VI.8.19; compare V.3.13, V.5.5, VI.8.8, and VI.8.18.

76 Plotinus also tries to explain more precisely why the experience is ineffable: see, for example, VI.9.10, V.5.10, and V.3.14.

77 Rist (1967a, p. 221) argues that ineffability is more prevalent in Plotinus: "We often speak of Plotinus' account of the mystic vision. And it is certainly true that, following the *Symposium* . . . Plotinus very frequently uses such language. . . . But faithful to Plato though he may wish to be, Plotinus cannot remain satisfied with this language. The aim of the mystic is not a *seeing*, but a *being*. It is not vision but union which is the goal and end of life. Hence Plotinus has to say, as has often been noticed, that this language of vision, of seeing, of contemplating, is inadequate." However, I believe Plotinus is being faithful to Plato and using the concept of ineffability in the same way.

78 Compare A.H. Armstrong (1945, p. 133), who argues that, though we see purification and unification of the soul as requirements in Plato's *Phaedrus* and *Symposium*, neither Plato nor Socrates were brought to mystical union or even the desire of it. Obviously, I disagree with Armstrong on the latter points.

79 I cannot easily find a commentator who mentions this requirement for Plato. But see Boas (1921, p. 328), who states while commenting specifically on the Sun Simile, that one must be made beautiful in order to see Beauty; and Gerson (1989, p. 94), who mentions *Republic* 443e1 and its point of "becoming one out of many" in the acquisition of virtue. Compare A.H. Armstrong (1945, p. 133).

80 See also *Laws* IV 716d4–7a4.

81 Compare *Republic* VII 521c5–8.

82 *Republic* VII 525a9, and see 525a–6b and 526d–7b. See also Findlay (1974, p. 21): "After the envisaging of all this ordered richness, the endeavor to reduce it to the formality and purity which could, on Plato's view, only be found in a philosophically transformed mathematics, and lastly the attempted derivation of all this ordered

purity from Principles or a Principle of such meta-mathematical purity as to achieve, on Plato's view, the necessary ineffability of a mystical Ultimate."

83 *Republic* VII 526c10.

84 Ibid., 528a9; see also e4.

85 Ibid., 527d1.

86 A.H. Armstrong (1976, p. 194) questions the possible difference between Plato and Plotinus on whether dialectic and the pursuit of the ultimate experience is better practiced as a group activity or as an individual one, and ultimately argues that they have similar views on this question. Gaiser (1980, pp. 14–5) mentions *Parmenides* 136e in the context of the truth's being attainable only after prolonged dialectic.

87 Reason, Spirit, and Appetite.

88 See, for example, *Republic* IV 443c–e, as well as Gerson (1989, p. 94); Hitchcock (1985, pp. 75–80); and Reale (1997, pp. 206–7); I agree with their comments.

89 Commentators have also mentioned these two as requirements: (1) Love: Hadot (1993, p. 56): I'm inclined to argue that love is merely part of our hardwiring for Plato (and Plotinus), being part of our desire for the Good; namely, it is not something to develop separately, as goodness, for instance. I contest Hadot's additional objection that Plato and Plotinus do not have the same view of love (see 'On Love' in chapter 4); and (2) Politics: Organ (1991, p. 22).

90 Kenney (1997, p. 336) states that the whole text of the *Enneads* gives us the requirements of the experience: "Plotinus does not function in the *Enneads* as an interpreter of his own experiences, from which he derives his theology. Instead we find in the texts a program for achieving the same cognition, the same enlightenment that Plotinus himself attained." O'Daly (1973, pp. 85–6) apparently believes that the experience of the One is inevitable, which does not seem warranted from Plotinus' text (see I.6.8.25–7).

91 For other commentators on purity in Plotinus, see A.H. Armstrong (1945, p. 133) and Majercik (1995, p. 48).

92 For more on Plotinian purity, see especially IV.7.10.27–32; see also II.9.15.22–7.

93 Here Plotinus is paraphrasing Plato's *Timaeus* 50d–e, as A.H. Armstrong (1988b, p. 328) states.

94 This passage seems to allude to meditation. Also, though A.H. Armstrong (1974, p. 182) is certainly right in saying, "In [V.1.2–4] we have what looks like a program of spiritual exercise for such men by which they can attain experience of the higher world," Plotinus certainly discusses the requirements in many other passages throughout the *Enneads*.

95 While discussing why not everyone attains the vision, Plotinus alludes to the problem partially being due to the body, and that by renunciation, the vision is possible (VI.9.4.15–35).

96 Mayhall's (2004, p. 88) note is representative of similar comments: "Plotinus, unlike Plato, adopts a much more thorough attempt at mystical experience in this attempt to abandon things material." In my view, Plato warns against the body and urges us to purify ourselves of it as much as possible, to the same extent as Plotinus.

97 Wallis (1972, p. 85) mentions virtue as being equally important as the intellectual component of dialectic to Plotinus.

98 For other commentators on the unity requirement, see A.H. Armstrong (1945, p. 133); Blumenthal (1996, p. 95); Fuller (1938, p. 285); Helleman-Elgersma (1980, p. 457); and McEvilley (2002, p. 190): "only a unified act of knowing can know the One, to know this knowledge is to be it, and hence to know oneself."

99 Boas (1921, p. 328) mentions this point in Plotinus and believes, as I do, that we can find this view in Plato. I disagree with Rist (1967a), however, because he takes Plotinus to task for allegedly changing what Plato said about working on statues: "[T]here are cases where Plotinus, for some reason which we cannot be sure we understand, actually changes what Plato says. A striking example of this has been pointed out by A.H. Armstrong [1961, p. 112], who observes that whereas in the *Phaedrus* (252d7) Plato describes the process of doing good to one's beloved as 'working on a statue' . . . Plotinus in I.6.9.13 exhorts the searcher for the Good to go on 'working at *his own* statue' (p. 183). He returns to this point: 'But the conflict of Goodness and Beauty in *Ennead* 5.5.12', or the matter of 'working on one's own statue' in Plotinus' version of the *Phaedrus*, are the real tests. In the case of the latter we might say that Plotinus was working from memory, that he forgot exactly what Plato had said, that 'it was something about working on statues.' But how curious that a man who is said to have found the whole truth in Plato and who is quite capable of quoting accurately should not bother to look up the text if he thought that accuracy was of tremendous importance" (p. 186). Contra Rist, the main point is not whether Plotinus used Plato's expression in an identical way, but whether Plato believes that one must work on one's metaphorical statue in order to see or know the Good, and I believe, based on the previous passages on virtue and goodness, that Plato would definitely agree with Plotinus' claim here. Rist's charge is especially stunning (at least to me), given that he says (at 1967a, p. 182) that Plotinus regards himself as a philosopher but not a scholar.

100 See also V.1.1.31–35.

101 Compare especially V.5.12.1–5, VI.7.15.31–2, and V.3.8.45–9; note, however, that in V.5.10.1–8, Plotinus questions whether we can capture the Good's power as a whole or in part, and argues that if we captured it fully, we'd be identical with it, which is impossible. This implies that we may partially capture its power.

102 See Dodds (1951, p. 286; 1960, p. 4) and Gurtler (1992, p. 457).

103 On this point, see A.H. Armstrong (1976, p. 194) and Wallis (1972, p. 85); compare Bussanich (1994, p. 5302).

104 See also VI.9.11.1–4.

105 Sinnige, 1999, p. 19.

106 Ibid.

107 Ibid.

108 Organ, 1991, p. 22.

109 See also *Theaetetus* 172c–7b for the way in which philosophers appear ridiculous to the multitude.

110 Compare *Theaetetus* 172c3–6; see also *Republic* VII 520a–d with 517c–e.

111 Findlay, 1974, p. 154.

112 Gaiser, 1980, p. 24.

113 Ibid.

114 Organ, 1991, p. 21.

115 To my knowledge, no commentators have raised this issue in English-language scholarship.

116 Some commentators seem to suggest that Plato and/or Plotinus have imagined what they discuss; for instance, Abhayananda (1994, p. 103): "[Plato] held that all particular forms, thoughts, and acts approach perfection only insofar as they approach fidelity with those original Ideal forms. It was a notion born, not of vision, but of imaginative speculation; yet it was a notion which seemed to answer some important questions,

and which fired the imagination of other philosophers of his time as well." And Miles (1999, p. 173): "The compelling attractiveness of [Plotinus'] vision, his imagining the real, is instructive" (see also Shorey 1938, p. 40).

117 For passages concerning the Good, where Socrates says that he is only giving his opinion and is not sure if his account is exactly the way things really are, see *Republic* VI 506b–7a and VII 517b.

118 Note that Plotinus does his best to argue for many aspects of his view, for example, that materialism is wrong, or that there must be a One beyond Intellect; given the prevalent view that Plotinus has had (or definitely claims to have had) an experience of the One, then the fact that Plato also makes arguments for his position does not necessarily show that Plato did not experience the Good.

119 Bowe (2003, p. 19). See also Findlay (1974, p. x), who boldly states that Plotinus' reading of Plato "represented what almost anyone with any interpretative flair must arrive at, if he read the main speculative passages in the Dialogues and Epistles with some care, and was willing to 'put two and two together.' My remark does not, of course, apply to those unable or unwilling to draw conclusions from more or less palpable hints, or constitutionally unable to understand metaphysical or mystical utterances, or to enter into mystical feelings, but such classes of persons should certainly never engage in the interpretation of Plato." So according to Findlay, the anti-mystical Platonic interpreters are just wrong.

120 Inge (1936, p. 136).

121 The following commentators actually refer to Plato as a rational mystic: Findlay (1974, p. 21, emphasizing the math requirement, p. 298; 1978, p. 15–16); Inge (1936, p. 137); Mayhall (2004, p. 9); Notopoulos (1944, p. 240), implied; Russell (1917, p. 8); Sinnige (1999, p. 14); and Unger (1952, p. 239). Interestingly, Garvie (1937, p. 425) says Plato is "not the practical" mystic, by which I confess I am not sure what he intends.

122 See, for example, Sinnige (1999): "There is a mysticism built upon the desire of knowledge and aiming at a state of bliss in which the soul may know her first and divine origin. This state of bliss is reached at the end of a long journey of detachment and philosophical meditation … [This first kind of mysticism] may be called the rational method, and is best exemplified in Plato. Contemplating the many manifestations of goodness and beauty in the visible world, the philosopher becomes aware that all of them represent a unique principle of perfection (*Symposium*). Rising above these visible instances he may come to see what is above the visible Forms and even at the other side of the principles of existence and 'at the other side of Being' (*Republic* VI 509)" (p. 14). And: "The other kind of mysticism is not built upon desire of knowledge in the first place. It takes the human heart as its home with its ineradicable desire of the real and eternal existence. What it strives after is a State of the Union-in-love with God, lover of the soul. … The western medieval mystics tirelessly give evidence of this ruling force, a deep affection for their suffering Lord. No philosophy is needed. The loving heart finds its way to the beloved by unfailing intuition. … For Plotinus there is no Savior who as a living person may be loved by the meditating mystic, when he tries to realize the presence of the living God and the soul. But a clear affirmation is found of the principle that 'in the center of our own being' the presence of the ultimate and universal is to be found. One of our specific points in the philosophical system of Plotinus is the importance of the judgments and feelings of the individual person" (p. 15). See also Boodin (1929, p. 495: "Plato is looking for the intelligible, not for an emotional intoxication. He,

therefore, chooses as the field of investigation the realm of structure"); Carter (1975, p. 268); and Majercik (1995, p. 40). I do not believe that Plato fails to describe the vision of Beauty in emotional terms (as well as in epistemic ones), that Plotinus' system is not built upon the desire for knowledge, and that no philosophy is needed on Plotinus' view.

123 See, for example, More (1923, p. 243); Shorey (1895, pp. 28–9; 1938, p. 44); and Zeller (1931, pp. 290–1).

124 R. Weiss (2001).

125 I agree with Bussanich (2004, p. 2) when he says: "Plato's own revelatory experiences motivate his use of images and symbols which themselves constitute a trail left by his fellow travellers [sic] on the journey to truth."

126 If I have it right, Plato does not have *beliefs* about reincarnation, recollection, souls, dialectic, the Good, and the rest; he has knowledge that they are true. I hold this, in spite of his not providing an account—as he demands from the true dialectician in *Republic* VII 534b–c—of every one of his claims in the dialogues. Moreover, if we look to Plato's Divided Line Analogy, he can be read as pushing for more than just rational, scientific belief or understanding; there he maintains that even studying mathematics (and, perhaps by inference, science, and logic)—though important to understand in theory as well as in practice—is not itself sufficient for knowledge. He faults mathematics for using unquestioned assumptions and visible diagrams, concluding that this is the cognitive ability of understanding, while lauding dialectic for proceeding to an unassumed first principle, labeling this knowledge. This implies that knowledge is perhaps not scientifically provable, not necessarily logical, and not even necessarily rational. Bussanich (2004, pp. 9–10) gives yet more evidence of nonrational practice in Plato: "There is likely to be something such as a path to guide us out of our confusion" (*Phaedo* 66b2–3). Now, this path is usually construed as an intellectual enterprise which aims at rational discursive knowledge. But the Socratic path also involves the practice of meditative withdrawal and self-concentration (64e5–6, 65c7–9, 66a, e2–4, 67c1, 79d, 81bc), which is synonymous with the "practice of dying" (67e, 81a1–2).

127 Compare Thorp (1994, p. 4): "Plato considers that knowledge in the strong sense, knowledge of the [F]orms, is infallible [*Republic* V 477e6]. A very great deal of scholarly ink has been expended over the difficulty of understanding why a dialectical method of enquiry which proceeds by making assumptions and testing them should ever be able to yield infallible certainty. In such an epistemological approach nothing is ever final, all is subject to question and revision. But the difficulty vanishes—I mean the difficulty of interpretation—if we realize that the infallible certainty is the product of mystical intuition, and that one of the standard features of this experience is precisely the sense of unshakable certainty which surrounds it. *The anhypothetical [sic] principle of knowledge is a different kind of knowing, the product of a mystical experience. Just understand that Plato was a mystic, and take him seriously as one, and the long difficulty about dialectic and certainty vanishes*" (emphasis added; see p. 6 as well). Against my view, the Alexandrian Press (1985, pp. 5–6) states without argument: "The Immortal Plato is the Master Philosopher and Idealist, while the 'Divine' Plotinus is that Master of Philosophic Religious Mysticism. This is the distinction between them. . . . [Plotinus] was a true Mystic; that is, one who was conscious of the immanence of the divine in the human, and of the spiritual in the material. He not only knew the *truth* of what he taught but also the *reality* of it; and because of this, the world of Sense held no attractions for

him save in so far as it could express the world of Spirit" (1985, pp. 5–6; compare Field 1934, pp. 285, 290). It is curious how the Alexandrian Press can confirm that Plotinus knows the truth and reality of his system, and can also know that Plato does not. Everything they say here about Plotinus also seems to be Plato's view.

128 A.H. Armstrong (1945, but not thereafter).

129 Ibid., 1947 and thereafter.

130 Ibid., 1945, pp. 138–9. See also Bréhier (1958, p.p 147–8), who asks what place his experience has in Plotinus' philosophy, and answers that many interpreters have concluded that there is only a loose connection between the experience and his philosophy. Katz (1950b, p. 19) says that Plotinus "knows he cannot rest his case on" his experience, even though he states that people who have had it will know what he is talking about. I concur with Katz that, philosophically, Plotinus cannot rest his case on the experience, but that does not imply that this experience did not inform him of the One's existence and its qualities. Katz (1950b, pp. 23–4) further claims that Plotinus did not have a special experience, and that the experience is not the same as Plotinus' interpretation of it (and that Plotinus' interpretation of his experience is not correct.) The former claim is not provable, and the *Enneads* say quite the opposite; the latter Katz bases on "(1) showing that the assumption of transsensible realities can be seen to arise on purely conceptual grounds and (2) by showing that the descriptions which Plotinus gives of alleged *special* experiences can easily be seen to refer to experiences that are *in kind* not different from sense experiences and which hence do not seem to warrant the assumption of *levels* of experience" (24). My response to (1) is that Katz cannot prove whether Plato himself had the experience that informed him of a transcendent Good in order to have that conception of the Good. And with regards to (2), an intellectual experience of becoming one with, or having a vision of, something that is beyond being is not conceivable as a sense experience; if anything qualifies as an experience that is different in kind from a sense experience, this is it. See also Turnbull (1948, pp. iii–v).

131 Gerson, 1994, p. 218.

132 Ibid.

133 Ibid.

134 Ibid., (pp. 215–6) is aware of this passage and also correctly notes that it is Plotinus' view that "no one *should* be content with anything less than Union with the One, so long as he is capable of it" (p. 188).

135 Gerson, 1994, p. 218.

136 Ibid.

137 Ibid.

138 Ibid., p. 224.

139 A.H. Armstrong, 1945, p. 138.

140 Ibid., 1947, p. 183. See also: "Plotinus takes very seriously his philosophical duty of arguing for the transcendence of the One. But it seems to me also clear that the impulse to argue this way comes from his experience, and that he does not think that any of his hearers or readers will be ultimately satisfied or totally convinced of the truth of what he is saying until they have shared that experience, as he exhorts them so insistently to do" (1974, pp. 192–3).

141 Bussanich (1988, p. 5). I also heed his point that Plotinus states that we can experience the other ontological levels (Nous, the All-Soul) as well, and that these are significant (1994, p. 5305); Plotinus just does not urge us as much to have these other experiences as he does concerning the One or Good.

142 Ibid., p. 5300. He also notes that the idea that Plotinus is a mystic and philosopher bothers some (1997, p. 341) but that most Neo-Platonist scholars believe that Plotinus is both (p. 339).

143 Dillon, 1988, p. 356. For the other commentators mentioned with whom I agree (only in these passages listed here), see Dodds (1928, pp. 140–1; 1951, p. 248 with p. 265n. 78; 1960, p. 7); Katz (1950b, pp. 19, 25); Kenney (1997, p. 335); Majumdar (2005, pp. 131–2); More (1923, pp. 178–9); Organ (1991, p. 28); and Rist (1967a, p. 183; 1989, p. 190).

Chapter 2

1 In this subsection, I agree with Menn's excellent work (1995, p. 19) and his analysis of "*Sophia*-and-*nous*" (except perhaps his claim that the latter is a Form).

2 Compare *Timaeus* 28c6–8 and 30b.

3 See also especially V.8.5.15–7, I.2.6.12–5, and V.9.11.24–7; compare I.2.7.6–7 and I.4.9.14–21. For other references to wisdom's association with the management of "the All" (here, the universe), as parallel to *Philebus* 30c, see II.9.8.8–16, III.2.13, V.1.4.1–10, and VI.6.18.29–35. On the general point, compare A.H. Armstrong (1945, p. 139), who argues that Nous "is conceived by Plotinus entirely in the true Platonic tradition, as the summit of the natural hierarchy of being and knowledge."

4 Rappe, 2000, p. ix; see also p. xiii. The same objections and comments as in the text apply to her comments there, and on my view, everything that she states about the Neo-Platonists' views of truth, philosophy, tradition, language, and identity theory of truth are all Platonic.

5 See also *Theaetetus* 176c1–3.

6 J. Armstrong, 2004, pp. 175–6. I note here that he contrasts the picture in the *Phaedo, Phaedrus*, and *Republic* with the "good human life," which "involves the application of one's knowledge to the world of change, creating harmonious mixtures of limit and unlimited as an intelligent craftsman" (p. 176). I believe that this is Plato's ideal for all human life, throughout his work, and see no conflict or incompatibility between what J. Armstrong calls "the ideal life" and "the good human life."

7 J. Armstrong, 2004, p. 171.

8 See also I.2.3.21–2.

9 Anton, 2010, pp. 12–13.

10 Hadot, 1993, p. 72.

11 Rist, 1964, p. 191.

12 Re: Rist's allusion to the non-dual aspect of the ultimate experience (mystical union and union in the Plotinian sense), see Yount, 2014 (pp. 127–8).

13 Hitchcock, 1985, p. 68.

14 One might think that knowledge of the Good just *is* knowledge of all the Forms, as opposed to knowledge of the Good's *entailing* knowledge of all the Forms. This issue is related to whether the Good just is all of the Forms collectively and what Plato and Plotinus intend by claiming that the Good or One is beyond being, with which I dealt with in Yount (2014) on pp. 6, 10, and pp. 2–14, 30, 33, 35, 36–40, 47, 104–5, 148n. 6, 149n. 15, 153–4n. 39, 154–6n. 44, and 168n. 127, respectively.

15 See also VI.9.11.45–51. Rist (1973, p. 79) mentions Plotinus' view that one's awareness of one's goodness or wisdom does not make one better off; one is equally good or wise, respectively.

16 See also *Euthydemus* 280b and *Republic* IX 585b.
17 If the wise are happy, it stands to reason that Plato says that few people are wise [*sophia*] at *Republic* IV 429a. It also works with Plato's claim in the *Timaeus* (88b) that wisdom [*phronēsis*] is one of two natural desires in humans, given what he says about all living things' desire being for the Good, as well as the claim that the lover of wisdom desires all, and not part, of wisdom [*sophia*] at *Republic* V 475b. For claims about Reason's being wise [*sophia*] and exercising forethought on behalf of the whole soul, see *Republic* IV 441e; compare *Republic* IV 442c–d.
18 See also I.3.6.8–14, III.2.9.19–27, and VI.9.11.45–51.
19 Ciapolo (1997, pp. 496–7) raises this issue: "If *eudaimonia* is achieved only by those who enjoy a super abundance of life, because they alone are endowed with intellect, and if the One-Good is above life (insofar as It is the source of life, presumably even superabundant life), then what the human soul enjoys and its mystical union with the Primal Reality must be a state beyond life and beyond *eudaimonia*. The reason for this is that *eudaimonia* is dependent on intellect, while the mystical union is supra-intellectual (since such mystical union no longer involves a duality of knower and known)." Since Plato and Plotinus seem to agree that the Good is beyond being and life, Ciapolo's comments apply equally to Plato on my view.
20 Compare *Symposium* 209a5–8 (presumably, on Plato's view, a just and temperate soul is also a pure soul).
21 See also I.2.7.6–7, I.6.6.12–3, I.4.16.10–7, and IV.4.12.4–5.
22 Compare A.H. Armstrong (1976, p. 194).
23 See also *Meno* 88e–9a (where Plato repeats this thesis, but adds that part or all of virtue must then be wisdom), *Symposium* 209a5–8, *Republic* IX 591b, and *Laws* III 689d and 693c.
24 Compare Anton (2010, pp. 12–13), which I argue against.
25 Plato also makes the somewhat related claim in the *Euthydemus* and *Meno* that if wisdom (*phronēsis* and *sophia* in the former, *phronēsis* in the latter) leads, then its possessor will make greater use of goods like wealth, health, good looks, and so on (*Euthydemus* 281d with 279a–b) and the wise person will make better use of wealth and other so-called goods (*Meno* 88e). Can we find this claim in Plotinus? Yes, but the evidence is a bit more indirect, in part because Plotinus tells us (in a Platonic way) that we should not even be concerned with health or wealth, but only the way in which we can meet the requirements of being able to have the vision of the Good (see, for example, I.4.16.1–9 and V.9.11). At I.4.15.1–6, however, Plotinus asks whether two wise [*sophia*] men are equally happy, if one possesses natural goods and the other possesses the opposites; he answers in the affirmative, provided that they are equally as wise. He continues, that as long as these goods have nothing to do with wisdom, virtue, the vision of the Good, or the Good, they will amount to nothing (see also I.5.8.13–9). From one perspective, this quote shows an apparent incompatibility with Plato's view; namely, because wise men can be equally wise whether or not they have natural goods, natural goods are not made greater (as Plato says) through wisdom. However, both philosophers believe that happiness is a state or a disposition and not a process; if happiness is a state, then if one is happy, it does not matter if one is wealthy, healthy, and the rest (as both philosophers also state). Moreover, they believe wisdom produces happiness, which implies that wisdom helps one choose the actions and use one's possessions in the best way so as to lead one to happiness, all of which is compatible with what Plato says in the *Euthydemus* and *Meno* passages.

26 I agree with the following Platonic commentators on this issue: Allen (1983, pp. 193–4) and Findlay (1974, p. 293; but note 1978, p. 28, where I admit that the Good may be beyond knowledge). Compare Rist (1964, pp. 91–2).

27 Compare *Charmides* 174b11–d1, which helps show that everything that Plotinus says about Plato is not only found in the middle dialogues, as some commentators have mentioned.

28 Luban, 1978, p. 162.

29 Other noteworthy comments: (1) Gosling (1999, p. 55) calls Plato's statement that "real knowledge is of *the* good" one of four "strange" things that Plato says. (2) Hampton (1990, p. 93) has a developmental view of the Good, arguing that in the *Philebus*, Plato holds that the highest knowledge is realizing that the Good is an organic whole, and the ideal good life is the properly arranged knowledge and pleasure types in imitation of the Forms. He then adds that this is not the Neo-Platonic goal of contemplation that seeks mystical union with the One. My reply is that in saying what he does about goodness and the Good in the *Philebus*, Plato has not thereby changed his mind about what is said about the Good in the *Republic*. After all, after writing the *Philebus* (according to most commentators' opinions), Plato wrote the *Laws*, which are meant to be the laws of the republic, which will have the educational program detailed in the *Republic*. More importantly, I believe that Plato only refers to the Form of the Good (at most) twice in the *Philebus*: 15a and 61a. His references to the good in the *Philebus* are similar to those made about good and bad in *Republic* X (608d–9a); namely, they apply to sensible instances, or "life on earth," and not the Form of the Good in general. (3) Rawson (1996, p. 107) believes there is a conflict between the Good's being the supreme object of knowledge and desire; for now, I will only state that if there is a real problem here, both Plato and Plotinus have it, because I have shown that they both hold that ultimate knowledge is of the Good, and will show that all souls desire the Good. Lastly, (4) while discussing whether Plato is a mystic, Rogers (1936, pp. 77–8) argues that in general (excepting the *Symposium* and *Phaedrus*), the Platonic philosophical goal is contemplation, scientific thinking and science, so Plato is not a mystic. He is not accounting for the *Symposium* or *Phaedrus* that he mentions, and he is not accounting for the *Republic*'s "mystical" statements about the Good in its central books or his "science-degrading" statements (viz., the discussion of the line's top two subsections in the Divided Line Analogy, where science seems to be second best, under dialectic that only deals with Ideas). But why, prima facie, would a mystic be prohibited from contemplating the Good or scientific thinking? Why are these mutually exclusive categories, per Rogers?

30 I agree with Findlay's (1975a, p. 673) statement that Plato and Plotinus have the same view of knowledge of the Good's being above Being, and with A.E. Taylor (1918, p. 631) that the ecstatic state is not the goal for Plotinus. Robin (1928, pp. 372–3) also acknowledges that knowledge of the One is possible for Plotinus. In addition, I agree with McGroarty (2006, p. 174) that Plato and Plotinus have the same view of the Good's being the greatest form of knowledge.

31 Compare II.9.18.40–8 and VI.7.26.1–2.

32 First, I disagree with Hardie (1936, p. 118), as his comments may apply to Plotinus. That is, Hardie was admittedly arguing specifically about Proclus in what follows, but I want to dispel the notion that he is correct *if he were* making the same claim about Plotinus. Hardie states: "There is a quite definite hiatus between the teaching of the *Republic* and the full-blown Neoplatonic doctrine of the derivation of intelligence and its objects from [1] an unknowable first principle. [2] The doctrine that the Good can

be known only by an immediate contact which transcends intelligence is not that of the *Republic*. [3] Rather, the Good is implied to be the supreme object of intelligence as the Sun is of vision (516b). [4] The process of dialectic would fail to reach its consummation if the Good were impenetrable to the human intellect" (my numbered brackets). Re: (1): We have seen that Plotinus does state that we can know the Good, just as Plato has; however, we'll see there is the possibility that we cannot know the Good/One (for *both* philosophers). Re: (2): The Good is the source of knowledge and truth; it is commonly held that for Plato, knowledge is of the Forms; if the Good causes the Forms to exist, then we can infer that, for Plato, the Good is in some sense transcending Being (or Nous). Re: (3): I agree, keeping in mind that Plotinus uses the vision metaphor as well. Re: (4) We must analyze how it is possible for Plotinus and Plato to state that dialectic is the best part of philosophy that enables us to achieve knowledge of the Good while they both also claim that knowledge of the Good is possible for humans. Second, Harris (1976, p. 7) confuses me with this statement: "In some respects Plotinus' way of salvation is reminiscent of Plato's theory of knowledge, since Plato places intuition higher than discursive reason. Plotinus' theory of knowledge, however, goes considerably farther than the limits of Plato's epistemology. . . . In Plotinus, as we have just seen, true knowledge passes on beyond general knowledge to a direct knowing of the Ultimate. Although this view is not inconsistent with Plato's epistemology, it is a rather radical development of it in view of the more cautious limits that Plato imposed upon knowing." Harris does not show why Plotinus "goes considerably farther than the limits of Plato's epistemology," since the Good is the ultimate in Plato's philosophy just as much as it is for Plotinus. In Plato, "true knowledge passes on beyond general knowledge to a direct knowing of the Ultimate," to use Harris' words about Plotinus. Lastly, I fail to see how Plotinus goes beyond Plato's cautious epistemological limits (whatever these limits are, exactly). See also Robin (1928, pp. 369–70) who argues that the goal is to soar to the infinite for Plotinus, but not for Plato.

33 Katz, 1950b, p. 85n. 28.

34 Zeller, 1931, p. 290. Zeller's second objectionable statement about Neo-Platonists is: "The kernel of philosophic thought lies no longer in knowledge of the object but in the state of the soul of the subject which is exalted to its highest bliss, the ecstatic union with God, by means of asceticism and pursuit of knowledge" (p. 291). Again, Plotinus states that knowledge of the Good is ultimate; as for the state of the soul's being exalted to its highest bliss, both philosophers say happiness is a state and that asceticism is necessary for the experience.

35 For commentators who basically note Plato's view here, see Findlay (1978, p. 126); Gadamer (1986, p. 89); Gerson (1994, p. 67); Gosling (1999, pp. 55–6; but the claim is "strange"); Rawson (1996, p. 106; the "Good is more valuable" than knowledge because it causes it); Reeve (2003, p. 43); and Shorey (1895, pp. 36–7). I appreciate Menn's (1995, pp. 55–6) explanation of the analogy with vision in the Sun Simile and its connection to the causation of knowledge and *noesis* by the Good. Mohr (2005, p. 79) argues that Plato's move here, that the Good is the cause of truth and knowledge, unsuccessfully avoids the problem of the causal inertness of the Forms. Shorey (1895, p. 65) asks the humorous question as to whether Plato's statements that the Good is beyond knowledge, truth, and being, are daemonic hyperbole, or "pious ejaculations thrown out at an object, forms of emotional expansion" or whether they have any definite significance; he then argues that the *Philebus* provides the key to interpreting the *Republic* VI statements: "the Good, though nearly akin to knowledge, is not mere

knowledge any more than it is mere pleasure, but is a mixture of many elements, owing its acceptability to a causal principle which combines these in due proportions." My reply to Hampton (1990, p. 93) in p. 219n. 29 works equally well here against Shorey.

36 See also VI.9.6.48–57 and III.9.9.1–18.

37 Compare VI.9.5.10–2, where Plotinus states that knowledge is of rational principles (or Forms).

38 See also V.5.12.37–40.

39 For further Plotinian affirmations of the details of Plato's Sun Simile, see especially I.7.1.20–8; see also II.9.4, V.5.7, V.6.4, and VI.7.21, for the metaphor of the Good or One's giving off light and being the sun, as well as there being a lord of light.

40 For commentary on the Divided Line Analogy in general, see Des Jardins (1976); Ferguson (1963, pp. 188–91, 191–3); Grube (1966, p. 25); Hill (2002, pp. 9–10, 118–19); H. Jackson (1882); Joseph (1948, p. 42); Luban (1978, p. 162); Morrison (1977, pp. 212–3); Murphy (1951, pp. 159, 163, 170); Owen (1953, p. 94); Raven (1953, p. 22); N. Smith (1998, pp. 292–4); and Stocks (1911, p. 88). For arguments against the degrees of reality view in Plato, see Penner (2006, pp. 252–7). For the connection (or not) between the Divided Line and the Cave, see Joseph (1948, p. 41); Raven (1953, p. 30); Reeve (1988, frontispiece; I disagree with his rendering of the sun outside the cave's being equivalent to the Forms in his chart); and Robinson (1941, pp. 192–5). For commentary on the relation (or lack thereof) between the Sun Simile, the Divided Line Analogy, and the Cave Allegory, see Ferguson (1963, p. 188) and Raven (1953, p. 32).

41 The following commentators agree with me that the Good is the unhypothetical first principle of the Divided Line Analogy: Allen (1983, p. 193); Murphy (1951, p. 174); Nettleship (1925, p. 256; compare p. 253); Penner (2006, p. 250); Reeve (2003, p. 42); Robinson (1941, p. 165; 1953, pp. 108–12); Sayre (1983, pp. 198–9); and White (1976, p. 100).

42 Incidentally, Inge (1929a, p. 234n. 2) points out that Plotinus uses *dianoia* and *noēsis* in the same way as Plato does (substituting one for the other, generally using them interchangeably).

43 B.D. Jackson (1967) argues that Plotinus "tries to define a mode of awareness that transcends the top of Plato's divided line. In VI.9.4 he says that awareness of the One comes neither by *episteme* nor *noesis* but by a presence transcending knowledge" (p. 322). Plato and Plotinus both claim (or imply) that the experience of the Good is knowledge and perhaps not knowledge, a vision, a touching, so we cannot simply state that Plotinus has a Line-transcending awareness in his philosophy that Plato does not have. In fact, it seems that the Good is not on the line in Plato's Divided Line because it is said to be not being but beyond being at *Republic* VI 509b8–9; so whatever awareness Plotinus believes there is to experience such a thing seems to be necessary on Plato's view as well. See also Wolfson's (1952, p. 126) interesting discussion that seems to say that Plato and Plotinus have the same view.

44 I am in good company here: Desjardin (2004, p. 231); Menn (1995, pp. 55–6); Miller (1986, p. 175); Mohr (2005, pp. 219, 222, 248–9); Rein'l (1956, p. 53); A.E. Taylor (1956, pp. 230–2); and Thorp (1994, p. 4). More specifically, see Mohr's (2005, pp. 248–9) excellent analysis of *apoblepein*, as evidence that knowledge is a form of direct acquaintance for Plato, which also implies that this knowledge is non-discursive.

45 For additional Platonic passages where he refers to the vision of the Good, see *Phaedrus* 277d–e, *Republic* VII 516b–c, 516e–7c, 518a–b, 518d–9b, 520c, 526d–e,

532a–d, 533a, 540a–c; compare *Republic* VI 500d, VII 508b–c, 533b–d, X 615a; *Letter* VIII 357a–d; *Epinomis* 986c–d, 988e–9a; and *Alcibiades* I 134d.

46 See A.E. Taylor (1956, pp. 230–1) for his argument that Beauty is like the Good for Plato, so when he uses the "touch" metaphor for Beauty, it applies equally to the Good. I agree with Taylor's argument in theory, but wish to stick even more closely to the text here.

47 From *haptō*, meaning to fasten, or bind fast.

48 Thorp (1994, p. 3) called my attention to this passage, for which I am grateful. See also *Phaedo* 79d1–7, *Phaedrus* 249d4–e4, and *Letter* VII 344d1–5, *Cratylus* 404d1–3 and 412b–c.

49 That is, Plotinian commentators do not dispute Plotinus' use of the vision metaphor, but whether Plotinus uses it differently than Plato. E.g., Wolfson (1952, p. 126) agrees with me that Plotinus and Plato are on the same page on this issue; Majercik (1995, p. 48) and Meijer (1992, p. 263) do not. Moreover, Majercik (1995, p. 51) mentions that Plotinus uses the vision and touch metaphors.

50 For additional Plotinian passages where he claims that a *vision* of the Good may be had, see I.4.13, I.4.15, III.5.3, III.8.10, V.1.5, V.2.1, V.5.10, V.6.5, and VI.9.3. Compare de Vogel (1986, p. 215).

51 De Vogel (1986, p. 215) notes that Plotinus uses the touch metaphor with respect to the intelligible objects in general (as well as the Good, which I am noting in the text).

52 To my knowledge, Plotinus only uses this metaphor (with *epaphē*) with respect to the Good one other time at VI.9.9.17–9; compare VI.9.7.16–26.

53 See also Rist: "There is one very curious feature of this matter which must now be considered. In all the passages we have looked at Plotinus refers to what he sees, to his vision of the Good. . . . Henry remarks that 'it is noteworthy that a Greek philosopher should prefer, in describing the mystical union, expressions which are more appropriate to the sense of touch than to the sense of vision.' . . . Why does he think of it as strange? Surely because he is thinking, as is not at all surprising, of Plato, of the Sun in the *Republic* and of the general significance of light-metaphors both in orthodox Platonism and probably in the writings of Posidonius. There seems to be more than a matter of words involved here. If we attempt to draw a general picture of Plotinus' descriptions of and allusions to ecstasy, of the highest attainment of the philosophic life, we soon come to realize that it is erroneous to suggest that there is an ultimate parallelism between what Plotinus is describing and the description of the vision of beauty and the *Symposium*. We see that vision is not the ultimate achievement for Plotinus; his aim rather is union, which he tends to describe in a language of touch and contact. Yet Porphyry, we recall, says that Plotinus followed the patterns of contemplation laid down in the *Symposium*, and when Plotinus alludes to his *personal* experiences specifically, he uses the language of vision too. 'He who has seen it knows what I mean.'" (1967a, pp. 197–8). It is interesting that Rist suggests here that the vision is not ultimate, since Plotinus is pretty clear (see p. 69 and p. 222n. 50 for "vision of the Good" references to Plotinus) that the vision is ultimate.

54 Miles, 1999, p. 170.

55 See Harris (1976, p. 7); McEvilley (2002, p. 101; recollection is non-discursive as well), Mohr (2005, p. 227); and A.E. Taylor (1956, p. 231); compare Thorp (1994, p. 4) and de Vogel (1986, p. 50), who both claim that the knowledge of the Good is not the same kind of knowledge as that of the Forms. I disagree with Sayre (1987, pp. 70–1), who argues that Plato believes, unlike in the *Republic*, that the Good can be reached by argument in the *Philebus*. Sayre is ignoring the Divided Line Analogy, where dialectic

is said to be the method of the topmost section of the line by which one may arrive at the Good somehow, and the passage where Plato states that a true dialectician must be able to give an account of the Good (*Republic* VI 511b3–c2). These considerations also count against Gadamer (1986, p. 31).

56 Lachterman (1989–90, p. 141).

57 Mohr, 2005, pp. 245–6.

58 On this issue, I agree with Harris (1976, p. 7: "Plato places intuition higher than discursive reason"; Katz (1950b, pp. 63–4; but see p. 25: "His rationalism ends by denying human reason in favor of some superhuman reason (*nous*). Rationalism thus becomes superrationalism, which is in fact the partial abdication of reason"); Rappe (2000, pp. xiii, 20–1; I extend her statements to include Plato, which she may or may not endorse); and Whittaker (1961, p. 100). Compare Cornford (1939, pp. 132, 133n. 2); who argues that Socrates' trance in the *Symposium* was discursive (he was, among other things, "*thinking* about something"), and since mystical union transcends the discursive, Socrates is not a mystic.

59 See also VI.9.6.48–57 and III.9.9.1–18.

60 Mayhall, 2004, p. 9.

61 Ibid.

62 Friedländer, 1969, p. 63.

63 See Findlay (1978, p. 28), who says the Good "will hardly in fact be an Idea at all, and will in a sense be beyond ideal Being or Knowledge or beyond even the act of naming." Friedländer (1969, p. 63) states that there can be no knowledge of what is beyond being (we'll see Rawson repeat this as a possibility). Lynch (1959, pp. 88–9) states that "The Good is above all our knowing and there can be no scientific knowledge of it" because there "can be no scientific knowledge of strict unity." And Reeve (2003, p. 43) seems to hint at the paradox raised here. Compare Gonzalez (1998, p. 217: "the paradox is that the good is so essential to our knowledge that it does not seem to be itself knowable" but "knowledge of the good clearly cannot be an empty knowledge of knowledge").

64 Rawson (1996, p. 103) notes that the good is beyond Socrates' understanding in the *Republic*, but this does not take a stand on the present issue, of whether knowledge of the Good is really not possible in theory.

65 Plato, via Socrates, via Diotima, states that one *knows* Beauty at *Symposium* 210c–e (which is *just* before he discusses the vision of Beauty's *not* being knowledge, in the quotation that follows in the text), and 211d (leaving aside the *Republic* V passages).

66 Perhaps an even more apt translation for *tis epistēmē* is "some branch of knowledge," but the point is the same either way.

67 Louth (1981, pp. 11–12) notes the "no knowledge" point here as well, arguing that there will be no logos of Beauty, and then suggests that we can ask the same question of the Form of the Good in the *Republic*; he then argues that the vision of Beauty in the *Symposium* transcends knowledge just as the vision of the Form of the Good transcends knowledge in the *Republic* (pp. 12–13).

68 Grube/Reeve translates this sentence as follows: "in the knowable realm, the form of the good is the last thing seen, and it is reached only with difficulty" (*Republic* VII 517b8–c1), rendering *mogis* by "reached only with difficulty," but an equally plausible rendering is "hardly" or "scarcely," so Shorey's translation of the same passage ("in the region of the known the last thing to be seen and hardly seen is the idea of good") is reasonable. Moreover, *mogis* modifies *horasthai* (to see), which implies that it is either hardly seen, or seen with difficulty. Nevertheless, Desjardin (2004, p. 231) reminded

me of several passages in the *Phaedrus* where Plato says that even the best of us "does have a view of Reality, just barely" because of our unruly "horse" (248a5–6); "their experience is beyond their comprehension because they cannot fully grasp what it is that they are seeing" (250a7–b1); and "the senses are so murky that only a few people are able to make out, with difficulty, the original of the likenesses they encounter here" (250b3–5).

69 See also VI.7.41.25–38.

70 See Gadamer (1986, p. 28): "One should be aware that Plotinus takes a new step when he also calls the 'One' *epekeina noēseōs* (beyond all thinking), and when he takes all being and all thinking too as a pointer into transcendence. In the context of the *Republic*, in contrast, the good is presented as the unifying one of the many. In other words, the good is articulated precisely in respect to the inner duality and dialectical function of the one which Plotinus' double 'beyond' [beyond being (*ousia*) and beyond thought (*noēsis*)] is specifically intended to exclude." If the Platonic Good is beyond being, then Plato has the same issues as Plotinus, especially given my points in favor of the idea that we cannot know the Good. So Plotinus has not necessarily taken a new step, as Gadamer claims.

71 See Hardie (1936, p. 118), and "the requirement that the guardian should know the good is incompatible with Neoplatonism" (p. 136), which shows that Hardie misses that both philosophers state (or imply) that the Good is both knowable and not knowable.

72 Shorey, 1938, pp. 53–4.

73 Rawson, 1996, p. 104.

74 Ross, 1951, p. 97.

75 Rist, 1964, p. 58.

76 At least one other issue will be shown to be inconsistent on both philosophers' views: they both claim that the Good is both a being and not a being but beyond being.

77 I agree with Thorp (1994, p. 4) that knowledge of the Forms is infallible; and with Mohr (2005) that the Platonic notion of "giving an account" does not equate to one's being able to give a definition (pp. 244–5), nor does it imply that one has discursive knowledge (pp. 246–8; Mohr cites Platonic passages in support of these claims). I disagree with Fine (1978, p. 124), who defends the view that knowledge is of propositions for Plato; I view Forms, as Penner does, as real natures of what things really are, and hence as non-propositional objects (see *Symposium* 211a–b).

78 See also *Symposium* 211c6–d1.

79 For a similar passage, see *Republic* VI 511b–c. See also VII 533b–c and 533e–4b, where Socrates recaps what was claimed in the Divided Line Analogy, and explicitly uses "knowledge" (*epistēmēn* at 533c5 and at 534a4–5) to describe the higher sections of the line. Also, Plato states that Reason is purified and sees clearly when it beholds reality (*Republic* VII 527d7–e3).

80 I take More's (1923, p. 247) comment to apply to Plotinus as well as to Plato (though I doubt More would so take it): "Genuine Platonism holds, on the contrary, that there is a truth dependent on our right apprehension of the power and operation of the eternal and impersonal Ideas; it holds that our happiness depends on the discovery of, and our obedience to, such truth."

81 Compare IV.6.2.18–22.

82 See also VI.1.6.11–3.

83 Harris, 1976, p. 7; compare Gerson, 2005, p. 268.

84 For some relevant passages that lead up to this one, see *Philebus* 55d and 58b–d.

85 Harris (1976, p. 3), Rist (1964, p. 21), and Sumi (1997, p. 412) basically agree with two kinds of knowledge, but the latter two seem to ignore attaching the "opinion" label to the favored phrase "sense knowledge."

86 For another passage on opiners' dreaming about being versus one's having a true waking vision, see *Republic* VII 533b–d. Mohr (2005, p. 246) adds: "We should not expect a description of the Good at the end of the process," that is, the transition of "waking" from the "dream." If Mohr is correct, this may help defend Plato from not giving a full account of the Good, as many have noted and often lamented.

87 Compare especially V.5.11.11–22.

88 I applaud Mohr's (2005, p. 222) taking Plato seriously when he says that opinion and knowledge have different faculties *and* different objects, even though I am still sorting out the details of exactly what Mohr says there.

89 Compare *Phaedrus* 273d3–6. For where Plotinus explains how one can know things external to one's soul, see IV.4.23.

90 I agree with Inge (1929a, p. 152) on this issue.

91 See also I.3.4.1–23.

92 See also VI.6.8.7–8. Compare what Plotinus says about false beliefs at III.5.7.49–51.

93 Rist, 1967a, p. 234; see also pp. 235, 237, and 239.

94 I disagree with the following commentators: Anton (1992 or 2000); Bréhier (1958); Cornford (1939, p. 132); Dodds (1928, p. 141); Harris (1976, pp. 3–4, 6–7); Meijer (1992, pp. 299–300); More (1923, pp. 204–5); Overstreet (1909, p. 4); Pistorius (1952, p. 28); Rist (1964, pp. 91–2); Robin (1928, pp. 369–70); Shorey (1938, p. 37); Sinnige (1999, p. 19); and Zeller (1931, pp. 290–1).

95 Findlay, 1978, p. 165.

96 Mohr, 2005, pp. 227–8.

97 Gaiser, 1980, pp. 14–15, 27.

98 Luban (1978, p. 167); Mohr (2005, p. 245); Murphy (1951, p. 174); and de Vogel (1986, p. 47); compare Nettleship (1925, p. 253).

99 I agree with these commentators as well: Mohr (2005, p. 251), who connects dialectical realization of one Form (Beauty) with the realization of other related Forms (for example, Temperance and others); Murphy (1951, p. 181), who claims that dialectic clarifies, as opposed to proves or disproves, mathematics; and Thorp (1994, p. 4), who claims that mysticism interpretively explains Plato's view of dialectic.

100 He mentions dialectic in the *Euthydemus*, *Gorgias*, *Cratylus*, *Phaedrus*, *Republic*, *Theaetetus*, *Sophist*, and *Philebus*; the most discussion is in the *Republic*.

101 See also *Republic* VII 533c7–d4 and 518d3–7; compare McEvilley (2002, p. 433).

102 Plato repeats the point that only dialectic advances to the first principle at *Republic* VII 533c–d.

103 See also *Phaedrus* 265e–6d and *Sophist* 253d–e; compare *Parmenides* 135d–6c, and 136d–e.

104 It is interesting to note that there is much discussion and debate about Socratic *elenchus*, its nature and purpose; this passage, however, seems to imply that Plato thinks that dialectic also accurately describes what Socrates is doing in the early dialogues as much as *elenchus* does. Regrettably, there is not space to develop this point here.

105 Moreover, in the *Sophist*, Plato implies a connection between the practice of dialectic with the "cleansing" (purification) of the soul: "The method aims at acquiring intelligence, so it tries to understand how all kinds of expertise belong to the same kind or not. And so for that it values them all equally without thinking that some of

them are more ridiculous than others, as far as their similarity is concerned. . . . You just asked about what name we call all the capacities that are assigned to living or nonliving bodies. As far as that's concerned, it doesn't matter to our method which name would seem to be the most appropriate, just so long as it keeps the cleansing of the soul separate from the cleansing of everything else. For the time being, the method has only tried to distinguish the cleansing that concerns thinking from the other kinds—if, that is, we understand what its aim is" (*Sophist* 227a10–b4, b6–c6). Note also that if we may infer that this "method" is dialectic, then dialectic is itself a purification.

106 Anderson, 2004, p. 68.

107 Sayre, 1987, pp. 70–1.

108 For instance, "The important point remains that the Good is reached by argument, and not submerged in a flurry of images as was its fate in the *Republic*" Sayre (1987, p. 71). Plato explicitly states that dialectic can reach the Good at *Republic* VII 534b–d.

109 A.H. Armstrong argues that both philosophers agree on the importance of dialectic (1967b, p. 235); and philosophy and dialectic are equally social for each philosopher (1976, p. 194), with which I agree. Inge (1929b, p. 106) states: "Plotinus follows Plato closely in his treatment of dialectic" (compare 1936, p. 137). Lloyd (1990, p. 164); Majumdar (2007a, p. 15); Overstreet (1909, p. 4); and Wallis (1972, p. 85) also basically state that Plotinus and Plato have the same view of dialectic. Shorey (1938, pp. 49–51) argues that Plotinus followed Plato more closely on dialectic than other Neo-Platonists did. I agree with what Katz (1950b, pp. 23, 25) says about Plotinus' view of dialectic, except that I take what he says there as applying to Plato as well (it is apparent that Katz does not concur with my view).

110 Curiously, Majercik (1995, p. 50) mentions Plotinus' endorsement of dialectic as being most important to have the ultimate experience, but fails to mention that Plato says the same thing in the *Republic*.

111 Anton, 2000, p. 51.

112 See Bréhier (1958, p. 4) and Robin (1928, pp. 369–70).

113 I agree with Bussanich (1994, p. 5303): "The preparatory study Plotinus has in mind is rational or discursive thinking, not the direct intellectual vision found in the intelligible world." Lloyd (1990, p. 165), however, claims that there are two kinds of dialectic, one of which is non-discursive: "This second type of dialectic is non-discursive by ruling out not just inference but the transition from subject to predicate and definiendum to definiens. Indeed, it rules language itself; it consists of the Ideas, which are, of course, thoughts, not the Ideas *and* knowledge of them. This is already implied by the thesis that they are not outside Intellect, for it implies that as they really are they are not prior to knowledge, and it is as they really are that the undescended Intellect presents them." Both Plato and Plotinus believe that discursive dialectic eventually takes one to the vision of the Good (which itself is non-discursive), so deciding this issue is indeed tricky.

114 See Shorey (1938, p. 37, implied, pp. 38–40); after repeatedly criticizing the Neo-Platonic reading of Plato (and quoting *Phaedrus* 247c), Shorey puzzlingly concedes: "Accepted in this way, Neo-Platonism is perhaps the most beautiful of philosophic systems" (p. 42).

115 See Anton (2000, p. 66). Of course there is a sense in which both philosophers are claiming that dialectic takes its practitioner beyond logic, since Plato states in the Divided Line Analogy (and Plotinus confirms) that dialectic goes beyond

mathematics and logic, to Ideas and beyond Ideas, to the unhypothesized first principle (the Good), which is beyond being. I can respond to this kind of criticism by admitting that both accounts are ultimately supra-logical, but still argue that both philosophers hold the same view; namely, that dialectic itself is a rational discursive process that has as its end a non-discursive vision of the Good. The latter claim is true for both philosophers as well. See also Anton (2000, p. 62), where he says that Plotinus' dialectic has as one of its functions "a way to theoretical discovery and construction," which acknowledges a logical component to dialectic for Plotinus.

116 See Sinnige (1999, p. 19) and Zeller (1931, pp. 290–1), who charge that Plotinus is not describing a Platonic intellectual process of ascent, and that Neo-Platonists doubted the possibility of theoretical knowledge of the ultimate basis of being, respectively.

117 Taking the virtue of wisdom to be equivalent to one's having the vision of the Good, the following commentators agree that the culmination of dialectic is a vision of the Good: Laguna (1934, p. 452) and Rist (1964, p. 91): compare Harris (1976, pp. 6–7).

118 Thanks in part to this Plotinian quotation, I believe Cornford is mistaken when he states: "Nor has any mystic ever suggested that the proper avenue to [Plato's] supreme experience lies in a fifteen-years course of pure mathematics and dialectic, followed by fifteen years of subordinate office in the State. There is no evidence that either Socrates or Plato ever had that experience which was really the core round which Plotinus constructed his theology. Had any such tradition been known in ancient times, the Neoplatonists would have made the most of it" (1939, p. 132). Technically, in the case of Plotinus anyway, Cornford is partially right. Plotinus did not explicitly state that potential knowers of the Good should practice mathematics for fifteen years and then dialectic, subsequently serving the State for fifteen years. However, Plotinus makes it clear that mathematics is important for philosophers and tried to found Plato's ideal state based on his *Laws*, so we can safely infer that he did endorse Plato's guardian regimen. I instead concur with Rist (1964, p. 91), who specifically mentions Plotinus' endorsement of studying mathematics before dialectic.

119 Anton (2000, p. 54). Similarly, Anton (1992, p. 10 or 2000, p. 53) claims that Plotinus constructed a system to make Being humanly accessible by removing all differences between human and divine intellect, but in so doing Plotinus assigned to dialectic tasks and functions that Plato's philosophy of Forms did not require. As for unifying oneself, both philosophers seem to advocate this in order to know the Good or One. Even granting that Anton is correct in his Plotinian interpretation, he has not shown that dialectic must necessarily have a different function for Plotinus.

120 Bréhier, 1958, p. 141.

121 Dodds, 1928, p. 141; compare More (1923, pp. 204–5).

122 Harris, 1976, p. 3; compare More (1923, pp. 204–5).

123 For references to dialectic in Aristotle, see, for example, *Metaphysics* I 987b, IV 1004b, XIII 1078b.

124 Harris goes further to state that Plotinus rejected Aristotle's logic (which is puzzling if he liked his dialectic as much as Harris suggests) and in the end devised his own Aristotelian-type dialectic (1976, pp. 3–4). These charges are a mystery to me, given the parallels that I have found in the Platonic and Plotinian texts.

125 Meijer, 1992, pp. 299–300.

126 Pistorius, 1952, p. 28.

127 See Yount, 2014, pp. 69–73.

128 Rist, 1964, pp. 91–2.

129 Ibid., p. 92.

130 See especially VI.7.15.9–10 and III.5.9.53–4; see also VI.7.16, VI.7.18; compare I.7.2, VI.7.17, VI.7.20–1; see also Yount, 2014, pp. 4, 14, 16, 37–8, 147–8n. 2, 148n. 4.

131 Anton (1992, pp. 24–5) lists five functions of dialectic, all of which are equally Platonic and Plotinian, in my view: (1) To say what each thing is, how it differs from other things and what it has in common with them; (2) To name the class to which each thing belongs, where it stands in its class, if it really exists, how many things really exist and how many do not as being other than real beings; (3) To say what is good and non-good and what things come under the good and its contrary; (4) To say what is unchangeable and what is not, and so with certain knowledge, and not opinion; and (5) As a science dialectic ceases to concern itself with the sensible world and establish itself in the intelligible realm.

132 I do not have the space to address Gulley's (1954, p. 2) specific arguments, that "the doctrine of the *Phaedo* (73 c ff.) shows an inadequate appreciation of the problems involved in assigning a role to sense-experience, and is seriously inconsistent with what Plato says elsewhere, in the *Phaedo* and in other dialogues, about the senses and sensible images; [and] that the revised and more responsible presentation of this doctrine in the *Phaedrus* is self-contradictory."

133 See also Mohr (2005, p. 227) and Shrine of Wisdom (1936, p. 57). I tentatively agree with Mead (1912, p. 176) that the primary purpose of recollection is not to recall previous earthly lives, though I think Plato and Plotinus might in fact think that such recollection is possible.

134 R. Weiss, 2001, pp. 7, 63–76. Anderson (2004, p. 73) says that the doctrine is only a metaphor but was mistakenly taken literally by the Neo-Platonists, but that he prefers a "more logical interpretation." On the (literal) assumptions that Forms exist, immortal souls exist, and reincarnation is true, all of which Plato believes, it seems logical to interpret recollection as being literally true.

135 Rawson, 2006, p. 137.

136 In fact, Gully (1954) rightly counter-argues that Plato never abandoned recollection, since he mentions it in the *Statesman*, *Sophist*, and *Timaeus*. Related to Rawson's claim that Plato does not bring up recollection as often as he should is his point: "If the *Phaedo* alone in the Platonic corpus had not survived his Academy, we could not think that Plato had a *doctrine* of recollection at all. . . . We would naturally consider recollection just one of Plato's various provisional models for exploring how philosophical inquiry requires active employment of native mental resources" (2006, p. 138). The fact that Plato mentions the view here and elsewhere, however, shows that we should take Plato as being serious about this doctrine. Mohr (2005, p. 217) questions why Plato does not explicitly mention recollection in the *Republic*, but then basically shows why the doctrine might implicitly be there (p. 219), so I do not take Mohr as going as far as Rawson does in his "sparseness" of recollection charge.

137 Rawson, 2006, p. 139.

138 See also ibid., p. 142.

139 Ibid., p. 138; see also p. 141.

140 Meno's Paradox is a two-horned dilemma created by asking the question: "Why should we look for knowledge of X?" since either (1) we already know X, in which case we do not need to look for it, or (2) we do not know X, in which case we also will not know (a) the means to gain that knowledge or (b) the moment at which we arrive at possessing knowledge. The paradox occurs at *Meno* 80d5–e5.

141 Compare *Symposium* 207e–8a.

142 See also *Laws* V 732b5–d7.
143 I agree with Wallis (1972, p. 80) and Wolfson (1952, p. 127) that Plotinus has the same view of recollection that Plato does.
144 See IV.7.12.8–11, V.3.2.7–14, V.9.13.7–12, IV.3.25.27–35, V.8.2.45–6, II.9.16.43–56, III.7.1.20–5, III.5.1.30–6, IV.6.3, V.1.1.1–3 (quoted or summarized in the text), and IV.4.5, IV.4.6, and II.9.12.
145 See also I.6.8 and V.1.1, where Plotinus metaphorically alludes to returning to the Fatherland and asks why we have forgotten our Father, respectively, which implies that we can recollect this somehow as well.
146 Gerson, 1994, pp. 179–80. He also argues: "Plato holds that in recollection we are led to recover the knowledge we had in a discarnate state. For Plotinus, the only discarnate state we have is that of our intellects or ideal selves. But these do not descend. Therefore, the recovery of knowledge, if there be such, has to be differently construed" (ibid., p. 180). Though I cannot point to the Platonic passage that states that human intellects never descend and I concede that most scholars deny that this position is Platonic, one might argue that this position is plausibly Platonic when we think, for instance, of Plato's sea god Glaucus passage, where Plato says we must look to the way in which the soul is one, and not to all of that which the soul puts on in its incarnation/descent; put this thought together with the principle of like knows like, and that the soul and Forms are immaterial, that all souls are in some sense one and that the soul (and more specifically Reason) is the most divine part of humans, and the view that Reason (or intellect) never truly descends at least seems more plausible on Plato's view, even if we cannot conclude that for certain. Moreover, we might ask, how can the part of the soul (Reason, or the part of Reason that knows the Forms) *really* descend to the point where it does not know the Forms in any sense, if Plato states that every soul knows the Forms, in some sense? Conversely, how do we know that Plato is stating that Reason descends to earth with a human soul, to the point where no part of it remains with the Forms, especially given that it always knows the Forms in some sense, and that Plotinus makes claims about the bad soul's descent and the good soul's ascent? Moreover, if we add that Plotinus says the same things about reincarnation as Plato, the fact that Plotinus says that intellect does not descend is not conclusive evidence that Plato cannot have the same view. These considerations make me doubt Gerson's conclusion that the Plotinian recovery of knowledge must be construed differently from Plato (as well as Gerson's questioning as to whether there *is* such knowledge recovery on Plotinus' view—it seems clear that there is).
147 See also V.1.11 and I.2.4.
148 Inge, 1929a, p. 227. Watson (1928, p. 491) apparently made this very claim before Inge: "Plotinus transforms the 'reminiscence' of Plato into a doctrine of 'innate ideas,' potentially present in the soul. The term 'memory,' he says, is improperly ascribed to the intellectual energizing of the soul in accordance with its innate principle. This was not understood by 'the ancients.' Their mistake arose from the fact that the soul does not always bring its latent powers into play, and indeed cannot bring them into action on its first arrival in the world." However, a cursory reading of IV.3.25 shows that Plotinus is merely making the argument that one cannot have memory of timeless, eternal beings—Forms—or of an experience that has nothing external to it, just as Plato says at *Philebus* 34a3–4, that memory is the preservation of perception, which in turn occurs "when the soul and body are jointly affected and moved by one and the same affection." Thus we see just how closely Plotinus is following Plato here, and by no means transforming his view of either recollection or memory.

149 See also I.3.2.1–4; and see V.9.5.29–32, where Plotinus connects recollection with the phrase "I searched myself"; compare V.3.8.49–53.

150 For more on the recollection of beauty, see V.5.12 and I.5.9.

151 Pistorius, 1952, pp. 98–9.

152 Due to space constraints, I cannot show that Plato and Plotinus seem to allude to and endorse meditation, if not something very close to it. For Plato, in the *Phaedo*, Socrates and Simmias link the avoidance of the hindrance of the body in pursuit of knowledge of the Forms with purification, and name this experience: "to gather [the soul] and collect itself . . . and to dwell by itself" (*Phaedo* 67c8–9). See also *Phaedo* 67c5–d3 with *Phaedrus* 249e4–5; *Phaedo* 65e7–6a10; *Laws* VIII 837b8–d1. I concur with Bussanich (2004, pp. 9–10), that this process that Plato is referring to is an internal process in consciousness, and that it has positive results in the form of wisdom and knowledge. Plotinus believes the gods of heaven (presumably souls of stars) contemplate and are always wise, with nothing to prevent them from contemplating: "Their thinking is always right in the calm and stability and purity of Intellect, and they know all things and are acquainted, not with mortal matters, but with their own divine ones, with all which Intellect sees. The gods who are in heaven, since they are free for contemplation, continually contemplate, but as if at a distance, the things in that higher heaven into which they raise their heads" (V.8.3.25–30). See also VI.4.15.18–32, V.1.2.11–7 and V.1.12.10–21; Plotinus also agrees with Plato that withdrawing from the body was a step in the direction towards knowledge and wisdom: see I.6.6.6–8, 13–6; see also IV.3.19.24–7. McEvilley (2002, pp. 589–90) adds V.8.9, where he alludes to direct intuition and IV.8.1, where Plotinus describes being lifted out of his body and having a vision of an awesome beauty. I disagree with Louth (1981, p. 41), who, after quoting I.6.8–9, states that Plotinus' encouragement for withdrawal is more intense than in Plato: "There is much that is familiar in this passage, much that reminds us of Plato: the image of flight, from the *Theaetetus*, then, more strikingly, the echoes of his Diotima's speech in the *Symposium*; only here, significantly, it is not just human beauty that awakens the soul's love, but also the beauty fashioned by the arts. But, despite similarities, the feel is different. *The emphasis on withdrawal into oneself is much stronger*; and the vivid image of making one's soul as a sculptor does a statue is new and striking" (emphasis added). My reply is that Louth is not taking into account the *Phaedo* "concentrate the soul itself by itself" passages, and I stress the fact that just because Plato only heavily refers to concentrating the soul itself by itself in one dialogue in no way implies that he does not any longer hold that view as he writes other dialogues. He may have simply felt that he made that point sufficiently and left it at that. A.H. Armstrong (1967b, p. 260) denies that Plotinus endorses meditation; but compare 1976, p. 194, where he does grant that Plotinus' "general conception of the philosophic life is one of withdrawn solitary concentration, as the *Enneads* repeatedly make clear." Again, I am taking "withdrawn solitary concentration" to be the equivalent to meditation; perhaps my disagreement with Armstrong is only semantic.

153 Due to space constraints, I cannot show that Plato and Plotinus do not essentially differ on their view of divination. Plato believes that the liver is the seat of divination (*Timaeus* 70d7–2b5); Plotinus claims that divination is possible and explains vaguely how it works (see III.3.6.22–8 with III.1.3.9–16), but does not include the liver in his explanation. However, Plotinus does mention the liver as the seat of desire (IV.3.19.23 and IV.4.28) and in conjunction with prayer (IV.4.41), which agrees

with Plato's view. Platonic commentators have basically ignored this feature of Plato's thought, while Plotinian commentators (all of whom I agree with) who have mentioned this aspect of his thought mainly argue that Plotinus is not a theurgist (Dodds, 1947, p. 57; 1951, pp. 285–6), that magic is partially effective but not on the wise man (A.H. Armstrong, 1947, p. 194), and that magic has nothing to do with the ultimate experience (Dodds, 1951, p. 286).

154 For Plato's laws concerning prayer at sacrifices and what to tell the poets who compose them, see *Laws* VII 801a5–b4.

155 See, for example, A.H. Armstrong (1938, p. 194; 1947, p. 194).

156 Plato states this, among other places, at *Laws* IV 716c2–3.

157 See Rist (1967a, pp. 211–12) for his claim that the Sages pray to the One. This seems questionable, since Plotinus mentions the heavenly bodies (or gods or God) as being responsible for responding to prayers (see IV.4.40–1), but "God" for Plotinus usually refers to Nous or Intellect, while it can also refer to the One.

158 A.H. Armstrong, 1938, p. 193; compare p. 192.

159 Moreover, A.H. Armstrong (1967b, p. 260) seems to deny that Plotinus endorses prayer. Perhaps his view is that, for Plotinus, prayer was useless to anyone, no matter the petitioner's goodness or lack thereof.

160 I concur with Mohr (2005, p. 222) that Plato is serious when he states that opinion and knowledge are different faculties and have different objects.

161 See also *Theaetetus* 187a–b, where Socrates states that they must not look to sense perception in order to find knowledge; see *Timaeus* 51d–2d for an argument that true opinion is distinct from understanding because they have a different origin (true opinion comes about from persuasion; mind, from instruction) and nature (true opinion is without reason, can be overcome by persuasion, and many humans possess it; mind is always accompanied by true reason, immune from persuasion, and only gods and very few humans possess it); compare *Republic* VI 508d4–6. Thus, Plato seems to hold this view that opinion and knowledge have separate objects in his later dialogues as well.

162 See also the Divided Line Analogy (*Republic* VI 509e–10a, and VII 533e–4b, when he recounts the divisions of the line), where Plato makes the distinction between two levels of opinion as well.

163 I concur with Inge (1929a, p. 152) that Plotinus follows Plato on the issue of opinion.

164 See also V.9.7.

Chapter 3

1 See Yount, 2014, pp. 22–5.

2 For all souls being one, see Yount, 2014, pp. 95–7; for Plotinus' claim that there are Forms of individuals, see ibid, p. 126.

3 See Yount, 2014, pp. 57–64.

4 See Yount, 2014, p. 78.

5 For these last three claims, see Yount, 2014, pp. 119–21.

6 In the MacKenna translation, Plotinus often refers to happiness as the Term, meaning the goal or end of life; that is, the Term is the Authentic Good of every living thing. Of course, this is no different than what we read in Plato.

7 Compare *Charmides* 173c–d.

8 *Republic* VII 517c4–5; adapted from Grube/Reeve.

9 Katz (1950b, p. 63) also rightly adds: "To attain this higher knowledge is for Plotinus not only an intellectual but also a moral matter"; Gerson (1994, p. 189) is correct that a person's opinion about whether or not he is happy does not decide the matter for Plotinus (and I add Plato); using More's (1923, p. 247) characterization of genuine Platonism, "that our happiness depends on the discovery of, and our obedience to, such truth [of the power and operation of eternal . . . Ideas]," Plotinus is a genuine Platonist. For more on *eudaimonia* and the ultimate experience, see Ciapolo (1997, pp. 496–7).

10 Plotinus also states at I.5.10.14–5 that the wise and good man gains benefit from actions based on what he has, neither from the simple fact that he acts nor the action's circumstances.

11 Gerson (1994, pp. 189–90) rightly notes that the happy Plotinian man desires necessities of life because they are instrumental to his existence (I.4.7.13); I only add that this is also true of Plato, and that the happy man does not seek to extend his life just for the sake of living longer. I disagree with Field (1934, p. 290), that the highest good is for a person to cooperate in the realization of the ideal community: instead I contend that happiness (via knowing the Good) is the highest good for a person to achieve; however, once this is achieved, the happy person will attempt to make others happy and "lead them out of the cave" depending on the others' proclivities, interests, abilities, and whether they currently reside in the ideal state.

12 See also *Symposium* 205a1 and 204d–e.

13 See ibid., 206c1–e3 for a passage where Diotima treats Beauty also as some thing, as opposed to beautiful things that we want to be drawn near to, for instance.

14 See also ibid., 204e2–7 with 206a3–8, where Diotima says that people love the good and want it to be theirs.

15 See also *Laws* IV 716d–e.

16 See also I.4.4.18–28. Later in I.4.4, Plotinus repeats the claim that the good man is happy due to what he has and is; see III.8.6 for Plotinus' claim that we act for the sake of some good and to possess the good in action.

17 Compare III.2.9.8–10, assuming that those who possess the good life also possess happiness; also compare I.4.4.

18 I agree with Bobonich (2002, p. 6) on this point: "Since Plato thinks that there is a very close connection between being virtuous and having a happy or flourishing life, non-philosophers' lack of virtue has starkly negative implications for their happiness."

19 See also *Letter* VIII 355a–c.

20 I agree with Carone (2005, p. 74) here, while adding my own passages to support her claim, as well as Kolb (1974, p. 137).

21 See also *Timaeus* 90b–d, where Plato states that one who consistently loves knowledge and wisdom and uses one's reason is singularly happy; see *Laws* V 730c for Plato's claim that valuing and possessing truth leads to happiness. Compare *Laws* VIII 840b–c, where Plato says we must conquer lust for happiness—Reason would play a role in such a conquering; and *Republic* V 473c–e, for Plato's claim that there is no other way for happiness in either private or public life unless philosophers become kings (or kings become philosophers), implying that Reason must be in charge for happiness to occur.

22 See also I.4.3, for a passage that claims that we cannot deny happiness to the irrational kind of lives (plants and animals) while allowing it to the rational kind of life (human life).

23 Plato also says that the possession (*hexis*) of the Good is deserving of higher honor than either knowledge or the truth, at *Republic* VI 509a5, which also certainly implies happiness.

24 Note that one cannot be truly just or get the benefits from knowing justice—and therefore be truly happy—without knowing the Good (*Republic* VI 504e–5b).

25 We've already seen Plotinus refer to happiness as a state at I.4.16.10–3; see also especially I.5.7.20–2 and I.5.10.20–3; and I.5.1, compare Gerson (1994, p. 212). Ciapolo (1997, p. 489) believes that Plotinus has a different view from Plato: "Plotinus's position on *eudaimonia*, as well as his view of its relation to seriousness and true life, while profiting from Platonic, Aristotelian, and Stoic insights, is nevertheless an original one. For him, perfect and superabundant life is to be found in *Nous* and in the intelligible nature of man. Both *Nous* and human beings (that is, the inner man in each human being) are life, while all other living things merely have life, precisely because they are less perfect and dimmer versions of Primal Life, the life of *Nous*. Hence, *eudaimonia*, the good state of one's inner reality, is identical with the attainment of identity with that One-Good by any being which has life superabundantly, that is, possesses an intelligible nature." However, I argue that they agree that our soul can "rise" to the level of *Nous* and be godly; in general, none of these claims are un-Platonic, and Ciapolo never returns to this point in her work to detail the way in which Plotinus' view differs with that of Plato.

26 I would like to note that no commentator has really brought out these kinds of claims systematically, to my knowledge; this is necessary for my project however, to show its similarity to Plotinus' view.

27 I take the *Menexenus* to be an authentic dialogue, in part based on Brandwood's stylometry (1992) and on Cooper's (1997, p. 950) evidence that Aristotle cites it several times as being by Plato, but acknowledge the possibility of its being inauthentic—see Cooper (ibid.) for considerations against its authenticity; thankfully, however, we have plenty of additional textual evidence for this section's thesis even if I cannot count on its authenticity.

28 See also *Phaedo* 84a9–b3.

29 See also: "Not that human affairs are worth taking very seriously—but take them seriously is just what we are forced to do, alas." (*Laws* VII 803b3–5)

30 See also *Republic* X 605c–d for Homer's effect on our Reason with his tragedies and our praise for how well he can affect us thereby, and 606a–c for Plato's claim that poets satisfy and delight our Spirit and relaxes our hold on Reason, so we think that pleasure is a gain, when really thereafter it is very difficult to restrain our grief over our own sufferings. Compare *Laws* V 732b–d, where the Athenian claims that we should restrain unseasonable laughter and tears, conceal excess joy or grief, whether we have good or bad fortune, and hope that God will lighten our troubles.

31 See also Gerson (1994 pp. 189, 282n. 9) and de Vogel (1986, p. 220) on this point. A.H. Armstrong (1947, pp. 194–5) curiously claims: "Plotinus is closer to the Stoics again in his account of the order and harmony of the material universe and the way in which it affects human life," and: "The wise man is beyond the reach of suffering not because his body cannot suffer but because he is utterly detached in spirit." However, Plato says much the same thing, and holds with Plotinus that we are most our Reason.

32 See also II.9.9, III.2.5, and III.2.15.

33 See also III.2.6.

34 See also I.4.11, where Plotinus claims that the "unconscious" Sage is misunderstood by the layperson; if laypersons grant inner happiness to the Sage, they cannot ask about outer activities and their effect on his happiness.

35 See pp. 209–10n. 51 to be adequately versed on the Bull of Phalaris torture device; then read I.4.13.3–12 for the full impact of Plotinus' claim.
36 See Anton (2000, pp. 141, 144) and A.H. Armstrong (1961, p. 113). Anton (2000, p. 141) adds that Plotinus holds that love is superior to dialectic in aiding us to "return to the One"; however, their views on dialectic are similar, as is their view on desire of the Good, so this claim is not un-Platonic on its face.
37 One can still submit that Plato would not chafe at the suggestion that the Good is love, when put in the context of its being an object of universal desire of all living things, which is the spirit of what Plotinus is saying; but see pp. 127–8 below for more on the context of Plotinus' passage on the Good and love. Moreover, both philosophers generally view love as being a lack, so we can be relatively assured that this statement that the Good is love and loves itself is a quirky, perhaps metaphorical statement, also keeping in mind the many other passages where Plotinus denies oneness, being, and other characteristics of the One, as does Plato (see Yount, 2014, pp. 30–9).
38 Rist, 1964, pp. 84–5.
39 Ibid., p. 97; in fairness, Rist also states that Plato did not follow up on the love qua giving/creation aspect to its logical conclusion.
40 Ibid., 1973, pp. 85–6.
41 See, for example *Republic* VI 508d–9a; compare VII 517c.
42 I suggest that, given that "God" is best interpreted as the Good at *Republic* X 596a–7e (see Yount, 2014, pp. 7–8, 19, 41–2, 78–9, 81, 191–2n. 55, 192n. 56), Plato can be interpreted as attributing wishing and willing to the Good.
43 Plato repeats Love's parental qualities of wisdom/resource (father) and lack of either (mother) at *Symposium* 204a–b.
44 I agree with Mortley's (1980, pp. 51–2) and Witt's (1931, p. 105) description of Plotinus' view of Love, but add that nothing that they say there is un-Platonic; I disagree with Anton (2000, p. 150), who claims: "Plotinus borrows nothing from the Socratic, or rather Diotima's view of eros as daimon, whether divine or human," since we see that Plotinus, quoting Plato, refers to Love as a guardian and Love as a god (see III.5.2.1–9 and III.5.4.24–5).
45 *Phaedrus* 242d.
46 Ibid., 265c.
47 *Symposium* 203b–e.
48 Ibid., b–c.
49 For more on Resource qua rational principle(s) and Poverty, see III.5.9–10.
50 See Majumdar (2007a, p. 220n. 61) for the way in which Plotinus uses "Poverty" differently in different places.
51 For Plato, see *Symposium* 203b–e. Plotinus not only affirms that Love yearns for the Good in this passage, but claims that Poverty symbolizes Matter, at III.5.9.42–57 (where matter is referred to once as "indefiniteness").
52 See also *Symposium* 204b4–7.
53 This treatise is designated as III.5.10 in the MacKenna translation, but III.5.9 in the OCT and A.H. Armstrong editions; the latter designation is used here.
54 See also *Symposium* 205e–6a and 206e. Compare *Republic* III 403a7–8.
55 I agree with Anton (2000, p. 162): "The carrier on which the soul is to rise to these ultimate heights of experience [with the One] is provided by the power of eros. . . . Only through the noetic fulfillment can any individual complete the requisite preparation for the ecstatic experience that eros alone brings."

56 Though it is not entirely clear to me, I believe the referent of "It" here is Being.

57 See also III.5.10. Compare III.5.1 for another passage on pure love desiring beauty alone; and VI.9.9 for a passage on our true desire's not being earthly beauty but veritable love's being of Beauty There.

58 I agree with Friedländer (1969) on his detailing of Plato's task and his description of the paths to knowledge (p. 40) and the characteristics of the experience (pp. 65–6), and add that we find these paths and experiences in Plotinus as well; with Penner (1987, p. 127), that Plato's ascent is from nominalistic love of beauty; and see Rawson (1996, p. 108) for a parallel passage in the *Republic* (VI 490b) to the *Symposium*. I disagree with Findlay (1978, p. 102; compare p. 101), who states that the principle of Beauty in the *Symposium* (210e–1b) does not differ from the Goodness elsewhere spoken of, since it covers all the virtues and forms of knowledge: I fail to see this written in the *Symposium*, though I grant that the experience is described by Plato certainly seems to be life-changing.

59 I agree here with Edwards (1993, p. 486) in his description of Plotinian beauty; and with Meijer (1992, pp. 299–300) that there are no Plotinian dialectics that lead to Beauty, but that this is consistent with Plato's view in the *Phaedrus*. We can use Meijer's point to address Anton's (2000, pp. 141–2) assessment that Plotinus says that love is superior to dialectic in returning the philosopher to the One. I also deny Anton's (2010, p. 12) claim that Plotinus, with his "new dialectic and reconstituted Eros leave behind both the *Republic* and the *Symposium* to enter the world of the *Timaeus* only to transform what was left of the Pythagorean *cosmos* into the infinite domain of the One"; Plotinus affirms all the chief claims of the *Symposium* and *Republic* concerning Beauty and the Good. Moreover, Plotinus did not transform the Timaean cosmos into an infinite empire of the One [that is, we have seen that Plato and Plotinus agree on the natures of God/Nous/Demiurge (see Yount, 2014, pp. 69–89), as well as the All-Soul in the *Timaeus* (see ibid., pp. 92–3, 97)]. Furthermore, I disagree with Bréhier (1958, p. 87), who claims that, where Plato arrives at the Idea of Beauty Itself, Plotinus arrives by the same path to Intelligence (which is *identical* to Beauty). However, Plotinus certainly differentiates Nous/Intellect from Beauty, and the Good from Beauty (see Yount, 2014, pp. 51–6), but there is nothing to prevent either thinker from also claiming that Nous or the Good are beautiful. Friedländer (1969, pp. 55–6; compare pp. 57–8) claims that Plotinus rejects/ignores the first step of the Ladder, sexual love, which leads to a contempt of the body which we do not find in Plato; however, Plotinus' text contains this step, even if he is not anxious to provide as much detail as Plato may have in the *Phaedrus*, for instance; and see Mortley's (1980, pp. 50–1) response to Friedländer. Hadot (1993, pp. 52–55) makes the same kind of charge as Friedländer, adding that Plotinus changes love into a solely mystical ascent to the Good. But Plato also describes the fourth kind of madness which involves love and being possessed in order to come to know goodness in some sense (*Phaedrus* 256a–b; compare 239c–d, 248d, 249d–e, 276c, 277d–e, 278a, and *Republic* III 403a); Plato says that the Good and Beauty are similar but not identical, so this experience in the *Symposium* is pretty philosophically close to what is described in the Cave Allegory, though there are certainly differences; and I have defended the view that Plato is a mystic to the same extent as Plotinus. Hadot (1993, p. 56) also details several differences between Platonic and Plotinian love: the former is masculine in tone, the latter feminine; however, despite the tone, they describe the same ascent to the same entity, so the love has the same effect; Platonic love rises through intellectual operations to the contemplation of Beauty—Plotinian love waits for ecstasy and divine

invasion; however, Plotinus describes the same Ladder and contemplation, and there is nothing in Plato that describes the vision of Beauty as being inevitable if one simply follows the prescribed steps; Platonic love after reaching Beauty produces science, education and the organization of the state; Plotinian love refuses to return to day-to-day activity unless it is forced by human condition needs; however, Plotinus wanted to found Plato's ideal state, and claiming to have had the very experience Plato describes here, Plotinus himself actually founded a school as Plato did. I am confused by Mortley's (1980, pp. 50–1) view, because he says that Friedländer is wrong that Plotinus ignores all the steps of the Ladder, but also says that Plotinus "is only concerned with the spiritual goals of *eros*" (p. 50). Perhaps this is compatible with Plato's view that the *goal* of ascent is knowledge or vision of Beauty, but each thinker's Ladder begins with physical love. Lastly, Rist (1964, pp. 187–8) argues that the Platonic Ladder of Love gives no support to a doctrine of ecstasy or of the ecstatic knowledge of God in the Plotinian sense; however, I read Plato's *Symposium* and *Phaedrus*, for example, as giving us plenty of reason to believe that the experience of Beauty is ecstatic; and nowhere does Plotinus state that if one has a vision of Beauty, he therefore knows God. Further, Rist claims that the *Symposium* is also describing the ascent to the Good as much as it is the Beautiful; so, given that Plotinus refers to the One as God, perhaps the Platonic passage *can* be so read.

60 Compare VI.9.9, VI.7.31, V.3.9 and III.5.2.

61 See Yount, 2014, pp. 55–6.

62 See also *Laws* V 739b–e for a passage that seems to imply that friends/lovers [*philoi*] are gods or sons of gods.

63 For further passages on passion, relating to sex and love, see I.1.5, I.2.3, I.2.5, I.6.6–7, III.5.1, IV.4.28, VI.7.22, and VI.9.4.

64 See V.8.10 for a passage that alludes to two of Plato's four kinds of madness—that of being possessed by Apollo and of the Muses.

65 See I.8.14, IV.3.7, IV.8.1, IV.8.4.

66 A.H. Armstrong (1961, p. 113) acknowledges this point on which Plotinus agrees with Plato. I concur with Mortley (1980, p. 51) that both thinkers claim: "sexual love could be described as a *misplaced* activity," but only if we construe this as sexual love between two partners who believe that procreation or physical love is the only rung on the Ladder of Love. I disagree with Friedländer (1969, pp. 55–6; compare pp. 56–8), who argues that Plotinus sublimates and desensualizes the Platonic world, omitting the preliminary stages of the ascent in the *Symposium*; my replies are to claim that at *Symposium* 210a–e, at any rate, Plato's world is already desensualized: at the very first stage, one is to love one body *and* beget beautiful ideas there, and thereafter only intellectual activity is described; moreover, III.5.1.55–65 pretty clearly shows that Plotinus does not disdain all sexual intercourse. I also disagree with Robin (1928, p. 371), who says that Plotinus wants to go beyond Plato's erotic in the *Symposium*—beyond intelligibility; Robin, however, fails to explain 211a–b, where Plato clearly states that the vision of Beauty is not one kind of knowledge.

67 See also VI.5.10 and III.5.1–3 for additional Plotinian evidence that love can also be a manifestation of our desire for the Good.

68 Plotinus also mentions pure love's attraction to authentic Beauty in other passages in III.5.1 and III.5.2.

69 Rist, 1967a, p. 184.

70 Wallis, 1972, p. 86.

71 For more on Plato's endorsement of asceticism, see *Phaedo* 65b–d and 114d–5a.

72 I agree with the following commentators on this issue: A.H. Armstrong (1945, pp. 133, 139–40; 1967b, p. 224); Atkinson (1983, p. 219), that Plotinus follows Plato in associating purification with separation from the body; Gerson (1994, p. 199); Meredith (1993, p. 51); Shorey (1938, p. 43); and Wallis (1972, p. 3). My previous arguments highlight my disagreement with the following authors: Harris (1976, pp. 6–7), if I understand him correctly as implying that for Plotinus (but not Plato), the salvation process begins with self-purification; Hathaway (1969, p. 20), that Plotinus, qua Neo-Platonist, demoted moral or political virtues to minimal conditions of the purification or theological virtues (see, for example, IV.7.10.40–52); Mayhall (2004, p. 88), that Plotinus' attempt (via his "ethics of escape") to abandon things material contrasts with Plato's concern of making this present life better (philosopher-king's governing of the ideal state); Meijer (1992, p. 290), who implies (from what I can tell) that Plotinus (and not Plato) holds that earthly life is not to be enjoyed, and we should liberate ourselves from earthly things; Rist (1964, p. 110), who argues that "Plotinus is more rigorous than Plato in applying the Platonic purifications" because Plato only urges us to purify the soul to make it Goodlike qua Being, but Plotinus applies it to the Good beyond being; lastly, Rist (ibid.) also says that Forms are outside the purified soul for Plato but inside for Plotinus.

73 See I.6.6.3–6; compare *Phaedo* 69c and I.2.3; moreover, Plotinus claims that purification produces the virtues at I.2.7. Compare *Gorgias* 507a–c.

74 For further Plotinian passages on purity and separation from the body (and its emotions and affections), see especially I.6.5.54–8 and IV.7.14.

75 For Plotinus' even more explicit claim that purification has the Good for its goal, as do the virtues, see VI.7.36.

76 For further Plotinian passages on purity and separation from the body, see especially III.6.5.15–22; and I.1.10, I.1.12, I.2.3–5, I.2.7, I.8.4, I.8.8, III.6.5, IV.7.14, V.8.11, VI.8.14; compare III.3.2.

77 Compare IV.4.45.47–52; compare III.3.5.

78 For instance, Plotinus refers to the One as "the Pure" (I.6.7.10; see also VI.9.3); that the pure soul is just (and thereby ruled by Reason) (I.2.5; compare II.1.9); before this incarnation some of us were pure souls in Nous (VI.4.14; compare VI.7.6); and a pure soul is at the level of godhood (VI.9.9). There is no reason to believe that Plato would disagree with any of these claims.

79 See Findlay (1978, p. 240): "The religious significance of Platonism . . . as the ultimate extension of the quest for the Well-formed and Good . . . is the guiding Principle of Mind and Thought."

80 Compare *Gorgias* 507a–c, where doing what is just by the gods, piously, and the doer of just and pious deeds must be just and pious.

81 For another reference to laws concerning impiety, see *Laws* X 907b–d.

82 See *Timaeus* 68e–9a for Plato's claim that we must seek the divine in all things for the sake of the blessed life if we wish to apprehend or receive or have any share in higher things.

83 A.H. Armstrong (1947, p. 180; see also 1967b, p. 259) claims: "Plotinus's religion is his philosophy and his philosophy is his religion"; Miles (1999, p. 170) states that for Plotinus, philosophy is not purely intellectual but a spiritual discipline; I agree with both of these statements and only add that they are certainly true of Plato's thought.

84 For more on the Gnostics' irreverence, see II.9.8, where Plotinus avers that it is blasphemous to question the beginning of the eternal, or to imply that a changing Being creates.

85 See also III.2.10, for Plotinus' claim that heaven's movements allow us to do impious actions (that is, we are not *determined* to perform impious actions).
86 Other passages that make the same kinds of points include I.3.1, I.6.7, VI.7.30, VI.8.19, VI.9.4, VI.9.7, VI.9.8, and VI.9.9–10. For a uniquely Plotinian claim that a unified person is immune from magic, see IV.4.44.
87 But see Yount, 2014, pp. 127–8.
88 See Yount, 2014, pp. 26–48.
89 See, for instance, *Republic* VI 508c–d.
90 Plato: *Laws* V 726a–7a and 743e; IX 870b–c; Plotinus: V.1.1–2.
91 I also endorse Miles' (1999, p. 170) echo of Hadot's claim that for Plotinus, philosophy was a way of life and a spiritual discipline, and, I only add (which they may not agree with, of course), just as it was for Plato.
92 Anton, 2010, p. 9.
93 See Yount, 2014, p. 87, for their similar cosmology; see ibid., pp. 69–78 for no essential differences with respect to Nous.
94 I do not agree with Bobonich (2002, pp. 7–8), who argues that Plato changes his mind from the *Phaedo* and *Republic* to the *Laws*: from believing that at least some non-philosophers are capable of being genuinely virtuous (taken here as being a good person) and living happy lives, to denying that claim because the non-philosophers' problem in the *Phaedo* and *Republic* originate in a fundamental cognitive defect, being unable to appreciate and value what is genuinely valuable. At *Laws* IV 720, Bobonich continues, that Plato condemns the procedure of threatening the citizens with penalties and turning to another law, while the legislator should instead "try to persuade the citizens to act in a manner that the laws require" (p. 8). After stating that non-philosophers can be genuinely virtuous, Bobonich changes his claim to "at least some non-philosophers can—albeit partially and imperfectly—come to appreciate and respond to genuine value" (p. 10). This is not the same claim, and precisely the question at issue. Though Bobonich argues that in the *Laws* Plato is not endorsing the basic elements of the *Republic*, in part by his argument that the *Laws* V 739a3–40a2 "endorses the community of property, women and children, and the goal of making the city as unified as possible," including the producer class, unlike in the *Republic* (p. 11), I believe the *Laws* is still endorsing the *Republic*'s basic structure. The *Laws* passage is merely giving hypotheticals—"If this situation exists somewhere now, or if it should ever exist some day, if women were common"; it is not proposed as a law, but a goal to attempt to reach. Moreover, Plato made the same arguments regarding community property, women and children (as Bobonich notes), as well as the goal of making the city as unified as possible, so the *Laws* do not represent a major change in thought; I fail to see where Plato says in the *Republic* that the guardians would not or could not in any way attempt to persuade, or that they would *only* threaten citizens, for example (and the noble lie comes to mind, which is a form of persuasion). Without such a prohibition, Bobonich's claim does not convince me. Lastly, see Stalley (1983), who argues that the citizens in the *Laws* might become virtuous only if their desires and passions are disciplined, obeying the law by habit (p. 9), and that there is no reference to the kind of virtue mentioned in the *Republic* for the philosopher-king, but maybe to the virtue of the auxiliary (pp. 56–7); compare Shorey (1903a, pp. 87–8). Similarly, Carone (2005, p. 53): "Plato's ethics in the *Timaeus* take us away from the elitism of the *Republic*, presenting instead an independent way to happiness that is available to everyone. . . . because everyone can share the universe as a common paradigm, and internalize its order." Surely Plato is

only urging everyone to assimilate to the harmonies and universal revolutions (*Timaeus* 90d), just as he urges everyone in general to be philosophers in other dialogues, though he realizes that most will not heed his advice. Lastly, see Gerson (1989, p. 100n. 25), for the technical point that "the 'perfect man' at 499b2–3 is not identified with the philosopher"; Gerson is correct that this phrase does not *have* to apply to the philosopher, but Plato can easily be interpreted as saying there that the men (and actually women) *who would be guardians/philosophers in the ideal state* will not be perfected unless uncorrupted, reluctant-to-rule philosopher-kings rule. Either way, this is a minor point.

95 Compare *Epinomis* 979b–d. Also, see *Gorgias* 526b–d for the Platonic claim that philosophers go to the Isles of the Blessed upon their death. I cannot find a similar claim in Plotinus, but they seem to share similar views concerning the good soul's fate.

96 Again, I find myself disagreeing with Bobonich (2002), who claims that Plotinus radicalizes what we find in Plato that only a philosopher can genuinely live well and lead a happy, flourishing life (pp. 1–2); and that genuine happiness requires that the sage transcend civic/ethical virtues via godlike contemplation and only the sage can do so (p. 4). Re: (1), admittedly Plato claims that each class of the ideal state will be as happy *as possible*, given the goal of the ideal state's being the happiness of the whole state in general (*Republic* IV 420b–1c, VII 519e–20a). The major point that I believe is missed by those who discuss the "problem of returning to the cave" for the philosopher is the point that, for Plato [let alone Plotinus], true happiness is a state, achieved by knowing the Good, which cannot be affected thereafter. Thus when Plato says that the philosopher would rather be contemplating, they are not made truly *unhappy* by the compulsion to rule; it is like saying that they really hate to eat; no, they just would rather not have to deal with necessary pleasures, but they are not thereby truly unhappy when they eat. We find no evidence in later dialogues that Plato changes his view of happiness or its link to the Good (if it is true happiness), even if others are said to be relatively happy. Re: (2), I cannot find passages where Plato claims that the non-philosopher is capable of rightly contemplating God, especially given his passages that one must be virtuous, godlike, or goodlike in order to see the Good (which is referred to at least once as God in *Republic* X). Moreover, knowing the Good is something that requires one to transcend civic virtues, since the Good is the source of the Forms, though, as Plotinus says (and in Bobonich' words), "civic or ethical virtues are products of the contemplative ascent of the philosopher" (and as Plato implies in the *Symposium*).

97 See also I.4.5, and I.4.7–9; for more on the Sage's control of fear, see I.4.15.

98 See Miller (1995, p. 238); I slightly disagree with J. Armstrong (2004, pp. 171, 175–6), who claims that becoming godlike for Plato in later dialogues entails improving the sensible world (*Timaeus*, *Philebus*, and *Laws*), as opposed to fleeing it (*Phaedo*, *Phaedrus*, and *Republic*), because, as I have shown, becoming divine is something the philosopher does in the *Republic*, and philosopher-kings are certainly committed to improving the sensible world in ruling the ideal state.

99 For more on becoming like god in Plato and Plotinus, see Meijer (1992, p. 329). For more on being god, see O'Daly (1973, p. 55); re: Plotinus and de Vogel (1986, pp. 228–9), even Plato seems to suggest that we become god (see *Laws* VII 792c10–3a5). In addition, see Rist (1964, p. 109), who—assuming Grube is right that we must lose ourselves more and more in the contemplation of truth, on Plato's view—claims: "We have no grounds on which to charge Plotinus with deviation from Plato if we

find him teaching the transcendence of the self. Our only criticism can be that perhaps he is more optimistic than Plato in his belief that such a divine state can be attained during this life." I hesitate to accept Robin (1928, pp. 370–2), on blending with absolute unity; Rist (1964, pp. 94, 187, 191); Majercik (1995, p. 48); and Organ (1991, p. 22)—we might become the Good on Plotinus' view—interpret that for Plotinus (and not for Plato), uniting with the One is the goal (and the universe is wholly derived from the One for Plotinus), but for Plato, we merely "might know the Good" (p. 22); Rist (1964, p. 94) adds that for Plato, we are "separated from the Gods by the barrier of lifelessness." I disagree with Organ and Rist, because I have shown that the ultimate goal for both philosophers is for us to have an experience of the Good; we do not know if the experience is a non-dual one for Plato, so we cannot assume that they differ on this point. I am not, however, denying that Plotinus states that we should unite with the One; I am only trying to suggest that whatever he means by that may be exactly what Plato has in mind when he says we should have a vision/knowledge of the Good (and that Plotinus says these things as well).

100 The first way of life is living according to the pleasures of the material realm; the second is living a nobler life but being unable to see the Forms.

101 For a similar passage to this, see II.3.9. Plotinus more closely echoes what Plato says in the *Theaetetus* about becoming like god, at I.2.3.11–22. For additional "become godlike" passages, see I.6.9, I.2.7, and VI.7.5; and see the famous last sentence of the *Enneads* (VI.9.11.49–51).

102 For the main passages where Plato discusses the ideal state, its classes, and the training of the guardians, see *Republic* III 414c–5d, 416c–7b, IV 420b, 421c, 427e, 431b–d, V 451d–2a, 455c–e, 456a–7d, 459d–e, 462a–b, 473c–e, VI 488a–9c, VII 519e–20a, 520e–1b, 525a–6b, 526d–e, 528a–c, 533c–d, 534e–5a, 539d–40e, VIII 544e–5a, IX 592a–b; *Timaeus* 17c–9b; and *Laws* I 632b–d; IV 711d–2a.

103 Majumdar (2007b, p. 158) interestingly describes the philosopher-king as "the leader of a mystical theocracy." I agree with Shorey (1903a, pp. 87–8) that the unity of Plato's thought extends from the *Republic* to the *Laws*, in that Plato does not change the curriculum away from dialectic; I agree with Carone (2005, pp. 12–13), that in the *Republic*, Plato does not say that the lowest class will be educated, but then widens education to more people in his late dialogues; but since he did not say that the lowest class would not be educated, we cannot infer that Plato changed his mind on this point. It is especially noteworthy, that someone as seemingly taken with Platonism as Findlay (1974) makes such disparaging claims against the Kallipolis: "there is little even of inspirational value" in the *Republic*'s recommendations and that proof that it would never work is found in Plato's not being able to turn Dionysius into a philosopher-king (p. 159); that the *Republic* is "in many ways a strange book" and not a manual of practical politics (p. 209); and that it is a "punishment" to read the *Laws* (p. 333). The contrast with Plotinus is obvious. Lastly, Leys (1965) argues that Plato does not have a complete political philosophy based on Leys' definitions thereof, and Sparshott (1967) extends these thoughts.

104 See also other *Republic* passages, such as Plato's Shipmaster Analogy in VI 488a–9a; his view that if a true philosopher lives in a non-ideal state, he should lay low and keep himself free from iniquity until death in VI 496c–7a; VI 500d; and VII 540d–e.

105 I agree with these commentators on these points: Anton (2010, p. 10), that we can understand why Plotinus did not work out a political theory, given his circumstances; and Mayhall (2004, p. 89), that there is a movement in Plotinus from an ethics of escape to an ethics of compassion. I somewhat disagree with Zeller's (1931, p. 291)

general point: "In one respect neo-Platonism shows a far-reaching modification of real Platonism. The social and political ideas to which, in the *Republic* at least, Plato had sacrificed the individual are replaced in neo-Platonism by an individualistic tendency." I believe that while Plotinus did not explicitly endorse every idea of the *Republic*, he does not necessarily have a different view than Plato regarding the importance of the individual to gain knowledge of the Good. Based on the idea that Plotinus wanted to found a city based on Plato's laws, and those laws were communitarian in nature, we do have a periphrastic Plotinian endorsement of sacrificing the individual.

106 Theiler (1960, p. 67).

107 See, for example, Anton (2010, p. 9); A.H. Armstrong (1967b, pp. 213–14); Bobonich (2002, p. 4): "Plotinus holds that the wise person will transcend political concerns"; Majumdar (2007b, p. 145), this is one of the "central difference[s]" between the two; Mayhall (2004, p. 88); Rist (1996, p. 389); and Santayana (1913, pp. 595–6): Plotinus "had no courage for such a legislative vision as that of Plato's *Republic*" because he was focused on the mystical ascent.

108 *Life*, ch. 12.

109 See Hadot (1993, pp. 97–9), who says that the *Life* ch. 12 passage concerning Platonopolis is "enigmatic" (p. 97), asking many questions about it, but still admits that "the astonishing aspect of Plotinus' project is its dimensions. We are not talking about a tiny community, but about an entire city, whose inhabitants were to live according to the laws of Plato" (p. 98). This is all I am assuming about Plotinus' intent. O'Meara (2003) posits that perhaps Plotinus is discussing the descent of the philosopher-king here (p. 74) as Plato does, and suggests that Plotinus would admit philosopher-queens (p. 85). See also O'Meara (1999, p. 279) and Rist (1964, pp. 171–3). Anton (2010) makes two claims with which I disagree: First, Plotinus "cherished the hope for a Platonic *polis*. But his disciples, friends and interlocutors bore little resemblance to Socrates' companions in or out of the dialogues" (p. 9). Unfortunately, this is irrelevant to investigating whether he believed that philosophers make the best rulers, or whether Plotinus had the same political philosophy as Plato did. Second, Anton claims that Plotinus was not a Platonist because he was neither a politician nor a critic of diverse constitutions as Plato was (p. 11). However, Plato was not a politician but did try to found his ideal state (which are both true of Plotinus), and the fact that Plotinus did not criticize the different constitutions that Plato criticized tells us nothing. For example, Plotinus may have thought Plato's arguments were perfectly adequate. Gerson (1994, p. 201) says: "It is a very good thing that he was denied his dream of setting up a separate Platonic state," which I only bring up to contrast with Plotinus' apparent endorsement of Plato's Kallipolis. Katz (1950b, pp. 71–2) suggests that Plotinus only wanted to establish his school in relative seclusion in the country, but the laws of Plato entailed more than only philosophers being citizens, so this possibility is too narrow.

110 Plotinus endorsed aristocracy in general, however: he echoes the spirit of Plato's shipmaster passage in the *Republic* VI 488a–9c, at IV.4.17.19–35. Thus, I am thoroughly puzzled by Hardie's (1936, p. 129) comment: "the requirement that the guardian should know the good is incompatible with Neoplatonism," at least as it applies to Plotinus.

111 O'Meara (1999, pp. 281–3).

112 Some commentators seem to forget that Socrates says that he's following his divine sign and not going into politics, as well as urging the wise person to avoid politics

(*Apology* 31d–32a), and that Plato says much the same (*Letter* VII 324b–6b, *Republic* VI 496c–7a), except, of course, that Plato lays out his ideal state and its laws. Since Plotinus tried to found a state based on Plato's laws and mentions the possibility of a philosopher-king's not being interested in ruling, this is much the same; for example, see Plato's discussion of compelling the guardians to rule (*Republic* VII 519d–20a), as O'Meara (1999, p. 283) alludes to). Also, O'Meara (1999, p. 279) discusses Plotinus' penchant for dissuading a pupil from political involvement—Zethus (*Life*, ch. 7) and lauds Senator Rogatianus' renunciation of political life and asceticism. However, this is consistent with what Plato says about his own divine sign: metaphorically, the best the philosopher can do in a non-ideal state is to lay low behind a metaphorical wall (*Republic* VI 496a11–e2).

113 See also, for example, VI.4.15.

114 As to whether the philosopher actually has wisdom (namely, knowledge of virtue) or merely the virtue proper to his class, see Gerson (1989, p. 96); that every class of Kallipolis is virtuous, see ibid., p. 92; for Plato changing his mind on the notion of virtue of the different classes, see Bobonich (2002, p. 7).

115 Compare Bobonich (2002, pp. 1–2, 4).

116 Compare I.2.4 and II.9.9.

117 See also *Republic* V 479e–80a; compare *Timaeus* 46c–e.

118 See also II.9.9, II.9.18, III.5.3, III.8.8, IV.4.1, IV.8.7, V.1.4; compare I.2.7, I.8.4, III.7.5, III.8.10, IV.3.24, IV.4.35, IV.8.8, V.3.9, V.5.6, V.8.4, VI.7.30; for Plotinus' non-philosopher passage, see III.8.4.31–6, which implies that philosophers *do* contemplate and do so properly.

119 Carone (2005, p. 74) also sees this view in the *Timaeus*; Gerson (1989, p. 97) correctly sees the equivalence in Plato's view of following one's Reason, wisdom, justice, and virtue in general; and Kolb's (1974, p. 137) statement is also apt: "As for men, they should live according to the best part in them, their souls, which are closest to the timeless nature of the Forms."

120 Compare *Republic* IX 581b and 582e–3a.

121 Gerson (1994, p. 271n. 40) reminds us that the good Plotinian man is not a composite of man and soul (I.4.14.1–4); and de Vogel (1986, p. 228) cites that involuntary action does not occur when the pure Soul has the leading part (III.1.9.9–14). I do not concur with Sinnige (1999, p. 19), who argues that, for Plato, the intellectual ascent is rational, via knowledge and philosophy; but in Plotinus it is an "existential process, which has its roots in the deepest of human emotions, not in theoretical distinctions." Indeed, Plato also describes the emotional effects of experiencing Beauty and the Good and the importance of dialectic.

122 Compare I.3.3, III.1.9, III.1.10, III.4.6, III.8.4, and III.8.6.

123 See also *Republic* VI 485a–d, 489e–90c, and 501d.

124 For further passages on learning, see IV.4.12 and VI.7.36; for more on the truth, see I.3.4; compare I.3.5.

125 I agree with Friedländer (1969, p. 64), that one of the paths to knowledge for Plato is liberating oneself from the chains in the cave, but not that this in itself is sufficient; and Raphael (1984, p. 93), that the cave symbolizes the ascetic aspects of Platonism very appropriately, among other things. I disagree with H. Stewart's (1915, p. 603; compare p. 613) view: "It is plain, of course, that to place Plato definitely among the ascetics involves large discounting of some of his dialogues in the light of others which we take to be more faithful to his deepest thought" and: "Readers of the *Protagoras* and the *Republic* will want much persuasion before they agree that the

author was next of kin to the saints of the desert." Unquestionably, Plato urged philosophers and people in general to be temperate and avoid unnecessary bodily pleasures, *even in* the *Protagoras* and *Republic*: those bodily pleasures that led to more future pain, for example, in the *Protagoras*, are not to be pursued; unnecessary pleasures are hindrances to the philosophical life in the *Republic*.

126 See also *Phaedo* 67d, 82b–d, 83a–d, *Gorgias* 492d–4a, *Republic* VI 485d–6c, IX 571b–d, and *Theaetetus* 176a–b.

127 I agree with A.H. Armstrong (1947, p. 195), the wise man's body cannot suffer because he is utterly detached in spirit; Gerson (1994, p. 193), that for Plotinus the way to escape evil is to escape from the body (I.8.7–8); and Hadley (1997, p. 454) that Plotinus does speak positively about the body. My own example: since the universe is the best and we choose our body/life, then in some sense it is good—but both philosophers downplay focusing on the body and believing that it is more important than the soul. Lastly, I agree with Tinsley (1954, p. 46), that they have the same view of flying away from earth (first found in *Theaetetus* 176a–b). On the other hand, I do not concur with Mayhall (2004, p. 88), who argues that Plotinus is much more thorough in his attempt to abandon things material, whereas Plato is concerned with making this present life better. Plato is pretty clear that we should not focus on the body even in the *Republic*, and arguing that Plotinus does not believe that we should be concerned with improving present life is not true; he holds with Plato that the philosophical ideal is the best way in which to guarantee such improvement. Shorey (1938, pp. 40, 43) wrongly implies that asceticism is not a part of Plato's view, calling it one of the aspects of Neo-Platonism, as if it does not occur in Plato. Tinsley (1954, p. 47), despite his agreeable remark just mentioned in this note, goes on to state that a main feature of Neo-Platonism is a "contempt for the human being (especially the body)." On the contrary, with Plato, he claims that being a human is the highest being on earth, with something divine about it—though I would agree with the statement that we should have a certain amount of contempt for the body, on both of their views. Lastly, de Vogel (1986, pp. 230–1) pushes the positive aspects of Plato's account of body; for example, the prescription of gymnastics in the *Republic* and the listing of the body as the second most valuable possession in the *Laws*, while Plotinus was much more reserved about his praise (except when responding to the Gnostics). Plotinus states that a person who does not use the gym only has himself to blame if he is assaulted (III.3.8). He thus implicitly agrees with Plato that one needs to pay attention to one's body to some extent, even though it should not be the primary focus of one's life; even an unhealthy good person has nothing to worry about or fear.

128 See also I.3.3; compare I.6.8, VI.4.16, VI.5.12 and III.6.5.

129 See Mill (1979, pp. 8–11).

130 See also I.4.14.

131 See also *Euthyphro* 12b, *Phaedo* 82b–3c, *Republic* X 613a, 618b–9b, and *Letter* VIII 355a–c.

132 Note that the last sentence of this quotation actually seems to assume something like Plato's Kallipolis, where Plotinus is referring to the rulers and artisans. For other passages on wealth and poverty's not being relevant to the philosopher's life, see I.4.4, I.4.5, and 1.4.7–9.

133 For another passage that heavily implies that the Sage does not care about his reputation, taking the case of the Sage's losing his rule over cities and people, as well as not receiving a proper burial, see I.4.7.

134 More, 1923, p. 240.

135 J. Armstrong (2004, p. 179) also finds this claim in the *Laws* ("Few are guardians"), though ordinary citizens will learn math and astronomy. And I agree with de Vogel (1986, p. 230): "This is certainly not a doctrine for everyone, and Plato was the first to know that. What he meant by 'knowledge of the Truth' was certainly a spiritualist ideal, accessible only to the small number of those who were able to see it." My chief opponent here is Carone (2005), who makes the following claims: the unexamined life of the *Apology*, where "no one, not even the craftsman or the stranger, was regarded as exempt from such a challenge," contrasts with the *Republic* where autonomous human fulfillment is rare (p. 7). However, Socrates does not claim that everyone is a (true) philosopher, any more than Plato does in the *Republic* V, while discussing the lovers of sounds and sights. And: "Plato's ethics in the *Timaeus* takes us away from the elitism of the *Republic*, presenting instead an independent way to happiness that is available to everyone. . . . because everyone can share the universe as a common paradigm, and internalize its order" (p. 53; compare pp. 68–78). However, I read Plato at *Timaeus* 44a–c as saying that the body is unintelligent at first, that it is only after returning several circles to their natural form and correcting revolutions that one can be deemed an intelligent being, and with true nurture and education he turns out "perfectly whole and healthy" (44c1). I also interpret that harmony (akin to our souls' revolutions) and rhythm were given to humans because: "With most of us our condition is such that we have lost all sense of measure, and are lacking in grace" (47d7–e2), which does not imply that people are generally wise and happy, even if he is recommending that we harmonize ourselves and enjoy certain rhythms. Moreover, Timaeus states: "Of true belief, it must be said, all men have a share, but of understanding [*nou*], only the gods and a small group of people do" (51e5–6), which implies that when he refers to rational humans in the previous passages, he is not claiming that every human is entirely rational. Lastly, Timaeus says: "If a man has seriously devoted himself to the love of learning and to true wisdom, if he has exercised these aspects of himself above all, then there is absolutely no way that his thoughts can fail to be immortal and divine, should truth come within his grasp. . . . Constantly caring for his divine part as he does, keeping well-ordered the guiding spirit that lives within him, he must indeed be supremely happy" (*Timaeus* 90b6–c2, c3–6). Each man should learn and bring his soul into conformity with the harmonies and revolutions of the universe and: "When this conformity is complete, we shall have achieved our goal: that most excellent life offered to humankind by the gods, both now and forevermore" (90d5–7). These latter two passages heavily imply that the person must love knowledge and wisdom, which is the purview of the philosopher and not the average person, even though Plato admittedly urges every person to assimilate the universe's revolutions. Throughout Plato's corpus, we get prescriptions for us to be virtuous, be philosophers, and have a certain metaphysics and epistemology, none of which means that the average person will accept any of these recommendations, but which does mean, on Plato's view, that such a person will not be ultimately happy.

136 Compare *Sophist* 254a8–b2 (with thanks to Mohr 2005, p. 250), *Republic* V 476b, VI 493e–4a and 495a–b.

137 On this point I agree with Robin (1928, p. 371) and Tinsley (1954, p. 48).

138 Compare III.3.4.13–8.

139 See also *Phaedrus* 237b–d and 265d–6d; compare *Parmenides* 135d–6c and 136d–e.

140 Compare I.3.6 and VI.1.1.

141 I agree with Kolb (1974, p. 138) on the Platonic importance of the mathematization of the Forms, and Murphy (1951, p. 156) on the importance of math in the Platonic regimen for "enlightenment"; for the view that Plato has the same number theory from *Republic* VII to the *Philebus*, see Mohr (2005, p. 229); compare Reeve (2003, p. 39). Interestingly, Russell laments: "It is noteworthy that modern Platonists, almost without exception, are ignorant of mathematics, in spite of the immense importance that Plato attached to arithmetic and geometry, and the immense influence that they had on his philosophy. This is an example of the evils of specialization: a man must not write on Plato unless he has spent so much of his youth on Greek as to have had no time for the things that Plato thought important" (1945, p. 132). I just want to stress that this point makes Plotinus more of a Platonist than modern Platonists, if Russell is correct—and I think he is for the most part, even today—since Plotinus obviously knew Greek and was a mathematician according to Porphyry: "He had a complete knowledge of geometry, arithmetic, mechanics, optics, and music" (*Life*, ch. 14).

142 See also *Philebus* 57b–d, and *Republic* VII 525a–d and 526c–e.

143 I agree with Rist (1964, p. 90) that although Plotinus does not put as much emphasis (in terms of mentioning often, according to me) as Plato on the exact sciences, "he still insists that they are necessary." I take issue with Bréhier (1958, p. 4), who states, for instance, that Plotinus fails to mention the Demiurge's not creating according to an ideal model; on the contrary, Plotinus explicitly mentions and endorses this very point at V.8.8.7–20. Bréhier then charges that Plotinus does not endorse the geometrical construction of the elements in the *Timaeus*, which is certainly not an assertion that a disciple of Plato would make, given that he denied non-geometricians entrance to the Academy; I have two replies: first, a lack of explicit endorsement of the geometry of the elements does not imply that Plotinus disagrees with Plato on this issue, and second, besides VI.3.16.20–4 and I.3.3 (compare V.9.11), see especially *Life*, ch. 14.

144 See also I.3.3; compare V.9.11.

145 By "virtue is one," I intend only what the introductory statement of this section states, realizing that there are obviously many interpretations on this issue and that I cannot go into great detail here about all of them. Nonetheless, for more on the distinction and argument between the unity of virtue and the unity of virtues, see Penner (1973, especially pp. 162–6; 1992, pp. 127–8), who argues for the former view. See Gerson (1989, pp. 85–7, 91, 97), who claims that the virtues are a unity; Irwin (1977, p. 86; compare p. 89), who argues that Plato's *Laches* argues that all "virtues" are really a single virtue, knowledge of good and evil, and that other dialogues suggest the same conclusion; Shorey (1903b, p. 7), that virtue in its essence is one; and Vaughan (1999), who argues that virtue is one at least in the early dialogues. I disagree with Cooper (1984, p. 3) that there is a different theory of virtue from the *Protagoras* versus the *Republic*, but will not defend that view here. Gerson (1989, p. 92) raises an interesting problem, that if Plato uses "virtue" univocally, then, since each class of the ideal state is said to possess virtue, each class is truly virtuous. I have two responses: without knowledge of the Form of the Good, nothing is useful or beneficial, and there is no such education for any class other than the rulers. Courage can still be cultivated, and the auxiliaries may still be good approximations, taking orders in how to train, when, where to fight from the rulers, but this is not knowledge of things to be feared, or of pleasures and pains. I think one can still refer univocally to wisdom, courage, and the rest, even if this is true. Plato does make the distinction between civic and

philosophic virtue, so he has different kinds of virtue and even different levels thereof. Finally, on the general point of ethics, I disagree with Kraut (1992, pp. 2–14) that the difference between Socrates and Plato is the emphasis on ethics in the early dialogues. Socrates is just as interested in exploring epistemology, discovering knowledge (even if it concerns virtue), and in metaphysics: he wants to discuss the nature of piety, what it really is in itself, and he arguably has a metaphysical view about Forms at that point. Also, Plato does not cease discussing ethics—it pervades the *Phaedo*, *Republic* (where the virtue is justice), *Phaedrus*, *Philebus*, and *Laws*, but is still present in the *Theaetetus*, *Statesman*, and *Timaeus*.

146 For other passages where Socrates discusses parts of virtue, see *Euthyphro* 12b–e and *Laches* 190c–d, 198a, 199c–e. I take no interpretive stance on whether virtue has parts per se or is just one; my interpretation tries to charitably reconcile what Plato says about virtue's being one in *Laws*, with the general point that virtue is also somehow one in the *Protagoras*.

147 Note that Laws XII 963c5–4a8 by itself does not show that Plato believes that virtue is one; continue reading the passage for that evidence.

148 See also *Meno* 72e–6b, where Socrates demands that Meno give him one definition of virtue—the one Form that all virtues have in common.

149 The Athenian also constrains his guardians to know how the fine and the good are one (as well as many), at *Laws* XII 966a–b.

150 See VI.7.36, I.2.7 and I.3.6, for instance.

151 See *Menexenus* 241c–2a, *Gorgias* 527e, *Cratylus* 411a, *Symposium* 203e–4a, 208e–9c, *Republic* IV 430d–e, VI 504d, 506d, *Statesman* 306b, *Laws* I 632e–3a, VI 770b–1a; compare *Republic* VII 518d–9a.

152 I can also infer from Plato's Cave Allegory that once one sees the "sun" (the Good), one has already seen the "things themselves," the "stars," and the rest of the objects outside the cave (the Forms). There is nothing in Plotinus' writings to my knowledge that would contradict this view.

153 Plato: *Protagoras* 360e–1a, 361c; *Meno* 71a, 72a-3a, 74a-b, 79b–d, 87e, 100b; and *Laws* XII 963c–d; Plotinus: I.2.1, I.2.6, I.6.1, I.8.8–10, VI.9.1, VI.7.27; compare I.2.3, II.9.15.

154 That Virtue is a Form and one (that is, without parts, since Forms do not have parts) does not imply the other way in which we are viewing virtue as one—namely as one thing with many parts: these are mutually exclusive ways in which virtue is one.

155 I can interpret this statement in at least two ways: first, we must possess every *part* of virtue, thereby having full virtue (and we only have one part of virtue—relative virtue—until we possess full virtue); or second, that we can possess one virtue without the others, so that virtue is not one. I prefer the first interpretation.

156 See also *Laws* III 696b–e; compare X 906b. See *Symposium* 212a; compare Findlay (1978, pp. 101–2) for Plato's claim that the vision of Beauty Itself quickens one with the true or perfect virtue, as Plotinus also implies.

157 Plotinus also uses the word "perfect" in the context of virtues in I.3.6.

158 See also III.4.6 and I.2.4.

159 Irwin, 1977.

160 I agree with J. Armstrong (2004, p. 182) that the *Laws* show a deep connection between metaphysics and ethics; Gerson (1989), that Platonic knowledge of virtue is not the spurious or demotic virtue of *Phaedo* and *Republic*, respectively (p. 96), virtue is the knowledge of good and evil and other doctrines—for example, no one errs willingly—are inseparable parts of one doctrine (p. 97), and, more hesitatingly:

"[The virtuous person knows that his] own good is identical with goodness. This is the knowledge that is necessary and sufficient for virtue" (p. 98); Irwin (1977, p. 86; but see pp. 251–4 where he denies the same of Plato), that virtue equals knowledge of good and evil; and Shorey (1903b, p. 7), that Plato always maintained that virtue is insight or knowledge and can in some sense be taught. I am not sure about Menn's (1995, p. 19) claim that sophia-and-nous is a virtue in the *Philebus*. Lastly, Gerson (1989, p. 87) claims that Plato seems to think all virtues are one, even though the idea that there is one type of knowledge that amounts to temperate and just behavior sounds implausible, though I believe he agrees with me that this is precisely what Plato is claiming.

161 One might argue that Plato does not actually say this, but rather suggests it as one hypothesis or explanation. I read Plato's *Meno* 99e4–100b6 as saying, in effect: "If our reasoning about virtue's teachability and its relation to knowledge is correct, then it seems to follow that virtue is a gift from the gods." But I attempt to resolve this seemingly odd conclusion on pp. 149–51 below.

162 See *Theaetetus* 176a–d, for Plato's claim that knowledge of the claim that we should become as godlike and just as possible is wisdom and virtue, and not to know this is ignorant and base. For a passage where Plato states that excellence of thought can be useful or harmful depending on the soul's conversion, see *Republic* VII 518d–9a; for Plato's definition of right and wrong, see *Laws* IX 863e–4a.

163 See *Protagoras* 320b–c: Socrates says he does not believe that virtue is teachable.

164 Homer, *Odyssey*, 10.494.

165 Reuter (2001, p. 78) discusses the "virtue is a gift of the gods" passage and argues: "The conclusion of the *Meno* will not be understood until we have a clear understanding of a Platonic notion of goodness." I agree with this interpretation, of course, but I came to this conclusion on my own before reading Reuter's view.

166 A.E. Taylor, 1930, pp. 266–7.

167 Remember that knowledge of the Good is alternatively described as a vision thereof.

168 My view admittedly equates the vision or experience of the Good with virtue or one's being truly virtuous, as well as one's possessing knowledge of good and evil, even though (as above) paradoxically there is some reason to question whether we can have knowledge of the Good.

169 Addressing my objectors, Anton (2010, pp. 12–13) argues that Plotinian "wisdom" shifts to meaning an instrument for understanding the goal of the return to the One (so wisdom "must perform radically new tasks, beyond what Plato and Aristotle . . . expected"): however, wisdom is viewed in the same way according to both philosophers, and virtue is a result of knowledge of the Good. Hathaway (1969, p. 20) claims that Neo-Platonists transformed the Socratic teaching, demoting the moral or political virtues to minimal conditions of the "purification" or theological virtues; for now I can say that they each have the same view of purification and that civic virtue (as discussed in terms of reincarnation) is not the highest level of virtue for them. Rist (1964, p. 182; compare p. 191) calls Plotinus' view "quasi-Platonic," where virtue is some kind of intellectual condition, intuiting the Forms, above all moral or civic judgment, and virtue is now a mystical/supra-sensible description of the functioning and nature of Being. However, I believe we see the same kind of view in Plato's Cave summary, that we must have a vision of the Good in order to act wisely in private or public. Similarly, Rist (1964, p. 184) claims: "For Plotinus, both virtue and knowledge are surpassed in the mystic union." Again, Rist's claim is best interpreted as Plato's view as well. Lastly, Rist (1964, p. 191) argues: "For Plato virtue

means being like the Platonic God; for Plotinus it means that state which leads to union with the One. We have seen in what sense, for Plato, virtue is knowledge: it is knowledge of the kind that guarantees action. For Plotinus, virtue—if we may use the word at all of the crown of philosophy—is creativity, since the One is eminently creative" and for Plato, virtue is knowledge, but for Plotinus it is love. However, I have shown that they have similar views on becoming godlike and have addressed the non-dual aspect of the ultimate experience (Yount, 2014, pp. 127–8). I fail to see how Plato's vision of the Good guarantees action: if it did, he would not have to discuss the compulsion of the philosopher-kings to return to the cave, at *Republic* VII 519d–20b. Plotinus certainly holds that the Good-seer will be a good person with good actions, just as Plato holds. Lastly, love is not a virtue for Plotinus any more than it is for Plato, and as Rist says, virtue for Plotinus is ultimately non-discursive knowledge (intuition) of the Good/One, which is Plato's view (as argued above).

170 Plotinus does, however, come pretty close to discussing whether virtue is teachable at VI.9.4.11–6, where he states that teaching is relevant to the road and traveling, but attaining the vision of the One is for those who wish to attain it in advance of the teaching. I take Plotinus' statement to be compatible with my reading of Plato's *Meno*, especially with Plotinus' not claiming that virtue is teachable per se, since one's goal (as with Plato) is the vision or knowledge of the Good or One. See also I.3.3.

171 A.E. Taylor, 1930, pp. 266–7.

172 See also *Laws* X 904a–c; compare *Republic* I 353d–e.

173 Plotinus does appear to consider that some virtues are bodily, and others are intellectual at VI.3.16.9–13, but the context is a discussion of Qualities, Aristotle's categories, and Plotinus states shortly after this quotation that (some) beauty as a quality is bodily, but that Reason-Principles are intellectual. Plotinus thus does not mention any virtues such as justice, specifically, and we see elsewhere that Plotinus declares that Virtue is a Form, so this quotation is not contradictory to Plato. See also Gerson (1994, p. 199), that virtue is a habit—*hexis*, though an odd habit—for Plotinus which intellectualizes the soul (VI.8.5.35–6).

174 See also *Republic* II 364c–d for the claim that vice is easy and toil is set before those who wish to be virtuous, and *Laws* IV 718d–9a; compare *Republic* X 608b.

175 See also I.6.8.25–27; compare III.3.4.

176 For more on the virtue of citizens in the *Laws*, see Stalley (1983, pp. 9, 56–7); I hesitate to endorse Gerson's (1989, p. 96) idea that the specific knowledge that is virtue is "in a way quite simple," because knowledge of the Good seems to give one a lot of information, as it were, but perhaps it is simple.

177 See also *Republic* III 395b–d, where Plato states that the guardians should not imitate mere civic liberty but brave, temperate and pious men; *Statesman* 290b–c, where civil servants are distinguished from rulers; compare *Republic* VI 500c–d. Gerson (1989, p. 100n. 26) alerted me to these additional "demotic virtue" passages: *Phaedo* 68c–9d, 82a–b, and *Republic* X 619d1.

178 I am in agreement with: Harris (1976, pp. 6–7), salvation begins with purification and civic virtue; Majumdar (2007b, p. 145), the practice of civic virtues "becomes a vital aspect of the process of divinization"; McGroarty (2006, p. 174), Plotinus agrees that knowledge of the Good comes after civic excellence; Plass (1982, p. 242), "Plotinus follows Plato in allowing substantial value to civic virtue (III.4.2.28)"; Pistorius (1952, p. 143), Plotinus adopts the four Platonic cardinal (civic) virtues: wisdom, courage, temperance, and justice; Rist (1964), Plotinus frequently emphasized the Platonic distinction between civic and philosophic virtue (p. 169; but see p. 182) and

that "natural virtues" at I.3.6 are civic virtues (p. 173); de Vogel (1986, p. 222), they have the same view that social virtue should always be present in a philosopher's life and it was in that of Plotinus; and Vorwerk (2001, p. 40), Plotinus follows Plato in the distinction between civic virtues and philosophic or "major virtues" (as he refers to them at I.2.1.22), and that when one possesses the philosophic/major virtues, this contributes to one's assimilation to Nous. O'Meara (2003, p. 41) argues that Plotinus follows Aristotle in excluding moral virtue from the divine based on I.2.1, whereas Plato attributes virtues to the divine; but Plotinus says there that we must be made godlike in some way by possessing civic virtues, and he thinks that the gods have the virtues of wisdom and justice. I disagree with Bobonich (2002, pp. 1–2), who argues that Plotinus radicalizes the "only philosophers can be truly happy" view; but I do not think that either Plato or Plotinus belittle civic virtue or say that the civically virtuous go badly astray; they merely prize philosophic virtue more and say that ultimate happiness can be found in the latter. Bobonich's (p. 4) claim that Plotinus' belief that genuine happiness requires the sage to transcend civic virtue just seems true of Plato's view as well. Dillon (1996, p. 331) puzzlingly states that Plotinus builds on a distinction made especially in Plato's *Phaedo* between civic and cathartic virtue, which is not found in Plato as such. My response, assuming "cathartic" refers to purification, is to deny this claim by citing *Phaedo* 67a2–b2, b10–d3, 68c–9d, 82a11–c1, *Republic* III 395b–d, X 619d1, and *Statesman* 290b–c; compare *Phaedo* 65b–d and 114d–5a, *Republic* VI 500c–d, *Sophist* 226e–7c, and *Timaeus* 89a–b. Gerson (1994, p. 211) claims that (1) it is repugnant for Plotinus to have the view that an indifferent, detached contemplator is better than a beneficent contributor to a community; and (2) Plotinus' condemnation of individuals who fail to honor themselves is inconsistent with *Laws* V 731d6–2b4. Re: (1), it is not clear that Plato would not have the same view, given that the best person is the philosopher who has seen the Good, *whether or not they are rulers in his ideal state*. After all, Plato does not claim that the guardian who is ruling at the time is a better person than the ruler-in-waiting. Re: (2), both thinkers have the same view that soul is the most divine thing about humans, and Plotinus has the same view as Plato on the over-concern of one's body and self-love. See also my response to Hathaway (1969, p. 20) on p. 247n. 169. Lastly, one might believe that Plotinus extends Plato's view by what he says about his degrees of virtue doctrine (civic versus philosophic virtues); I believe that many of the main features of this doctrine appear in Plato, but I will leave it an open possibility that Plotinus innovates here.

179 The "likeness," "flight to God" Platonic passage he is discussing is *Theaetetus* 176a–b; "civic virtue" is explicitly mentioned at *Republic* IV 430c; and the purification passage is *Phaedo* 69b–c. A.H. Armstrong (1966a, p. 135) says that civic virtue is not mentioned in the *Republic* passage in the way that Plotinus takes it, but we can find what Plato says in spirit when he predicts that the person who follows the laws of the city and gets along with everyone well will be reincarnated as a bee or some other like being.

180 See also I.2.1, I.2.2 (for a good explanation of civic virtue), and I.2.3.

181 The OCT gives 22 references in the *Enneads* to *Theaetetus* 176a–c.

182 See Reuter (2001, p. 94).

183 See also *Theaetetus* 176a9–b2, where Plato states: "Escape means becoming as like God as possible; and a man becomes like God when he becomes just and pure, with understanding [*phronēseōs*]," and *Laws* VII 792c–e, where Plato avers that being temperate is godlike.

184 See Rist (1962b, p. 169).
185 See also especially I.2.1.46–52 and II.9.15.38–40; and VI.8.6; compare III.9.2.
186 Compare Bobonich (2002, p. 6): "Since Plato thinks that there is a very close connection between being virtuous and having a happy or flourishing life, non-philosophers' lack of virtue has starkly negative implications for their happiness." Depending on the extent of the lack of virtue, Plotinus certainly agrees about the relative unhappiness of the non-philosopher's life.
187 One might raise the objection that in Plotinus' endorsement that virtue is sufficient for happiness, he ignores the *Philebus*, which avers that the happy person (the possessor of the human good) requires or possesses beauty, proportion, and truth, in addition to intellect, science, pleasure (64e–6e), even though reason is far superior to and more beneficial to humans than pleasure (66e). My reply is that Plotinus believes, with Plato, that the truly happy person has seen the Good, and therefore knows goodness, truth, beauty, true pleasure, intellect (Nous), and *has* intellect/mind (as he puts it at *Timaeus* 51e). Plotinus also holds that knowing the Good entails acting wisely in private and public. Lastly, Plotinus also maintains with Plato that true pleasures accompany the happy person. This is not to say that Plotinus in no way (in the details) moves Plato's view into a new direction; only that much of what we see both philosophers claim about virtue's sufficiency for happiness is similar.
188 See also *Letter* VII 344b; compare *Phaedo* 114d–5a, where Plato makes the connection between the good fate of one's soul, asceticism, knowledge, and virtue, and *Epinomis* 979b–d.
189 Compare I.6.6.
190 Plotinus also agrees that wealth or lack thereof is irrelevant to the Sage's quest and life, at II.9.9.
191 For other Platonic passages on justice's relation to virtue, see *Meno* 78d–9a; for a claim that the best warrior is courageous as well as just, temperate and wise, see *Laws* I 629e–30b.
192 See also *Protagoras* 330b–e, *Greater Hippias* 287c, *Phaedo* 75d, 76d–7a, *Republic* II 358c–d, V 476a, 479a, 479e, VI 501b, VII 517e, X 612a–b, *Parmenides* 130b, 131a, 135c–d, *Phaedrus* 247d, *Philebus* 62a; compare *Laws* VI 757e.
193 See *Protagoras* 330b–d and *Greater Hippias* 287b–c.
194 See *Cratylus* 412c–3d.
195 Rist (1964, p. 68) raises the criticism (after citing Plotinus' definition of justice at VI.6.6.37–8—justice is an active actuality, or perhaps a sort of disposition of intellect, but it is not the thought of justice) that, "this definition could never have been given by Plato" but humanizes Plato's thought. However—aside from the fact that it is literally true that Plato could not have said this, since Aristotle coined the term *energeia*—given that Plato does describe justice as all parts doing their own, this is an *energeia*-like definition. Moreover, Justice qua Form causes everything just to be just, so in this sense it is an active actuality and not a "motionless, unchanging" separated entity. In short, I believe that Rist is exaggerating the difference here between the thinkers.
196 See also IV.7.7, V.5.1, V.6.6, V.8.10, VI.6.6, VI.6.14, VI.6.15, and VI.7.33.
197 See *Laws* I 644d–5c, VII 803c, and X 902b.
198 Compare A.H. Armstrong (1947, pp. 194–5) and Gerson (1994, p. 201).
199 See other parts of III.2.17, as well as II.3.8, III.2.6, III.2.8, III.2.9, and V.8.4 (in this latter passage, Plotinus claims metaphorically that Justice is assessor to Zeus).

200 See J. Armstrong's (2004, pp. 171, 181–2) view of justice, gods, and humans in the later dialogues.
201 See also *Philebus* 39e, where Plato says that a just, pious, good person is dear to the gods.
202 See also I.8.6 and IV.4.45.
203 Here I agree with Gerson (1989, pp. 92, 95, 97) and Hitchcock (1985, p. 76): the just man will be one.
204 For passages that state that a just person follows his/her Reason, see *Republic* I 353d–4a, IV 441d–e, 442c–d, 443c–4a; compare I 350c–d, IV 444b, VI 500b–d, IX 571d–2b, IX 590c–e, *Sophist* 247a, and *Timaeus* 42b–e. For analogous Platonic passages, where the city is just when it obeys the lovers of wisdom (or the class that follows Reason most), see *Republic* IV 433b–e, IV 435b–c, V 462a–b; compare *Meno* 73a–b, *Symposium* 209a–b, *Republic* VI 500b–d, IX 590c–e, and *Laws* IV 714c.
205 Plato also makes analogies in the *Gorgias* about justice and the soul: Justice is to the soul as medicine is to the body (464b–d); and rhetoric is to justice what cookery is to medicine (465c).
206 See *Republic* IV 433b–e, 434a, 435b–c, 442c–d, and 443c–4a.
207 See *Gorgias* 507a–8c and *Laws* III 696c.
208 Compare VI.2.18, I.2.5, III.6.2, and VI.4.15.
209 Elsewhere (e.g. VI.8.5) Plotinus implies that justice is good order.
210 Plotinus confirms that he believes that a sound mind is one that follows its Reason, that is, a sound mind is just (based on I.2.3); see III.6.2.29–32.
211 See also *Gorgias* 527b–c, e3–7, *Republic* I 345a, II 357d–8a, V 451a, IX 589c, X 612c–e, and *Laws* V 731e–2a, XII 964b; compare *Gorgias* 478b, *Laws* II 662d–3d, V 728c, XII 937d–e, *Letter* VII 344a–b, and *Epinomis* 979b–d.
212 See also *Gorgias* 476e; compare *Epinomis* 988e.
213 Here I am in agreement with A.H. Armstrong (1947, pp. 194–5), except that he feels that Plotinus got his view from the Stoics, whereas I see this view in Plato; and I agree with Gerson (1994, p. 201).
214 See also III.3.4, where Plotinus declares that degradations in future incarnations (say from human to ox) are just for certain souls, and IV.3.16; compare III.2.4.
215 Plato also states that we must think the opposite of the just man, namely that if an unjust man is wealthy or healthy, these conditions will serve to be evil to him (*Republic* X 613b). See also *Apology* 44a-b and *Laws* II 661b–c.
216 More specifically, none of the following will harm the Sage, according to Plotinus: Wealth, poverty or murder (II.9.9); death of loved ones (I.4.4); sickness (III.2.5); or loss of property (III.2.15); and there is no envying the fool of the "lures" of being handsome, powerful and rich, including even the ruling of the entire human race (I.4.14).
217 For additional passages where Plato construes temperance qua mastering one's pleasures and desires, see *Protagoras* 358b–c with 357b–7e, 352a–2e, and 353c–e; *Republic* III 389d–e, 402e–3a, IV 430e–1b; compare *Laws* I 636d–e.
218 See *Republic* III 403a7–8 and *Protagoras* 352a–2c; compare *Republic* X 604b–d.
219 This interpretation is confirmed in the *Republic* V 431e–2b and 442c–d.
220 See *Laws* I 626e and 644b.
221 I concur with Rist (1967a, p. 135) that both thinkers have the same view (that passions overtaking Reason is a bad thing); I do not see the justification for Turnbull's (1948, p. ii) view: "Perhaps the greatest addition which he has made to Platonism is that the Soul is itself transformed in its passage from darkness to light," because it

assuredly is a transformation for one to go from alternately obeying one's appetites, emotions and reason indiscriminately to only obeying Reason, having seen the Good, on Plato's view. Lastly, I believe, *contra* Pistorius' (1952, p. 143) view of Plotinus, that "In the absence of the body there will be no passions. Temperance will therefore be unnecessary," holds true of Plato as well.

222 See *Phaedo* 66d7–e1 and 67a2–4.

223 Compare III.1.1 and IV.7.7, where Plotinus argues that if the soul were a body, the phrase "master of itself" and/or temperance itself would not make sense; VI.8.13, where he claims that Intellect is master of itself; and I.2.6.

224 See I.2.3.15–6, I.2.1.18–9, I.6.5.8–18, I.4.8.24–30, I.2.5.3–16 with I.6.6.1–3; compare I.1.12, III.1.10, IV.4.17, IV.4.28, VI.8.5, and IV.8.6.

225 Vorwerk (2001, p. 30) holds that Plato asserts in his later dialogues the basic ideas about self-knowledge rejected in the *Charmides*, a thesis with which I agree. See also Gerson (1989, p. 98) on self-knowledge's being equivalent to knowing that goodness is one and that one is essentially a rational soul.

226 I believe that even Irwin's (1977, p. 88) view that temperance is said to be the knowledge of good and evil (*Charmides* 174b11–6a5) can be interpreted in Plato's philosophy overall (especially as in the *Republic*) as being another way of saying that knowledge of the Good (and its privation) amounts to temperance as well.

227 Cf V.8.11.31–3. On this issue, I agree with Dodds (1960, p. 4), that returning to the One is a recovery of one's true self; Meredith (1993, p. 51), that we need to be reminded of our true selves and be purified to be true to ourselves—though this sounds tautologous; Rappe (2000, pp. 19–20), that philosophical insight and self-knowledge are one and the same for Plotinus qua Neo-Platonist (adding that it applies equally to Plato); and Vorwerk (2001, p. 44–5), to the extent that I understand his view, that Plotinus apparently agrees with Plato's overall view of temperance. I am not sure I agree with Rist (1973, p. 81), that self-knowledge is necessary but only a stage, where dualism is still present and must be transcended. On one hand, it seems that self-knowledge would be dual in nature; on the other hand, by referring to *wisdom* as self-knowledge, where wisdom is equivalent to one's knowing the Good (and implies a unified soul), one cannot truly know oneself unless one knows the Good, which just *is* that transcendent experience Rist refers to.

228 See also V.3.4 and I.2.7.

229 Plato: *Gorgias* 507a–8c, *Laws* V 733e–4c, *Protagoras* 332a–b with 333b–c; compare *Republic* X 618e–9b; I argue that for Plotinus, happiness results from wisdom and knowledge, wisdom can only happen with knowledge of the Good or One (which in turn implies that one is temperate), happiness results from one's possessing the virtues, the temperate are guided by Reason, and happiness occurs when Reason guides the soul.

230 For Plato's discussion, see *Phaedo* 61e–3a, and compare *Crito* 47d–8a and *Gorgias* 507b; for Plotinus' view that one should not commit suicide as long as there is hope of philosophical progress, see I.9.1.18–9. Here I agree with Inge (1929b, p. 174), that they basically have the same view on suicide, and McGroarty (2006, p. 199), that suicide can be done in specific cases, on which Plotinus and Plato basically agree; as opposed to Rist (1967a, p. 175), who believes that suicide is never acceptable for Plotinus.

231 For this particular claim in Plato, see *Republic* III 405c–d, and 406d–8b, and *Timaeus* 89a5–d1. Compare *Laws* I 646c. For the definitive Plotinian passage on suicide, see I.9.1.18–9, which I take to be consistent with Plato's view that one should not receive

excessive, futile medical treatment, especially given Plotinus' claim: after asking whether suicide might be permissible if the Sage loses his reason, he answers in part that this loss must be classed with the inevitable; see I.9.1.14–5.

232 Plato: *Laws* VII 803b3–5 and *Republic* X 604b–c; Plotinus: III.2.15.21–9, and the remainder of III.2.15.

233 See Cherniss (1954) for the interesting point that the motion of evil souls causes positive evil, but they do not intend the evil as evil, keeping in mind that no one errs willingly (p. 254), and that the vicious soul is morally responsible for the positive evil and for its ignorance of the truth (p. 257).

234 See also, for example, *Phaedrus* 237d–8c, 246a–b, 253c–4e, 255e–6b, *Republic* IV 439d–e, IX 571c–d, and X 602d–3d; compare *Laches* 191c–e.

235 See Gerson (1994, pp. 193–4) on similar points; Hadley (1997, p. 453) reminds us that Plotinus does speak positively of the sensible realm, but goes too far when he diagnoses Plotinus' reputation as follows: "It may be that Plotinus is often taken as an enemy of things bodily and visible because of his association with Plato, who often suffers being labeled a dualist, or because of his reputation as a father of western mysticism." Since we see the same passages in Plato as in Plotinus, this reputation is entirely justified, which is not to say that Plato does not speak positively of the sensible realm in places as well, to the point where de Vogel (1986, p. 230) defends Plato's positive view of the body. I disagree with Inge (1929a, pp. 256–7), who says that Plotinus does not like Plato's disparagement of the material world, so he likes the *Timaeus*' way of handling the issue, as opposed to the *Phaedrus*. He also says that Plotinus is attracted to the Platonic passages where Matter is assumed to be a defilement to the spiritual principle (p. 259), which certainly harks back to Plato's attitude in the *Phaedrus* and other dialogues. Plotinus seems to endorse both views, in short. Rist (1996, pp. 391–2) states of Plotinus' view: "Material objects in the body, far from evil in themselves insofar as they exist, are a source of temptation, perhaps of almost inevitable temptation, to the soul." I only add that I see nothing un-Platonic in this description.

236 See also I.8.8.40–4.

237 Compare IV.8.5.

238 Plotinus is referring to *Phaedrus* 248c8.

239 See also V.1.1.

240 See also III.3.4, I.8.4, I.8.14, and I.1.9.6–14; compare I.1.9.1–3.

241 The unjust life is compatible with a vicious soul's life, because it is a life where one does not obey one's Reason.

242 For a claim that men should never be trained to evil ways, see *Laws* IV 706d.

243 For Plato's claim that the best nature will fare worse under bad education than the average nature, see *Republic* VI 491d–e.

244 Compare *Republic* II 360e.

245 Plotinus also refers to the "earth-bound man" who is handsome, powerful, and rich who rules all humans as a fool of such lures at I.4.14, which implies that these so-called goods will not really benefit this man but will only serve as a means to make him even more unjust (since he is "earth-bound" and concerned only for what is important to a non-believer in Forms, for instance). Compare III.2.13.

246 See also III.2.9.19–28; compare I.8.2.7–15 and IV.3.18.1–7.

247 Mohr (2005) rightly says about the view of the *Timaeus*: "The phenomena are, on their own, a spontaneous source of disorder and positive evil" (p. 144), and it is the "sheer corporeality of the phenomena" from which positive evil arises (p. 145).

Hackforth (1946, p. 118) argues that all moral evil involves ignorance (including the apparently inconsistent passages in the *Sophist* and *Laws* IX); and in my view Majumdar (2007b) wrongly states that it is humans in the cave and not ignorance that keeps the cave prisoners down (p. 153), *and* that the Good is the cause of even the ignorance in the cave (p. 156).

248 See also *Republic* X 609b–c; compare *Euthydemus* 281d–e, *Republic* IX 585b, *Timaeus* 86b–c, *Sophist* 228c–d, *Philebus* 48c, 49d–e, and *Laws* III 689a–c, VIII 831c–e. Moreover, at *Lesser Hippias* 372e–3a, Socrates states that Hippias would greatly benefit Socrates if he could cure his soul of ignorance, which implies that ignorance is a great evil of the soul.

249 Note that Plato argues at *Phaedo* 82d–e that we wallow in ignorance until philosophy takes over the soul, which is an alternative way of saying that until we have knowledge of the Good and/or follow our Reason, we are ignorant.

250 See also *Republic* IV 444b6–7 with 439e6–40a3, and *Timaeus* 86b–c. Compare Plato's Leaky Jar Analogy at *Gorgias* 492e–3d; *Republic* IX 586a–c, X 606d–e, *Phaedrus* 238b–c, 277d–e, *Timaeus* 70b–d, *Sophist* 228d–e, *Philebus* 47e–8a, *Laws* III 689a–c, VIII 831b–e, 837c–d, and IX 863b–4a.

251 Plato also claims that ignorance or lack of self-control causes intemperance at *Laws* V 734b–c, and argues that ignorance of what is and is not to be feared is cowardice at *Protagoras* 360c.

252 See also *Sophist* 230a–b and *Laws* IX 863c.

253 I agree with O'Brien (1971, p. 139): "Matter and weakness [jointly] in the soul are part causes of evil in the soul." If I understand Majumdar's (2007b, p. 155) view—that the Good is the source of evil in Plotinus (but not Plato), because he has a monistic nature of Good whereas Plato has a dualistic Good—I disagree based on my adduced passages.

254 See also III.6.2; compare IV.4.44.

255 See Rist (1967a, p. 135).

256 See also III.1.9, III.1.10, and VI.6.1.

257 Compare I.1.9 and IV.4.44.

258 One might wonder what ignorance Plotinus is referring to; one of his examples is when he wonders what has caused our souls to forget God and be ignorant of both God and themselves (V.1.1.1–5), and ignorant of their origin (V.1.1.8–9). One can see the way in which this kind of ignorance could lead to false opinions about, say, bodily reality and pleasures, or the importance of fame or money. I cannot find a place in the *Enneads* where Plotinus states that ignorance is thinking you know something when you do not (compare the end of VI.8.1 though), as Plato states in the *Sophist*, but I also cannot see how such a notion fails to be Plotinian.

259 See especially I.4.15, I.6.5–6, IV.8.2, VI.5.15, as well as I.1.2, I.1.4, I.2.3, I.2.5, I.8.15, III.6.3–4, IV.8.3, V.5.4, and VI.7.34.

260 See also *Laws* X 888d, 902e–3a, and 907b–d; compare 891c–d. For other Platonic passages on impiety, see *Gorgias* 479b–c, 505a–b, *Republic* III 417a, and V 461a–b.

261 For passages where Plotinus discusses the materialists' drifting far from God and losing one's thought of their origin in the divine, see VI.9.5 and V.1.1, respectively; for his claim that it is impious and irreverent to grant that less noble living things are nonetheless admirable in themselves, see III.2.7.

262 Compare *Laws* VII 792c–e.

263 I agree with Gerson (1994, p. 193); I disagree with Friedländer (1969, pp. 56–8), who claims that Plotinus' mystical union leads to a contempt of the delightful instrument

of the body, which is a notion of Eros far removed from Plato's, due in part to *Laws* V 731d6–2b4. This section also tells against the commentators who argue that Plato does not disparage the body as much as Plotinus does, or similar claims: Hadley (1997, pp. 453–4); Inge (1929a, pp. 256–7); Mayhall (2004, p. 88); and de Vogel (1986, p. 230–1).

264 See also V.9.1, III.6.6; compare V.1.1, VI.9.3, VI.9.5, III.6.2, IV.4.4, IV.4.18, and III.3.4.

265 See also I.8.4; compare I.1.9.

266 See *Republic* III 398c–9c and 399e–400d for the acceptable and forbidden modes and rhythms, respectively.

267 See also *Republic* III 401d–2a, *Laws* II 654e–5d; compare *Phaedrus* 258e–9d.

268 See also I.6.1, I.6.3, II.9.16, III.2.16, V.9.11, and VI.3.16; compare I.3.1, IV.4.31, IV.4.40, and I.4.1. For Plotinus' analysis of the syrinx, see III.2.17.

269 See also *Republic* III 400d–1d, X 597e–8d, 601b–c, 602a–b; *Sophist* 235d–6c, *Statesman* 284a–b, *Philebus* 59a, *Laws* VI 769a–d; compare *Philebus* 59a–c, *Laws* X 888e, 889a, and 892b.

270 Karelis (2006, pp. 320–1) notes that some poetry will be allowed, and that it is not qua imitation that poetry is to be banned; imitation is an accidental feature of poetry; Marshall (1922, pp. 468–9) states that Plato bans the dramatic poet; P. Murray (1996, p. 12) rightly claims that Plato consistently attacks the poet's lack of knowledge in the *Ion*, *Phaedrus*, and *Republic*; also: "Hymns to the gods and encomia to good men will be permitted in the ideal state, but there will be no place for poetry as we know it" (p. 15). Joseph (1948, p. 38), speaking broadly, states that Plato banished poetry from the ideal state, which is not technically true.

271 P. Murray (1996, p. 16). He goes on to claim that Plato is equally hostile towards poetry in the *Laws* as he is in the *Republic* (1996, p. 30); see also Nehamas (1988, p. 230n1), who cites passages containing heavy censorship of poetry in the *Laws*. In addition to my point that poetry's not being completely banished, Nehamas (p. 216) adds that a careful reading of Plato shows that he outlaws neither painting nor sculpture.

272 The following commentators have the view that Plotinus has a different view than Plato or simply mention it as a defining characteristic: Alexandrakis (2004, p. 188; cites V.8.1; compare p. 190); A.H. Armstrong (1967b, p. 233); More (1923, p. 185); Rist (1967a, pp. 183–4); and Wallis (1972, pp. 86–7). The remainder of this paragraph is my attempt to show that we find the same view in Plato, though it is admittedly less obvious.

273 I credit Rist (1967a, pp. 183–4) for pointing this passage out to me.

274 Cairns refers to Plato as a philosopher-poet in Hamilton and Cairns (1961, p. xv). A philosopher, using words, imitates Forms in her speech (see the *Phaedrus*, for example), and poetry is an art for Plato. Though Plato disparages poets' work when it does not speak the truth or elevate the soul, we have an example of an artist according to Plato (Plato himself), who can aid in leading someone to the truth by an artificial product (his writings, even though they have flaws and dialectic is superior).

275 Here I agree with: A.H. Armstrong (1967b, p. 233), that Plotinus "is only interested in the beauty of art, or of nature, as a help in our ascent to the intelligible beauty and beyond it to its source, the Good," but I think this is also true of Plato, since the Good in some way causes images all the way down into the cave, and the artists in the cave desire the Good, so even as they deal with or create images or art, they seek the Good; O'Meara (1993, p. 72), that for Plotinus art does not deliberate (from

Aristotle), but this seems consistent with Plato's claims that the poets are divinely inspired but cannot explain their work well; Tate (1932, pp. 165–6): "Neo-Platonic views of art appear to me quite in accord with Plato's doctrine" because, for example, Plotinus recognizes "the distinction between the imitation which is once-removed and that which is twice-removed from the ideas. They differ from Plato only in taking a slightly more lenient view of the art which is twice-removed (imitative in the bad sense). But Plotinus' view that 'the arts create much from themselves' is simply the Platonic attitude towards genuine art." I disagree with Anton (1967, p. 94; 2000, p. 125), who argues that, even though Plotinus' view of art does admit that its creations are imitations, his aesthetics cannot be fully understood apart from his ontology of emanation. I think we should not take the metaphor of emanation as being literal or as a distinguishing mark from Plato's view. Anton also claims that Plotinus modeled his view of beauty after the *Symposium* and not the *Republic* (pp. 95–6)—if that is true, my general argument that they have the same view stands. I also reject the claim that Plotinus on this issue is rightly called a Neo-Platonist, as opposed to being a Platonist (p. 101n. 20); A.H. Armstrong (1967b, p. 232) [and Gerson (1994, p. 213); compare O'Meara (1993, pp. 95–6)] claims: "Plotinus, unlike Plato, puts the beauty of art on a level with the beauty of nature as a way to the intelligible beauty." However, Plato would not dispute that if beautiful art can raise one to thinking of intelligible beauty, then it is a good thing, but since they both hold that the lowest rung of the Ladder of Love is appreciating/loving one beautiful person, even beautiful nature is to be transcended on their view, so this is not a major point of difference between them. Plotinus also argues that living beauty is more glorious than dead ones, and even that living ugly humans are more attractive than sculptured handsome ones, at VI.7.22.24–36, so we have reason to be more cautious than Armstrong et al. on this point. Lastly, if I am reading Karelis (2006, p. 315) correctly, Plotinus counters *Republic* X's view of art because he thinks that art provides an even *truer* representation of the Forms than ordinary reality; however, I do not see that in Plotinus' text, though, as A.H. Armstrong (1967b, p. 233) points out, Plotinus does say that sometimes art can improve on nature (V.8.1.36–40). Compare More (1923, p. 184) on this issue, that Plotinus was more Platonic than Plato on art; I am not sure what to make of that claim.

276 For further Plotinian passages on the sense world's being an image of the Forms, artistic representations not properly being called images, and where Plotinus rejects Forms of imitative arts, see Gerson (1994, pp. 89, 261n. 57); for nature's non-artisanal production, see O'Meara (1993, p. 76).

277 See also IV.3.10.17–9; V.9.11, V.8.1; compare V.9.14 and IV.4.31.

278 Compare his biography, where he strongly objected "to sitting to a painter or sculptor," reasoning that the body was just an image, and the painting or sculpture would just be a lasting image of the image of the soul, so that artwork is not something worthy to gaze at (*Life*, ch. 1). Those commentators, such as Fuller (1938, p. 310), who believe that Plotinus does not scorn art as an imitation as much as Plato need to explain this passage, as well as IV.3.10.17–9, where Plotinus says that art pieces are "dim and weak imitations, toys not worth much."

279 Though this is less tentative, since we know that Plotinus wanted to found Platonopolis based on Plato's laws, this implies that poetry would be restricted in the ways in which Plato restricts it.

280 I agree with: Carone (2001, p. 123: "[Even when] the lower parts win, synchronic belief-*akrasia* does not occur because the soul has been made to believe at that time

that what the lower part believes to be best is actually best all things considered," because an ignorant soul can have many false beliefs and sublimate its Reason to Appetite and/or Spirit; compare Kahn (1987, p. 85); Hitchcock (1985, p. 81): "The good as Plato understands it is not the goal of human beings only but of every soul, including those of animals and gods." I also incline toward the view that plants in some sense desire the Good as well; Lesses (1987, p. 147), that the *Republic*'s account of motivation in the discussion of weakness of will is surprisingly Socratic; Morrow (1929, p. 345) gives a nice explanation of desire of the Good: "The ultimate object of the soul's quest is the Good . . . not simply the subordination of knowledge to morality, or of science to human welfare, but the complete contentment of the whole man—reason, imagination, and emotion"; and Shorey's (1895, pp. 32–3; compare p. 48) Unitarian view of pleasure and the Good across the *Protagoras*, *Gorgias*, and *Republic*, compare Lesses (1987, p. 147). For an argument that Plato uses *boulēsis* (wish) differently in the *Protagoras* than in the *Gorgias*, see Gulley (1965, p. 82); for an argument that Plato's notion of goodness is incomplete and that therefore his *summum bonum* rests on a logical mistake, see Hitchcock (1985, p. 82); for arguments that Socrates and Plato have different views of desire for the Good, see Irwin (1977, p. 224) and Penner (1992, pp. 128–9). I disagree with: Menn (1992, p. 572), who implies that only a perfectly rational soul desires the Good by participating in Nous. I take Plato as holding instead that every soul desires the Good, and ignorant souls are just very bad at securing their good (and they do not err willingly); Rawson (1996), who is struck by "The fact that the Good is [the] supreme object both of knowledge . . . and of desire, given Plato's painful awareness of conflicts between reason and desire" (p. 107): even the ignorant soul has Reason, which is divine and wants what is best for itself, even as it has and fulfills unnecessary appetitive desires, so this should not be too striking; and Rawson (1996, pp. 110, 115n. 25), that desire of the Good (and maybe even just desire, in the *Symposium*) entails true belief: yet in the *Republic* 505e, the (presumably unknowing) soul is said to be "confused" and "unable to grasp [the Good's] nature."

281 Plato uses "we all desire to be happy" as a premise at *Euthydemus* 282a–c; compare *Laws* III 687d.

282 Remember that the Good may not be known because it is not a being (*Republic* VI 509b8–10).

283 See also *Euthydemus* 278e3–9a4, of which Reeve (2003, p. 52) reminded me. Penner (2003, p. 217) doubts that Plato is claiming that every soul: "seeks a perfect object in some world beyond this, in an effort to escape from this world and what is useful and beneficial in it." I believe that Plato is more widely claiming that every soul does seek the Good (namely, the beyond being source of the Forms), because, as Plato says in the Cave summary, it is the source of all that is right and beautiful, and provides ethical truth as well (VII 517c), so to benefit from or use any other knowledge we might have rightly, we must "possess" it as well (VI 504e–5b); however, I agree that the Good is not in another world any more than X is in a different world than its shadow.

284 For further Plotinian passages related to this topic, see Gerson (1994, pp. 62, 152, 155); moreover, I agree with the following commentators on this issue: Findlay (1976, p. 28); Gerson (1994, pp. 198, 222); and Merlan (1967, p. 353).

285 See also V.1.6, VI.5.1, VI.6.18, VI.8.7, and III.5.3; compare VI.9.9, V.6.5, III.8.7, V.5.4, and VI.7.31.

286 See Penner (2006, p. 251) for a defense of egoism in Plato and Socrates, and that it is not best interpreted as selfishness; see Findlay (1978, p. 202) for the same kind of view in the *Laws*.

287 For example, Plotinus says that being is indifferent at III.7.6.14 and that the maker of beautiful works is neither indifferent nor ugly, at V.8.2.27–31.

288 See also I.7.1 and III.8.5.

289 Compare VI.8.13.

290 Plato: *Republic* VI 505d–e; Plotinus: I.6.7.

291 Plato also uses plants as an example of a well-conditioned body being heated and blown by the wind, right alongside a well-conditioned body that is not moved by food, drink, and toil, at *Republic* II 380e–1a.

292 Findlay (1978, p. 202) alludes to an argument in the *Laws* (or at least one that the Athenian desires to be made): "Proving that all self-motion, however distorted or misguided, is ultimately for the sake of the Good." This implies that Plato is arguing that every self-mover—that is, every soul including plants and animals—desires the Good, though admittedly this may not be what Findlay had in mind. I agree with Hitchcock (1985, p. 81) that the Good is the goal of animal and god souls, and not merely humans, but I also add plants.

293 This passage refutes at least half of Inge's (1929a, p. 209) analysis of Plotinus and Plato: "The energy of the Universal Soul descends as low as vegetable life, and slumbers even in inorganic nature. Here Plotinus frankly leaves Plato, who allowed souls to animals, but not to vegetables or minerals." Plato clearly refers to trees, plants and seeds as a "third kind of soul"; and see *Sophist* 265c–d, which describes things that grow and are fusible beneath the earth, which might refer to minerals. Even if, as is perhaps likely, the *Sophist* passage does not refer to minerals, it is not a major difference between their views if we have no view given by Plato on minerals, whereas we do from Plotinus.

294 See also especially VI.5.1.8–14; and VI.6.18.

295 Compare I.4.2.

296 Plato on free will: *Phaedo* 68a, *Republic* X 617d–e, *Laws* IX 861a–b, 861e–2c, and X 904a6–c4. Plotinus: III.2.10.1–3, 7–11; compare III.1.9 and III.1.10.

297 On this issue, I agree with: Carone (2001) that the *Protagoras* and *Republic* are consistent and that the latter is a continuation and elaboration of what Plato says in the former (pp. 108–9), that Plato uses *epithumia* the same way in the *Charmides* and *Republic* (p. 117), that each part has beliefs about the Good and that neither synchronic belief-akrasia nor knowledge-akrasia are possible in the *Republic*, as they are not in the *Protagoras* (pp. 123–4, 147), and that there is some cognitive element in the lowest desires late in the *Republic* (p. 124); Cherniss (1954, p. 254), that evil souls do "not intend as evil the evil that they cause"; Gerson (1989), that Plato holds that no one errs willingly all the way through the dialogues, and it is a fundamental Platonic doctrine (p. 88), "There is in fact a much greater continuity in the *Republic* with the doctrines of the *Protagoras* and *Gorgias* than is usually realized" (p. 91), and no one errs willingly is part of a Platonic doctrine package, with claims such as virtues are a unity and virtue is the knowledge of good and evil (p. 97); Hackforth (1946, p. 118): "It is universally agreed that Plato inherited from Socrates, and consistently maintained to the end, the doctrine that no man does evil of set purpose" [except that it is not universally agreed—see, for example, Penner (2000, pp. 170–1, 189) discussed further in this note]; Shorey (1903b, p. 7): "Plato always formally maintained that all wrongdoing is involuntary"; Mohr (2005,

pp. 144–5) rightly states that we even see something akin to the "no one errs willingly doctrine" in the Atlantian account (*Timaeus* 25c) and *Critias* 121a–b, which describes their evil as being due to ignorance. For more on akrasia and its issues in Plato, see Price (1995, pp. 94–103); compare Kahn (1987, p. 85) and Lesses (1987, p. 147); Penner (1992, pp. 129–30); compare A.E. Taylor (1956, pp. 259, 259n. 1), on the *Protagoras*, who argues that the major difference between Socrates and Plato is on the issue that no one errs willingly: "'Knowledge is strong' means different things in Socrates (*Protagoras*, *Euthyphro*, and *Meno*) and Plato (*Republic*)." Penner (2000, pp. 170–1, 189) believes that Plato changed his mind at *Republic* IV 437d–8a by endorsing brute irrational desires. I cannot spend too much space here going through all the details of this argument and its related texts, but I will briefly state three considerations in favor of my view that Plato is not changing his mind in Book IV: (a) Plato states at *Republic* VI 505d–6a that every soul pursues the Good and does not want the semblance of goodness, so it is strange to think that Plato has changed his mind from the *Meno* and *Gorgias* in *Republic* IV, and then apparently changes it back in Book VI and for the rest of the dialogues; (b) Plato states in the *Timaeus* and *Laws* that no one errs willingly as well; and (c) Plato has Socrates himself bring up the idea of one's possessing courage, having to fight against and rule over *desires* (*epithumiais*) at *Laches* 191e5 (and fears, pains, and pleasures at *Laches* 191e5–6), which, on Penner's reading, is not supposed to be a dialogue in which either there are *desires*, because (on Penner's view) there is only one *desire* for the good. That is, one should not be able to fight against irrational desires (where Plato uses *epithumia* for "desire" in the *Laches* and for Appetite, the part of the soul, in *Republic* IV). It is important to note that in the *Meno*, in his argument that everyone desires the good, Plato uses *epithumounta* and *epithumētēn* (and derivatives) for "desire" from *Meno* 77b4–8a8, but near the end of the argument, he uses *bouletai* for "wish" at 78a6–7, and b5 (as he does at *Gorgias* 467c–8b and 509d–e). First, note that Plato uses *epithumiais* in the *Laches* passage, which is the same Greek in the *Meno* for the "desire of the good" argument on Penner's view. Second, since Plato interchanges *bouletai* with *epithumounta*, then one cannot draw a meaningful distinction between them in this argument. Lastly, compare *Protagoras*, where knowledge prevails over "everything else" (357c4), which refers to passion (*thumos*), pleasure, pain, love, and fear (352b7–8). It is puzzling how the view that all desire is for the good is compatible with the possibility of one's prevailing over passion, pleasure ("if the pleasant is the good," at 358b6–7), or love. The points concerning fighting against or prevailing over desires or passion are compatible with there being parts of the soul, including Reason, Spirit, and Appetite, for which *Republic* IV 437d–8a argues. See also Carone's (2001) argument against this kind of view. Suppose one advocates the view that *Republic* IV endorses akrasia (and the *Protagoras* does not), but that it is still true that no one errs willingly (as long as we interpret that claim as saying that our will is in our Reason, but our appetites belong to Appetite); then acting against one's Reason is still possible. Notwithstanding this note, the general analysis of this section concerns the impossibility of erring willingly and my contention in this note is only sketch towards a claim. Nonetheless, if my view is implausible, it does not bear on the general point that Plato and Plotinus have the same view, for one can merely set aside the early dialogues and compare the middle and later claims about erring by choice. In any case, since Plotinus believes in the same three parts of the soul—so the alternative explanation remains a viable option—and as Plotinus makes similar claims about erring willingly, it remains plausible to argue that Plato and Plotinus have the same view on the general issue.

298 I thank Penner for pointing out this passage and interpretation.

299 See also *Gorgias* 468c5–7.

300 See also *Timaeus* 86b3–7 and 87a7–b4.

301 See also *Laws* IX 860d5–6.

302 See also Ibid., X 885b and 902a8–b3a, where in the latter passage, Plato implies that he does not agree that one can know a better course and not take it, just as he said in the *Protagoras* at 358b–c.

303 Here I agree with Gurtler (1988, p. 201) and de Vogel (1986, p. 228); and see Gerson (1994, pp. 135 and 268n. 16) for more analysis and passages related to this topic.

304 Compare IV.8.5.7–8, where Plotinus states that the soul unwillingly descends, and cites as proof the fact that everything that goes to the worse, unwillingly does so. Also, Plotinus defines voluntary action strictly speaking as an action that is performed by following Reason at III.1.9, and states that when it is hindered from its own action and does not follow Reason, the soul suffers, at III.1.10.

305 See also II.9.15.34–8.

306 See also I.8.8.40–4.

307 See *Philebus* 36b–d; compare 42a–d.

308 See Ibid., 51b; compare 66c; and *Republic* IX 584b–c.

309 See Ibid., 51b.

310 See A.E. Taylor (1956, p. 260) for his argument: "Neither Protagoras nor Socrates is represented as adopting the Hedonist equation of good with pleasure"; and I agree with Shorey's (1895, pp. 32–3) general stance of the unity of Plato's thought concerning pleasure and Good across the *Protagoras*, *Gorgias*, and *Republic*.

311 See *Republic* VIII 561c, IX 586a–7a, *Philebus* 40a–1b, 61d–e, 63b–c, *Laws* I 631e–2a, 635b–d, II 653a–c, V 733e–4c, and *Letter* III 315c; compare *Republic* II 357b–c.

312 See also *Timaeus* 81e and *Philebus* 42a–d.

313 Compare the Leaky Jar Analogy at *Gorgias* 493a–4a.

314 Compare *Laws* I 631e–2a.

315 For an interesting discussion as to a problem that Plotinus has in trying to accommodate Plato's view that Nous has pleasure, see McGroarty (2006, pp. 169–70; but see p. 171); I believe that Plato is referring to the pleasures of intellect as they occur in humans, for instance, in the *Philebus*, and not the pleasures of Nous, which is equivalent to God or the Demiurge. McGroarty predicates Plotinus' "problem" on the claim that Plotinus needs to "remain true to Plato's general view of pleasure as replenishment of a lack" (p. 169). This is not true, however, of the pleasures of knowledge or pleasant smells, as Plato says, so even if Plato states that Nous has pleasure of some sort, we should most charitably interpret that as meaning that Nous has knowledge, and not that Nous enjoys bodily pleasures in some way.

316 See also II.9.16.39–43; compare VI.7.27 and VI.7.29–30.

317 Plato: *Laws* X 902e4-3a6; Plotinus: V.1.7.33–5 (where Kronos is Intellect or Nous), I.2.7.3–4; compare III.2.1.18.

318 See also *Protagoras* 352b–3b, 357a–e, *Gorgias* 493a–4c, 496d–7a, 497c–e, 499b–500a, *Phaedo* 65c, 83b–e (the rivet passage), *Republic* VI 505b–d, 508d–9a, VII 519a–b, X 606a–e, *Phaedrus* 237d–8b, 250e–2b, *Timaeus* 86b–e, *Sophist* 228b, *Philebus* 11b–c, 22b–e, 31a–b, 31e–3a, 36b–d, 37c–8b, 40a–1b, 42a–d, 46d–8a, 60a–b, 61a, 64a, 65b–d, 67a–b, *Laws* I 633d–e, 649d, II 653a–c, 667d–8a, III 689a–c, VI 782c–3b, VII

792c–3a, IX 863b–d, *Letter* III 315c and *Letter* VIII 354e–5a. Compare *Republic* III 402e–3c, IX 587b, *Phaedrus* 240a–b, *Laws* I 631e–2a, 644c–d, and *Cratylus* 403c–d.

319 Compare the Leaky Jar Analogy at *Gorgias* 493a–4a.

320 See also I.6.5, I.4.2 (parallel to the *Philebus*' pleasure versus intellect discussion), II.9.15 (for an interesting argument against Epicurus and even more the Gnostics for their views on pleasure), I.6.6 (for a claim that temperance takes no part in pleasure but breaks away from them as being unclean), IV.8.2, VI.8.8, V.1.1, V.5.12, VI.4.15, VI.7.24 and VI.7.25 (more on Plato's *Philebus*), and VI.9.11 (where godlike men are said to take no pleasure in the things of earth). Compare IV.4.17, IV.4.25, I.5.6, and I.8.7–8. I agree with Rist (1996, pp. 391–2): "Material objects in the body, far from evil in themselves insofar as they exist, are a source of temptation, perhaps of almost inevitable temptation, to the soul." I have a mixed evaluation of Inge (1929a), because I agree that Plotinus is attracted to many Platonic passages where Matter is assumed to be a defilement of the spiritual principle (p. 259), but Inge also states that Plotinus does not agree with the *Phaedrus* ("disparagement of the material world") view, but is satisfied with the *Timaean* doctrine that the soul abides in the best (pp. 256–7); I see Plotinus as endorsing both positions and see no inconsistency in doing so. I disagree with: Friedländer (1969, pp. 56–8), who charges that the Plotinian mystical union with the One leads to a contempt of the delightful instrument of the body, which is far removed from Plato's view; they both have contempt for the body in the same way from all indications (and praise when used properly); Hadley (1997) wishes to focus on Plotinus' positive comments on the body (p. 454), arguing against the view that "Plotinus is . . . an enemy of things bodily and visible because of his association with Plato, who often suffers being labeled a dualist, or because of his reputation as a father of western mysticism" (p. 453). Both philosophers have some positive things to say about the body, but they both thoroughly agree that pursuing bodily pleasures is not the way to happiness; Mayhall (2004, p. 88), who claims that "Plotinus, unlike Plato, adopts a much more thorough attempt at mystical experience in this attempt to abandon things material"; that we see this view to abandon things in material is, to my mind, pretty obvious; and de Vogel (1986, pp. 230–1), who (like Hadley in reverse) wants to emphasize the positive comments of Plato toward the body; my replies to Inge and Hadley (*mutatis mutandis*) apply to her view as well.

321 Plotinus here refers to love as a pleasure, as Plato does at *Phaedrus* 250c–2b.

Chapter 4

1 Yount, 2014, pp. 124–30.

Bibliography

Primary Sources

Aristotle

Barnes, Jonathan, ed. (1984), *The Complete Works of Aristotle: The Revised Oxford Translation*, Bollingen Series LXXI. 2 vols, Princeton: Princeton University Press.

Cicero

Cicero (1903), *The Fourth Verrine of Cicero*, F.W. Hall, ed., New York: The MacMillan Company.

Plato

Adam, James, ed. (1902), *The* Republic *of Plato*, Vol. II (repr. 1929), Cambridge: Cambridge University Press.

Burnet, J. (1900–7), *Platonis Opera*, 5 Vols, Oxford: Clarendon Press.

Cooper, John M. and D.S. Hutchinson, eds (1997), *Plato's Complete Dialogues*, Indianapolis: Hackett Publishing Company, Inc.

Denyer, Nicholas, ed. (2001), *Plato*: Alcibiades, New York: Cambridge University Press.

Gould, G.P., ed. (1914–35), *Plato*, Loeb Classical Library. 12 vols. [v. 1, trans. H.N. Fowler, 1914 (repr. 1982); v. 2, trans. W.R.M. Lamb, 1924 (repr. 1977); v. 3, trans. W.R.M. Lamb, 1925 (repr. 1983); v. 4, trans. H.N. Fowler, 1926 (repr. 1977); v. 5, trans. Paul Shorey, 1930 (repr. 1982); v. 6, trans. Paul Shorey, 1935 (repr. 1987); v. 7, trans. H.N. Fowler, 1921 (repr. 1987); v. 8, trans. H.N. Fowler and W.R.M. Lamb, 1925 (repr. 1975); v. 9, trans. R.G. Bury, 1929 (repr. 1989); v. 10, trans. R.G. Bury, 1926 (repr. 1984); v. 11, trans. R.G. Bury, 1926 (repr. 1984); v. 12, trans. W.R.M. Lamb, 1927 (repr. 1986)], Cambridge: Harvard University Press.

Hamilton, Edith and Huntington Cairns, eds (1961), *The Collected Dialogues of Plato* (repr. 1996), New York: Pantheon.

Jowett, Benjamin (1953), *Plato: Dialogues; translated into English with analyses and introductions*, 4 vols. 4th ed. Oxford, Clarendon Press.

Reeve, C.D.C. (2004), *Plato*: Republic, Indianapolis: Hackett Publishing Company, Inc.

Zeyl, Donald J. (2000), *Timaeus*, Indianapolis: Hackett Publishing Company, Inc.

Plotinus

Armstrong, A.H., trans. (1966a), *Plotinus*, Loeb Classical Library. Vol. I. 2nd edn. (repr. 1995), Cambridge: Harvard University Press.

Armstrong, A.H., trans. (1966b), *Plotinus*, Loeb Classical Library. Vol. II. (repr. 1979), Cambridge: Harvard University Press.

Armstrong, A.H., trans. (1967a), *Plotinus*, Loeb Classical Library. Vol. III. (repr. 1980), Cambridge: Harvard University Press.

Armstrong, A.H., trans. (1984a), *Plotinus*, Loeb Classical Library. Vol. IV, Cambridge: Harvard University Press.

Armstrong, A.H., trans. (1984b), *Plotinus*, Loeb Classical Library, Vol. V, Cambridge: Harvard University Press.

Armstrong, A.H., trans. (1988a), *Plotinus*, Loeb Classical Library, Vol. VI, Cambridge: Harvard University Press.

Armstrong, A.H., trans. (1988b), *Plotinus*, Loeb Classical Library, Vol. VII, Cambridge: Harvard University Press.

Henry, Paul and Hans-Rudolf Schwyzer, eds. (1964, 1976, 1982), *Plotini Opera*, 3 vols. (*editio minor* = H-S_2), Oxford: Clarendon Press (v. 1, *Enneads* I–III); (v. 2, *Enneads* IV–V); (v. 3, *Ennead* VI).

MacKenna, Stephen, trans. (1992), *Plotinus*: The Enneads, Burdett: Larson Publications.

MacKenna, Stephen, trans. and John Dillon, ed. (1991), *Plotinus*: The Enneads, New York: Penguin Books.

O'Brien, Elmer, trans., ed. (1986), *The Essential Plotinus*, 2nd ed., Indianapolis: Hackett Publishing Company, Inc.

Turnbull, Grace H., comp. (1948), *The Essence of Plotinus: Extracts from the Six Enneads and Porphyry's Life of Plotinus*, Stephen MacKenna, trans., New York: Oxford University Press.

Secondary Sources

Abhayananda, S. (1994), *History of Mysticism: The Unchanging Testament*, 2nd ed., Olympia: Atma Books.

Alexandrakis, Aphrodite (2004), "Plotinus, Marsilio Ficino, and Renaissance Art," in Liana Cheney and John Hendrix (eds), *Neoplatonic Aesthetics: Music, Literature, and the Visual Arts*, New York: Peter Lang, 187–95.

Alexandrian Press (1985), *The System of Plotinus*, Edmonds: The Alexandrian Press.

Allen, R.E. (1983), *Plato's Parmenides. Translation and Analysis*, Minneapolis: University of Minnesota Press

Anderson, Albert (2004), "Plato's Heritage in the Arts: Form as Essence," in Liana Cheney and John Hendrix (eds), *Neoplatonic Aesthetics: Music, Literature, and the Visual Arts*, New York: Peter Lang, 67–77.

Anton, John P. (1967), "Plotinus' Conception of the Functions of the Artist," *The Journal of Aesthetics and Art Criticism*, Vol. 26, No. 1 (Autumn), 91–101.

Anton, John P. (1992), "Plotinus and the Neoplatonic Conception of Dialectic," *The Journal of Neoplatonic Studies*, Vol. 1, No. 1 (Fall), 3–30.

Anton, John P. (2000), *Archetypal Principles and Hierarchies: Essays on Neoplatonic Themes*, Binghamton: Global Publications.

Anton, John P. (2010), "Is Plotinus a Platonist?" *Philosophein* Issue 2 (June), 6–15.

Appleby, Peter C. (1980), "Mysticism and Ineffability," *International Journal for Philosophy of Religion*, Vol. 11, No. 3 (Autumn), 143–66.

Armstrong, A.H. (1938), "The Gods in Plato, Plotinus, Epicurus," *The Classical Quarterly*, Vol. 32, No. 3/4 (July–Oct.), 190–6.

Armstrong, A.H. (1940), *The Architecture of the Intelligible Universe in the Philosophy of Plotinus: An Analytical and Historical Study*, Cambridge: Cambridge University Press.

Armstrong, A.H. (1945), "Platonic Mysticism," *The Dublin Review*, Vol. 216, 130–43.

Armstrong, A.H. (1947), *An Introduction to Ancient Philosophy* (repr. 1983), Totowa, NJ: Littlefield, Adams & Company.

Armstrong, A.H. (1961), "Platonic *Eros* and Christian *Agape*," in A.H. Armstrong (1979: 105–21).

Armstrong, A.H. (1967b), *The Cambridge History of Later Greek and Early Medieval Philosophy*, Cambridge: Cambridge University Press.

Armstrong, A.H. (1974), "Tradition, Reason and Experience in the Thought of Plotinus," in A.H. Armstrong (1979: 171–94).

Armstrong, A.H. (1976), "The Apprehension of Divinity in the Self and Cosmos in Plotinus," in A.H. Armstrong (1979: 187–98).

Armstrong, A.H. (ed.) (1979), *Plotinian and Christian Studies*, London: Variorum Reprints.

Armstrong, John M. (2004), "After the Ascent: Plato on Becoming Like God," *Oxford Studies in Ancient Philosophy*, Vol. 26, 171–83.

Atkinson, Michael (1983), *Plotinus:* Ennead *V.1: On the Three Principal Hypostases*. Michael Atkinson, trans., New York: Oxford University Press.

Benitez, Eugenio E. (1995), "The Good or The Demiurge: Causation and the Unity of Good in Plato," *Apeiron*, Vol. 28, No. 2 (June), 113–40.

Blumenthal, Henry J. (1966), "Did Plotinus Believe in Ideas of Individuals?" in Blumenthal (1993: 61–80).

Blumenthal, Henry J. (1996), "On Soul and Intellect," in Gerson (1996: 82–104).

Boas, George (1921), "A Source of the Plotinian Mysticism," *The Journal of Philosophy*, Vol. 18, No. 12 (June 9), 326–32.

Bobonich, Christopher (2002), *Plato's Utopia Recast: His Later Ethics and Politics*, Oxford: Clarendon Press.

Boodin, J.E. (1929), "Cosmology in Plato's Thought (I.)," *Mind*, New Series, Vol. 38, No. 152 (Oct.), 489–505.

Bowe, G.S. (2003), *Plotinus and the Platonic Metaphysical Hierarchy*, New York: Global Scholarly Publications.

Brandwood, Leonard (1992), "Stylometry and Chronology," in Richard Kraut (ed.), *The Cambridge Companion to Plato*, New York: Cambridge University Press, 90–120.

Brisson, Luc (1995), "Premises, Consequences, and Legacy of an Esotericist Interpretation of Plato," *Ancient Philosophy*, Vol. 15, 117–34.

Bussanich, John (1988), *The One and Its Relation to Intellect in Plotinus: A Commentary on Selected Texts*, Philosophia Antiqua: A Series of Studies on Ancient Philosophy, W.J. Verdenius and J.C.M. Van Winden (eds), Vol. XLIX, New York: E. J. Brill.

Bussanich, John (1994), "Mystical Elements in the Thought of Plotinus," *Aufstieg und Niedergang der romishen Welt: II*, Vol. 36, No. 7, 5300–30.

Bussanich, John (1996), "Plotinus's Metaphysics of the One," in Gerson (1996: 38–65).

Bussanich, John (1997), "Plotinian Mysticism in Theoretical and Comparative Perspective," *American Catholic Philosophical Quarterly*, Vol. 71, No. 3 (Summer), 339–65.

Bussanich, John (1999), "Socrates the Mystic," in John J. Cleary (ed.), *Traditions of Platonism: Essays in Honour of John Dillon*, Brookfield: Ashgate Publishing Co., 29–51.

Bussanich, John (2004), "Beyond Reason: Plato's Mythical Imagination," *Ninth Annual University of Arizona Colloquium on Ancient Philosophy*, 1–27.

Bussanich, John (2005), *Plato's Cosmology and Its Ethical Dimensions*, New York: Cambridge University Press.

Carone, Gabriela Roxana (2001), "*Akrasia* in the *Republic*: Does Plato Change His Mind?" *Oxford Studies in Ancient Philosophy*, Vol. XX (Summer), 107–48.

Carter, Robert Edgar (1975), "Plato and Mysticism," *Idealistic Studies*, Vol. 5, No. 4 (Sept.), 255–68.

Cherniss, Harold F. (1944), *Aristotle's Criticism of Plato and the Academy*, Vol. I, Baltimore: The Johns Hopkins Press.

Cherniss, Harold F. (1945), *The Riddle of the Early Academy*, New York: Russell & Russell (reissued 1962).
Cherniss, Harold F. (1954), "The Sources of Evil According to Plato," in Vlastos (1978b: 244–58).
Ciapolo, Roman T. (1997), "The Relation of Plotinian *Eudaimonia* to the Life of the Serious Man in Treatise I.4 (46)," *American Catholic Philosophical Quarterly*, Vol. 71, No. 3 (Summer), 489–98.
Cooper, John M. (1984), "Plato's Theory of Human Motivation," *History of Philosophy Quarterly*, Vol. 1, No. 1 (Jan.), 3–21.
Cornford, Francis MacDonald (1939), *Plato and Parmenides* (repr. 1950), London: Kegan, Paul, Trench, Trubner & Co., Ltd.
Desjardin, Rosemary (2004), *Plato and the Good: Illuminating the Darkling Vision*, Boston: Brill.
Dillon, John (1988), "The Mind of Plotinus," *The Proceedings of the Boston Area Colloquium in Ancient Philosophy*, John J. Cleary (ed.), Vol. III (1987), Lanham: University Press of America.
Dillon, John (1992), "Plotinus at Work on Platonism," *Greece & Rome*, 2nd Ser., Vol. 39, No. 2 (Oct.), 189–204.
Dodds, E.R. (1928), "The *Parmenides* of Plato and the Origin of the Neoplatonic 'One'," *The Classical Quarterly*, Vol. 22, No. 3/4 (July–Oct.), 129–42.
Dodds, E.R. (1947), "Theurgy and Its Relationship to Neoplatonism," *The Journal of Roman Studies*, Vol. 37, Parts 1 and 2, 55–69.
Dodds, E.R. (1951), *The Greeks and the Irrational*, Berkeley: University of California Press.
Dodds, E.R. (1960), "Tradition and Personal Achievement in the Philosophy of Plotinus," *The Journal of Roman Studies*, Vol. 50, Parts 1 and 2, 1–7.
Duncan, Patrick (1940), "Socrates and Plato," *Philosophy*, Vol. 15, No. 60 (Oct.), 339–62.
Earle, William (1976), "Phenomenology of Mysticism," *The Monist*, Vol. 59, No. 4 (Oct.), 519–31.
Edman, Irwin (1925), "The Logic of Mysticism and Plotinus," *Studies in the History of Ideas*, Vol. II, New York: Columbia University Press, 51–81.
Edwards, Mark J. (1993), "A Portrait of Plotinus," *The Classical Quarterly*, New Series, Vol. 43, No. 2, 480–90.
Ferguson, John (1963), "Sun, Line, and Cave Again," *The Classical Quarterly*, New Series, Vol. 13, 188–93.
Field, G.C. (1934), "Great Thinkers: (II) Plato," *Philosophy*, Vol. 9, No. 35 (July), 282–92.
Findlay, John N. (1974), *Plato: The Written and Unwritten Doctrines*, New York: Humanities Press.
Findlay, John N. (1975a), "The Three Hypostases of Platonism," *The Review of Metaphysics*, Vol. 28, No. 4 (June), 660–80.
Findlay, John N. (1975b), "The Rationality of Mysticism," in John Howie and Thomas O. Buford (eds), *Contemporary Studies in Philosophical Idealism*, Cape Cod: Claude Stark and Company, 133–48.
Findlay, John N. (1976), "The Neoplatonism of Plato," in R. Baine Harris (ed.), *The Significance of Neoplatonism*, Norfolk: International Society for Neoplatonic Studies, 23–40.
Findlay, John N. (1978), *Plato and Platonism: An Introduction*, New York: Times Books.
Fine, Gail (1978), "Knowledge and Belief in Republic V," *Archiv Fur Geschichte der Philosophie*, Vol. 60, 121–39.
Fox, Adam (1957), *Plato and the Christians*, London: The Camelot Press Ltd.

Friedländer, Paul (1969), *Plato: Volume 1: An Introduction*, Hans Meyerhoff, trans., 2nd ed., Princeton: Princeton University Press, 1969. (Originally published by Bollingen Foundation, New York, New York, 59th in a Bollingen Foundation series.)
Fuller, B.A.G. (1938), *A History of Ancient and Medieval Philosophy*, New York: Henry Holt and Company.
Gadamer, Hans-Georg (1986), *The Idea of the Good in Platonic-Aristotelian Philosophy*, P. Christopher Smith, trans., New Haven: Yale University Press.
Gaiser, Konrad (1980), "Plato's Enigmatic Lecture 'On the Good,'" *Phronesis*, Vol. 25, No. 1, 5–35.
Gale, Richard M. (1960), "Mysticism and Philosophy," *The Journal of Philosophy*, Vol. 57, 471–81.
Garvie, Alfred E. (1937), "Reflections on Plato's '*Republic*,'" *Philosophy*, Vol. 12, No. 48 (Oct.), 424–31.
Gerson, Lloyd P. (1989), "Plato on Virtue, Knowledge, and the Unity of Goodness," *Essays in Ancient Greek Philosophy III: Plato*, J.P. Anton and A. Preus (eds), Albany: State University of New York Press, 85–100.
Gerson, Lloyd P. (1994), *Plotinus: The Arguments of the Philosophers*, Ted Honderich (ed.), New York: Routledge.
Gerson, Lloyd P., ed. (1996), *The Cambridge Companion to Plotinus*, New York: Cambridge University Press.
Gerson, Lloyd P. (1997), "The Study of Plotinus Today," *American Catholic Philosophical Quarterly*, Vol. 71, No. 3 (Summer), 293–300.
Gerson, Lloyd P. (2005), "What is Platonism?" *Journal of the History of Philosophy*, Vol. 43, No. 3 (July), 253–76.
Gonzalez, Francisco J. (1998), *Dialectic and Dialogue: Plato's Practice of Philosophical Inquiry*, Evanston: Northwestern University Press.
Gosling, J.C.B. (1999), *Plato: The Arguments of the Philosophers*, Ted Honderich (ed.), London: Routledge & Kegan Paul.
Grube, G.M.A. (1966), *Plato's Thought*, 4th printing, Boston: Beacon Press.
Gulley, Norman (1954), "Plato's Theory of Recollection," *The Classical Quarterly*, New Series, Vol. 4, No. 3/4 (July–Oct.), 194–213.
Gulley, Norman (1965), "The Interpretation of 'No one does wrong willingly' on Plato's dialogues," *Phronesis*, Vol. 10, 82–96.
Gurtler, Gary M. (1988), *Plotinus: The Experience of Unity*, New York: Peter Lang.
Gurtler, Gary M. (1992), "Plotinus and the Platonic *Parmenides*," *International Philosophical Quarterly*, Vol. 32, No. 4, Issue No. 128 (Dec.), 443–57.
Hackforth, Reginald (1946), "Moral Evil and Ignorance in Plato's Ethics," *The Classical Quarterly*, Vol. 40, No. 3/4 (July–Oct.), 118–20.
Hadley, Douglas (1997), "Plotinus's Defense of the Sensible: The Metaphysics of Image and Dance in *Ennead* II.9 (33)," *American Catholic Philosophical Quarterly*, Vol. 71, No. 3 (Summer), 453–68.
Hadot, Pierre (1993), *Plotinus or The Simplicity of Vision*, Michael Chase (trans.), Introduction by Arnold I. Davidson, Chicago: The University of Chicago Press.
Hampton, Cynthia (1990), *Pleasure, Knowledge, and Being*, Albany: State University of New York Press.
Hardie, W.F.R. (1936), *A Study in Plato*, New York: Oxford University Press.
Harris, R. Baine (1976), "A Brief Description of Neoplatonism," in R. Baine Harris (ed.), *The Significance of Neoplatonism*, Norfolk: International Society for Neoplatonic Studies, 1–20.

Harvey, Andrew (ed.) (1996), *The Essential Mystics: The Soul's Journey into Truth*, San Francisco: Harper.

Hathaway, R.F. (1969), "The Neoplatonist Interpretation of Plato: Remarks on its Decisive Characteristics," *Journal of the History of Philosophy*, Vol. III, No. 1 (Jan.), 16–26.

Helleman-Elgersma, Wypkje (1980), *Soul-Sisters: A Commentary on* Enneads *IV 3 (27), 1-8 of Plotinus*. Amsterdam: Rodopi N.V.

Hick, John (2000), "Ineffability," *Religious Studies*, Vol. 36, No. 1 (March), 35–46.

Hill, Stephen, ed. (2002), *The Power of Plato: An Anthology of New Translations*, London: Duckworth Publishers.

Hitchcock, David (1985), "The Good in Plato's *Republic*," *Apeiron*, Vol. 17, 65–92.

Inge, William Ralph (1929a), *The Philosophy of Plotinus: The Gifford Lectures at St. Andrews, 1917–1918*, 3rd ed., Vol. I, New York: Longmans, Green and Co.

Inge, William Ralph (1929b), *The Philosophy of Plotinus: The Gifford Lectures at St. Andrews, 1917–1918*. 3rd ed., Vol. II, New York: Longmans, Green and Co.

Inge, William Ralph (1936), "The Place of Myth in Philosophy," *Philosophy*, Vol. 11, No. 42 (April), 131–45.

Inge, William Ralph (1948), *Mysticism and Religion*, (repr. 1976), Westport: Greenwood Press, Publishers.

Irwin, Terence H. (1977), *Plato's Moral Theory: The Early and Middle Dialogues*, (repr. 1979), Oxford: Clarendon Press.

Jackson, B. Darrell (1967), "Plotinus and the *Parmenides*," *The Journal of the History of Philosophy*, Volume V, 315–27.

Jackson, Henry (1882), "On Plato's *Republic* VI 509D sqq.," *The Journal of Philology*, Vol. 10, No. 19, 132–50.

Jessop, T.E. (1930), "The Metaphysics of Plato," *Journal of Philosophical Studies*, Vol. 5, No. 17 (Jan.), 36–50.

Joseph, H.W.B. (1948), *Knowledge and the Good in Plato's* Republic, London: Geoffrey Cumberlege, Oxford University Press.

Kahn, Charles H. (1987), "Plato's Theory of Desire," *Review of Metaphysics*, Vol. 41 (Sept.), 77–103.

Kahn, Charles H. (1996), *Plato and Socratic Dialogue: The Philosophical Use of a Literary Form*, New York: Cambridge University Press.

Kaplan, Abraham (1958), "Philosophic Sense and Mystic Sensibility," *Proceedings and Addresses of the American Philosophical Association*. Vol. 32 (1958–59), 41–64.

Karelis, Charles (2006), "Plato on Art and Reality," *The Journal of Aesthetics and Art Criticism*, Vol. 34, No. 3 (Spring), 315–21.

Katz, Joseph (1950a), *The Philosophy of Plotinus*, New York: Appleton-Century-Crofts, Inc.

Katz, Joseph (1950b), *Plotinus' Search for the Good*, New York: King Crown's Press.

Kellenberger, J. (1979), "The Ineffabilities of Mysticism," *American Philosophical Quarterly*, Vol. 16, No. 4 (Oct.), 307–15.

Kenney, John Peter (1997), "Mysticism and Contemplation and the *Enneads*," *American Catholic Philosophical Quarterly*, Vol. 71, No. 3 (Summer), 315–37.

Kolb, David A. (1974), "Time and the Timeless in Greek Thought," *Philosophy East and West*, Vol. 24, No. 2, Time and Temporality (April), 137–43.

Kraut, Richard (1992), "Introduction to the Study of Plato," in Richard Kraut (ed.), *The Cambridge Companion to Plato*, New York: Cambridge University Press, 1–50.

Lachterman, David, "What is 'The Good' of Plato's *Republic*?" *St. John's Review*, Vol. 39, 139–71.

Laguna, Theodore de (1934), "Notes on the Theory of Ideas," *The Philosophical Review*, Vol. 43, No. 5 (Sept.), 443–70.
Lamprecht, Sterling P. (1927), "A Type of Religious Mysticism," *The Journal of Philosophy*, Vol. 24, No. 26 (Dec. 22), 701–15.
Lesses, Glenn (1987), "Weakness, Reason, and that Divided Soul in Plato's *Republic*," *History of Philosophy Quarterly*, Vol. 4, No. 2 (April), 147–61.
Leys, Wayne A.R. (1965), "Was Plato Non-Political?" in Vlastos (1978b: 166–73).
Livius (2015), Livius.org: http://www.livius.org/sh-si/sicily/sicily_t08.html [accessed December 18, 2015].
Lloyd, A.C. (1990), *The Anatomy of Neoplatonism*, Oxford: Clarendon Press.
Lodge, Rupert C. (1966), *Plato's Theory of Ethics: The Moral Criterion and the Highest Good*, New York: Archon Books.
Lounibos, John (1984), "Plotinus: Pagan, Mystic, Philosopher," in Robert C. Smith and John Lounibos (eds), *Pagan and Christian Anxiety: A Response to E.R. Dodds*, Lanham: University Press of America, 131–66.
Louth, Andrew (1981), *The Origins of the Christian Mystical Tradition: From Plato to Denys*, Oxford: Clarendon Press.
Luban, David (1978), "The Form of the Good in the *Republic*," *The Journal of Value Inquiry*, Vol. 12, 161–8.
Lynch, William F. (1959), *An Approach to the Metaphysics of Plato through the* Parmenides, (repr. 1969), Westport: Greenwood Press, Publishers.
Majercik, Ruth (1995), "Plotinus and Greek Mysticism," in Donald H. Bishop (ed.), *Mysticism and the Mystical Experience: East and West*, Selinsgrove: Susquehanna University Press, 1995, 38–61.
Majumdar, Deepa (2005), "Alone to the Alone: The Ascent to the One in Plotinus," in Robert Berchman and John Finamore (eds), *History of Platonism: Plato Redivivus*, New Orleans: University Press of the South, 131–46.
Majumdar, Deepa (2007a), *Plotinus on the Appearance of Time and the World of Sense: A Pantomime*, Burlington: Ashgate Publishing.
Majumdar, Deepa (2007b), "Mysticism and the Political: Stairway to the Good in Plato's Allegory of the Cave: Two Models of Numinous Politics (Part I)," *Philotheos: International Journal of Philosophy and Theology*, Vol. 7, 144–59.
Marlow, A.N. (1954), "Hinduism and Buddhism in Greek Philosophy," *Philosophy East and West*, Vol. 4, No. 1 (April), 35–45.
Marshall, Henry Rutgers (1922), "The True, The Good and the Beautiful," *The Philosophical Review*, Vol. 31, No. 5 (Sept.), 449–70.
Mayhall, C. Wayne (2004), *On Plotinus*, Belmont: Thomson-Wadsworth.
McEvilley, Thomas (2002), *The Shape of Ancient Thought*, New York: Allworth Press.
McGroarty, Kieran, trans. (2006), *Plotinus on* Eudaimonia*: A Commentary on* Ennead *I.4*, New York: Oxford University Press.
Mead, G.R.S. (1912), "The Doctrine of Reincarnation Ethically Considered," *International Journal of Ethics*, Vol. 22, No. 2 (Jan.), 158–79.
Meijer, P.A. (1992), *Plotinus on that Good or the One* (Enneads *VI, 9): An Analytical Commentary*, Amsterdam: J.C. Geiben.
Menn, Stephen (1992), "Aristotle and Plato on God as Nous and as the Good," *Review of Metaphysics*, Vol. 45 (March), 543–73.
Menn, Stephen (1995), *Plato on God as Nous*, Carbondale and Edwardsville: Southern Illinois University Press.

Meredith, A. (1993), "Plato's 'Cave' (*Republic* vii 514a–517e) in Origen, Plotinus, and Gregory of Nyssa," in *Studia Patristica*, Vol. 27. Papers presented at the 11th International Conference on Patristic Studies held in Oxford 1991. Elizabeth A. Livingstone (ed.), Louvain: Peeters Publishers.

Merlan, Philip (1967), "Plotinus," in *The Encyclopedia of Philosophy*, Paul Edwards (ed.), Vol. 6, New York: Macmillan Publishing Co., Inc.

Miles, Margaret R. (1999), *Plotinus on Body and Beauty: Society, Philosophy and Religion in Third-Century Rome*, Malden: Blackwell Publishers, Inc.

Mill, John Stuart (1979), *Utilitarianism*, George Sher (ed.), Indianapolis: Hackett Publishing, Inc.

Miller, Mitchell (1986), *Plato's Parmenides: The Conversion of the Soul*, University Park: The University of Pennsylvania Press.

Miller, Mitchell (1995), "The Choice between the Dialogues and the 'Unwritten Teachings': A Scylla and Charybdis of the Interpreter?" *The Third Way: New Directions in Platonic Studies*, Francisco J. Gonzalez (ed.), London: Rowman & Littlefield, Inc., 225–43.

Mohr, Richard D. (2005), *God and Forms in Plato*, Las Vegas: Parmenides Publishing.

More, Paul E. (1923), *Hellenistic Philosophies*, Princeton: Princeton University Press.

Morrison, J.S. (1977), "Two Unresolved Difficulties in the Line and Cave," *Phronesis*. Vol. 22, 212–31.

Morrow, Glenn R. (1929), "The Theory of Knowledge in Plato's Seventh Epistle," *The Philosophical Review*, Vol. 38, No. 4 (July), 326–49.

Mortley, Raoul (1980), "Love in Plato and Plotinus," *Antichthon*, Vol. 14, 45–52.

Murphy, N.R. (1951), *The Interpretation of Plato's* Republic, Oxford: Clarendon Press.

Murray, Gilbert (1912), *Four Stages of Greek Religion*, New York: Columbia University Press.

Murray, Penelope ed. (1996), *Plato on Poetry*: Ion, Republic *376e–398b9*; Republic *595–608b10*, New York: Cambridge University Press.

Nails, Debra, and Holger Thesleff (2003), "Early Academic Editing: Plato's *Laws*," in Samuel Scolnicov and Luc Brisson (eds), *Plato's Laws: From Theory into Practice*, International Plato Series, Sankt Augustin: Academia Verlag, 14–29.

Nehamas, Alexander (1988), "Plato and the Mass Media," *The Monist* 71, 214–34.

Nettleship, Richard Lewis (1925), *Lectures on the* Republic *of Plato* (repr. 1897), London: MacMillan and Company, Ltd.

Notopoulos, James A. (1944), "The Symbolism of the Sun and Light in the *Republic* of Plato II," *Classical Philology*, Vol. 39, No. 4 (Oct.), 223–40.

O'Daly, Gerard J.P. (1973), *Plotinus' Philosophy of the Self*, Shannon: Irish University Press.

O'Meara, Dominic J. (1993), *Plotinus: An Introduction to the* Enneads, Oxford: Clarendon Press.

O'Meara, Dominic J. (1999), "Neoplatonist Conceptions of the Philosopher-King," in Johannes M. Van Ophuijsen (ed.), *Plato and Platonism. Studies in Philosophy and the History of Philosophy*, Vol. 33, Washington, DC: The Catholic University of America Press.

O'Meara, Dominic J. (2003), *Platonopolis: Platonic Political Philosophy in Late Antiquity*, New York: Oxford University Press.

Organ, Troy Wilson (1991), *The One: East and West*, New York: University Press of America.

Overstreet, Harry Allen (1909), "The Dialectic of Plotinus," *University of California Publications in Philosophy*, Vol. 2, No. 1 (May 15), 1–29.

Owen, G.E.L. (1953), "The Place of the Timaeus in Plato's Dialogues," *The Classical Quarterly*, New Series, Vol. 3, No. 1/2 (Jan.–April), 79–95.

Penner, Terry (1973), "The Unity of Virtue," *Philosophical Review*, reprinted in Hugh Benson (ed.), *Essays on the Philosophy of Socrates*, Oxford: Oxford University Press, 1992, 162–84.

Penner, Terry (1987), *The Ascent From Nominalism: Some Existence Arguments in Plato's Middle Dialogues*, Boston: D. Reidel Publishing Company.

Penner, Terry (1992), "Socrates and the Early Dialogues," in Richard Kraut (ed.), *The Cambridge Companion to Plato*, New York: Cambridge University Press, 121–69.

Penner, Terry (2000), "Socrates," in Christopher Rowe and Malcolm Schofield (eds), *The Cambridge History of Greek and Roman Political Thought*, New York: Cambridge University Press, 164–89.

Penner, Terry (2003), "The Forms, the Form of the Good, and the Desire for Good in Plato's *Republic*," *The Modern Schoolman*, Vol. 80, 191–233.

Penner, Terry (2006), "The Forms in the *Republic*," in Gerasimos Santas (ed.), *Blackwell Guide to Plato's* Republic, Malden: Blackwell Publishing, 234–62.

Pistorius, Philippus Villiers (1952), *Plotinus and Neoplatonism: An Introductory Study*, Cambridge: Bowes and Bowes Publishers, Ltd.

Plass, Paul (1982), "Plotinus' Ethical Theory," *Illinois Classical Studies*, Vol. 7, No. 2, 241–59.

Pond, Enoch (1856), *Plato: His Life, Works, Opinions, and Influence*, Boston: G.W. Cottrell.

Price, A.W. (1995), *Mental Conflict*, New York: Routledge.

Raphael (2005), *Initiation into the Philosophy of Plato*. New York: The Aurea Vidya Foundation, Inc.

Rappe, Sara (2000), *Reading Neoplatonism: Non-discursive Thinking in the Texts of Plotinus, Proclus, and Damascius*, Cambridge: Cambridge University Press.

Raven, J.E. (1953), "Sun, Divided Line, and Cave," *The Classical Quarterly*, New Series, Vol. 3, 22–32.

Rawson, Glenn (1996), "Knowledge and Desire of the Good in Plato's *Republic*," *Southwest Philosophy Review*, Vol. 12, No. 1 (Jan.), 103–15.

Rawson, Glenn (2006), "Platonic Recollection and of Mental Pregnancy," *Journal of the History of Philosophy*, Vol. 44, No. 2, 137–55.

Reale, Giovanni (1997), *Toward the New Interpretation of Plato* (10th ed.), John R. Catan and Richard Davies (trans. and eds), Washington, DC: The Catholic University of America Press.

Reeve, C.D.C. (1988), *Philosopher-Kings: The Argument of Plato's* Republic, Princeton: Princeton University Press.

Reeve, C.D.C. (2003), "Plato's Metaphysics of Morals," *Oxford Studies in Ancient Philosophy*, Vol. 25 (Winter), 39–58.

Rein'l, Robert (1956), "Naturalism and Supernaturalism in East and West," *Philosophy East and West*, Vol. 6, No. 1 (April), 49–67.

Reuter, Mark (2001), "Is Goodness Really a Gift from God? Another Look at the Conclusion of Plato's 'Meno'," *Phoenix*, Vol. 55, No. 1/2 (Spring–Summer), 77–97.

Rist, John M. (1962a), "The Indefinite Dyad and Intelligible Matter in Plotinus," *The Classical Quarterly*, New Series, Vol. 12, No. 1 (May), 99–107.

Rist, John M. (1962b), "Theos and the One in Some Texts of Plotinus," *Medieval Studies*, Vol. 24, 169–80.

Rist, John M. (1964), *Eros and Psyche: Studies in Plato, Plotinus, and Origen. Phoenix*: Supplementary Volume VI (repr. 1991), Ann Arbor: UMI Out-of-Print Books on Demand.

Rist, John M. (1967a), *Plotinus: The Road to Reality*, Cambridge: Cambridge University Press.

Rist, John M. (1967b), "Integration and the Undescended Soul in Plotinus," *The American Journal of Philology*, Vol. 88, No. 4 (Oct.), 410–22.

Rist, John M. (1973), "The One of Plotinus and the God of Aristotle," *Review of Metaphysics*, Vol. 27, 75–87.

Rist, John M. (1989), "Back to the Mysticism of Plotinus: Some More Specifics," *The Journal of the History of Philosophy*, Vol. 27, No. 2 (April), 183–97.

Rist, John M. (1996), "Plotinus and Christian Philosophy," in Gerson (1996: 386–413).

Robin, Léon (1928), *Greek Thought and the Origins of the Scientific Spirit*, New York: Alfred A. Knopf.

Robinson, Richard (1941), *Plato's Earlier Dialectic*, Ithaca: Cornell University Press.

Robinson, Richard (1953), "Hypothesis in the *Republic*," in Vlastos (1978a: 97–131).

Rogers, A.K. (1936), "Plato's Theory of Forms," *The Philosophical Review*, Vol. 45, No. 1 (Jan.), 61–78.

Ross, Sir David (1951), *Plato's Theory of Ideas*, (repr. 1963), Oxford: Oxford University Press.

Runciman, Walter Garrison (1959), "Plato's *Parmenides*," *Harvard Studies in Classical Philology*, Vol. 64, 89–120.

Russell, Bertrand (1917), *Mysticism and Logic*, (repr. 1959). London: G. Allen & Unwin.

Russell, Bertrand (1945), *A History of Western Philosophy* (16th printing), New York: Simon and Schuster.

Santas, Gerasimos (1983), "The Form of the Good in Plato's *Republic*," in John P. Anton and Anthony Preus (eds), *Essays in Ancient Greek Philosophy*, Vol. 2, Albany: State University of New York Press, 232–63.

Santayana, George (1913), "Dr. Fuller, Plotinus, and the Nature of Evil," *The Journal of Philosophy, Psychology and Scientific Methods*, Vol. 10, No. 22 (Oct.), 589–99.

Santayana, George (1936), *Obiter Scripta*, New York: Charles Scribner's Sons.

Sayre, Kenneth M. (1983), *Plato's Late Ontology: A Riddle Resolved*, Princeton: Princeton University Press.

Sayre, Kenneth M. (1987), "The *Philebus* and the Good: the Unity of the Dialogue in which the Good is Unity," in John Cleary (ed.), *Proceedings of the Boston Area Colloquium in Ancient Philosophy*, Vol. 2, Lanham: University Press of America, 45–78.

Seeskin, Kenneth R. (1976), "Platonism, Mysticism, and Madness," *The Monist*, Vol. 59, No. 4 (Oct.), 574–86.

Sells, Michael A. (1994), *Mystical Languages of Unsaying*, Chicago: The University of Chicago Press.

Sheldon, Wilmon H. (1952), "What Is Intellect? Part Two," *Philosophy East and West*, Vol. 2, No. 2 (July), 129–43.

Shorey, Paul (1895), "The Idea of Good in Plato's *Republic*," in Paul Shorey, *Selected Papers*, Vol. 2, New York: Garland Publishing, Inc., 1980, 28–79.

Shorey, Paul (1903a), *The Unity of Plato's Thought*, Chicago: The University of Chicago Press.

Shorey, Paul (1903b), "Plato's Ethics," in Vlastos (1978b: 7–34).

Shorey, Paul (1938), *Platonism: Ancient and Modern*, Berkeley: University of California Press.

Shrine of Wisdom, eds (1936), *The Human Soul in the Myths of Plato* (repr. 1984), Hertfordshire: The Garden City Press Ltd.

Sinnige, Th. G. (1999), *Six Lectures on Plotinus and Gnosticism*, Boston: Kluwer Academic Publishers.

Slaveva-Griffin, Svetla (2009), *Plotinus on Number*, New York: Oxford University Press.

Smith, Nicholas D. (1998), "Plato's Divided Line," in *Plato: Critical Assessments. Volume II: Plato's Middle Period: Metaphysics and Epistemology*, New York: Routledge, 292–316.

Snell, Laird Wingate (1944), "My Mystical Experience," *The Hibbert Journal*, Vol. 43, 148–56.

Sparshott, F.E. (1967), "Plato As Anti-Political Thinker," in Vlastos (1978b: 174–86).

Stace, W.T. (1967), *A Critical History of Greek Philosophy*, New York: St. Martin's Press.

Stalley, R.F. (1983), *An Introduction to Plato's* Laws. Indianapolis: Hackett Publishing Company.

Stewart, Herbert L. (1915), "Was Plato an Ascetic?" *The Philosophical Review*, Vol. 24, No. 6 (Nov.), 603–13.

Stewart, J. A. (1917), "Socrates and Plato," *Mind*, New Series, Vol. 26, No. 104 (Oct.), 393–406.

Stocks, J.L. (1911), "The Divided Line of Plato *Rep*. VI," *The Classical Quarterly*, Vol. 5, 73–88.

Sumi, Atsushi (1997), "Plotinus on *Phaedrus* 247d7–e1: The Platonic *Locus Classicus* of the Identity of Intellect with the Intelligible Objects," *American Catholic Philosophical Quarterly*, Vol. 71, No. 3 (Summer), 404–20.

Tate, J. (1932), "Plato and 'Imitation,'" *The Classical Quarterly*, Vol. 26, No. 3/4 (July–Oct.), 161–9.

Taylor, A.E. (1918), "The Philosophy of Proclus," *Proceedings of the Aristotelian Society*, New Series. Vol. 18, 600–35.

Taylor, A.E. (1930), *The Faith of a Moralist: Gifford Lectures Delivered in the University of St. Andrews, 1926–1928*, Series II: Natural Theology and the Positive Religions. London: MacMillan and Co., Ltd.

Taylor, A.E. (1956), *Plato: The Man and his Work*, New York: Meridian Books.

Taylor, Thomas, trans. (1816), *The Theology of Plato* (repr. 1995), Somerset: Prometheus Trust.

Theiler, W. (1960), "Plotin zwischen Platon und Stoa," *Les Sources de Plotin* (Entreteins sur l'antiquite classique V), Fondation Hardt: Vandoevres-Geneva, 63–103.

Thorp, John (1994), "Sex and Mysticism in Plato," paper for a joint meeting of the *Society for Ancient Greek Philosophy* and the *American Philological Association* in Atlanta, GA, 1–10.

Tigerstedt, E.N. (1974), *The Decline and Fall of the Neoplatonic Interpretation of Plato: An Outline and Some Observations*, Helsinki: Societas Scientiarum Fennica.

Tigerstedt, E.N. (1977), *Interpreting Plato*, Uppsala: Almqvist & Wiksell.

Tinsley, E. J. (1954), "Mysticism – Neoplatonic and Christian," *The Hibbert Journal*, Vol. 53, 43–50.

Turnbull, Grace H. (1948), *The Essence of Plotinus*, New York: Oxford University Press.

Ullman, Robert and Judyth Reichenberg-Ullman (2001), *Mystics, Masters, Saints, and Sages: Stories of Enlightenment*, Berkeley: Conari Press.

Underhill, Evelyn (1974), *Mysticism*, New York: New American Library.

Unger, Eric (1952), "Use and Misuse of the Unknown," *Philosophy*, Vol. 27, No. 102 (July), 238–43.

Vaughan, Barry F. (1999), "The Unity of Virtue Revisited: A Resolution to a Socratic Enigma," dissertation, Ann Arbor: UMI Dissertation Services.

Vlastos, Gregory (1965), "Degrees of Reality in Plato," in Renford Bambrough (ed.), *New Essays and Plato and Aristotle*, London: Routledge.
Vlastos, Gregory (1991), *Socrates: Ironist and Moralist Philosopher*, Ithaca: Cornell University Press.
Vogel, C.J. de (1969), "What Was God for Plato?" in *Philosophia: Part I: Studies in Greek Philosophy*, Assen: Van Gorcum, 210–42.
Vogel, C.J. de (1986), *Rethinking Plato and Platonism*, in *Mnemosyne*, Supp., v. 92. Leiden: E.J. Brill.
Vorwerk, Matthias (2001), "Plato on Virtue: Definitions of *ΣΩΦΡΟΣΥΝΗ* in Plato's *Charmides* and in Plotinus *Enneads* 1.2 (19)," *The American Journal of Philology*, Vol. 122, No. 1 (Spring), 29–47.
Walker, Merle G. (1938), "The One and Many in Plato's *Parmenides*," *The Philosophical Review*, Vol. 47, No. 5 (Sept.), 488–516.
Wallis, R.T. (1972), *Neoplatonism*, London: Duckworth.
Watson, John (1928), "The Philosophy of Plotinus," *The Philosophical Review*, Vol. 37, No. 5 (Sept.), 482–500.
Weiss, Rosalyn (2001), *Virtue in the Cave: Moral Inquiry in Plato's* Meno, New York: Oxford University Press.
White, Nicholas P. (1976), *Plato On Knowledge and Reality* (repr. 1980), Indianapolis: Hackett Publishing Company.
Whittaker, Thomas (1961), *The Neo-Platonists: A Study in the History of Hellenism* (4th ed.), Hildesheim: Georg Olms Verlagbuchhanlung.
Witt, R.E. (1931), "The Plotinian Logos and Its Stoic Basis," *The Classical Quarterly*, Vol. 25, No. 2 (April), 103–11.
Wolfson, H. A. (1952), "Albinus and Plotinus on Divine Attributes," *The Harvard Theological Review*, Vol. 45, No. 2 (April), 115–30.
Yandell, Keith (1975), "Some Varieties of Ineffability," *International Journal for Philosophy of Religion*, Vol. 6, No. 3 (Fall), 167–79.
Yandell, Keith (1979), "The Ineffability Theme," *International Journal for Philosophy of Religion*, Vol. 10, No. 4, 209–31.
Yount, David J. (2014), *Plotinus The Platonist: A Comparative Account of Plato and Plotinus' Metaphysics*, New York: Bloomsbury.
Zeller, Eduard (1931), *Outlines of the History of Greek Philosophy* (13th ed.) (repr. 1980), revised by Wilhelm Nestle, trans. by L. R. Palmer, New York: Dover Publications, Inc.

Index Locurum

VI:

PORPHYRY

Life of Plotinus

General Index

Printed in Dunstable, United Kingdom

75327277R00181